THE EVOLUTION OF WESTERN THOUGHT

Volume 1: From the Ancient World to Late Antiquity

A rich and immersive reinterpretation of the history of western thought, this volume – the first in a major trilogy – explores the transmission and development of philosophical ideas from Plato and Aristotle to Jesus, Paul, Augustine, and Gregory the Great. Christopher Celenza recalibrates philosophy's story not as abstract argumentation but rather as lived practice: one aimed at excavating wisdom and shaping life. Emphasizing the importance of textual tradition and elucidation across diverse contexts, the author shows how philosophical and religious ideas were transformed and readjusted over time. By focusing on the centrality of Christianity to western thought, he reveals how ancient ideas were alchemized within religious frameworks, and how – across the centuries – ethical and intellectual traditions intersected to shape culture, memory, and the pursuit of sagacity. Ever attentive to ongoing conversations between past and present, this expansive intellectual history brings perspectives to the subject that are both nuanced and fresh.

Christopher S. Celenza is Dean of the School of Arts and Sciences and a professor of History and Classics at Johns Hopkins University. A former director of the American Academy in Rome, he has also held fellowships from the Guggenheim Foundation, the American Council of Learned Societies (ACLS) and the Fulbright Foundation. He is a scholar whose wide interests and expertise span Renaissance thought, classical tradition, and intellectual history. His many books include *Machiavelli: A Portrait* (Harvard University Press, 2015), *The Intellectual World of the Italian Renaissance: Language, Philosophy, and the Search for Meaning* (Cambridge University Press, 2017), and *The Italian Renaissance and the Origins of the Modern Humanities: An Intellectual History, 1400–1800* (Cambridge University Press, 2021).

THE EVOLUTION OF WESTERN THOUGHT

A New History, from Antiquity to the Early Modern Era

Volume 1
From the Ancient World to Late Antiquity

CHRISTOPHER S. CELENZA

Johns Hopkins University

CAMBRIDGE UNIVERSITY PRESS

Shaftesbury Road, Cambridge CB2 8EA, United Kingdom

One Liberty Plaza, 20th Floor, New York, NY 10006, USA

477 Williamstown Road, Port Melbourne, VIC 3207, Australia

314–321, 3rd Floor, Plot 3, Splendor Forum, Jasola District Centre, New Delhi – 110025, India

103 Penang Road, #05-06/07, Visioncrest Commercial, Singapore 238467

Cambridge University Press is part of Cambridge University Press & Assessment, a department of the University of Cambridge.

We share the University's mission to contribute to society through the pursuit of education, learning and research at the highest international levels of excellence.

www.cambridge.org
Information on this title: www.cambridge.org/9781009699174

DOI: 10.1017/9781009699167

© Christopher S. Celenza 2026

This publication is in copyright. Subject to statutory exception and to the provisions of relevant collective licensing agreements, no reproduction of any part may take place without the written permission of Cambridge University Press & Assessment.

When citing this work, please include a reference to the DOI 10.1017/9781009699167

First published 2026

A catalogue record for this publication is available from the British Library

A Cataloging-in-Publication data record for this book is available from the Library of Congress

ISBN 978-1-009-69917-4 Hardback

Cambridge University Press & Assessment has no responsibility for the persistence or accuracy of URLs for external or third-party internet websites referred to in this publication and does not guarantee that any content on such websites is, or will remain, accurate or appropriate.

For EU product safety concerns, contact us at Calle de José Abascal, 56, 1°, 28003 Madrid, Spain, or email eugpsr@cambridge.org

For Winston Tabb, in gratitude

CONTENTS

Preface		*page* ix
Acknowledgments		xiii
Note on Biblical Sources		xv
1	Introduction: Philosophy, Conversations, Wisdom, Traditions	1
2	Plato: Philosophy, Conversation, and the Nature of Reality	25
3	Plato: Wisdom Is about Examples	46
4	Aristotle: From Observation to Ethics	72
5	The Shape of the Good Life: Virtue, Friendship, and Contemplation in Aristotle	87
6	Strands in the Fabric: Judaism, Hellenistic Thought, Rome	106
7	Christianity	134
8	The Death of Christ	158
9	Vessel of Election, Light of the Gentiles	169
10	Augustine, Platonism, and Conversion	195
11	Augustine, the *City of God*, and History	224

| 12 | Endings and New Beginnings: Gregory the Great and Beyond | 240 |

Epilogue — 269

Bibliography — 273
Index — 299

PREFACE

The Evolution of Western Thought: A New History from Antiquity to the Early Modern Era, Volume 1, *From the Ancient World to Late Antiquity* offers readers a new way of appreciating the development of western intellectual history and philosophy from ancient Greece to the end of antiquity and the beginning of the Middle Ages. It is the first of what I anticipate will be a three-volume series.

This book's story begins with Plato and Aristotle, travels through Judaism and Rome, spends significant time with early Christianity (Jesus Christ and Paul) and Saint Augustine, and concludes in the seventh century with Gregory the Great. My method is to focus closely on key texts, drawing readers in through the richness of the authors' language and placing their ideas in historical context. Throughout, a few guiding ideas shape the project.

First, philosophy – following its ancient etymology as the love of wisdom – deserves to be considered more broadly than is customary. Especially in premodern times it was often a lived practice as much as a written one – a practice that shaped the lives and emotional worlds of its practitioners. It was interwoven at times with literature, religion, and the arts. Looked at in this way, philosophy focuses on human beings, their lives, and their place in the cosmos – questions that still animate us today.

Second, genre matters. For the most part what we have from Plato are dialogues, from Aristotle, lecture notes, and from any number of early Christian thinkers, letters, sermons, and commentaries. The format of the written works can shape both the ideas they contain and how they were understood over time.

Third, Christianity features prominently. In late antiquity Jesus Christ was sometimes portrayed as a philosopher, clothed in a garment called the *pallium*. That symbolic image reminds us that some early Christians saw their faith as continuous with philosophical inquiry. Christianity helped popularize philosophical ideas – especially those associated with Plato – and created new contexts for engaged thinking across cultures, geographies, and social classes. And though early Christians could not escape some of the cultural conditions of their era, the idea of equal human personhood emerged powerfully, both in the Gospels and the work of Paul of Tarsus. Though varied across regions and centuries, Christianity was a cultural mainstay, and its central narrative – Jesus Christ's life, death, and resurrection – was widely shared and endlessly interpreted. Jesus Christ was also seen as divine, and belief in him reshaped individual lives and entire societies. Whatever one's faith commitments may be, these are cultural realities that deserve serious engagement. We should understand religion in general, and Christianity specifically in the traditionally western context, as real phenomena that possess density, richness, and subtlety. Reducing Christianity to a cause of past wrongs elides that richness and complexity.

None of this is to idealize the past. The ideal of fundamentally equal human personhood – central to Christianity and with a long genealogy in western thinking – was rarely realized fully. But it remains a powerful aspiration. However much we may differ on how to enact it, this ideal should continue to animate our aspirations.

Recent histories of philosophy – by Anthony Gottlieb, A. C. Grayling, Anthony Kenny, Peter Adamson, the team of Matthew Sharpe and Michael Ure, and others – have contributed richly to the field. My project differs: It is not a disciplinary history of philosophy, nor a critique of academic philosophy. Rather, it hopes to add something complementary – attuned to the porous boundaries between philosophy, literature, and religion, and attentive to the lived dimensions of thought.

My own training in the history of Italian Renaissance humanism has taught me the value of stepping outside one's disciplinary comfort zone. Figures like Angelo Poliziano challenged the academic boundaries of their day, arguing that humanistic inquiry – rooted in philology – could bridge disciplines and offer a wider perspective on human wisdom. His example reminds us to remain intellectually adventurous.

I've also found inspiration in thinkers like Eric Adler, Danielle Allen, William Egginton, Rita Felski, Mark Lilla, Martha Nussbaum, and Michael Roth, who have called for a renewed sense of shared purpose in the humanities and in society at large – one that fosters community through liberal education rather than fragmenting into endless specialization. Different though they are, these scholars offer pragmatic and generous visions, grounded in the idea of the "general welfare." My project belongs in this neighborhood, though it has a more historical and textual focus.

The term "western thought" deserves some explanation. The figures highlighted in this book – Plato, Aristotle, Cicero, Jesus Christ, Paul, Augustine, Gregory – are considered foundational to the west. Taken on their own, sometimes strange-to-us terms, they are worth encountering, rediscovering, and understanding in their monumentality. By monumentality I mean something like the meaning of the Latin term *monumentum*. The word can mean a physical monument, to be sure, but it is more broadly connected to memory. The Roman poet Horace wrote that in his poetry he had completed a "monument more lasting than bronze" (*exegi monumentum aere perennius*, Horace, *Odes* 3.30.1). He meant that his words would last even longer than physical structures and that they, and he, would be remembered.

The historical figures noted here (as well as some others you will encounter in this book) meet that criterion of monumentality by any fair measure. The traditions they represent are worth revisiting not because they are always perfect or unproblematic, but because their ideas have had enduring influence and raise perennial questions: What is a human being? What is human nature? Do we have free will? What are the duties of citizenship? What is our place in the universe? What does it mean to be happy, and how do we get there? How should we pursue wisdom? Is there something beyond us – beyond our lives as lived and, yes, beyond our eventual but inevitable deaths?

To be sure, the term "western" can obscure as much as it reveals. If we look at almost any epoch of western history, we find fruitful encounters among people of different backgrounds. Jesus Christ – a Middle Eastern Jew – was, of course, not geographically western, even as his life and doctrines inspired, shaped, and framed the outlook not only of countless western thinkers but also that of majorities of people in the premodern places traditionally identified as western. Augustine was North African. And any number of other "western" thinkers hailed from backgrounds and cultures not associated with western Europe. The Egyptian city of Alexandria fostered rich cultural interchange, nurturing many forms of philosophical thinking. The transmission of ancient texts through Syriac, Arabic, and Hebrew traditions was vital to their survival. And so on. While the term "western" is meaningful and convenient shorthand, it must be understood as culturally and geographically complex, not as a simple or exclusive heritage.

Some today argue for discarding the term altogether. But, as philosopher Lucy Allais has noted, to do so would risk denying the global relevance of ideas that emerged within western contexts but belong to all of humanity. These ideas are not proprietary. They are part of a larger, shared human inheritance.

Much recent humanities scholarship in the United States has focused on alterity, disruption, revolution, and the margins. That work has yielded important insights. But it is time to revisit the core: the texts, thinkers, and ideals that shaped enduring traditions of inquiry, reflection, and moral imagination. As Michael Roth once wrote in the *Chronicle of Higher Education*, perhaps we should seek to see ourselves as "explorers of the normative" rather than as only critics of normativity.

This book represents one such effort. The thinkers and texts explored here still speak to us today. Durable, sometimes shimmeringly transcendent, often complicated, they offer critically interesting perspectives, insight, and even enchantment. I hope to share that excitement with the reader, sometimes by close reading, other times through broader vistas. The goal is not only to understand the past, but to let it inform a richer present.

ACKNOWLEDGMENTS

It is a pleasure to acknowledge the people and institutions that have contributed to this project. Scholars who have read all or part of this book include: Scott Bruce, Greg Bucher, Stephen J. Campbell, Anthony B. Cashman, William Egginton, Chris Frilingos, Craig Gibson, Hahrie Han, Elizabeth McCahill, Suzanne Marchand, Dean Moyar, Denis Robichaud, Philip M. Spector, Jenna Storey, and Vaclav Zheng. All have improved the book, and I am profoundly appreciative of their suggestions and critiques. At Johns Hopkins University, teaching together with Earle Havens helped this project in many ways, as did dialogue with several colleagues.

I thank my wife, Anna Harwell Celenza, not only for reading and bettering this book, but also for thirty years of love, friendship, and partnership, through thick and thin.

No one could write about much of what this book covers and not be immeasurably indebted to the visionary work of Peter Brown. I also wish to acknowledge the influence of two scholars sadly no longer with us: John O'Malley, SJ (d. 2022), whose incisive writing, intellectual adventurousness, and generosity were never short of inspirational; and J. G. A. Pocock (d. 2023), whose focus on language and its shaping effect on intellectual history is foundational. At a greater distance are scholars whom I have never met but whose work has been important in shaping my outlook: Pierre Hadot (d. 2010), Diarmaid MacCulloch, Alasdair MacIntyre (d. 2025), Martha Nussbaum, Armando Petrucci (d. 2018), Richard Rorty (d. 2007), and Charles Taylor.

I am deeply grateful to Beatrice Rehl, at Cambridge University Press, for her editorial vision and partnership. To my colleagues in the Dean's office at

Johns Hopkins, thank you for your generous collaboration, creativity, and companionship.

Finally, I dedicate this book to Winston Tabb, Dean Emeritus of the Sheridan Libraries at Johns Hopkins, who embodies the highest ideals of learning, humanity, and service to others.

NOTE ON BIBLICAL SOURCES

Citations from the Greek New Testament are to the Nestle-Aland edition: Eberhard Nestle, Erwin Nestle, Kurt Aland, Barbara Aland, Johannes Karavidopoulos, Carlo M. Martini, and Bruce M. Metzger, eds., *Novum Testamentum Graece*, 28th rev. ed. (Stuttgart: Deutsche Bibelgesellschaft, 2012).

Citations from the Latin Vulgate are to Robert Weber and Roger Gryson, eds., *Biblia Sacra Iuxta Vulgatam Versionem*, 5th ed. (Stuttgart: Deutsche Bibelgesellschaft, 2007).

Biblical citations in English are to the Douay-Rheims translation, in Swift Edgar and Angela Kinney, ed. and trans., *The Vulgate Bible: Douay-Rheims Translation*, 6 vols., Dumbarton Oaks Medieval Library (Cambridge, MA: Harvard University Press, 2010–2013). I use the Douay-Rheims translation because it derives from the Latin Vulgate, the biblical text most widely received and interpreted by western medieval Christian readers. One of this book's guiding aims is to explore the ancient Christian past as it was transmitted, understood, and lived within the intellectual and devotional horizons of the medieval Latin West. Where the Douay-Rheims diverges in meaningful ways from the Greek New Testament (as represented in the Nestle-Aland edition), or from the Hebrew or Greek traditions underlying (what Christians knew as) the Old Testament – including the Septuagint – I note those differences.

I

INTRODUCTION

Philosophy, Conversations, Wisdom, Traditions

THIS IS A BOOK ABOUT PHILOSOPHY, BUT PHILOSOPHY IN A slightly different key. There has been a long-standing tendency, in academic circles, to separate philosophy from religion, even as this separation would not have seemed self-evident to many thinkers of the past. We are all creatures of habit, and no habits seem more ingrained than those cultivated in academia. In this case, the habits go back to the eighteenth century. It was then that the modern historiography of philosophy was set on its course, a course that continues today in one important respect: It has shaped definitively what "counts" as part of the history of philosophy and who counts as a philosopher.

The word philosopher means "lover of wisdom" and combines two Greek roots, *philia*, which means "love," and *sophia*, which means "wisdom." In a tale that became proverbial in Greco-Roman antiquity, it was Pythagoras who invented the term philosopher, when he was asked by a king whether he was wise (*sophos*). In what ancients considered a sign of humility, he answered that he was not a *sophos* (a wise man) but instead a *philosophos* (a lover of wisdom).[1] Those who recorded this anecdote about Pythagoras had no writing of his to go on, since Pythagoras wrote nothing. Instead, he was satisfied to have inspired a circle of followers, a school, as it were, whose members passed down his doctrines, imitated his style of life, and continued the project he had begun. Consideration of Pythagoras is meaningful because, when we normally think of philosophy, we tend to default to written works and the arguments they contain. However, if we

---

[1] Cicero, *Tusculan Disputations*, ed. and tr. J. E. King (Cambridge, MA: Harvard University Press, 1945), sec. 5.8, pp. 432–433; Cicero and other ancient thinkers attributed this anecdote to Heraclides of Pontus (390–310 BCE) . For literature, see Christoph Riedweg, "Zum Ursprung des Wortes 'Philosophie' oder Pythagoras von Samos als Wortschöpfer," in Anton Bierl and Joachim Latacz, eds., *Antike Literatur in neuer Deutung* (Munich and Leipzig: Saur, 2004), 147–182.

step back from writing for a moment and think twice about that word, "argument," the parameters of philosophy start to shift.

As to written works, western philosophy was about two thousand years old before the introduction of printing with moveable type, which began (in the west) in Germany in the 1450s and spread thereafter throughout Europe.[2] People wrote before then, of course. But imagine (for a moment) the absence of the internet, printed books, and all the other associated technologies that we take for granted in our world of reading and writing. Consider, instead, that you are an author living in a world where the only books are handwritten ones. What sort of range do you imagine your written work will have? A more penetrating question is: What sort of range *can* you imagine your work will have? Under those conditions, if you were a person in search of wisdom who also wanted to teach, your interactions with those you taught, your followers, would have been at least as meaningful as your written works.[3] It is not that you wouldn't care about your writing – if you were in fact someone who cared about writing. It is just that it all would have mattered differently. You would have had no way to imagine thousands of exact copies of your work, even less to envisage the immediate, worldwide diffusion of your written words that current technology permits. The local would have mattered greatly.

Then, there is this word "arguments," as in the phrase "verbal arguments" or "philosophical arguments." It is a signifier for approaching incontrovertible truth through words. A thinker's argument is better, the more it has an internal logic that is sound and, indeed, the more it reflects a coherence with what that thinker may write or say elsewhere. This conception – that careful argumentation is central to philosophy – is an important one, and it has always been a part of philosophy.[4] But it is not the only part. It is fair to say that an overreliance on analyzing argumentation has led to, not so much mis-readings of the history of philosophy, but limited readings.

---

[2] For literature on printing in the west, see Adrian Johns, "The Coming of Print to Europe," in Leslie Howsam, ed., *The Cambridge Companion to the History of the Book* (Cambridge: Cambridge University Press, 2015), 107–124. Printing with moveable type appeared earlier in Asia, though it was not the preferred mode of reproducing writing; see Tsien Tsuen-Hsuin, *Chemistry and Chemical Technology, Part 1: Paper and Printing*, volume 5 of Joseph Needham, ed., *Science and Civilization in China* (Cambridge: Cambridge University Press, 1985), p. 2.

[3] Cf. Raffaella Cribiore, *Listening to the Philosophers: Notes on Notes* (Ithaca: Cornell University Press, 2024), esp. 1–13.

[4] See John M. Cooper, *Pursuits of Wisdom: Six Ways of Life in Ancient Philosophy from Socrates to Plato* (Princeton: Princeton University Press, 2012) for an eloquent statement of this perspective.

Plato, for example – the first thinker you will meet in this book – wrote dialogues of literary beauty, which in addition to detailed verbal argumentation often included character sketches, especially of his beloved teacher, Socrates. The argument-centered way of reading the history of philosophy tends to skip the literary side of Plato and pass lightly over the character sketches, analyzing instead the different verbal arguments the characters in a Platonic dialogue make. But Plato took care that his dialogues were enticing and contained portraits of people for a reason: He believed that philosophy was as much about finding models for life as it was about the niceties of logical language. Hence the use of Socrates – his life and, especially, the way he chose to die – as an exemplar for living. Works of philosophy needed to be persuasive to do the work Plato intended them to do: to change people for the better. Style was and is meaningful.[5]

To read Plato without taking these factors into account – to dissect his work, to leave out what he deliberately included – is to miss the idea that philosophy was about finding the right style of life, an enterprise certainly less exact than analyzing argumentation but no less important.[6] So, this approach is what this volume will present. It will be more weighted toward ethics and less inclined to epistemology and metaphysics than normal accounts of the history of philosophy. Accordingly, since religion touches those parts of people's psyches that dispose them to behave in certain ways, Christianity will figure prominently.

---

[5] Malcolm Schofield, *How Plato Writes: Perspectives and Problems* (Cambridge: Cambridge University Press, 2023) offers a wealth of useful perspectives on these issues. See also Myles Burnyeat, "First Words: A Valedictory Lecture," *Proceedings of the Cambridge Philological Society* 43 (1998), 1–20; and David Sedley, "The Stoic-Platonist Debate on *kathēkonta*," in Katerina Ierodiakonou, ed., *Topics in Stoic Philosophy* (Oxford: Clarendon, 1999), 128–152.

[6] See Juliusz Domański, *Philosophy, Theory or Way of Life? Controversies in Antiquity, the Middle Ages, and the Renaissance*, tr. Matthew Sharpe, Andrew B. Irvine, and Matteo Stettler (Leiden: Brill, 2024), an English translation of Domański's *La philosophie, théorie ou manière de vivre? Les controverses de l'Antiquité à la Renaissance* (Fribourg: Cerf – Editions Universitaires, 1996); Hubertus Drobner, "Christian Philosophy," in Susan Ashbrook Harvey and David G. Hunter, eds., *The Oxford Handbook of Early Christian Studies* (Oxford: Oxford University Press, 2008), 672–690; Pierre Hadot, *Philosophy as a Way of Life: Spiritual Exercises from Socrates to Foucault* (Oxford and New York: Blackwell, 1995); Pierre Hadot, *The Selected Writings of Pierre Hadot: Philosophy as Practice*, ed. and tr. Matthew Sharpe and Federico Testa (London: Bloomsbury, 2020); Alexander Nehamas, *The Art of Living: Socratic Reflections from Plato to Foucault* (Berkeley: University of California Press, 1998); Matthew Sharpe and Michael Ure, *Philosophy as a Way of Life: From Antiquity to Modernity* (London: Bloomsbury, 2021); and Justin E. H. Smith, *The Philosopher: A History in Six Types* (Princeton: Princeton University Press, 2016).

Here, by the way, is why we need to understand the eighteenth- and nineteenth-century contexts that have shaped traditional views of the history of philosophy. For it was then that a basic framework arose that tended to focus on "philosophy as argumentation," instead of "philosophy as the search for a style of life." Three factors were decisive: the impact of the work of the philosopher Descartes (1596–1650), a history of philosophy by a little-known thinker named Johann Jakob Brucker (1696–1770), and the rise of modern research universities in the nineteenth century.

As to Descartes, his legacy is what matters.[7] In his lifetime, his work was subject to debate. And the truth is that he considered himself more a scholar of the natural world than a philosopher of the mind. Nevertheless, a few generations after his death, a consensus emerged around some of what he had discussed in his two most famous works: The *Discourse on Method* and the *Meditations*.[8] He wrote the *Discourse* in French and the *Meditations* in Latin, but both circulated in translation in various languages. In them, he proposed something that in hindsight seems radical and new concerning the human mind. Living in a society suffused with skepticism, he began by asking what it was that he knew with certainty about himself.[9] The more he asked himself that question, the harder it became to assert that he had certain knowledge of much of anything at all beyond mathematical propositions. One's senses often fail one, for example. How can one be certain – certain in the way one is about the truths of mathematics – that anything one sees, or hears, or touches, is what one believes it to be? Moreover, we dream, and what we dream seems real. But then we wake up and realize it was all just an illusion.

Given this inherent uncertainty about the world, Descartes decided to suppose (for the sake of argument) that he should consider nothing the senses presented him as true. Moreover, he should count everything that had ever entered his mind as "no more than the illusions" of his dreams.[10] In other words, unless he could be immediately and unreflectively

---

[7] For recent literature, see Stephen Nadler, Tad M. Schmaltz, and Delphine Antoine-Mahut, eds., *The Oxford Handbook of Descartes and Cartesianism* (Oxford: Oxford University Press, 2019).

[8] For his works, see Descartes, *Oeuvres*, ed. Charles Adam and Paul Tannery, 11 vols. in 13 (Paris: Vrin, 1973–1976), henceforth abbreviated as AT; and Descartes, *The Philosophical Writings of Descartes*, 3 vols., tr. John Cottingham, Robert Stoothoff, Dugald Murdoch, and (for vol. 3), Anthony Kenny (Cambridge: Cambridge University Press, 1985–1991), henceforth abbreviated as CSM.

[9] See Richard Popkin, *The History of Scepticism: From Savonarola to Bayle* (Oxford: Oxford University Press, 2003), esp. 143–173.

[10] *Discourse*, pt. 4, sec. 32, in CSM, 1: 127.

convinced of a principle as being true – self-evidently true – he would not admit that principle into his thinking. But then he was struck by something that met that criterion of certainty: Even as he found himself trying to "think everything false," he was still the one who was thinking. As he wrote in French, *je pense, donc je suis* – "I think, therefore I am," a phrase that also gained currency in Latin, as *cogito, ergo sum*. That he was thinking and was sure he was thinking meant also that he was a thinking *being*, meaning he could at least be sure that he himself existed. It was this principle, incontrovertible as it was, that he could accept as the "first principle" of the philosophy he sought to create.[11]

This assumption had another consequence, one that entailed Descartes' injecting a kind of mystery into the history of philosophy, a mystery that shaped it decisively thereafter. Taking this realization that he was a thinking being as a point of departure, Descartes wrote: "From this I knew that I was a substance whose whole essence or nature is to think, and which does not require any place, or depend on any material thing, in order to exist. Accordingly, this 'I' – that is, the soul by which I am what I am – is entirely distinct from the body."[12]

Here is what was new, in two connected parts. First, the essence of a person is the "soul." Descartes uses the French word *âme*, for soul, drawn from the Latin *anima*. That term traditionally had been used in different ways: to mean "wind" or "breath"; to indicate the "breath of life" in something that was alive; to signify the "animating force" in anything that was alive (hence the Latin word *animal* – a "living being", i.e., a being endowed with *anima*); to point to a principle of motion; and in the Christian tradition to denote a person's immortal "soul." More on that in a moment.

Second – and again as to what is new – Descartes is saying that this essence of a person is immaterial. Now, it might sound surprising to readers accustomed to the traditional notion of an immortal soul (drawn from Plato, as we shall see, and becoming a cornerstone of Christianity) that this idea was new. But, both in its articulation and considering the context in which Descartes enunciated it, it was new. Before Descartes, the soul was imagined as a kind of semi-physical spirit, a notion embedded in the core meaning of the word *anima*: "breath." Importantly, it was believed that the soul could have effects in the physical world, the world of phenomena: the things we perceive with our senses. The Christian concept of the Resurrection, too, points in the same direction: At the end of time, when God so decrees, souls

[11] Ibid.   [12] *Discourse*, pt. 4, sec. 33, in CSM, 1: 127.

will be reunited to their bodies – literally, as if it were impossible to conceive of an immaterial soul forever separate from its physical form. True, this belief is still part of Christian theology. Descartes' innovation was that he defined things in such a way that those older associations eventually passed away, at least as assumptions held by intellectuals interested in how the world works.

In his *Meditations*, Descartes uses the Latin word *mens*, "mind." About it he says that, in contrast to body, which is always divisible, the mind is "utterly indivisible."[13] Further, he writes that, when he considers himself as a "thinking thing," he understands himself "to be something quite single and complete."[14] The most authentic part of who you were was completely non-material.

One would not want to give the impression that there was no genealogy behind Descartes' vision. There was a tradition concerning the soul's incorporeality, especially in the work of Plotinus, the third-century CE Platonist.[15] In the thirteenth century, Thomas Aquinas stressed that the soul was both the form of the body and incorporeal.[16] Descartes, however, posited that the soul and the body were separate substances, with the soul being a *res cogitans* (a "thinking thing") and the body being a *res extensa* (an "extended thing"), meaning that the body takes up space and is divisible into parts. Moreover, by the era of Descartes, something like a modern conception of the "self" was coming into view. In Descartes' wake, the "mystery" alluded to above had to do with how the core part of who you are, a "self," could know things about and within an external, material world to which it was fundamentally unconnected. That is what was new.

So, how did this mind – this "self," we might say – know things about the world? It was this question that became the defining one for philosophy thereafter. Or it might be more accurate to say that this "epistemological paradigm" became the framework for those who, in the nineteenth century and later, taught and studied philosophy in university contexts.[17] As the

---

[13] Descartes, *Meditations*, AT, 7: 85–86; CSM, 2:59.
[14] Descartes, *Meditations*, AT, 7: 85–86; CSM, 2:59.
[15] Plotinus, *Enneads*, 7 vols., ed. and tr. A. H. Armstrong (Cambridge, MA: Harvard University Press, 1966–1988), 4.7 (vol. 4, pp. 338–391).
[16] Thomas Aquinas, *Summa theologiae*, 5 vols. (Ottawa: Institut d'études médiévales, 1941–1945), 1.75.1.
[17] See Knud Haakonssen, "The History of Eighteenth-Century Philosophy: History or Philosophy," in Knud Haakonssen, ed., *The Cambridge History of Eighteenth-Century Philosophy*, 2 vols. (Cambridge: Cambridge University Press, 2006), 1: 3–25, esp. 13–25. The influence of Victor Cousin is meaningful in valorizing the primacy of Descartes as a starting point for modern philosophy as an endeavor that departed from the medieval "soumission à une autorité autre que raison" and progressed to the modern "soumission à la

norms behind histories of philosophy solidified, and as "natural philosophy" broke away from philosophy writ large and became the modern natural sciences, more historiographic attention fell on metaphysics and epistemology, less on ethics and morals.

None of this transformation happened overnight. People rarely realize they are living through revolutions.[18] Indeed, Descartes faced objections to his ideas from contemporaries. Offering a sign of what he considered the enterprise of philosophy to be about (conversation, rather than proclamation), he had his *Meditations* published along with those objections, having solicited reactions from his contemporaries.[19] Moreover, for him, these considerations about mind, though necessary, were secondary. He saw his true enterprise as that of "natural philosophy," what we would today call natural science. He hoped to sweep these questions about knowledge – What is a mind? What can we know? – out of the way and get down to the business of investigating the physical universe. But, alas, that for which he was remembered, over time, was this new idea of the mind. It was the essence of the self, distinct from the body, and thus a puzzle.

And it is at this moment that the eighteenth century comes into play. We can turn specifically to the decade of the 1740s, a moment notable for two reasons. First, by then nearly a century had passed since Descartes' death. Was the soul material? Immaterial? By now, one just didn't ask those questions much anymore. What had been the locus of debate and controversy in Descartes' day had become something like settled opinion.[20] "Natural philosophy" was separating itself ever more from philosophy. It was becoming its own set of fields – chemistry, physics, biology, and so on – with newly evolving norms for judging progress, evaluating truth claims, and coming together in disciplinary communities of like-minded peers.

A corollary of what Descartes was propounding – that the essence of humanity, the mind, was fundamentally separate from the physical universe – was that the physical universe existed apart from humanity. It was there. And

---

seule autorité de la raison"; see Cousin, *Cours de l'histoire de la philosophie* (Paris: Didier, 1841), pp. 358–398, at p. 362.

[18] See Daniel Garber, "Descartes, the Aristotelians, and the Revolution that did not Happen in 1637," *The Monist* 71 (1988), 471–486; Hans-Peter Schütt, *Die Adoption des "Vaters der modernen Philosophie"* (Frankfurt am Main: Klosterman, 1998).

[19] Desmond M. Clarke, *Descartes: A Biography* (Cambridge: Cambridge University Press, 2006), pp. 199–212; it is worth noting that in a late treatise, the *Passions of the Soul*, Descartes proposed that a physical organ (the pineal gland) served as the mediator between mind and body: Descartes, AT, 11: 359–356; CSM, 1: 343–347; see Jonathan Westphal, *The Mind-Body Problem* (Cambridge, MA: MIT Press, 2016), esp. 1–23, at p. 19.

[20] Cf. Schütt, *Die Adoption*, 17–48.

even if we weren't there, it would exist without us.[21] That postulate entailed a momentous assumption for us human beings interested in figuring out how the physical universe worked. The natural scientist could dispense with God as an active participant in the world.[22] This is not to say that everyone became an atheist. It was just that one could assume, as a natural scientist, that there were rules as to how the world worked and that one's job was to find them. Descartes had squared this circle by arguing that to comprehend God's perfection was to understand that, when He set the world up eons ago, He created all its laws and rules and didn't need to intervene thereafter. What kind of truly perfect entity would create a system and then need to tinker with it all the time? By the middle of the eighteenth century, most "natural philosophers" shared that assumption in such a way that it barely needed articulation. Most of "philosophy" was then on a trajectory to think ever more deeply about what that "mind" was and, especially, how this immaterial mind knew things in the world, material as it was. Descartes' basic assumption became somewhat *de rigueur*. Most of "philosophy" was then on a trajectory to think ever more deeply about what that "mind" was and, especially, how this immaterial mind knew things in the world, material as it was.

What mattered was setting philosophy on a new foundation, one on which it could build useful edifices, with assumptions and postulates that were rigorous and well argued. And this is where the second element appears that made the 1740s important. For it was then that Johann Jakob Brucker began publishing volumes of his epochal *Critical History of Philosophy*, or *Historia critica philosophiae* in Latin.[23] Though this Lutheran pastor from Augsburg also published a German version, it was the Latin text that had Europe-wide diffusion, given that Latin was still a major language of learned communication at the time. Brucker's enterprise was ambitious – to cover all of what one could properly call philosophy in the west, from antiquity until his own day. His influence was far-reaching.

In the introduction to his work, Brucker foregrounded his objectives with lucidity and honesty. He enunciated goals for the historian of philosophy,

---

[21] This Cartesian propensity later developed into a veneration of what Daston and Galison term "structural objectivity"; see Lorraine Daston and Peter Galison, *Objectivity* (Brooklyn: Zone Books, 2007), pp. 253–307.

[22] See the classic study, Alexandre Koyré, *From the Closed World to the Infinite Universe* (Baltimore: Johns Hopkins University Press, 1968).

[23] Johann Jacob Brucker, *Historia critica philosophiae a mundi incunabulis ad nostram usque aetatem deducta*, ed. Richard H. Popkin and Giorgio Tonelli, 2nd ed., 5 vols. (Leipzig: Weidemann and Reich, 1766–1767; repr., Hildesheim: Olms, 1975).

Introduction: Philosophy, Conversations, Wisdom, Traditions

even as he wove into that vision the state at which philosophy had arrived in his era. For example, Brucker wrote that the terms "philosopher" and "philosophy" had been used too promiscuously in the long history of the ever-evolving discipline. No longer could one apply the label "philosopher" to a poet or to someone else who just seemed wise. Now, philosophy needed to be about "systems" of thought, whose elements cohered internally. Each system will have its own critical principles. Brucker expressed himself distinctly (with some terms highlighted for emphasis):

> So that, therefore, a sound, correct judgment might be able to be drawn out of the **expressed opinion** of the philosophers, an **entire system** must be **excavated** from their writings, to such an extent that, above all else, the **general principles** may be excavated that, like a **foundation**, underlie the entire edifice of their teachings. The final result is that those **conclusions** that flow freely from those sources **may be built** on top of the general principles, like a superstructure.[24]

As mentioned, Brucker wrote this text in Latin. It is worth diving in for a moment, to see what he really had in mind.

First, for "expressed opinion" Brucker used the word *sententia*. It can mean "opinion," "sentiment," "judgment," or "thought," among other things. I added the adjective "expressed" in the translation because Brucker is pointing toward texts in all their complexity. If Plato wrote dialogues, that is what you had as a source. But there was within those literary, multi-faceted works, which contained many different opinions, a "system." It was your job, as a historian of philosophy, to "excavate" that system. You needed to find its "general principles," which Brucker theorizes here with an architectural metaphor: Those principles are like a "foundation." From the outside of any edifice, you might not always see the foundation, of course. But it was there, and your job was to find it. Why? So that the "conclusions" could be "built" – conclusions that flowed from those sources.

What he is saying is evident: Philosophy is not about literary art or genre. It is instead about fundamental principles that might, indeed, lie hidden in

---

[24] Brucker, *Historia critica*, 1:15, my tr.: "Ut itaque de sententia philosophorum sanum rectumque iudicium ferri queat, totum ex eorum scriptis systema ita eruendum est, ut ante omnia principia generalia, quae fundamenti loco toti doctrinarum aedificio subiiciuntur, eruantur, et his demum illae superstruantur conclusiones quae ex istis fontibus sponte sua fluunt." There is now an excellent study and English translation of Brucker's "Preliminary Discourse" and a bit more from the *Historia critica* in Jacob Brucker, *Critical History of Philosophy: "Preliminary Discourse" and "On the Socratic School,"* ed. and tr. Leo Catana (Oxford: Oxford University Press, 2024).

the work of a past author. To find what that thinker's "system" was, one needed to dig those principles out. One did not need much in the way of context. Was the thinker writing a dialogue in which he deliberately inserted different and sometimes discordant opinions? Was he writing in an era when everything was handwritten, so that it would be hard to imagine that one's work would circulate endlessly in the same form in which one wrote it – an assumption that would indeed change what one wrote, how one wrote it, and so on? Did he include literary flourishes, adorning his philosophical writings with the jewels of rhetoric and poetry? Questions of that sort did not need to be foregrounded in Brucker's view.

Brucker's work was a triumph. Abridged and translated into other languages, it became a standard reference text, and it may serve for us as a stand-in for other histories of philosophy that followed it. These had varied emphases and sometimes different grounding assumptions, but they were similar in one important respect: They led to the creation of a canon of "philosophers," a canon that continues to shape the way the history of western philosophy is conceived.[25]

This canon represents the most meaningful consequence of Brucker's work. He was writing in the eighteenth century, so it goes without saying that approaches to the history of philosophy have changed over time, that there were national differences in European traditions, and that the field of philosophy and its relation to its histories has always been a complicated subject.[26] But there is the stubborn fact that, if a thinker did not make it into the eighteenth-century canon of who "counted" as a philosopher, that thinker still has little chance of getting a hearing today.

---

[25] See Leo Catana, *The Historiographical Concept "System of Philosophy": Its Origin, Nature, Influence and Legitimacy* (Leiden: Brill, 2008); Christopher S. Celenza, "What Counted as Philosophy in the Italian Renaissance? The History of Philosophy, the History of Science, and Styles of Life," *Critical Inquiry* 39 (2013), 367–401; Brian Copenhaver, *Philosophy as Descartes Found It* (Oxford: Oxford University Press, 2024), esp. 10–13; Mario Longo, "Storia 'critica' della filosofie e primo illuminismo: Jakob Brucker," in Gregorio Piaia and Giovanni Santinello, eds., *Storia delle storie generali della filosofia*, 5 vols. (Brescia: La Scuola, 1981–1995), 2: 527–635; Wilhelm Schmitt-Biggeman and Theo Stammen, *Jacob Brucker (1696–1770): Philosoph und Historiker der europäischen Aufklärung* (Berlin: Akademie-Verlag, 1998).

[26] See Leo Catana and Mogens Laerke, "Historiographies of Philosophy, 1800–1950," *British Journal for the History of Philosophy* 28 (2020), 431–441, and the associated articles published in that issue; Dmitri Levitin, *Ancient Wisdom in the Age of the New Science: Histories of Philosophy in England, c.1640–1700* (Cambridge: Cambridge University Press, 2015); Richard Rorty, J. B. Schneewind, and Quentin Skinner, eds., *Philosophy in History* (Cambridge: Cambridge University Press, 1984).

Accordingly, a major consequence of the Brucker moment is that we are missing large swaths of time from the "history" of philosophy.[27] And time, of course, is primarily what history busies itself about. If we think of philosophy as the enterprise of searching for human wisdom, then it cannot be the case that there are centuries in which philosophy didn't happen.

To give one example that is relevant to this book, much of late antiquity (the third to seventh centuries CE) is largely missing from most accounts, as is early Christianity. This is not to say that thinkers from those eras have not been studied. It is to say that the presentations of them, their thought, and their ways of life have been incomplete. They are not presented, in other words, in ways that would have been recognizable to them. One cannot boil religion and individual spirituality down to "arguments" or "principles," for example. Yet, to address the work of a later Platonic thinker like Plotinus (203–270 CE), "excavating systems" of principles is misleading. He did indeed have what a later era might have called a coherent system of thought, but it was in service of one particularly important aim: to reach the divine. Non-Christian Platonist though he was, he evolved his thinking in service of religion.

Also – and just to stick with Plotinus for a moment – Plotinus did not care all that much about writing. A philosopher named Porphyry, who was Plotinus' student and biographer, noted that Plotinus did not write down his lectures and needed encouragement to do so.[28] When he did, he would occasionally misspell things and sometimes write inelegantly. And yet, no one was considered more of a philosopher than Plotinus. He was inspiring in his continuous search for wisdom, charismatic as a teacher, and someone whose reputation was good enough that people came from far and wide to study with him. Philosophy, for him, was a living enterprise, its success judged not by responses to one's arguments in writing but by how one's live teaching served as a vehicle of growth, inspiration, and meaning for one's students and followers.

This emphasis – on lived philosophy rather than written philosophy – deserves attention. True, our sources are, for the most part, written sources. But it is what we do with them and how we read them that matters. Moreover, what we count as a source is significant. This is where one word

---

[27] Cf. the graphic representation of the canon in Josh Platzky Miller and Lea Cantor, "The Future of the History of Philosophy," in *The Philosopher* 111 (2023), www.thephilosopher1923.org/post/the-future-of-the-history-of-philosophy.

[28] Porphyry, "Life of Plotinus," in Plotinus, *Enneads*, 7 vols., ed. and tr. A. H. Armstrong (Cambridge, MA: Harvard University Press, 1966–1988), 1: 2–87, at p. 29.

in this Chapter's title, "conversation," deserves special emphasis. It is not only that much of what authentically counted as philosophy in the premodern west had to do precisely with conversation and oral expression. It is also meaningful to convey where those conversations went, whom they reached, and how they were communicated to variegated audiences. And here is where the impact of Christianity needs to be registered. It is not that historians of philosophy have not noted the presence of Christianity. But there has been a tendency to "dig the system out," as Brucker would have said, focusing on the arguments these thinkers made and forgetting by and large why they made them: to get closer to God and, eventually, to have their philosophy serve as support for theology.

The thinkers profiled in this book were involved in multiple conversations. Plato and Aristotle are central. Their work, as it was interpreted over time, was one source of later thinkers' joining a kind of never-ending dialogue. Jesus Christ must also count as part of the history of philosophy, as well as his most influential disciple, Paul. Christ's life provided an example of a lived philosophy and a style of life that became the basis for countless women and men over time, combining humility, wisdom that was accessible to all, and courage. His thought, expressed in the three synoptic Gospels of Matthew, Mark, and Luke and then refined in the Gospel of John, assumed shape in a durable and meaningful way in the work of Saint Paul. The Pauline letters, which became part of scripture, contained sophisticated and, occasionally, difficult-to-untangle interpretations of Christ's message, much of which had distant origins in Plato. What were these ideas? People have souls connected to the divine in some way. The divine will judge people's conduct, offering rewards or punishments after death for their conduct in life. The possession of those souls means that people are equal in essence in some way, whatever their material conditions are on earth. The divine is so great that we can barely conceive what it is or how to describe it. The enterprise of understanding these and other analogous positions ran through the history of western thought, a never-ending conversation fueled in the first instance by texts. But the conversation would have remained at the level of texts, and it would have accordingly been available only to a small stratum of elite thinkers, had Christ not entered the picture. People soon believed about him what he himself on occasion said: He was the divine made human. God became more than an intellectual principle. Rather, human beings could see themselves in God.

The perspective animating this book is this: for much of its history, western philosophy was a search for a style of life as much as it was and still is a search for coherent argumentation in writing. Someone could be considered "wise" and worth following and studying with even if that person did not write much or at all. If one accepts this premise as legitimate, then Christianity must be considered central to the shaping of western philosophy. Christianity was the vector that allowed ancient non-Christian philosophical ideas to gain acceptance and be adapted within the new religious and intellectual context. It became, eventually, what amounted to the official religion of western Europe. Finally, learning in western Europe was preserved in the early Middle Ages almost exclusively through Christian institutions.

I'd like to make clear that, in laying a fair amount of stress on religion and Christianity, my reasoning is not confessional. Rather, I have been inspired by scholarship in the history of science that stresses the reciprocities inherent to the production of knowledge. All knowledge-making, philosophy included, involves many voices. There are those who write, of course. They are the authors of the texts we study, and they deserve focus and attention as such. But like all authors they are embedded in dense webs of interactions. When it comes to the history of early modern science (for example), one scholar, Deborah Harkness, showed that in Elizabethan London, members of the artisanal class, merchants, midwives, and others were having conversations often parallel to those of better-known figures like Francis Bacon.[29] Bacon was the writer. Yet, he was surrounded by others whose voices formed part of the same conversations who may not have had an interest in permanent written commemoration. And there have been others, like Pamela Smith and Pamela Long, whose work has tended in similarly illuminating directions.[30]

Similar reciprocities and exchanges – between elite and nonelite, written and oral, individual and community – inflect Christianity and premodern western philosophy. Consider the mass appeal that Christianity eventually had (keeping in mind that it was multifarious and that determining actual versus theoretical orthodoxy in any era is a tricky business). Consider further how, as John Marenbon rightly stressed in his fine history of early medieval

---

[29] Deborah Harkness, *The Jewel House: Elizabethan London and the Scientific Revolution* (New Haven and London: Yale University Press, 2007).

[30] Pamela Long, *Openness, Secrecy, Authorship: Technical Arts and the Culture of Knowledge from Antiquity to the Renaissance* (Baltimore: Johns Hopkins University Press, 2001); Pamela Long, "The Contribution of Architectural Writers to a 'Scientific' Outlook in the Fifteenth and Sixteenth Centuries," *Journal of Medieval and Renaissance Studies* 15 (1985), 265–298; Pamela H. Smith, *The Body of the Artisan: Art and Experience in the Scientific Revolution* (Chicago: University of Chicago Press, 2004); Pamela H. Smith, *From Lived Experience to the Written Word: Reconstructing Practical Knowledge in the Early Modern World* (Chicago: University of Chicago Press, 2022).

philosophy, the Early Middle Ages saw absorption of many ancient philosophical notions through the prism of Christianity.[31] And finally, consider that many premodern western philosophers converged in one important, trans-historical place. That place was not physical. Instead, it was a place of books but then – beyond books – a place of memory and the mind: scripture, repetitively and ritualistically imbibed, until it fixed fast in one's memory.[32] In short, for much of the premodern western past, Christianity and scripture were "hard-wired" into the consciousnesses of many of those we study under the rubric of philosophy. It is difficult to imagine that kind of centrality today, but if we are to attain a persuasive picture of the past, we must endeavor to do so.

An academic reader might object that none of this is new, or interesting, or unusual. After all, most histories of western Europe include substantial reference to the "rise" of Christianity, and there is no history of western philosophy that does not refer to Christianity, as one moves from antiquity through the Middle Ages. All true. What is different about this book, however, is that the self-understanding of thinkers in the past will be what guides us, in the first instance. We won't be "digging an entire system" out of their works and thus leaving behind the rich soil in which these ideas flourished. Moreover, the search for human wisdom – for wise ways of life – does not progress in the same way as do the natural sciences. Only the most hidebound would not admit the stunning technical progress that has occurred since the scientific revolution. It is better to be alive when medical professionals understand the germ theory of disease than before they did. But philosophy is not that kind of thing. The big questions are still with us. Why am I here? How should I consider my obligations to my friends? How do I fit into society? What does it mean to live an ethical life? What, in our life, can we make of the meaning of death? Over time, the contexts have changed in which those questions have been asked, but the central questions of philosophy have not.[33]

Accordingly, with the impact of Descartes and Brucker in mind, there is a third and final lens through which we can view the need for the perspective this book offers. The rise of modern research universities in the early nineteenth century signals an important moment. It is the period to which

---

[31] John Marenbon, *Early Medieval Philosophy (480–1150): An Introduction* (London: Routledge, 1988).
[32] Cf. Mary Carruthers, *The Book of Memory: A Study of Memory in Medieval Culture*, 2nd ed. (Cambridge: Cambridge University Press, 2008).
[33] Cf. Richard Rorty, "The Historiography of Philosophy: Four Genres," in *Philosophy in History*, 31–48, esp. 58–59.

we owe most of our modern scholarly disciplines in their current form. No one would confuse the sorts of instruments that different scholarly fields possess today with those that existed in 1810. But there is a story here, and it is worth highlighting, because we owe more to this nineteenth-century period than commonly acknowledged.

That year, 1810, turns out to be highly significant. For it was then that a German thinker named Wilhelm von Humboldt (1767–1835) carried out a reform of educational life that went from the school system all the way up to the university.[34] The University of Berlin was in many ways his creation. And what was newest about it – and, indeed, what made it the model for much of modern western university life – was the creation of a new "philosophical" faculty.

Universities had their origins in Europe in the twelfth and thirteenth centuries (though one can point to the University of Bologna and its activities around the discipline of law a bit earlier and to Islamic *madrassas* earlier still).[35] When universities emerged, something like a standard pattern came into place. There was a "lower" faculty where one studied the liberal arts. Traditionally, these were seven: grammar, rhetoric, and logic on the verbal side, and arithmetic, geometry, music, and astronomy on the mathematical and natural scientific side. By the time medieval universities came into their own, the liberal arts were studied through the prism of Aristotle, many of whose works were translated into Latin in the twelfth and thirteenth centuries. If one completed the arts course, one would receive the title *baccalaureus artium*, or "bachelor of arts" (the ancestor of our B.A. degree). And if one stayed a little longer one would be designated *magister artium*, or "master of arts," a title that afforded a *licentia ubique docendi*, or a "license to teach anywhere," meaning that one could serve as a teacher of those same liberal arts, not only at one's home institution, but at others as well. There were also three "higher faculties," in which one could earn the title "doctor": medicine, theology, and law. These doctoral options took longer – often up to twelve years of additional study. And it was in these faculties that scholars labored on ever-more-complex questions related to

---

[34] See Christophe Charle, "Patterns," in Walter Rüegg, ed., *Universities in the Nineteenth and Early Twentieth Centuries*, vol. 3 of *A History of the University in Europe*, 4 vols. (Cambridge: Cambridge University Press, 1992–2010), 33–80, esp. 47–53; Johan Östling, *Humboldt and the Modern German University: An Intellectual History* (Lund: Lund University Press, 2018); Chad Wellmon, *Organizing Enlightenment: Information Overload and the Invention of the Modern Research University* (Baltimore: Johns Hopkins University Press, 2015).

[35] See Hilde De Ridder-Symoens, ed., *Universities in the Middle Ages*, vol. 1 of *A History of the University in Europe*, 4 vols. (Cambridge: Cambridge University Press, 1992–2010).

their disciplines. Some universities developed specialties, as Paris did in theology, or Bologna in law, or Salerno in medicine.

It was a successful model. From 1300–1500, the number of universities organized in this fashion grew significantly.[36] Though there were variations on the model and though it changed over time, the basic structure – a "lower" faculty for the liberal arts and "higher," professional faculties – continued in force for most of Europe's long early modern period.

However, by the late eighteenth century, attitudes toward academic disciplines were changing among practitioners. These changes, in turn, led to Humboldt's 1810 reform.[37] Driving change was the fact that by then the "liberal arts" had turned into something like what we refer to today as the "arts and sciences." Practitioners of the different disciplines saw them now as important not only for the formation of young people, but also as mature, research-oriented disciplines. These subjects, spanning the natural sciences to the humanities and social sciences, comprised the new "philosophical" faculty. The formation of this new faculty is why, even today, someone who receives a doctoral degree in chemistry, or history, or any other of the arts and sciences, has a "Ph.D." degree as a "doctor of philosophy," rather than as a doctor of chemistry, or of history, and so on.

Humboldt enunciated the aims of the sort of research to be carried out in the new university when he offered his thoughts on how one should conceive *Wissenschaft*. This wonderful German word means "science" in its broadest sense, referring to scholarly knowledge of all sorts, across all disciplines. Humboldt wrote that one should regard *Wissenschaft* as something not yet completely discovered, and never fully discoverable, but as something that must nonetheless incessantly be sought.[38] It is this lofty spirit that guided the university reform and, in its high-mindedness, made the scholar's life akin to a vocation and, indeed, a lifelong voyage of discovery.

This university model was generative. By the end of the nineteenth century, most other western European and North American universities adopted it in one form or another.[39] The basic idea was that universities

---

[36] From about fifteen to well over sixty; see Jacques Verger, "Patterns," in *A History of the University*, 1: 35–67.

[37] Most recently, see Östling, *Humboldt and the Modern German University*.

[38] Wilhelm von Humboldt, "Über die innere und äussere Organisation der höheren wissenschsftlichen Anstalten in Berlin," in Andreas Flintner and Klaus Giel Wilhelm von Humboldt, eds., *Werke in fünf Bänden*, 5 vols. (Stuttgart: J. G. Cotta'sche Buchhandlung, 1960), 4: 255–266, at 256.

[39] For Europe, see Rüegg, *A History of the University in Europe*, vol. 3; for the United States, see Roger L. Geiger, *The History of American Higher Education: Learning and Culture from the*

were about advancing human knowledge through research, often in teams led by powerful professorial figures. One of these figures, a German scholar of ancient Roman law named Theodor Mommsen, coined a term at the end of the nineteenth century to refer to this sort of work: *Grosswissenschaft*, or "big science," signaling academic projects that were so large that they needed teams of workers and a great, guiding idea supplied by a professorial leader.[40]

The big science model is especially well suited to natural sciences. Scholars in those fields – such as chemistry in nineteenth-century Germany and almost all lab scientists today – work in this fashion. A professor heads a lab, comes up with a guiding idea for a project and – in our current academic world – seeks funding to pursue that project. With that funding, if successful in the application bid, the professor funds postdoctoral scholars (young scholars who have completed a doctoral degree), doctoral students, and often undergraduate university students. It is the professor's project, the professor's lab, and the professor's idea. But the project could not come to fruition without the team of researchers working under the professor's direction.

This approach led to important discoveries in the nineteenth century (even as it does so today). But the humanities bore a burden. When it comes to the history of philosophy, two issues come to the fore. First: What sort of work in the humanities has the best chance of succeeding under this big research model? The answer: large projects whose participants will gather resources, edit texts, and create collections of texts, objects, and so on. The nineteenth century was a golden age for this sort of work. One could reach back to the French Enlightenment and the *Encyclopédie* of Diderot and D'Alembert, begun in 1751. That project was a private affair, with the editors charging for subscriptions and using the revenue to finance the ongoing work. But by the time the nineteenth-century university model became wedded to the humanities, big projects became one of the main goals of research. These were enterprises (which went beyond collections of texts, of course) so big they needed researchers, doctoral students, and junior faculty to carry them out. But each also needed one guiding mind to theorize and direct them.

Founding to World War II (Princeton: Princeton University Press, 2015), esp. 326–337; Emily J. Levine, *Allies and Rivals: German–American Exchange and the Rise of the Modern Research University* (Chicago: University of Chicago Press, 2021).

[40] Theodor Mommsen, "Antwort an Herrn Harnack," in *Sitzungsberichte der Königlich Preußischen Akademie der Wissenschaften zu Berlin* (Berlin, 1890), 791–793, at 792.

Accordingly, the humanities disciplines proceeded in some respects analogously to natural scientific disciplines. It would be an exaggeration to say that there was no deep reflection on the nature of the specific fields in question.[41] But it is true to say that the pressure – in the high-stakes, big research environment – to compete with the natural sciences was there. It meant, in general, that one came up with a large guiding concept and then, with that concept in hand, got to work.

Second, when it comes to the history of philosophy, the guiding concept was Brucker's, by and large. Philosophy was about rational principles, not literary context. It evolved progressively over time, meaning that one needed to tell a story of progress, a story in which some of the past context would necessarily fall away. And the historian of philosophy's job was to tell that story and, meaningfully, to focus on those figures and moments in the past that exemplified the story. Brucker himself was broad-minded, spending time (in the first volume of his magnum opus) on the origins of philosophy in non-western European realms (though we can note that the general title there is *De philosophia barbarica*). But as western European nationalisms came to the fore in the early nineteenth century, and as more thinking and practice went into the idea of the "west," some of those earlier and broader associations fell away. Brucker (and others of his generation) created frameworks first for what counted as philosophy – something that has changed since he wrote. He also validated a canon of who counted as a philosopher. That canon has remained more stable. Certain figures were left out – women, for example, in the German historiography of philosophy after Brucker.[42] Just as meaningfully, others – even standard, canonical figures – were read selectively. When this selectivity joined the practices and mentalities of the evolving research university, a picture of the history of philosophy solidified.[43]

---

[41] Wilhelm Dilthey comes to mind, as does Paul Deussen. On Dilthey, see Rudolf Makkreel, *Dilthey: Philosopher of the Human Studies* (Princeton: Princeton University Press, 1975); on Deussen, who made serious attempt to integrate Indian thinking into proto-global history of philosophy, see Suzanne Marchand, *German Orientalism in the Age of Empire: Religion, Race, and Enlightenment* (Cambridge: Cambridge University Press, 2009), pp. 300–312.

[42] Sabrina Ebbersmeyer, "From a 'Memorable Place' to 'Drops in the Ocean': On the Marginalisation of Women Philosophers in German Historiography of Philosophy," *British Journal for the History of Philosophy* 28 (2020), 442–462, esp. 451–453; Kristin Gjesdal and Dalia Nassar, eds., *The Oxford Handbook of Nineteenth-Century Women Philosophers in the German Tradition* (Oxford: Oxford University Press, 2024); see especially Gjesdal and Nassar's "Editors' Introduction," 1–21.

[43] See Ulrich Johannes Schneider, *Philosophie und Universität: Historisierung der Vernunft im 19. Jahrhundert* (Hamburg: Felix Meiner Verlag, 1999).

Moving away from selective reading helps us understand Plato more deeply. Plato took care to present opposing points of view, to set his arguments in a literary context, to use myths liberally as a teaching technique, and to offer exemplary character sketches, especially of Socrates. If one major thrust of Plato's work was to offer models for the power of rational argument, another – and they were linked – was to offer guides for living. So, in this first volume, there is substantial attention to Plato in that latter guise – as an author of literary philosophical work. It was work in which there were ambiguities, where one reader could plausibly come to conclusions different from those of another, and where philosophy's highest calling was as a guide for life. Similarly, there are two chapters on Aristotle's ethical work. There, he sketched how people who appear to live good lives do so in practice. What sorts of virtues do they possess? How do they acquire them?

So much happened between Aristotle's era and the emergence of Christianity that it would be impossible to cover it fully. But for the development of intellectual life, the central importance of Judaism; the philosophical stamp of the Hellenistic philosophical schools of Skepticism, Stoicism, and Epicureanism; and the imprint of the Roman world – its politics and its intellectual life – all need attention. Accordingly, there is a chapter devoted to these tiles in the mosaic.

Thereafter, Christianity looms large. Christianity served as the vector by which ancient philosophical ideas were transmitted, even as Christian thinkers changed those ideas and adapted them within their own frameworks. There are chapters on Jesus and the Jesus movement, along with analysis of how Paul foregrounded and shaped some of Christianity's most salient ideas.

Attention then turns to Augustine, a colossal figure, and the most important thinker in the transition between the ancient world and the Middle Ages. In his *Confessions*, he offered readers a moving and persuasive account of his conversion from spiritual rootlessness to the Christian faith. Like other contemporaries, he tried different ancient philosophies on for size, but (in his accounting) it was only when he gave himself to Christ that his anxieties were washed away, as he acquired purpose and conviction. The *Confessions* served as the exemplary model of conversion. Along the way, Augustine accounted for other forms of pagan thinking, presenting Christianity as a completion of tendencies that must always be incomplete until subsumed into the message of Christ.

A similar underlying view – of a process that was unfolding through time – can be seen in his other masterpiece, the *City of God*. This work saw Augustine wrestle with history. A common view in antiquity was that if your religion and your gods were stronger and better than those of your opponents, you would be able to triumph over them in battle, with your political realm eventually becoming dominant. It was a circular kind of thing, related to ancient public religiosity. Large, public, ritualized ceremonies of sacrifice seemed to propitiate your gods, and your eventual victories in battle showed that you had the right gods and the correct religion. But in its early years, Christianity was a religion of the humble, sparked by a dynamic and charismatic figure, Jesus, who said that the "last shall be first" and that the humble would inherit the kingdom of God.[44]

In the immediate aftermath of the sack of Rome in 410, Augustine needed to disconnect the success (or not) of political developments from religion. He posed the idea, derived from Jesus' preaching and solidified in Paul's Letters, that at some unknown time in the future, when God decided, earthly history would come to an end and Jesus Christ would return to judge the living and the dead. There was, accordingly, a "City of Man," meaning broadly the world of human politics, wars, changes in government, and so on. And there was a "City of God," the eternal realm in which the divine drama just alluded to would take place.

The history of Rome, a grand story that Romans had been telling themselves for centuries, saw Rome go from the workings of an isolated small tribe camping out on the banks of the Tiber River to one of the greatest empires the world had ever known. But in Augustine's view, inflected as it was by the eye of eternity, even that grand story seemed, if not small, then part of an evolution. This evolution was moving toward something bigger, better, and infinitely more important: God's providential judgment over both the lives of his creatures and their potential salvation. History had a direction, Augustine was saying. In doing so he implicitly rebuked one typical ancient view that history was cyclical, an endless rising and falling of powers. Yes, in the moment history might seem that way. But the City of Man, finite and limited by human time as it was, was little more than a blip in the eyes of God, who saw the past, present, and future as if in an eternal present and who, importantly, had a plan for humanity. If that plan was known ultimately only to him, we could still see signs and hints, as we went forward in the endless human pattern of interpreting ourselves, our society, and our world.

It would be difficult to overstate how influential the *City of God* turned out to be. Its unique depiction of the shape of history conditioned many

---

[44] Matt 19:30, 20:16; Mark 10:31; Luke 13:30; Matt 5:3, 5:5, 18:4, 23:12; Luke 6:20, 18:14.

Introduction: Philosophy, Conversations, Wisdom, Traditions 21

medieval views of history. We were moving toward a final judgment, time unknown. And if one senses similar teleologies in other later thinkers – Hegel and Marx, for example – those views are indebted to Augustine's early staking out of this ground.[45]

The book ends with Gregory the Great, pope from 590–604. An inheritor of the ancient and early Christian tradition, he fostered missionary work and served as a cultural translator for some of the more "high concept" thinking we see in Augustine. Gregory wrote in a simple Latin. He was speaking in the first instance to contemporaries in Italy, many of whom could not follow oratorical, high Latin, as they heard works read to them. Gregory was also directing his work to other parts of Europe, where Latin had never been a native language, places such as Germany or, farther afield and a place of special interest to him, the "insular" realms – the island nations of what we now know as England, Ireland, Scotland, and Wales. As missionaries traveled to those areas, so distant from Christianity's beginnings over a half a millennium earlier in the Middle East, newly converted monks and clerics often needed to learn Christianity's official language from the ground up. It was a new world and a new culture. It represents an appropriate point at which to bring this volume to a close.

Some concluding comments are needed. Looking into the past and into other cultures, we encounter difference and, at times, values starkly at odds with those we hold dear. Assumptions about people's roles that seemed routine and intuitively acceptable to people in the distant past may now seem beyond the pale, even as, certainly, those looking at us centuries and millennia from now will find similar discordances.

Take Paul, one of the thinkers we shall meet. One way he spread the new teachings of Christ was through letters that he wrote to communities and to disciples. In one, the Letter to the Galatians, he expresses the idea of the universality of Christ's new message and urges his readers not to hold fast to old customs. In this new dispensation, he writes, "there is neither Jew nor Greek, there is neither bond nor free, there is neither male nor female. For you are all one in Christ Jesus."[46] One often talks today about the intersection of race, class, and gender, and how they need to be accounted for together, if one is to understand how power and oppression are sometimes linked.[47] And

---

[45] Cf. Arnaldo Momigliano, *The Classical Foundations of Modern Historiography* (Berkeley: University of California Press, 1990), pp. 155–156.
[46] Gal 3:28.
[47] See Kimberlé Crenshaw, Neil Gotanda, Gary Peller, Kendall Thomas, eds., *Critical Race Theory: The Key Writings that Formed the Movement* (New York: The New Press, 1995), esp.

there they are, all three, with Paul recognizing that individuals differentiated themselves accordingly. In suggesting that if people accept the Christian faith, they will escape the prison-house of those categories, he is also looking forward (unintentionally of course) to much later theories of human rights, wherein simply by being human, one can be seen as entitled to certain rights, whatever one's race, class, or gender. He seems remarkably prescient and modern, able to look past the strictures of his contemporary culture and toward a different and more equitable time.

But then, in another Pauline letter (this one to Timothy), the author advocates for a form of gender discrimination when writing about the right ways to pray. We read, regarding men: "I want the men everywhere to pray, lifting up holy hands without anger or disputing."[48] The author then focuses on women, who should dress modestly. As the men lead the enterprise of prayer, "A woman should learn in quietness and full submission. I do not permit a woman to teach or to assume authority over a man."[49] Adam came first, he goes on, and Eve second. But it was not the first man, Adam, who was deceived and first sinned. Rather, it was the first woman, Eve, who did so (one recalls the story of Eve eating the forbidden fruit, introducing sin and disobedience to God into the world, and so on).[50] So, "women will be saved through childbearing" provided they live lives of faith.[51] Elsewhere, in his first Letter to the Corinthians, Paul says that women should remain silent in churches and should ask their husbands at home if they have a question.[52] In these cases, we see Paul as defender of the idea that men were the public actors, the ones who led. Women were expected to be silent and obedient.

Benefitted as we are by modern scholarship, it is worth noting that one can distinguish between Paul and "Paul." This is to say that textual scholars of the New Testament believe that there are seven letters in the Pauline body of texts that Paul himself wrote, and others penned by followers (the first and second letters to Timothy are among the latter).[53] Those indications are important as we seek the historical Paul's viewpoint – to understand Paul

---

Crenshaw, "Mapping the Margins: Intersectionality, Identity Politics, and Violence Against Women of Color," 357–383.

[48] 1 Tim 2:8.   [49] 1 Tim 2:11–12.   [50] Gen 2:4–3:24.   [51] 1 Tim 2:15.

[52] 1 Cor 14:33–35; cf. Leppin, *The Early Christians*, 129 with n.13. The association of women with silence was long-standing in ancient culture. Cf. Sophocles, *Ajax*, in Sophocles, *Ajax, Electra, Oedipus Tyrannus*, ed and tr. Hugh Lloyd-Jones (Cambridge, MA: Harvard University Press, 1997), pp. 27–163, at l.293 (p. 58), my tr., where a character is told that "silence is an ornament for a woman."

[53] See Arland J. Hultgren, "The Pastoral Epistles," in James D. G. Dunn, ed., *The Cambridge Companion to Saint Paul* (Cambridge: Cambridge University Press, 2003), 141–155, at 142–144 for a summary of the evidence.

as he understood himself, in so far as we can. But this book is as much about how Paul may have been read over time as it is about disentangling the knotty Pauline textual tradition. For the late ancient and medieval readers who read him, there was one Paul. So, one could plausibly come away from his letters with either of the two noted perspectives, the one universalist and stressing the inherent equality of all human persons, the other less so.

These contradictory images present us with a test case of how to read. Paul as defender of the equality of all persons versus Paul as enforcer of existing social prejudices: which to choose? In this book, part of what we will be doing is seeking context. In this case regarding Paul, we can say that in different letters he shows that women were clearly part of the early Christian community, often positively highlighting certain women by name and acknowledging their importance in the Jesus movement (see Rom, 16:1, highlighting a woman named Phoebe who served as a deacon, for example).[54] Still, the truth was that women's roles in his day were more restricted than they are in ours. Expecting someone from that era to align with current values seems misguided, just as it would be unreasonable not to note ancient prejudices and their subsequent effects. And yet, when we do see glimmerings of modern ideas – such as Paul's implicit recognition of the fundamental equality of all human beings and the complexities surrounding race, gender, and class – what are we to make of these moments?

The perspective behind this book is twofold. First, ideas matter. They have a way of traveling out of their original context, existing unmoored from whatever reality out of which they might have emerged and taking root in other eras and at other times, adopted and adapted by later thinkers in different contexts.[55] The "conversations" alluded to in the chapter's title point to this dynamic. The protagonists – the thinkers who enunciated the many ideas we shall encounter – were all historical figures, grounded in their environment, just as subject to blind spots induced by their culture as we are by ours. We will respect their contexts but also realize that the conversations occurred across different times and places, as thinkers looked backwards, added their own contributions, and – like improvisers in jazz – added something new, even when the underlying chords were similar.

---

[54] See Hartmut Leppin, *The Early Christians: From the Beginnings to Constantine*, tr. Kathrin Luddecke (Cambridge: Cambridge University Press, 2023), pp. 124–136; cf. Acts 21:9.

[55] Cf. J. G. A. Pocock, "*The Machiavellian Moment* Revisited: A Study in History and Ideology," *Journal of Modern History* 53 (1981), 49–72, at 52–53: "in civilizations employing complex literary traditions, patterns of language and thought outlive the authors who utter them in specific texts, and reappear in successive texts and contexts ... They are not merely epiphenomenal, and they have histories which display persistence as well as fluidity."

Second, we need to read generously. The conversations traced here shaped our world for better and, at times, for worse. We need to extend the same understanding of diversity that we prize today to thinkers of the past. In the Pauline dilemma above, which of the two sentiments does it seem better to focus on today? To me it seems obvious that we would want our own best work at least to get a hearing. Accordingly, in this case, more focus should fall on Paul's Galatians text – "neither Jew nor Greek," and so on – than on the (time-bound) comments regarding women's places in worship. None of this is to say we should read naively, or that – to recall Brucker – we should "dig out" from the thinking of the past only the things we wish to find. The same "Paul" (in the eyes of his late ancient and early medieval readers) who wrote the first statement also wrote the second. We need to acknowledge this point and understand the ramifications and consequences. But every thinker we shall meet in this book inhabited a world where norms concerning equality among persons and attitudes toward gender and power were radically different from current preferences. Some of those thinkers departed from the consensus of their era and contributed to some of the more humanity-affirming mindsets prized today. Others scattered seeds that would later grow. This process took time, effort, and imagination across centuries and among widely varied thinkers. Recognizing this fact, we should build constructively on the past, just as the thinkers under discussion did. This is precisely what this book attempts to do: to take what is best about this western philosophical past and to bring it into contact with our world today, in short, to continue the conversation.

2

PLATO

Philosophy, Conversation, and the Nature of Reality

Is reality immediately apparent to us? Or is it deeper and more mysterious than we commonly suppose? Does what we see and hear reflect reality? Or are our senses only imperfect guides? Is the world around us all there is? Or is there more, something beyond us? These questions, meaningful still, stood out in the work of Plato.

Plato lived in a time of cultural flourishing in Athens, Greece, at a moment marked by war and societal division. During his lifetime, Greek literature was in flower, with the tragic plays of Aeschylus, Sophocles, and Euripides performed at public festivals. Ancient sculpture thrived, as artists made statuary so lifelike it seemed almost miraculous. The philosopher Socrates, Plato's teacher, engaged in public discussions over virtue and vice, pressing his fellow interlocutors, sometimes to the point of exhaustion.

Athens was proud of being a democracy, a place where citizens could vote and participate in their own government.[1] As Plato came to maturity, however, Athens was in a bad way, politically, having suffered defeat in what is now known as the Peloponnesian War. The victor in that struggle was the city of Sparta, a place whose customs and laws could not have been more antithetical to those of Athens. Centralized where Athens was pluralistic, shunning luxury and the arts as Athens cultivated them, and organized around one central principle, militaristic strength, Sparta had come out on top in the almost thirty-year struggle. Tensions were high in Athens. And, in a culture such as theirs, where debate and critique played out in various public fora – from the organized, governmental parliament where all

---

[1] See Robin Osborne, ed. and tr., *Athenian Democracy*, 2nd ed. (Cambridge: Cambridge University Press, 2023), for sources and pp. 167–168 for further reading; John, Ma, *Polis: A New History of the Ancient Greek City-State from the Early Iron Age to the End of Antiquity* (Princeton: Princeton University Press, 2024), pp. 182–193.

citizens had the right to speak (the *boule*), to the more informal but no less important marketplace (the *agora*) – someone like Socrates, contrarian as he tended to be, was at risk. People making their own decisions about governance, the staple of democracies, is a virtue. But democracies sometimes make mistakes. One of those occurred, in Plato's view, when the Athenian government sentenced Plato's friend and mentor, Socrates, to death, after a group of private citizens indicted and prosecuted him, and he was convicted by a jury.

Socrates pioneered a style of doing philosophy that relied on continual questioning (a style to which we owe our phrase "Socratic questioning"). He had built up a following in Athens, serving as an inspiring teacher to many younger men, among whom Plato counted himself. Yet among some, Socrates had a reputation as a person whose constant questioning served no purpose or, worse, as an all-too-obvious critique of societal institutions. It was this latter tendency that pushed the Athenian government to its fatal sentence. A friend offered Socrates the chance to escape but he chose not to do so. Remaining as he did, he became a kind of martyr in social memory. Plato dedicated all his intellectual energy to honoring the memory of the teacher he loved. He did so in two ways.

First, there is the portrait of Socrates in Plato's dialogues. In them, Plato presents the image of Socrates that has endured through millennia: unattractive physically, but magnetic in person; unafraid to criticize institutions, but loving to his friends; a thinker who could speak learnedly about many subjects, even as he was concerned most of all with ethics and life in the world. And there was one more thing. Plato presents Socrates as possessing what we would today recognize as a conscience, which the character Socrates refers to as his *daimonion*, a word that can mean "something divine," or a "little spiritual presence" or more colloquially, a "little demon," though without the necessary associations of evil that the English word "demon" implies today. Socrates' *daimonion* would appear to him and warn him not to do certain things (it is thus that Socrates explains his avoidance of politics, for example).[2] His contemporaries may have interpreted this latter factor as Socrates claiming he was under divine inspiration, somehow superior to the rest of his fellow citizens and, accordingly, even more suspicious.[3] But for his student Plato, the *daimonion* is a lovable characteristic, individuating

---

[2] See Plato, *Apology*, in Plato, *Euthyphro, Apology, Crito, Phaedo*, ed. and tr. Chris Emlyn-Jones and William Preddy (Cambridge, MA: Harvard University Press, 2014), sec. 31c–d, pp. 158–159.

[3] See Plato, *Euthyphro*, sec. 3b–c, in Plato, *Euthyphro, Apology, Crito, Phaedo, Phaedrus*, 24–25.

Socrates. It represents one among many factors that make Plato's literary portrait of his friend and teacher so lasting.

There are other sources that attest to Socrates' centrality in Athenian cultural life. He appears as a character in a comic play by Aristophanes, *The Clouds*. There, Socrates seems a bumptious quibbler more concerned with doing things like measuring how far a flea could jump than with anything resembling a life of integrity.[4] And in the *Memorabilia* of his student Xenophon, Socrates emerges as a virtuous thinker.[5] Xenophon's Socrates is a man concerned with defending the existence of the divine, practicing self-control, and encouraging an ethical framework that stressed the links between what one did in the world and the way that activity contributed to the common good. But it was Plato's portrait that took hold, causing Socrates to be remembered as a signal figure in the history of philosophy.

The second "tribute" that Plato paid his teacher is more important. It has to do with genre. This factor, genre, does not often get its due in the interpretation of intellectual life and its written products, whether these are lengthy books or short epigrams, lapidary poems or, more to the point here, works of philosophy. Plato's choice to write in dialogues was precisely that: a choice, one that must be foregrounded to understand what he was up to.

What is it that dialogues do? What kind of thinking can they foster? The best way to approach these questions is to leap right into Plato's most famous dialogue, the *Republic*. Structured in ten "Books" (think of them as extended chapters), the *Republic* addresses the questions: What is justice? And does being a just person lead to being a fulfilled, or happy, person? Along the way, Socrates, the main interlocutor, leads a conversation that covers the structure of an ideal city, the afterlife, the place of the arts in society, the nature of the human soul, and much more.[6]

At the beginning of Book 7, Socrates reports something he said during a long, winding conversation concerning education and how people come to know things.[7] Examining the passage allows insight into key elements of

---

[4] Aristophanes, *Clouds*, lines 143–152, in Aristophanes, *Clouds, Wasps, Peace*, ed. and tr. Jeffrey Henderson (Cambridge, MA: Harvard University Press, 1998), pp. 26–27.

[5] Xenophon, *Memorabilia*, in Xenophon, *Memorabilia, Oeconomicus, Symposium, Apology*, ed. and tr. E. C. Marchant and O. J. Todd, and rev. by Jeffrey Henderson (Cambridge, MA: Harvard University Press, 2013), pp. 8–377.

[6] See G. R. F. Ferrari, ed., *The Cambridge Companion to Plato's Republic* (Cambridge: Cambridge University Press, 2007); Peter Adamson, *Classical Philosophy: A History of Philosophy without any Gaps*, vol. 1 (Oxford: Oxford University Press, 2014), pp. 144–151.

[7] Plato, *Republic*, 2 vols., ed. and tr. Chris Emlyn-Jones and William Preddy (Cambridge, MA: Harvard University Press, 2013), vol. 2, sec. 507c–517a.

Plato's philosophy, even as it serves as a springboard to a discussion of genre and to less familiar ways of viewing Plato's thinking. Here is Socrates:

> Imagine human beings as if they were in an underground, cave-like dwelling, with a long wide entrance facing the light along the whole length of the cave. They have been there since childhood shackled by the legs and the neck, so that they remain in the same spot facing only forward, unable to turn their heads right round because of the chains.[8]

The cited passage represents the beginning of the "allegory of the cave."

What is on view thus far is arresting, in two ways. First, the cave image begins with Socrates making a point about education to one of the dialogue's other interlocutors. Remember that fact, for we shall return to it. Second, the language asks us to imagine people literally in chains, imprisoned and shackled so that their heads can face only one way. It is an image designed to be memorable and startling, to force the other, fictional interlocutor in the dialogue to pay attention, and to compel the reader – you, the real, non-fictional interlocutor – to do the same.

The cave image grows clearer. Behind the chained human beings lies a light from a fire that burns above them. In between that fire and its accompanying light is a path leading up to a low wall, "just as puppeteers have a screen in front of the audience above which they present their entertainments."[9] It is not too hard to see where the image is headed. There are people behind that wall carrying statues and other representations of creatures fashioned out of wood and stone, some of which speak, others of which are silent. What is it, then, that the imprisoned people see? Or rather, what is it possible for them to see, given how they are situated face front? The answer is: shadows. They would see shadows of the objects that the puppeteers throw onto the wall in front of them. Moreover, they would think that what they saw was real and that the words they were saying about the shadows applied instead to real things.[10] Those unfortunate enchained people would be subject to misconceptions that were, to boot, even more powerful because there was no way of discerning anything else.

"Shadows." The Greek word that Plato uses, through his interlocutor Socrates, is *skia*. It is a common ancient Greek word, used often in proverbs.[11] Plato is connecting matters of the greatest moment (how we know

---

[8] Plato, *Republic*, 2: 514a–b, tr. modified.   [9] Ibid., 514b.   [10] Ibid., 515b.
[11] See for example Sophocles, *Fragments*, ed. Richard C. Jebb, Walter G. Headlam, and Alfred C. Pearson, 3 vols. (Cambridge: Cambridge University Press, 1917), fr. 13: "anthropos esti pneuma kai skia monon" ("man is only a spirit, a shadow").

what we believe we know, and whether what we believe we know is real) with ordinary, everyday language. Philosophy emerges from stories, stories that, if told correctly, should be available and understandable to everyone.

What would happen, Socrates goes on, if these unfortunate people were released from their chains? Imagine one of them who has been set free and made to stand up, turn around, and look at the light. The first reaction of this poor unfortunate would be pain and, indeed, a kind of blindness, as the unaccustomed exposure to light would create a glare. Let us say that someone has been leading this person toward the light and telling him that what he had seen before, while chained, was "nonsense"; whereas now the formerly chained person was seeing "more correctly." Let us say, too, that this guide asked the newly freed prisoner what each thing was that he was now seeing. What would the still confused man's reaction be? Socrates asks: "Don't you think that he would be **at a loss** and think that what he had seen before used to seem **truer** than what was being shown to him now?"[12]

The expressions highlighted in bold are meaningful. The word translated as "at a loss" derives from the Greek verb *aporein*, which means "to be uncertain," a verb from which the Greek noun *aporia* comes as well. It is a word sometimes used in English, especially in philosophical contexts. And it is important in helping us understand Socrates' style of inquiry. It represents a method that Socrates, in real life, had carried out orally, by means of face-to-face discussions, even as the best records we possess are those that Plato put into writing in his dialogues.[13]

The method (questioning leading to an *aporia*) is on display through Plato's dialogues and, indeed, in the *Republic* itself. An example: Early in the *Republic*, one question that preoccupies Socrates is the nature of justice. What is justice? How can we best describe it? One of the interlocutors, faced with Socrates' questions, suggests that justice has to do with giving back what one owes to another. Socrates then questions him with a neatly chosen example. Let us say you have borrowed weapons from a friend, and after a time, the friend wants them back. But in the interim between his loan to you and his request that you return them, the friend has gone mad. Can we really describe the act of returning the weapons when he is in that condition as a "just" thing to do? The answer, obviously, is "no." Accordingly, as to

---

[12] Plato, *Republic*, 515d, tr. modified, emphasis mine.
[13] See Andrea Nightingale, "Plato on *Aporia* and Self-Knowledge," in Andrea Nightingale and David Sedley, eds., *Ancient Models of Mind: Studies in Human and Divine Rationality* (Cambridge: Cambridge University Press, 2010), 8–26; David Wolfsdorf, *Trials of Reason: Plato and the Crafting of Philosophy* (Oxford: Oxford University Press, 2008), pp. 197–239; and E. N. Tigerstedt, *Interpreting Plato* (Stockholm: Almquist and Wissell, 1977), pp. 98–99.

the "what is justice" question, the interlocutor is facing an *aporia*. He is "at a loss." The result is that, in this example as in many others, the conversation needs to continue, so that, together, the interlocutors can proceed more precisely, honing their questions and answers – honing their language – in the hopes of seeking and finding human wisdom by getting closer to the truth.

Then there is "truth."[14] Note what Socrates suggests. The prisoner is newly freed and still unaccustomed to the light, to his new surroundings, and to the new-to-him world to which he has been exposed. In this condition, he may indeed think that the things that once surrounded him and that he used to observe – the things he saw in the cave, in other words – were "truer" than what he is being told he is seeing now. The Greek word in question is an adjectival form of the word *aletheia*, a word that indeed means "truth" but that also signifies "reality" and "appearance." What is at issue is twofold: first, how your perceptions match what appears to your senses and, second, how that appearance relates to reality. The underlying question is: What is reality?

Let us further suppose (Socrates goes on) that the partner induced the newly freed prisoner to look directly at the light – the real light, outside, rather than reflected light. Initially it would be too much, and the prisoner's eyes would hurt. He would turn away, veering back almost automatically toward what he previously believed to be true. But then let's say someone dragged the prisoner up anyway. At first, he would still be unable to see anything clearly. Socrates says: "Indeed, I think he would need to acclimatize himself if he's going to look at what is above."[15] What next? Well, he would start out by seeing "shadows" and then move outward to "reflections of people and other things in water, and later on the things themselves."[16] Plato, through his character Socrates, strategically employs the physical world in the story he is telling, stressing natural phenomena – water, reflections – that to any reader are intuitively familiar. The point is that a continuum of possible perceptions exists. These perceptions range from those that are almost automatic and most apparent, to those that are more removed, and that take work to perceive and to understand. The freed man would then look at the heavenly bodies, especially the moon and stars. Then, thus habituated, he would "be able to see the sun, not its reflection in water ... but by itself alone."[17] The discussion leads us (even as the prisoner

---

[14] Cf. Gregory Vlastos, "Degrees of Reality in Plato," in Gregory Vlastos, ed., *Platonic Studies* (Princeton: Princeton University Press, 1973), 58–75.
[15] Plato, *Republic*, 516a.   [16] Ibid.   [17] Ibid., 516b.

is led) to contemplate that there is a continuum in nature, the observance of which requires training.

Plato means to do more with this example. He has Socrates observe the consequences of the prisoner's viewing of the sun, pure and simple, not through a reflection but as it is. Once the prisoner has arrived at the ability to see the sun directly, he will then be able "to **infer**" that the sun "provides the seasons, and the years, and governs everything in the **visible world**, and is somehow responsible for all those things that they themselves" – the enchained prisoners – "used to see."[18] For the prisoner, this process of realization – in this case that the sun is, in some respects, the author of everything – proceeded through a process of reckoning. Indeed, the verb translated above as "infer" is *syllogizein*, in Greek, a verb that combines two roots: *syn*, which means "together" and *logos*, which means "word," "reason," "speech," and "argument," among other things.

The prisoner, then, under the tutelage of his guide, can see many facets of the visible world in a gradually more distinct fashion, moving from inchoate shadows to accurate reflections, to, finally, the things themselves. And he has done so in the "visible world," the Greek for which means more literally the "place that has been observed," meaning everything that can be perceived, everything apparent, everything, in other words, that is phenomenological. Also, the prisoner's process has been helped along by the persistent presence of the guide, who at each stage has pushed the prisoner a bit more – to look a little closer, to attend a bit longer, to observe ever more closely. We are in the realm of education, or at least in the realm of metaphors that have to do with education.

Socrates asks his interlocutor, what next? What would happen, that is, after the prisoner had, finally, grasped the truth? After he had realized that everything he knew was, essentially, a fiction and, more, that his fellow prisoners were themselves subject to the same delusion? The answer, though Plato does not word it this starkly, is that a conversion would occur. If, for instance, that formerly imprisoned man thought back on his old way of life, what seemed desirable then would seem so no longer. Back in the old community, perhaps his fellows used to give each other honors and prizes for their accomplishments. But those would not mean very much to our newly enlightened prisoner. Moreover, when he did return, his eyes, now accustomed to the bright light of the sun, would be plunged back into the realm of shadow. Accordingly, he would not be able to see as well as the

---

[18] Ibid.

prisoners. Unaware as they are of their true circumstances, they would ridicule him. Indeed, should someone try to free them from their chains and take them up to the light, they would resist mightily, since from everything they have seen, exposure to the world above leads to nothing other than confusion and blindness. That, in brief, is the basic story of the cave.

Socrates reveals the underlying meaning of this tale: "And if you take the upward journey and the seeing of what is above as standing for the upward journey of the soul to the intelligible realm, you will not mistake my intention..."[19] Through Socrates, Plato posits a world of hierarchy. On the low end are physical things most apparent to us. On the high end (up to this point in the discussion) there is "the intelligible realm." This expression's Greek words are *noētos*, which means "intelligible," "able to be understood," and "subject to the power of reason," and *topos*, whose basic meaning is "place," with all the connotations that word can possess. The word *noētos* embeds within it another Greek word, *nous*, which means "mind," "reason," "intellect," and, in short, what you need within you to be able to understand things. It applies to human capacity. Plato also employs it to suggest that there is some "place" or "realm" that has a certain character. If you can ascend there, the capacities of your mind to understand things will find their match in a place where the things that can be truly understood reside. This is the "intelligible realm." It is a "place" but not a physical location; a part of the universe at large but not a world we see or experience with our senses.

Socrates has explained the allegory thus far. He pauses for a moment, to say something that is, in one respect, almost a throwaway line. Regarding the veracity of what he has sketched, he says, "only God knows, I suppose, if this is entirely true."[20] The line applies both to the allegory just explained and to what he is about to say. And what he is about to say is momentous. It is a passage so important that it is worth quoting in full, with Socrates speaking as follows, with some key terms highlighted:

> This is how things appear to me: in the **knowable realm** the form of the Good is last among the things perceived and is seen with difficulty, but once seen, then this is to be reckoned as the cause of all that is **right** and **beautiful** for everyone. It gives birth to light and the source of light in the visible world, and it is itself the **source** of truth and understanding in the **intelligible realm**.[21]

---

[19] Ibid., 517b, tr. modified.   [20] Ibid., my tr.   [21] Ibid., 517b, tr. modified.

Anyone, Socrates goes on, who acts sensibly in private or public life will have seen the form of the Good.

As to the terms, first, there is the Greek substantive adjective *gnôstô*, translated here as "knowable realm," though it is worth mentioning that a more literal translation would be, simply, the "knowable." The Greek term enfolds within it the word *gnôsis*, whose range of meanings runs from "inquiry," to "knowledge" in the sense of being acquainted with something or someone, to "secret, hidden knowledge," to "knowledge," pure and simple. Plato is foregrounding a part of the universe where knowledge happens, the "knowable realm."

Then there is the "form of the Good." Here there are two key words in question, "form" and "Good." "Form," the translation used here for the Greek word *idea*, can also mean something like what we mean when the use the word "idea" (Plato expresses the same notion, that of "form," with another word as well, the Greek *eidos*, elsewhere in his work). "Form" – as a concept and category – represents one of the most important parts of Plato's thinking. We can best understand his concept of "form" if we think of it as the very essence of a thing, the ultimate answer to the question: What makes this thing what it is? However, when "form," understood in this way, is paired with "the Good," further questions emerge. How can you define an ultimate "good"? In the *Republic*'s analogy, Socrates is clear that the Form of the Good is, in some fashion, the cause of all good things. To understand this notion, and its importance in Plato's thought, we need to step back for a moment, to look at the educational environment in the era of Plato and Socrates.

When it came to education in Plato's era, no element was more central than persuasion, which relied on rhetoric.[22] Today, when we hear the word "rhetoric," common associations are often negative. "Empty rhetoric" signifies a profusion of words without content. "Mere rhetoric" means something similar: an artificial, hypocritical attempt to trick people with words. It can be surprising to modern readers to hear that rhetoric was the cornerstone of education in Plato's day. Those who provided that education were called "sophists" – again, a word that today rings negatively. One of the reasons that word has negative associations has to do with how Plato portrayed sophists.

---

[22] George A. Kennedy, *A New History of Classical Rhetoric* (Princeton: Princeton University Press, 1994), pp. 3–80; Henri Irenée Marrou, *A History of Education in Antiquity*, tr. George Lamb (Madison: University of Wisconsin Press, 1956), pp. 46–60; James J. Murphy, Richard A. Katula, Michael J. Hoppmann, *A Synoptic History of Classical Rhetoric*, 4th ed. (New York: Routledge, 2014).

The word in Greek, *sophistês*, derived from the Greek word *sophos*, which means "wise." And the word *sophistês* meant among other things "expert," and "master of one's specific craft." You could describe a good musician or poet as a *sophistês*. And you could use the word to describe an especially wise and skilled statesman.[23] The sophists of whom we are speaking now, however, were teachers of rhetoric. Shorn of its negative connotations, rhetoric is simply the art of persuasion. And in a preindustrial direct democracy, like Athens, persuading one's fellow citizens counted for a lot. Becoming a skilled orator could lead to political success and the skills that sophists taught were desirable.[24] Sophists were in such demand that they charged fees for education, a practice to which Socrates and Plato were averse, believing that true lovers of wisdom would not cheapen what they did by demanding money.[25] More importantly, the sophists also seemed to be relativistic (as we would term it today) when it came to ethics.[26]

It is surely true that, at the most basic level, sophists provided necessary education in a society where public speaking was important. Our source for seeing sophists as relativistic is owed mostly to Plato and his presentation of one of them, Protagoras. So, we should take some of what Plato said with the proverbial grain of salt. Still, what we do know about sophistic practices can be arresting.

Plato portrayed Protagoras in more than one dialogue. In one, Protagoras says: "Man is the measure of all things, of the things that are, that they are, and of things that are not, that they are not."[27] "Man" here means "human beings" at large. And the implication, if one follows the inexorable logic present in that pithy statement, is that there cannot be an objective criterion for determining what is or isn't true. Protagoras was also reported to have boasted that he could teach students how to make "the weaker argument also the stronger one."[28] Here too we see a tendency that could have troubling results if unchecked. Winning through persuasion seems all that

---

[23] Herodotus, *The Persian Wars*, 4 vols., ed. and tr. A. D. Godley (Cambridge, MA: Harvard University Press, 1926), 1.29, p. 32.
[24] See Jacqueline de Romilly, *The Great Sophists in Periclean Athens*, tr. Janet Lloyd (Oxford: Clarendon Press, 1992).
[25] Plato, *Apology*, 20b–21a, pp. 116–121.
[26] See Richard Bett, "The Sophists and Relativism," *Phronesis* 34 (1989), 139–169, for the complexities surrounding the term.
[27] Plato, *Theaetetus*, ed. and tr. Harold North Fowler (Cambridge, MA: Harvard University Press, 1921), sec. 152a, p. 40, tr. modified.
[28] See the testimony of Eudoxus (per Stephanus of Byzantium) in André Laks and Glenn Most, eds. and trs., *Early Greek Philosophy*, 9 vols. (Cambridge, MA: Harvard University Press, 2016), vol. 8, pp. 52–53.

matters, and the way one persuades people is to use purely human frameworks for judgment. Since human frameworks change – over time and by region – the implication is that there is nothing, really, that is universally true, only immediate contexts and episodes, each up for grabs in what amounts to a game of endless persuasion and dissuasion. It is not the case that all those termed sophists believed in this strong form of relativism.[29] But the tendency was marked enough that Plato could use it as something to fight against, all the while strengthening his own ideas. And his principal weapon was the theory of Forms.[30]

Take the Form of Beauty. All around us, we are surrounded by beautiful things: things that we see in the natural world, such as intricately patterned flowers, or butterflies; things that we hear, like music that touches us to such an extent that, once we have heard it, we cannot imagine that the music in question at one point did not exist. And then, too, there are people who surround us, some of whom we find physically attractive. If all those disparate things can be called beautiful, what is it then that they share? Plato's answer would be the Form of Beauty. More precisely, he would say that they "participated" in the Form of Beauty. The Greek word for participation, one that Plato used repeatedly, is *methexis*.[31] The basic meaning of the verb, *methechein*, on which this noun is based, is "to have a share of" or "to partake of." Accordingly, that flower that seems so beautiful partakes of the Form of Beauty, in the sense that it has, undoubtedly, a portion of beauty overall.

There is a divine element in play, for Plato, something that can be seen even more clearly when it comes to the question of physical love. You are attracted to a beautiful person, perhaps so much so that you seem to lose your faculty of reason for a time. You have desires for physical contact with that person. Since all of this is part of the natural world, Plato accepts the existence of physical love and desire. But he insists that, to understand beauty in its purest form – to approach the Form of Beauty – you need to train yourself to understand just what those desires represent. And what they represent is an inevitable feature of human experience, a lack of control, that must be tamed by education. For what that individual person's beauty represents, great as it is, is an imperfect manifestation of perfect, unsullied beauty in the realm of the Forms.

---

[29] Bett, "The Sophists and Relativism."
[30] In a rich literature, see most recently Vasilis Politis, *Plato's Essentialism: Reinterpreting the Theory of Forms* (Cambridge: Cambridge University Press, 2021).
[31] See e.g., Plato, *Phaedo*, 100c–101c, pp. 456–461.

Where then are these Forms? They reside, Plato tells us elsewhere, "outside the heavens."[32] We think of places as physical, but the type of place in question is not physical at all, for what is in this place has no color, no shape, and no solidity. There one finds intangible being, "that which truly exists, with which the class of true knowledge is concerned," something "visible only to the mind, the pilot of the soul."[33] Color, shape, and solidity are subject to the human senses. But our senses can deceive us. Our bodies fail, they grow ill, they decline over time. Plato is saying there exists a realm where those normal aspects of the human condition do not apply. It is a domain better than the one we inhabit, higher by any measure, unsullied by earthly desires, and subject to no normal human affection. So, when you see that beautiful person and feel physical desire for him or her, what that really signifies – what it should signify, Plato suggests – is a reminder of that other, better, eternal place. It is a reminder that the beauty in front of you, magnificent as it may seem, manifests eternal beauty only imperfectly.[34]

For Plato, it is against these sorts of eternal attributes that we should measure our earthly conduct, a notion that was alien to the sophists, whose main measure of success was earthbound. If sophists claimed to teach wisdom, Plato suggested that what they taught was, instead, little more than a knack – a purely technical skill of persuasion, with no grounding in any deeper source of wisdom, such as could be found were one to contemplate the Forms.

To return, then, to the allegory of the cave, the difficulty of the prisoner's plight is clear. It is hard for him to shed his normal conditions and arrive at the sun and just as hard, once he has seen it, to return whence he came. It is a central conflict in human life when it comes to education. Should education be practical, fitting students out for applied success? This was the way of the sophists. Or should education be based foremost on eternal truths, truths that require a great deal of mental discipline to comprehend, not to mention moral education toward the end of inculcating humility in the face of a complex world? This was the way of Socrates and Plato. The message is unequivocal: There is something divine that exists above, beyond, and apart from us, something that it is our obligation to try to understand, mysterious as it may seem when we first consider it.

---

[32] Plato, *Phaedrus*, in Plato, *Lysis, Symposium, Phaedrus*, ed. and tr. Chris Emlyn-Jones and William Preddy (Cambridge, MA: Harvard University Press, 2022), 247b, p. 416: "exo tou ouranou."

[33] Ibid., 247c, pp. 416–417, tr. modified.

[34] See e.g., Plato, *Symposium*, in Plato, *Lysis, Symposium, Phaedrus*, 210a–212a, pp. 272–279; and *Phaedrus*, 249c–250c, pp. 422–427.

Recall what the interlocutor Socrates said when discussing whether the allegory as he had outlined it was true: "Now only God knows whether this happens to be true." The word translated as "God" is *theos* in Greek, a noun used in the singular form. We should not make too much of this fact. Plato was a polytheist, as were his fellow Athenians. Moreover, the Athenian community possessed a rich religious life, predicated on a world suffused with divinities of all sorts.[35] Plato and his contemporaries believed in many gods, meaning that there were different divinities thought to govern different aspects of life: Poseidon was the god of the sea, who could protect seafarers who were friendly to him and worshipped him properly, even as he could summon storms to punish enemies. Hephaestus was the god of blacksmiths and artisans, who watched over trades and was also believed to make the gods' weapons. Demeter was the goddess of agriculture. Worship her correctly and you would enjoy good harvests that would yield abundant grain. Fail to do right by her, and your fields might not be fruitful, so that famine and blight served as signs of her anger. And so on. There were hosts of natural processes, all of which had gods connected to them.

If we shouldn't make too much of Plato's use of the term "God," we shouldn't make too little of it either. For Plato, the "divine" came to mean more than the seemingly mechanistic processes just outlined might connote. The two great epic poems authored centuries before Plato, Homer's *Iliad* and *Odyssey*, were central in Greek culture.[36] Those who were highly educated could recite, comment on, and link together the many episodes and characters included in those masterworks. The *Iliad* told the tale of the Trojan War, a struggle that broke out after a beautiful woman, Helen, who was married to the Greek king Menelaus, ran away with a Trojan, the young, handsome, impetuous Paris. The *Odyssey* centered on a Greek hero, the wily Odysseus, King of Ithaca, and his ten-year journey back home after the Trojan war. Each of these epic poems offered readers and listeners (for they were often recited by professional performers called "rhapsodes") numerous ways of engagement.[37] They taught examples of virtue and vice, as they focused on the characters of the heroes involved. They also taught

---

[35] See Robert Parker, *Polytheism and Society at Athens* (Oxford: Oxford University Press, 2005); Ma, *Polis*, 421–424.

[36] For recent excellent translations, see Homer, *The Odyssey*, tr. Emily Wilson (New York: Norton, 2018); and Homer, *The Iliad*, tr. Emily Wilson (New York: Norton, 2023); as well as Homer, *The Odyssey*, tr. Daniel Mendelsohn (Chicago: University of Chicago Press, 2025).

[37] Cf. Jonathan L. Ready and Christos C. Tsagalis, eds., *Homer in Performance: Rhapsodes, Narrators, and Characters* (Austin: University of Texas Press, 2018).

myths, as gods and goddesses entered and exited the stage, often accompanied by explanations of their attributes.

Telling the tales of these gods, the epic tradition also revealed something Plato and other early Greek philosophers found objectionable: In their passions, the gods seemed not like gods at all, but rather all too human. Hera, for example, the wife of Zeus (king of the gods), was subject to numerous jealousies as she plotted against his frequent extramarital lovers. Zeus had snuck down to earth and fathered Heracles, who would become a great hero. Hera sent two snakes to the infant Heracles's room to murder him (though the infant hero killed the snakes himself). Later Hera compelled Heracles to engage in twelve great tests, or labors, which she made progressively more difficult. If the "queen" of the gods was subject to such human passions, then what was Zeus, the king of the gods, doing mingling with human beings, seducing them, and participating in their petty wars? What kind of a "god" was this, subject to all the same passions that beset mortals? These were the sorts of questions Plato asked.[38]

There was something else, too. It is obvious from our everyday language that we think in comparative terms. We say that things are "better" and "worse" – comparative terms that imply hierarchy. If there is a hierarchy, there must be something that sits atop the hierarchy, something that is the best possible version of whatever thing there is in question. In one respect, this is what Forms are like for Plato: the best, most incorruptible version of a thing, its model. Though the tree you see before you will, at some point, wither away and die, there is a perfect "tree-ness" out there somewhere, of which your individual tree on earth is a copy – and an imperfect one at that. When it comes to material things, Plato never really resolved the problem of there being a possible infinity of forms. But his theory of Forms was more useful and durable when he discussed abstractions that nonetheless had meaning in everyday life. The Form of Beauty was one of these instances. Even more important was the Form of the Good. When you do good things, you are by your behavior participating in goodness, meaning, in the Form of the Good.

The form of the Good – recall what Socrates says about it at the end of the cave allegory: "in the region of what is known, the Form of the Good is the last among what is perceived." But then, once it is perceived, it is reckoned as the "cause" of "all that is right and good for everyone." The word translated here as "cause" is *aitia* in Greek, a word that also means "origin."

---

[38] See e.g., Plato, *Republic*, Book 3.

Plato is saying that it is hard work to see the Good. Once seen, the Good leaves an impression, one so strong that it overrides all your other perceptions and thoughts to such an extent that you understand – you *know* – that the Form of the Good is behind everything that human beings in their day-to-day interactions consider "right" (*orthôn* in Greek, which also means "straight," like a line, and "upright," as in upright behavior) and "good" (*agathon* in Greek, with all the many attendant shades of meaning that word can possess). The form of the Good, in other words, sits atop the hierarchy of Forms.

Now Zeus, in the realm of the gods, was also at the top of that hierarchy. But he did so many things that could not be called "good" that he should in no way serve as a model or be considered a cause of the things that are truly right and good in the world. True, the Socrates of Plato's dialogues pays respect to the Greek religious system, a system that intermingled religious rituals with public, political culture. As such, these gestures represented acts of citizenship as much as what we would today recognize as a religious or faith commitment. More centrally at issue is how the Form of the Good, described in the *Republic* and elsewhere in Plato's work in an almost mystical fashion, became the grounding for western idealism, a process in which Plato's reverence for a certain type of education plays a role.

To zoom back in, what the discussion at the end of the cave allegory reveals is that it is difficult to know the Good. It is unsurprising when, soon after the passage analyzed above, Socrates says: "Education is not what some people who desire to be authorities on it say it is. They claim, I imagine, that if there is no understanding in the soul, they are supplying it, as if putting sight into the eyes of the blind."[39] "Some people who desire to be authorities" – *tines epangellomenoi*, in Greek. These are the sophists, who stand accused of doing something Plato wishes to portray as impossible, as if moral education were something automatic, easy, a knack that allows you to infuse information into someone. Instead, it is far more complex, in Plato's view.

One way to understand his thinking is to focus on the Greek word used for "education:" *paideia*. The root of that word is *pais*, "child," so that in its most literal sense the word means the "rearing of a child." But it came to mean more in Plato's world, signifying a way to approach culture and, indeed, pointing toward the basic cultural equipment that educated people should possess.

---

[39] Plato, *Republic*, 518b.

The sophists represented a way of treating, supporting, and furthering culture that, from Plato's point of view, ignored the basic question of absolute truth. For Plato, this tendency was a negative one, ever in the realm of opinion, never in the world of true knowledge. Yet, there was also a more positive way to view the sophists. Protagoras's "man is the measure" pointed to a view of the world that was profoundly earthbound, relational, and human.[40] The grounding assumption? To achieve good in the world as it is, one needed to function within existing political structures, with all their imperfections. Moreover, the sophists taught the art of persuasion, and to persuade people one needs to see them, to pay attention to them, to understand that there is someone on the other end of what one is saying. If it was a view that could be abused, it was also a perspective that, when framed within a robust ethical context, could lead to the orator becoming one of society's most admired figures.

Later, in the second century BCE, a grave Roman military leader and political figure, Cato the Elder, reportedly said that an orator should be a "good man well skilled in the art of speaking," or a *vir bonus dicendi peritus*. The person who attributed this definition to Cato was an even later Roman figure, Quintilian (35–100 CE), who wrote a book that became famous called the *Institutio oratoria*, or *The Education of an Orator*. And the passage in question occurs toward the end of Quintilian's book where, attempting to sum up what he has been trying to do, he writes: "Let the orator, then, whom we have been trying to form, be such as Marcus Cato defined: a good man well skilled in the art of speaking."[41] The book takes as its subject matter the education of a boy, from his youth through manhood, along the way learning principles of language and public speaking. It is all about rhetoric. It was a rhetoric theorized not as an empty attempt to persuade but rather as an art that could, when used skilfully and leavened with moral education, serve as the glue that bound society together.

This was the polarity that the sophists and Plato set in motion. On the one hand, there was a practical focus on concrete results in human communities. On the other, there was a search precisely for ideal truth, however remote that ideal truth might seem, however it might need (as human logic dictates)

---

[40] See Mauro Bonazzi, *The Sophists* (Cambridge: Cambridge University Press, 2020); and cf. Bryan Garsten, *Saving Persuasion: A Defense of Rhetoric and Judgment* (Cambridge, MA: Harvard University Press, 2009).

[41] Quintilian, *Institutio Oratoria*, 5 vols., ed. and tr. Donald A. Russell (Cambridge, MA: Harvard University Press, 2001), vol. 5, 12.1, p. 196: "sit ergo nobis orator, quem constituimus, is qui a M. Catone finitur, 'vir bonus dicendi peritus.'"

to reside in a never-to-be-reached divinity, whose essence must perforce remain mysterious given the limits of our earthly knowledge.

It is worth returning to the cave allegory, to its end, where Socrates defines precisely what sort of education will be needed if a student is to be educated well. Remember, when it came to ultimate knowledge, the metaphor Plato chose was the sun – the biggest, brightest, most powerful of heavenly bodies as he would have understood them. Plato has Socrates, his spokesperson in the *Republic*, explain the allegory of the cave and suggest that the enchained prisoner is a stand-in for human beings. The liberated prisoner first sees the sun indirectly, discerning only the shadows it casts. Thereafter, there is a nearer approach, as the prisoner observes reflections of the sun. Then after hard work, he can see the sun itself, finally realizing it is a source of nourishment, power, and life. The allegory is about education. And there are those who mistakenly think education is something simple, the easy infusing of knowledge from one person to another. This is an error, to be sure, in Plato's view. But why?

One thing remains. It is the most important part, because it is the most immediate to us and to our human experience. This missing piece constitutes the central mystery of who we are and of what makes us alive, meaning full of life, possessed by life, energized by life. That one final factor, the part that is the real object of education, is the soul. The word Plato employs for soul is *psyche*, in Greek, when Socrates continues his thoughts on education. Having posed the stance of the sophists, that education can be something simple, that you can infuse knowledge into someone, Socrates says:

> However, our present **discussion** indicates that this **ability** exists in everybody's **soul**, as does the **instrument** by which each person learns. It is just as if the eye were unable to turn from the darkness toward the light in any way other than with the whole body. So too, it is with the whole **soul** that one must turn from the world of **becoming**, until the soul is able to contemplate reality and the most brilliant part of reality. It is this that we claim to the be the Good, right?[42]

This short comment reveals much of what later became understood as "Platonism," as well as key terms – interpretive hinges, as it were – that have led to misinterpretations.

To take the latter first, the word translated as "discussion" is *logos*, in Greek. Its most literal meaning is "word." It can also signify "argument" in the different senses that word implies, including in the way that it is used

---

[42] Plato, *Republic*, 518c, 2: 120–121.

today when speaking of a philosophical "argument," with the implication of a carefully constructed and internally coherent set of sentences. That sense is, at times, what Plato means when he uses the word *logos*. But it is too narrow to encompass Plato's meaning here.

The translation above, "discussion," gets us closer to what Plato meant, which was to foreground the importance of conversation and its centrality to the search for wisdom. The dialogue form points in that direction. As here in the *Republic*, so elsewhere: Plato often has his interlocutor Socrates lead his conversation partners in the direction he wants them to go. Yet the fact that Socrates often leads an interlocutor into an *aporia* yields a meaningful conclusion, banal as it may sound: Life is full of uncertainty and gaps in our knowledge, and conversation is the way out. *Logos* does not signify a tidy, syllogistic argument. It points toward the humanly inexact way that conversations proceed: with misunderstandings that must be worked out through further discussion, with a need for ever more dialogue, and with a faith that both interlocutors are working toward the goal of finding wisdom and truth, rather than simply advancing their own interests. "Like the wind," Socrates says elsewhere in the *Republic*, "wherever *logos* leads us, there we must go."[43] The implication is that the dialogue on the page must be played out in real life, both because of certain facts about the human condition (as Plato sees it), and because of the premises under which legitimate education occurs.

As to Plato's views on the human condition, three other words occur in the quoted passage that can show us the way. There is the "ability" that exists in everybody's "soul" along with the "instrument" by which each person learns. For "ability" the Greek word is *dynamis*, a word that connotes "motion" as well as "ability" and "capacity." The word for "soul" is *psyche*, which in early Greek signified simply "life" and in Homer, the "spirit," as in the "spirit" that would leave one's body upon death, or the "ghost" of departed ancestors.[44] Plato, however, uses the word to indicate the part of a human being that is immortal, or should be so considered. The *psyche*, as the central attribute of human life, was the answer to the question: What is it that makes a person alive? The *psyche* thus had attributes, such as the *dynamis* of which Socrates speaks. It was as much a capacity as a source of motion – a "dynamism," so to speak. And it had an "instrument" to help learning occur, the word for which in Greek is *organon*, a word that is like the English word "organ" in the sense of a bodily organ.

---

[43] Plato, *Republic*, 394d, 1: 254–255.
[44] See e.g., Homer, *Iliad*, 22.467; *Odyssey*, 9.523–524; 11.222; 24.1–10.

All of it together – the "whole soul" as Socrates says, alluding to the various attributes found in the soul – must turn away from the world of "becoming" until a key point is reached. This crucial moment occurs when the whole soul (meaning the human person) can endure contemplating "reality and the most brilliant part of reality." Our everyday life takes place in the world of becoming, where things are impermanent, where they are born, where they grow, where they die and then fade away. But there is another world, the world of "reality," as it is translated here, but which in Greek is simply, *to on*, which most literally means "being." It is this bifurcation that the human soul faces: between becoming and being, appearance and reality, change and permanence, humanity and divinity.

The human soul, then, is immortal, imbued with different capacities and, most importantly, in need of training. How should this training occur? Socrates says, regarding training: "of this very thing, therefore, there would be an art." The word for "art" is *technê*, which also means "craft." Socrates means that there must be a special "art" or "craft" of education itself, one that centers on what he describes as a *periagôgê*, a "turning around" – in this case, of the soul.

Notionally, Plato's *Republic* has to do with the foundation of a state: what sorts of institutions it needs, how its laws should encapsulate justice, and so on. Therefore, shortly after Socrates points out the features of the soul and its capacity for education, he highlights that those who watch over the state – its guardians, meaning people in the highest governance positions – must be educated in the way described.[45] They must be the ones who look toward "reality" or "the world of being" (that which is eternal) rather than only toward the "world of becoming" (the everyday, earthbound flow of events). They must be educated so that their highest, best capacities can be brought to full actuality. The *Republic*, as a text, returns to its progress, landing gently from its high-flying cave allegory and moving toward a discussion of the centrality of numbers and mathematics in education. Other topics, some as famous in the history of philosophy as the cave allegory, will emerge in Plato's masterpiece.

Reading Plato, it is tempting to boil down what he says into arguments, to remove from view many of the features that make his use of the dialogue form so meaningful and lasting: Socrates' occasional teasing humor, the interaction among the interlocutors, the brief character sketches that remind us that the individuals in the dialogues were, though presented in fictional

---

[45] Plato, *Republic*, 519c, 122–123.

settings, modeled on actual, real-life Greeks whom Plato knew, of whom he had heard, and with whom he had interacted.[46]

Erasing those seemingly minor features leads to a great, and fatal, error. It must be avoided, indeed nipped in the bud, whenever philosophy comes under discussion. For as much as philosophy is about arguments – about using precise language and logically structured language – it is also about something bigger, more immediately present to every human individual, and more important: the search for wisdom in human life. It is a search that, to be sure, has to do with the refining of one's individual capacity, language, and intelligence. But it is also a search that happens relationally, among people, and in conversation.

There is a moment, toward the end of the cave allegory, that is easy to miss but deserves our attention. Socrates returns to the part of the analogy that has to do with sight.[47] He says that, just as a person who has not yet been exposed to the brightness of the sun will be unable to see when thrust into its bright light, so too will a similarly disabling blindness occur, should a person accustomed to the light be thrust back into darkness. If that were to happen, if you were an observer with "any sense," you would recall that the eyes can become confused when passing from one extreme to the other.[48] Then, Socrates goes on, regarding the observer: "bearing in mind that the very same thing happens in the soul, when you see it bewildered and unable to see something clearly, you would not laugh irrationally."[49] The sensible observer would start to inquire. Has the soul – and of course the person who possesses it – come from a place of great illumination, needing now to accustom itself to the everyday world? Or has it come from a place of ignorance, so that it is now dazzled by the enlightened environment into which it is attempting to step?

It would be ponderous to continue spinning out Socrates' analogies, which are clear enough: The eyes represent the soul; the sun, the form of the Good. The more meaningful part of this last example is also its subtlest. Socrates is making a case that character and emotion matter. The "sensible observer" stands in for a good teacher. And the possession of good sense – intelligence – in this instance points not only to I.Q.-type intelligence. It also signifies that the observer has been educated fully, as a whole person, and has learned when it is appropriate to intervene and when it is more valuable to

---

[46] See Danielle S. Allen, *Why Plato Wrote* (Oxford: Wiley-Blackwell, 2013); Debra Nails, *The People of Plato: A Prosopography of Plato and Other Socratics* (Indianapolis: Hackett Publishing, 2002).

[47] Plato, *Republic*, 518a, 118–119.   [48] Ibid.   [49] Ibid.

show restraint and self-discipline: to listen, rather than to instruct; to elicit questions, rather than to demand answers.

It is this factor that deserves a renewed and more intense focus: the exemplary importance of character. There is no better place to turn for this important element of Platonic philosophy than to the dialogue *Phaedo*, which is set dramatically on the most painful night of Plato's life: the night before Socrates was put to death.

3

PLATO

Wisdom Is about Examples

A NOTEWORTHY SENTENCE APPEARS EARLY IN PLATO'S dialogue, *Phaedo*.[1] It runs as follows: "I have the time, and I will try to tell you the whole story, for nothing gives me more pleasure than to call Socrates to mind, whether talking about him myself or listening to someone else do so."[2] Who is speaking? What is the story in question?

The speaker is one of Plato's interlocutors who, as often, is based on a real historical figure.[3] In this case it is Phaedo, a native of Elis, a place notable for its sanctuary dedicated to Olympia, the residence of the gods, and accordingly a place that served as an early home of the Olympic games. Having suffered imprisonment in war, Phaedo had come to Athens, where he became close to Socrates. In this respect he was like other young men, Plato included, who fell under the sway of Socrates' gentle but persistent style of conversation, teaching, and friendship. Phaedo's history – the history, that is, of the real person – lies buried from view when he appears as a character in the dialogue. For Plato's earliest readers and listeners, those facts about Phaedo were known. To us, he simply appears as an interlocutor and a vehicle for Plato to tell his story.

---

[1] Plato, *Phaedo*, tr. G. M. A. Grube, in Plato, *Complete Works*, ed. John M. Cooper (Indianapolis: Hackett, 1997), pp. 49–100. For the Greek text, see Plato, *Euthyphro, Apology, Crito, Phaedo*, ed. and tr. Chris Emlyn-Jones and William Preddy (Cambridge, MA: Harvard University Press, 2017), pp. 292–523. Unless otherwise noted, I will cite from Grube's translation, and I will refer to section, rather than page numbers.

[2] Plato, *Phaedo*, 58d.

[3] See Debra Nails, *The People of Plato: A Prosopography of Plato and Other Socratics* (Indianapolis: Hackett Publishing, 2002); and David Sedley, "The Dramatis Personae of Plato's *Phaedo*," in Timothy Smiley, ed., *Philosophical Dialogues: Plato, Hume, Wittgenstein* (Oxford: Oxford University Press, 1995), pp. 3–26, esp. pp. 8–9.

The narrative is of great moment. It concerns the night before Socrates' death and how he chose to spend it. The quotation above is Phaedo's response to another of the many characters in Plato's cast of interlocutors, again a real person, Echecrates, about whom even less is known than about Phaedo. The dialogue begins, in fact, with no set-up at all: Echecrates asks whether Phaedo had been present during Socrates' last night and then becomes ever more intrigued once learning that Phaedo had indeed been in attendance. The *Phaedo* is thus a "dialogue within a dialogue," as Phaedo recounts the resonant conversations of that night, when Socrates, surrounded by his friends, expounded upon death. Though he had been sentenced to execution, it had been delayed, and Socrates found himself in prison. The delay was connected to a yearly ritual in Athens.

What was this ritual? Once, in the mists of time, the Athenians had been compelled by the King of Crete, Minos, to send a delegation there by sail, containing fourteen young people, seven male, seven female, to be sacrificed to the Minotaur, a monstrous offspring of Minos' wife Pasiphaë and a bull, whom a god had ordered Minos to slay. Minos disobeyed the command and did not slay the bull. The god punished him for his insolence by making Pasiphaë fall in love with the bull. She mated with the animal, and lo: There was born a vicious monster that, hungry for human flesh, needed propitiation. Under obligation to Minos and to Crete, the Athenians had to supply their portion each year. The Athenian hero Theseus, traveling with one of those delegations, rose up, slew the Minotaur, and saved the cohort of youths.[4] They prayed to Apollo, vowing that, if they were finally saved, they would send a delegation each year by sail to offer worship at Delos, Apollo's home. Further, they would keep Athens "pure" during that time. In practice, that meant not carrying out executions during the annual delegation to Delos.

Which is why, to close this mythic parenthesis — starkly unfamiliar to us but a basic part of how Plato's contemporaries understood their world — Socrates had been in prison for a long time and, now that the delegation had returned, found himself facing his fate the next morning. It is the story of this last night that Phaedo recounts to Echecrates.

---

[4] Apollodorus, *Library*, 2 vols., ed. and tr. James George Frazer (Cambridge, MA: Harvard University Press, 1921), 3.1 (vol. 1, pp. 296–307), Epitome, sec. 1 (vol. 2, pp.128–139); Plutarch, *Life of Theseus* in Plutarch, *Lives, Vol. 1, Theseus and Romulus, Lycurgus and Numa, Solon and Publicola*, ed. and tr. Bernadotte Perrin (Cambridge, MA: Harvard University Press, 1914), pp. 1–88; Ovid, *Metamorphoses*, 2 vols., ed. and tr. Frank Justus Miller and G. P. Goold (Cambridge, MA: Harvard University Press, 1977), 8.ll.1–182 (vol. 2, pp. 406–419).

A curious moment occurs early. Echecrates asks Phaedo who was present with Socrates on that fatal night. Phaedo tells him, offering a list of names of Athenians and "foreigners" (those from outside Athens), adding in between: "Plato, I believe, was ill."[5] What are we to make of this assertion? Plato wrote the dialogue, so we can be sure that what we encounter there is what Plato meant us to read. But *Phaedo* represents a capstone in a sequence of dialogues that Plato authored soon after Socrates died. Plato wanted to offer a portrait of his teacher and friend, one that would weave the story of Socrates' trial and death together with a depiction of what and how he thought and taught.

There were four of these dialogues, of which *Phaedo* is the last. In it, Plato's self-declared absence looms as a meaningful moment in his own transition from student to independent thinker. Like *Phaedo*, each of the other three dialogues involves a main interlocutor and, as in *Phaedo* and other Platonic dialogues, Socrates serves as the lead.

First, there was *Euthyphro*. In it, Socrates meets Euthyphro (a somewhat unserious young Athenian) near the *agora* – the marketplace that served also as a public square – and more specifically in that part of the public square where magistrates plied their trade. Piety forms the subject of this dialogue. What is it? How do we discern it? Are there universal definitions we can apply? Socrates queries Euthyphro on these topics, even as the dialogue ends with Euthyphro walking away from the conversation, claiming that he has business elsewhere. But there is a portrait emerging already of Socrates: a questioner who hopes to find universal answers to complicated ethical questions.

If *Euthyphro* presents a sketch of Socrates where a reader can observe him in action, the *Apology* complements that sketch in important ways. We listen almost exclusively to Socrates speaking. The work begins as follows: "I do not know, men of Athens, how my accusers affected you; as for me, I was almost carried away in spite of myself, so persuasively did they speak. And yet, hardly anything of what they said is true."[6] The word *apologia* in Greek possesses a specific meaning: not an "apology" in the way we think of that word in modern English but rather a "justification." In a legal sense, it signifies a "defense speech," which is what Socrates is delivering on his own behalf, to counter a charge that he broke a law forbidding impiety against the gods. He also takes the opportunity to explain what it is that he does: not, as some have accused him, of teaching how to make "the worse case the

---

[5] Plato, *Phaedo*, 59b.   [6] Plato, *Apology*, tr. Grube, in Plato, *Complete Works*, pp. 17–36, 17a.

stronger" – the classic reproach against sophists and one that some had hurled against Socrates – but rather something different.

He had heard from a friend who had visited the oracle at Delphi. The oracle's prophetic but sometimes puzzling utterances were regarded as enigmatic bearers of truth that needed to be discussed and unraveled to be understood. The oracle said that, among men, Socrates was the wisest. Thinking himself far from wise, Socrates wondered what this could mean. He went about testing the proposition by "examining" others considered wise. Doing so, he found that "those who had the highest reputation were the most deficient, while those thought inferior were the most knowledgeable."[7] This "discovery," as well as Socrates' method, did not win him friends among the powerful. Eventually Socrates ascertained what the oracle meant when it called him the wisest of men. Socrates had repeatedly avowed that he knew only one thing: that he knew nothing. This belief accorded with the oracle's estimation of human wisdom. It also buttressed Socrates' (and Plato's) sense that the wisdom of the crowd is more likely to lead one astray than to produce true wisdom. In his own defense, Socrates also says that far from being impious in his actions, he was instead being pious. The gods want human beings to be good, not to offer empty sacrifices.

Then there was the third of the "trial" dialogues, called *Crito*, named again after an interlocutor. Socrates has been sentenced, but the execution is not to be carried out for a while, given the ships going to Delos. Crito offers to gather Socrates' friends together, bribe the jailers, and spirit Socrates away. Thus, he might live in exile, away from an Athens that had condemned him without real cause. This is what is expected of friends, Crito says. They help each other in times of trouble. Moreover, Socrates' family will suffer great sorrow because of his death. It is unjust for Socrates to leave them bereft. Here too we see how Plato wants his contemporaries (not to mention posterity) to see and to remember Socrates. As Socrates converses with Crito and expounds his positions at length, the portrait that emerges is that of a citizen dedicated to justice and to law.

Socrates' accusers had made him out to be a thorn in the side of polite society. He questioned everything that was conventional and always insisted that what people customarily thought was incorrect. Plato has Socrates take the stage and correct the record. In his defense speech in the *Apology*, Socrates had mentioned his military service for Athens, stressing that he had not left his post during intense fighting at the battle of Potidaea. Here, in

---

[7] Ibid., 22e.

Crito, Socrates expands that duty-oriented trajectory and focuses on the importance of devotion to one's homeland and, foremost, to its laws. Socrates says, taking his point of departure from battle: "one must not give way or retreat or leave one's post, but both in war and in the courts and everywhere else, one must obey the commands of one's city and country, or persuade it as to the nature of justice."[8]

There are at least three ways to look at this and associated passages in Plato. First, we see Plato fleshing out his portrait of Socrates: Concerned with duty and principle, Socrates was inclined to sacrifice his own needs, comfort, and well-being for causes he deemed larger than himself. Perhaps this sense of self-sacrifice and self-scrutiny represented Socrates' own view of piety, wherein being radically honest about our human frailties served as a more appropriate sort of worship than empty ritual. Perhaps his view of piety pointed to a devotion to a humanly created abstraction, the law, which here emerges as a unique intellectual space, with a character that can be described as follows: One has a chance to alter the space within which the law resides and operates – by persuasion of one's fellow citizens, as Socrates says – but, should one fail to do so, one must accept the law's verdicts as absolute. One cannot have a productive, functioning society and simply decamp and go into exile if a verdict is reached that does not accord with one's immediate interest or preferred opinion. So absolute is this commitment that one should be willing, as is Socrates, to face death.

The second way to view Socrates' utterances is to reflect on a quotation by an eminent early twentieth-century philosopher, Alfred North Whitehead. He wrote: "The safest general characterization of the European philosophical tradition is that it consists in a series of footnotes to Plato."[9] Whitehead meant that Plato foreshadowed many of the characteristic concerns that have shaped western philosophy. In this latter instance, regarding law, Socrates' utterances adumbrate social contract theory: the idea that citizens of a polity willingly, if sometimes implicitly, enter into an agreement to abide by laws. These laws may restrict their freedom in an absolute fashion since each citizen cannot do whatever he or she wants at any given moment. But, by safeguarding the community, the agreed-upon laws ensure justice for the greatest number. And in truth, there are many other fixtures of our mental world that appear first in a robust way in Plato: the notion that we should believe in an objective, rather than just a relative

---

[8] Plato, *Crito*, tr. Grube, in Plato, *Complete Works*, pp. 37–48, 51c.
[9] Alfred North Whitehead, *Process and Reality: An Essay in Cosmology* (New York: MacMillan, 1929), p. 63.

good; that something of us survives after death; that there exists a world above and beyond our own, in which the divine has a superintending role; and the notion that "rhetorical" speech is somehow inauthentic, insincere, and liable to accusations of bad faith. These sentiments and more became something like strands in a richly textured fabric, each distinct in its own way but each, too, overlapping and woven together with others. Together they produced a powerful political, philosophical, and literary field on which contests over justice, rights, and many other contentious topics have taken place for well over two millennia.

There is, however, a third way to view Socrates, and it entails returning to the *Phaedo*. In one respect in the dialogue, Socrates hits the high points of Platonic philosophy in his discussions with his young friends, with extended discussions on the Forms and a beautiful, myth-laden tale of the immortality of the human soul. But in this other respect, there is a moment that deserves to be highlighted, wherein the portrait Plato paints of Socrates takes on a special relevance. Examining this moment will serve as a springboard to a consideration of the place of narrative, myth, and emotion in philosophy.

The episode in question occurs midway through the dialogue. At Socrates' urging, the interlocutors have been testing arguments for the immortality of the soul. They have come upon a snag: On the one hand, they concluded it reasonable to think the soul has some kind of existence separate from its human body and can be reborn into other bodies after death. On the other, what if the soul is damaged by successive births and rebirths, as it repeatedly experiences death? During that wearying cycle, could one of those bodily deaths prove too much for the soul, leading to its ultimate destruction?

They have arrived at this point by arguments. First, things seem to arise from their opposites: Certain things become smaller from having been bigger, death comes from life, even as life come from death.[10] Second, when we come to know something fully, we seem to have always known it, as if we are remembering what we had once forgotten.[11] When you are presented with two objects that are unequal to each other in size and you realize this fact intuitively, you also come to know the meaning of things being "equal" and, accordingly, you understand the form of the Equal itself, in which those two objects were participating. That knowledge is so intuitive and ineradicable that it seems as if you are recollecting it. And the time when you first came to know it was before you were born, when you were

---

[10] Plato, *Phaedo*, 70–72e. [11] Ibid., 72e–78b.

unencumbered by a body and just a soul existing among the Forms, earlier and pure and simple.

These arguments resonate as persuasive to the gathered interlocutors. Still, they have not solved the problem of whether there might be one final death in which a person's soul simply evanesces. This problem, a particularly fraught one, given that the interlocutors are talking with and about Socrates (who is indeed about to die), leads to a point of tension.

We arrive at one of *Phaedo*'s most significant moments. Plato's literary art is so formidable, pulling us backward and forward in time, that we barely notice that the entire dialogue is a deliberate construction, each piece integral to the larger whole. The two interlocutors with whom the dialogue began are, we recall, Phaedo and Echecrates who, in asking Phaedo to recount Socrates' final evening and its attendant conversations, had set the dialogue in motion. This Phaedo had done, so that the action moved from the present (Phaedo and Echecrates' conversation) to the past (Socrates' last night). Now the action moves forward, if ever so briefly, to the present, as Phaedo breaks his recounting of the conversation. He emphasizes how disturbed he and the other witnesses to Socrates' conversation were when they came upon, and could not surpass, the notion that one cannot be sure that one's soul is immortal. "We felt uncomfortable," Phaedo recalls. "We were thrown into confusion." "We had lost our conviction."[12] Echecrates, in response, says to Phaedo: "Tell me, by Zeus, how Socrates proceeded with the discussion."[13]

The word translated here as "discussion" is *logos* in Greek, that variable, brilliant, and elegantly slippery word that can mean "argument," "word," and "conversation." How did Socrates proceed? How did he carry the conversation forward when, of course, he knew that he would die soon and when, more to the point, he found himself among his young friends, whose impending bereavement hung like a cloud about to burst over their heads?

Here is what Phaedo says, in response to Echecrates' query (with some key terms highlighted):

> I have certainly often admired Socrates, Echecrates, but never more than on this occasion. That he had something to say was unsurprising. But the first thing by which I was struck was the pleasant, kind, and respectful way he received the young men's **discussion** and how sharply he was aware of the effect the **discussion** had on us, and how well he treated us and how

[12] Plato, *Phaedo*, 88e, tr. modified. [13] Ibid.

he **rallied** us, as if we had **fled** and been **defeated** and how he turned us around to follow up and consider the **discussion** together with him.[14]

The manifold resonances this passage possesses deserve explanation.

First, there are the words Plato chooses, each one of which had multiple shades of meaning. As to "discussion," the word in all three cases is, again, *logos* in Greek. You could make a case for translating the word here as "argument," as in a "philosophical argument." But doing so would blunt the vitality of Socrates' ensuing approach to the question of the soul's immortality. Then there are the words "rallied" and "fled," and "defeated," all of which would have evoked at least two possibilities in a contemporary reader's mind. The verb in Greek translated as "rally" is *anakaleô*, which indicates "calling out repeatedly," most literally, possessing also the medical meaning of "bringing someone back to health." And then the words for "fled" and "defeated" (the participles *pepheugotas* and *êttêmenous*, respectively) have all the resonances one can imagine, including those of soldiers on the verge of defeat and about to flee a battle, who need to be rallied to come back to their mission. Socrates as friend, healer, and general: All those images are enfolded in this brief citation.

Even more meaningful is the fact that Phaedo chooses to remember Socrates as a friend. Plato included this passage in his *Phaedo* for a reason. It is interstitial, breaking up the dialogue into different sections, to be sure. So, it has a structural role. But there is more to Plato's personality-revealing anecdote about Socrates than its structural function.

Immediately after Phaedo draws this short but evocative portrait of his old, now dead friend, Echecrates enthusiastically asks: "How did he do this?" Meaning: How did Socrates observe, countenance, and heal his young friends' distress? Phaedo responds: "I'll tell you. I happened to be sitting on his right ..."[15] Thereafter, the dialogue moves backward in time, to the conversation itself. But it is where the conversation goes that matters most.

Phaedo, the character in the dialogue, highlighted Socrates' care for his friends' souls. As we return to that night's conversation, Socrates encourages his friends to avoid making a crucial error. To Phaedo, he says: "Let us not become **misologues**, as those do who become **misanthropes**. For one could suffer no greater **evil** than hating **conversations**."[16]

"Misologues." We are yet again in the realm of *logos*. Here, it is paired with a Greek prefix derived from the verb *misein*, which means "to hate." A "misologue" is a "hater of *logos*," meaning a hater of conversation, which

---

[14] Ibid., 89a, my tr.   [15] Ibid., 89b.   [16] Ibid., 89c–d, my tr.

is to say, finally, a "misanthrope," a hater of one's fellow men, or better, of one's fellow human beings. The Greek word *anthropos*, or "man," signifies "man" as opposed to God, rather than man as opposed to woman. It is universalizing and should be understood today as referring to humanity at large. Socrates also stresses that it is an "evil" (the Greek word is *kakon*) to hate "conversations" (again, the root word is *logos*) in Greek. This is how Plato understands philosophy: as inquiring conversation, conversation that will, indeed, sometimes produce definitive solutions but that at other times will serve as a vector for human interaction. Hating conversation is something like hating people, so that conversation – with all its ambiguities, risks of fundamental disagreement, and possible impasses – exemplifies the essence of humanity.

The tradition that Plato made emblematic in his dialogues (in their open-ended form and in the portrait they paint of their central character Socrates) served as an important moment in the beginnings of western philosophy. Philosophy in this respect points not only to a trust in the power of human reason logically to identify, clarify, and solve problems. It also represents humility in the face of the world's complexity, as well as the concomitant need to work through that complexity in the company of others. Philosophy is not one or the other of the two: It is both.

As Plato moves toward the final trajectories of *Phaedo*, Socrates again takes the stage. He makes his commitments clear. If there are times – as there inevitably will be – when conversation and "argument" do not produce certainty, "we should not allow into our minds the conviction that argumentation has nothing sound about it."[17] Here again we encounter the word *logos*, this time translated as "argumentation." But it is the same word, capacious and mysterious all at once, whose implication for Socrates is this: Discussion and conversation are paramount.

When *logos* fails to produce certainty, what then? Rather than believing that all argument is in vain, "we should believe that it is we who are not yet sound and that we must take courage and be eager to attain soundness, you and the others for the sake of your whole life still to come, and I for the sake of death itself."[18] Note: Socrates cares for his young friends here, and their futures, but also for himself. Before our eyes he is becoming a person in the round, even as his leadership and self-sacrificing nature stand out.

"For the sake of death itself." Throughout the dialogue, death looms, a presence that is spectral yet not as threatening as it might seem. Socrates tells

---

[17] Ibid., 90e. [18] Ibid., 91a.

his young followers that philosophy is a preparation for death – a way of finalizing the soul's separation from one's troublesome body, with the latter being the source of physical desires, conflicts over resources, and misperceptions.[19] Now, here on earth, our senses can deceive us. Then, when we become a pure soul once again, we will be in direct contact with the Forms, with unmediated access to knowledge and truth. But for anyone, even a philosopher like Socrates, the magnitude of change that death introduces is so great that it warrants continued attention. Recall that the interlocutors left the question of the human soul's immortality in a state of anxiety. They had become convinced that there was something distinctive about the soul and that it could be considered as having prior existences in a cycle of birth, death, and rebirth. But they were not convinced that the same cycle would go on forever. As they faced the death of their beloved friend, the question of the immortality of the soul pressed upon them, as indeed it had on Socrates himself.

Phaedo's final section emerges as a cornerstone of the dialogue. Socrates details a myth about the soul and its fate after death. Before arriving there, however, he offers yet another story, this one about his own life, a story that – yet again in the Platonic corpus of dialogues – had a shaping effect on learned cultures to come. It is a story about enchantment and disenchantment, enthusiasm and disappointment, and about gradually dawning feelings of inauthenticity versus an authentic search for wisdom.

Socrates begins: "When I was young, I was wonderfully keen on that branch of wisdom that they call the 'investigation of nature,' for I thought it splendid to know the causes of everything, why it comes to be, why it perishes, and why it exists."[20] A wise person looks back on his life with the perspective of age. He is telling a story that begins with an early and excited passion to know things about the world. Note the expression "that branch of wisdom that they call the 'investigation of nature.'" As a kind of shorthand, we might have translated the Greek as, simply, "natural science." And yet, though that translation is defensible, it robs Socrates' utterance of the strangeness that we need to understand Plato in his fullness. What is translated here as "wisdom" is the Greek word *sophia*. And then for "investigation of nature," the two key words are *historia* ("investigation") and *physis* ("nature"). *Historia*, from which our word "history" derives, meant simply "investigation" or "inquiry." Socrates is saying that his early passion had to do with precisely the sort of inquiry from which he would learn two things:

---

[19] Ibid., 67e.   [20] Ibid., 96a, tr. modified.

how the world works and, more importantly, what the underlying causes were behind that functioning.

For a while, the excitement of the investigation spurred him on. Then there came a moment when knowing facts was no longer satisfying, since he had yet to understand the underlying causes of why the things he was examining were the way they were. After he abandoned the study of the natural world, owing to its unsatisfying nature, another impulse occurred: "It seemed best to me to take refuge in **words**, and to look for the truths of the realities within them."[21] "Words." Again, the term in question here is *logos*, here translated most sparingly. Socrates is saying that he moved away from natural investigation to something else. But what was that something else? If he moved toward "words," does that mean he decided that the best way to philosophize was to focus on language and its clarity (or potential lack thereof), as we describe the world? Or if the right resonance is instead "theories," does he mean that he was in search of ever more comprehensive and overarching theories of ultimate causation? Or does the truth lie somewhere in between?

It is only by following Socrates in his exposition that we can answer these questions. Narrating this carefully structured intellectual autobiography, Socrates (as Plato has portrayed him) has gained authority within the dialogue's dramatic structure. He presents himself as a character of constant questioning, both of himself and of the interlocutors around him. That nature gives him a standing, in this moment in the *Phaedo*, to reemphasize one of his earlier points: that the world of the Forms exists.

Socrates had introduced the Forms earlier in the dialogue, spending time defining them and linking them to learning and the doctrine of recollection – the notion that when you learn something, you are really remembering something you knew before you were encumbered by your body and its error-prone senses and irrational desires. Socrates now returns to that earlier conversation. It is a moment that occurs after the uncertainty surrounding the human soul's immortality and after the break in which Phaedo remembers Socrates' kindness and leadership. We observe a gentle sleight of hand on Plato's part, one that relies on the good will the reader has stored up regarding Socrates.

It was uncertainty concerning causation that had led Socrates to suffer dissatisfaction with "inquiry" in the natural world. It is with this issue that he begins, wanting to clear up uncertainty: "So that is why I am setting out to

---

[21] Ibid., 99e, tr. modified, using Emlyn-Jones and Preddy.

try to show you the **kind** of cause about which I have spoken so much ... and I will do so by **assuming** that there is a certain something we can call the Beautiful itself, by itself, the Good, the Great, and all the rest."[22] The word translated here as "kind" is the Greek *eidos*, which we can also translate as "form." And note that Socrates asks his fellow interlocutor to join him in "assuming" that the Forms – "the Beautiful," the "Great," the "Good," and so on – do indeed exist.[23] This is Plato's sleight of hand: If there had been uncertainty about the Forms in the dialogue's first part, now there is no longer; if the group of friends would have pressed Socrates even more vigorously earlier, now they will allow unchallenged the assumption that the Forms exist. This allowance is especially important given what is to come. For as Socrates explains to his friends, he now hopes to persuade them that the soul is immortal, so that both he and they can face his death in the belief that he will yet live – if not in this world, then in another.[24]

First, he offers the notion of participation, the idea that something is what it is because it takes part in, or "participates" in its Form. This notion, "participation" or "having a share in," represents the most basic reason for why a thing is what it is. There is a Form of Beauty. A person is beautiful in so far as he or she has a share in that ultimate beauty. Once you understand this type of cause – participation – it is difficult if not impossible to understand other explanations of causation. This difficulty manifests itself in what Socrates terms "wise" causes. He uses the adjective *sophos,* "wise," but with an ironic layering: those with whom he may earlier have studied, those "wise" men who explained causation through natural observations, had not provided accounts that could muster explanations as satisfying as Form-based accounts. You could say something becomes hot because it was touched by fire, but the more you thought about it, the more you would be asking ever more insistent questions: Where did fire come from? Why was it hot? For Socrates, it was hot because it participated in a Form of Heat. You could end the discussion there, but then you had to rest satisfied that you could never see or feel that Form of Heat. But it was there, somehow divine and beyond this world, like Beauty, the Good, and all the others, assuring us that somewhere, somehow, there was an objective, stable referent to which we could compare our inherently unstable earthly experiences.

---

[22] Ibid., 100b, my tr.
[23] "Assuming": this is a translation of *hypothemenos*, the aorist middle participle of the Greek verb *hypotithemi*. Another possible translation could be "proposing."
[24] Plato, *Phaedo*, 100b.

Socrates points out that the soul has a certain essence, which is, in a word, "life." There is an answer to the simple question, which Socrates poses to an interlocutor: "What is it that, when present in a body, makes it living?" Without hesitation, the interlocutor responds: "A soul."[25] The soul gives life. Accordingly, it cannot admit death into its being, or else it would not be what it is. It is "deathless," and must thus be the one thing, of all things, that can in no way admit destruction. Given that the soul is indestructible, Socrates says: "Then when death comes to a man, the mortal part of him dies, it seems, but the deathless part goes away safe and indestructible."[26] The interlocutors for the most part agree, though one of them, Simmias, has doubts.

Socrates' most stirring defense of the human soul's immortality begins. It is in this exposition that Plato, with Socrates as his spokesman, set the stage for doctrines and mentalities that later bestrode the stage of the theater of western thinking. Responding to Simmias, Socrates agrees that it is right to look at the problem of the soul from every angle, given its importance. For if the soul is immortal, "it requires our care not only for the time we call our life, but for the sake of all time."[27] Not caring for the soul represents, accordingly, a great danger. The reason? Everything the soul possesses when it goes into the "underworld" (that is, after death) is what we have given it in life: its "training" and "education."[28] Our soul is a gift so valuable that in life it requires care, work, and energy, so that when it leaves the mortal world, it will face its new life appropriately prepared. If it has not had the right instruction, the soul will face consequences. The latter we learn from a tale that Socrates tells.

A myth, this section of the *Phaedo* is not marked by Socrates' usual back and forth or by the dialectical style of reasoning in which one often finds him engaged. He speaks with authority to listeners avid to learn what they hope to hear: There will be a place after death where the good and bad receive their deserved rewards. The tale is by turns funny, quirky, and haunting.

Socrates asserts that after death, the soul upon entering the underworld encounters the "guardian spirit" that it had been assigned in life, as a kind of guide.[29] But there is a distinction to be made since, by the time lives have been lived, souls enter the underworld differently disposed. On the one hand, the "well ordered and prudent soul" will recognize its attendant spirit

---

[25] Ibid., 105c.
[26] Ibid., 106e; cf. Richard Bett, "Immortality and the nature of the Soul in the 'Phaedrus,'" *Phronesis* 31 (1986), pp. 1–26, at 5–6.
[27] Plato, *Phaedo*, 107c.   [28] Ibid., 107d, my tr.   [29] Ibid.

and follow it as a guide.[30] The Greek word for "well ordered" is *kosmia*, an adjective derived from *kosmos*, or as we know it, "cosmos." It is a word that indicates "order," in the first instance, as in a state that is "well ordered," where all the parts are attended to and where the whole, as the saying goes, represents more than the sum of the parts. It also indicates beauty (hence our "cosmetics"). And it is no accident that the word "cosmos" is also employed to refer to the universe as a whole.[31]

Considered in these terms, the universe would make no sense, if it were not well ordered. It would lack meaning, if it were not something whose apparent daily disorder we must try to account for and to study, so that we might understand the beauty, harmony, and order that underlie the seeming chaos the world presents us. It is that ability – to see, to hear, and to experience much – that marks a soul that can be described, in addition to *kosmia*, as *phronimos*: "prudent" or "practically wise. In life, a person with a well-ordered and prudent soul will have cultivated these positive qualities. In death that person's soul will be at peace, will follow its attendant spirit, and will be surrounded by other such spirits, gods, and positive elements.

On the other hand, there is another type of soul in another type of person, who like all mortal creatures will also face death. The good soul will experience pleasantness in the afterlife. "But," Socrates says, "the soul that possesses passionate attachment to the body ... hovers around the body and the visible world for a long time, resisting and suffering much, until it is led away by its appointed spirit by force and with difficulty."[32] It is somewhat macabre, this image put forth by Plato's Socrates: the poorly trained soul as ghost, unable to reconcile itself with death. Not having thought enough in life about the world to come, it cannot thrive in the heavenly realm. Thrashing, angry, the miserable soul is dragged away at the point of death.

This cosmic discomfort is not the only hardship one can suffer. Let us say that there is a soul that is "uncleansed" – *akatharton*, which also means "unpurified," "unpurged," and the like, suggesting a state arrived at by a lack of care. It joins that posthumous realm and the other souls there, after having lived a life in which its possessor committed horrible deeds, like murder and other "unclean" acts. In that case, "everyone flees this soul and turns away from it and is unwilling to serve as either its companion or its guide."[33] This fate seems a particular wretchedness: to be shunned and

---

[30] Ibid., 108a.
[31] See Thucydides, *History of the Peloponnesian War*, 4.76; Homer, *Iliad*, 14.187; Plato, *Republic*, 373c.
[32] Plato, *Phaedo*, 108b, my tr.   [33] Ibid., my tr.

alone, in a realm where there are others blessed with a social community of souls, who serve as friends and allies ready to guide them through a new and unfamiliar world. No, the bad actor's soul is condemned to live alone and wandering until, finally, it is compelled to go to its eventual "appropriate dwelling." Left grimly undefined, this place, we glean, is some kind of hell.

Then there is the fate of the blessed. They are accompanied by "gods as their companions."[34] They travel in the afterlife, to a splendid place, the likes of which we have not truly heard or imagined. What sort of place is this, an interlocutor asks Socrates. There follows a curious bit of Platonic narrative, one that reminds us of when, where, and how Socrates, Plato, and their fellow Greeks lived. Socrates says in response: "there are many wondrous places on the earth, and the earth is not such as those who discourse on it claim, when it comes to its nature and size..."[35] As Socrates describes how the dead will travel, where they will go, and what they will face, he offers more details about the "earth." It is round, a "sphere in the middle of the heavens."[36] And it is "very large."[37] We are familiar only with our relatively immediate surroundings, Socrates suggests to his fellow interlocutors. He refers to (what we now call) the Mediterranean Sea and says: "we live around it like ants or frogs around a pond."[38] Most important, both for our interpretation of Plato and for what will come after him, Socrates continues: On the earth, "many other peoples live in many such parts of it."[39]

There are two ways to look at this statement, one having to do with the *Phaedo*, the other more expansive. To take the latter first, Plato points to an idea that his student, Aristotle, later embraced more definitively: People are different and in different places they possess different ways of life or what we would call cultures. The sentiment also bespeaks a disciplined humility, as if to say that when we are interpreting our own surroundings, we should make sure to remember that there will be others who, owing to their own situation, may interpret the same things quite differently.

To move back to the dialogue, there is the matter of our own condition, that of "us Greeks," who serve here as a kind of stand-in for humanity at large. For as we learn from Socrates' continuing description, while we think we live on the surface of the earth, instead we inhabit only a "hollow" thereof. We see the real surface of the earth, far above us, in the same way that someone living in the ocean observes what lies beyond, and above, the water:

---

[34] Ibid., 108c, my tr.   [35] Ibid., my tr.   [36] Ibid., 109a, my tr.   [37] Ibid., my tr.
[38] Ibid., 109b., my tr.   [39] Ibid.

Seeing the sun and the other heavenly bodies through the water, he would think the sea to be the sky. Because he is slow and weak, he has never reached the surface of the sea or risen with his head above the water or come out of the sea to our region here. He has not seen how much purer and more beautiful it is than our own region, nor has he ever heard it from anyone who has seen it.[40]

One senses a refrain. It has grown so familiar and become such a key part of our collective consciousness that it is worth mentioning that Plato was one of the first western thinkers to articulate it so powerfully: There must be someplace better, purer, less marred by daily struggle and imperfection than the world we inhabit.[41]

Plato reinforces this sense of gradation with a series of metaphors, as he has Socrates return to the sea, as a comparator. Socrates says there is "nothing worth mentioning" there that compares in beauty with our own world – the sea being full of "slime, and caves," and other unappealing phenomena. Just so, the things in the upper world that we cannot see "are in their turn far superior to the things we know."[42] Up there, they have colors that are richer, plants that are more beautiful, and stones that we consider precious and rare as their normal, everyday stones. It is "a sight for the blessed," and counts also as a place inhabited by a special sort.[43] What sort are they? Well, there "are many other creatures on the earth, and also men, some living inland, others at the edge of the air," whose relation to the air is as ours to the sea.[44] Again, they are blessed in many ways. "The climate is such that they live without disease."[45] They see and hear better than we do, and their intelligence is superior. Not only do they have temples and groves dedicated to the gods, but they also communicate directly with those deities, who themselves inhabit those sacred places. These superior beings, in other words, are in direct contact with divinity.

So, there are different regions of the "earth," inhabited by different living things and, to some extent, by different sorts of human beings. Some happen to be close to divinity, so close that they see the gods, serve and honor them with temples and other religious appurtenances, and communicate directly with them. As to the different regions, Socrates says that they are connected below the surface of the earth. Channels and rivers large and small, hot and cold, serve as a means of those connections. Among those rivers four deserve special

---

[40] Ibid., tr. modified.
[41] Adumbrations in Homer, *Odyssey*, 4, ll. 561–569; Hesiod, *Works and Days*, ll. 167–173; Pindar, *Olympian Odes*, 2, ll. 59–80.
[42] Plato, *Phaedo*, 110a.   [43] Ibid., 111a.   [44] Ibid.   [45] Ibid.

mention. The biggest, which circumscribes the earth, is called Oceanus – ocean. Another, going in the opposite direction, is called the Acheron, which flows into a great lake, the "Acherusian lake." It is here where most souls arrive after death, who stay there for shorter or longer periods and are then "sent back to earth, to be born as living creatures."[46] A third winds between the first two and passes through an exceedingly hot region, running next to the Acherusian lake but not mingling with its waters, before flowing ever downward into Tartarus, "the deepest pit below the earth," as Homer had called it.[47] Hot and wild, this river is called the Pyriphlegethon ("flaming with fire," in Greek). The fourth major river, the Stygion, flows into a lake called Styx. The waters exit Styx into another river, Cocytus, which in Greek means "lamentation" or "wailing."[48]

These rivers delimit the major features of the underworld. When the dead arrive there, they are judged for what they did in life. People who led an average life are led into the Acheron, where they dwell for however long it takes them to be purified by "penalties for any wrongdoing they may have committed."[49] They are rewarded for their good deeds. Then there are those who have done things so heinous that they are deemed irredeemable in death. They are "hurled into Tartarus," never to be seen again.[50] Some others have committed terrible crimes, like murder or "doing violence to their father or mother," who are also flung into Tartarus but whom the current rejects after a year of suffering there.[51] Upon their release from Tartarus, they wind up in the Acherusian lake. There they "cry and shout" begging those against whom they had sinned to let them come out of the lake.[52] Should they succeed in their persuasion, they step out of the lake, their punishment ended. If not, they must return to Tartarus, to repeat the cycle of lament and suffering, yet again attempting to convince those they harmed to free them. The ancient culture of oratory reaches out even unto death, in the underworld, where to escape a cycle of punishment one must use powers of persuasion – rhetoric – to be forgiven.

Then there are those judged good. Those considered "extremely pious" go up "to a pure dwelling place and live on the surface of the earth" (remember that we in our daily existence live in a hollow, albeit unknowingly).[53] And then "philosophy" enters the picture. We learn from Socrates that "those who have purified themselves sufficiently by philosophy live in the future altogether without a body."[54]

---

[46] Ibid., 113a, tr. modified. [47] Homer, *Iliad*, 8.14. [48] Ibid., 22.409.
[49] Plato, *Phaedo*, 113e. [50] Ibid. [51] Ibid. [52] Ibid., 114a. [53] Ibid., 114c.
[54] Ibid.

The truly purified, those who have cleansed themselves by means of philosophy, live a life that is eternal and unencumbered by the frail physicality with which human beings are burdened. Thereafter, "they make their way to even more beautiful dwelling places which it is hard to describe clearly, nor do we now have the time to do so."[55]

"Hard to describe clearly." It is indeed hard to describe a place beyond all worldly human experience. And yet, the description that Socrates offered is also – like his more conventionally logical argumentation elsewhere – *logos*: inquiring conversation in the presence of friends. It is *for* them, in a fundamental sense and, in this case, carried out in the form of myth, rather than syllogistic reasoning. Then, too, there is Socrates as exemplar and, in this instance, as a friend so beloved that he can be pardoned for saying: "nor do we now have the time to do so." For this caesura in the story, his friends excuse Socrates, for the obvious reason that he is about to face death and is running out of time, his impending demise having loomed like a dark specter over the whole affair since the beginning, when we learned that the ships had come back from Delos.

As readers, we can accordingly also forgive Plato, the author, who left this myth behind, a myth voiced by a Socrates, who in the *Phaedo* achieves a kind of sanctity. In so doing, Plato solidified the image of his beloved teacher in ways that are as moving as they are lasting. Additionally, he laid the groundwork for much of western ways of thinking, Christianity included.

The dialogue moves to a conclusion. Socrates recommends that, given the picture he has sketched, "one must make every effort to share in virtue and wisdom in one's life, for the reward is beautiful and the hope is great."[56] Socrates also evinces modesty about what he has said. Doing so serves simultaneously to solidify his image and example – of a man dedicated to duty, piety, and humility – and to allow Plato to escape the iron grip of logical argument and make the case for something like faith. Socrates says:

> No sensible man would insist that these things are as I have described them, but I think it is fitting for a man to risk the belief – for the risk is a noble one – that this, or something like this, is true about our souls and their dwelling places, since the soul is evidently immortal; and a man should repeat this to himself as if it were an incantation, which is why I have been prolonging my tale.[57]

"My tale." The word for "tale" that Socrates employs is *mythos*, in Greek: "myth," "story," or in short an explanation that emerges from that place

---

[55] Ibid. [56] Ibid. [57] Ibid., 114c–d.

where reason takes us after it has reached its limits. We can reason about human life, and we can "know" things about it, meaning we can grasp how to do things in life and can give accounts of them. We cannot satisfyingly reason in the same way, with the same degree of certainty, about what happens after life ends. Accordingly, Socrates says that this tale is something to "repeat as if it were an incantation," a lengthy phrase in English and one that Greek, in its linguistic economy, accomplished with one verb: *epaeidein*, a word that has within it the root verb *aeidein*, "to sing." Socrates is pointing to that most basic of ritual elements, incorporated often into religions: repetitive song. Here it is intended to inculcate belief – faith, really – in the notion that our all-too-brief earthly existence will not be all that we have, that there will be something that lies beyond, and that – as Plato's Socrates has outlined it – we will be rewarded if we have behaved well in life, even as those who have not done so will suffer punishment.

There is little need to emphasize just how lasting this idea became. Though there were hints in earlier thinkers, it was only in Plato that the idea – immortality of the soul – was formulated in a way that allowed it to endure: literary work that lasted precisely because it engaged people's emotions as well as their intellects.

The end of *Phaedo* is resonant. Socrates is positively jovial as he readies himself to take his final leave from his friends. One should be of good cheer about one's soul, if one has lived a good life, a life carried out according to "moderation, justice, courage, freedom, and truth," which are what truly beautify the human soul.[58] He decides he should have a bath now, before he drinks the mandated death-dealing poison, so that his family will be spared the need of bathing his body after his death. He teases and jokes with his friends about his burial, implying with gentle humor that the rituals of burial do not matter all that much, if we have our eyes on the truth, which is this: "after I have drunk the poison, I shall no longer be with you but will leave you to go and enjoy the good fortunes of the blessed..."[59] To one of his concerned friends, he says about his own impending burial: "You must be of good cheer, and say that you are burying my body, and bury it in any way you like and think most customary."[60] Socrates here introduces a kind of otherworldliness, a casual disregard for some of humanity's most meaningful rituals and customs, when it comes to recognizing, commemorating, and accepting the loss of a loved one.

---

[58] Ibid., 114e–115a, tr. modified.   [59] Ibid., 115d.   [60] Ibid., 115d–116a.

And a loss it was. The camera, as it were, pans outward again, as Phaedo, the narrator, tells how he and the other friends reacted when Socrates left the room to go and have his bath: "So we stayed, talking among ourselves, questioning what had been said, and then again talking of the great misfortune that had befallen us."[61] What did these devoted friends think? It was as if "we had lost a father and would be orphaned for the rest of our lives."[62] Socrates saw his wife and children for one final time. Then, he was once more with his friends, a fact whose naturalness in the flow of the dialogue shows that the bonds of emotional intimacy that mattered most lay less with family and more with Socrates' male cohort of friends. A government official arrives, a representative of the judicial body whose members had ordered Socrates' execution. He is weeping since, despite his duty, he has come to know Socrates as "the noblest, the gentlest, and the best man" he has met in his difficult work.[63] This official says to Socrates: "try to endure what you must as easily as possible."[64] The official leaves. Socrates remarks to his companions that the official was pleasant and agreeable, always having stopped to talk to him: "How genuinely he weeps for me."[65]

Then, it is time: "Let someone bring the poison if it is ready."[66] One of the companions, Crito, makes a final attempt to keep Socrates with the group just a little longer. It often happens, he says, that those who have been similarly condemned feast and enjoy intimate companionship with their loved ones. Again, however, for Socrates, the ways of ordinary mortals are not his ways, the footsteps of the crowd not a trail he believes he needs to follow. He will take the poison, and he will do so now. The official in charge of administering it is summoned. He tells a placid Socrates that he should drink the poison and walk around until his legs feel heavy. Thereafter, he should lie down and the death-dealing substance will have its effect. Socrates takes the cup "cheerfully" and drains it."[67] It was at that moment when his comrades could no longer hold back their tears. Phaedo says: "my own tears came in floods against my will."[68] Phaedo covered his face, realizing only then that: "I was weeping for myself, not for him – for my misfortune in being deprived of such a comrade."[69] Socrates exhorts his young companions to buck up: "keep quiet and control yourselves."[70] This they did, only to watch as Socrates walked around until the poison began to have its intended effect. Socrates lay down, as he had been instructed to do, pressed his calves and the rest of his body, showing the companions that his

---

[61] Ibid., 116a. [62] Ibid., 116a–b. [63] Ibid., 116c. [64] Ibid., 116c–d.
[65] Ibid., 116d. [66] Ibid. [67] Ibid., 117b. [68] Ibid., 117e. [69] Ibid. [70] Ibid.

body was growing cold, and he said that when it reached his heart, he would be no more.

Before his life ended, Socrates uttered words that ring odd to our modern ears. He told his friend Crito: "Crito, we owe a cock to Asclepius. Make this offering to him, and do not forget."[71] The son of a god (Apollo) and a mortal woman, Asclepius was the symbolic overseer of medicine and healing. One would offer him a sacrifice (like that of the cock that Socrates suggests), if one were healed of something, or if one hoped to be healed, or even, as here, if one were about to take medicine. Hemlock, the poison Socrates drank, was indeed a medicine if taken in small quantities. When he was given the hemlock earlier, he had suggested he wanted to "offer a libation to some god," meaning, he wanted to pour a bit on the ground in a god's honor.[72] His jailer told Socrates he should not pour the libation, since those preparing the poison measured only so much as was necessary.

One scholar has suggested that Socrates' earlier, unfulfilled desire to offer that libation was completed, in effect, by his last request to Crito.[73] Others, since antiquity, have offered various explanations. Perhaps, for Socrates, human life itself, with all its vagaries and discomforts, became a disease. Accordingly, in his final words and with his request to Crito, Socrates might be thanking Asclepius for providing a medicine, here the hemlock that would heal the "illness" of being immersed in human life. Perhaps Socrates thinks that death may be likened to childbirth, so that his nod toward Asclepius represents a way of thanking the demi-god for permitting Socrates' "birth" into the new and better life that awaited him after he shed his body.[74] All of these explanations have something to recommend them. Given that Socrates was about as famous as one could be at the time of his death, and given the context of his time, it seems unlikely that Plato, in recounting Socrates' last words, would simply have made them up.[75]

Because all life is meaningful, so too is any death. The death of a beloved teacher and friend, to which that same person goes voluntarily, seems as dramatic and life-altering – for those who remain – as any other. Consequently, as the dialogue ends, the stakes rise. After Socrates besought Crito to sacrifice to Asclepius, Crito responded, reassuring Socrates that his

---

[71] Ibid., 118a. [72] Ibid., 117b.
[73] Colin Wells, "The Mystery of Socrates' Last Words," *Arion* 16 (2008), 137–148.
[74] Emily Wilson, *The Death of Socrates* (Cambridge, MA: Harvard University Press, 2007).
[75] See Glenn W. Most, "A Cock for Asclepius," *The Classical Quarterly* 43 (1993), 96–111, esp. 97–98.

wishes would be carried out. Crito adds: "tell us if there is anything else."[76] The answer? "To that question, there was no response."[77] This is, of course, the universal dyadic act of human death, whereby as in all dyads, both sides exert an action on each other. The living strain still to converse and to be present with the dying, even as those who die begin – sometimes lengthily, other times more abruptly – to pull away from life, creating a tension full of affect, emotion, and incipient memory, a memory that will be inscribed on the hearts of the living. And then there is that one moment when the conversation simply stops.

Phaedo our narrator (and Plato, our author) tell us Socrates moved one more time, a movement the viewers could detect, as Socrates lay under a cloth in which he had draped himself. The cover was removed, but by then Socrates' "eyes were fixed."[78] A more literal translation would be that Socrates eyes "stood still." The Greek verb employed here is *histêmi*, which at its most basic level means simply "stand" and which implies a lack of motion. For Plato, the soul was the source of motion, so that, when Socrates' eyes, part of his body, "stand still," it means that the soul has departed. What is left is a physical memorial of Socrates, but not Socrates. What animated him is elsewhere. There is "no response" possible anymore, and the conversation – the *logos* – with Socrates himself has come to an end.

When Crito saw this development, he closed Socrates' eyes. Here are the dialogue's final lines, as Phaedo, back in the present now, speaks to Echecrates: "This, then, was the end of our friend, a man who was, of those we have known, the best, and also the wisest and the most just."[79] This will be the memorial Plato erects to his teacher: one made not of stone, but of words. It is a portrait that for centuries shaped the way many people thought about philosophy, human conduct, and the nature of what it means to be human.

Almost two millennia later, a brilliant Dutch thinker, Erasmus of Rotterdam (1466–1536), compiled a series of *Adages*. These were proverbs, in both Greek and Latin, that he listed and then explained. In one of them, titled *The Sileni of Alcibiades*, the following Latin phrase appears: *Sancte Socrates, ora pro nobis*, or "Saint Socrates, pray for us." The "Sileni" were ancient figures linked to Bacchus, the god of reveling, merriment, and wine. They were often represented as carved wooden figures, Erasmus says, on an item that could be opened and closed. When closed, on the outside they looked like one thing, a "hideous flute-player," for example.[80] When

---

[76] Plato, *Phaedo*, 118a.   [77] Ibid., tr. modified.   [78] Ibid.   [79] Ibid., tr. modified.
[80] Erasmus, *Adages*, *II vii 1 to III iii 100*, tr. R. A. B. Mynors (Toronto: University of Toronto Press, 1992), 3.3.1, p. 262.

opened, however, they displayed a deity. The artist's trick – to conceal a deeper reality behind a playful façade or more meaningfully to conceal a larger truth underneath a humble surface – served as a reminder that many things were like this. The sacraments, for example. Erasmus says that "you see the water, the salt, the oil, you hear the words of consecration, and this is like seeing a Silenus from the outside. The power from heaven you neither hear nor see."[81] But that divine power is there, below the surface, resonating powerfully for those who have the disposition to appreciate it.

As to Socrates, he was known to be (conventionally) unattractive. In one of Plato's dialogues (the *Symposium*), Socrates is compared to a Silenus.[82] If his inner wisdom was not evident from his appearance, it reposed instead in his conversation, his prudence, and his interaction with others. If his sanctity was not appreciated by all during his life – as his condemnation would indicate – it became apparent instead in how he chose to die. To flee and go into exile, as he could have done, would have been to run from the rule of law. Though honoring the rule of law was a practice with comparatively little history behind it, Socrates nonetheless saw it as the foundation of human society. To despair at the manifestly unjust conviction would have been to deny the very part of being human – the mysterious, ineffable part – that seems to transcend our physical life.

Looking back, with the millennia of hindsight we are fortunate to possess, we can say that Plato's depiction of Socrates resonates for two reasons. First, there is what scholars of the ancient world have come to call "exemplarity," and more specifically, how this exemplarity interacts with the history of philosophy. True, in *Phaedo* as in the other Platonic dialogues, we find many logical arguments. With the willing help of his interlocutors, Socrates lays out certain premises from which conclusions emerge, sometimes positive and ending in the resolution of a question, sometimes more negatively, ending in an *aporia*. And yet, if we shift our gaze ever so slightly, open our eyes more fully, and observe more carefully, we see what Plato surely intended us to perceive: Socrates serves not only as an intellect, or a kind of disembodied, argument-generating computer, but more meaningfully as an example. It is this latter factor, his "exemplary" status, that makes a discussion of exemplarity and its relation to the history of philosophy important. We see a person who engaged in *logos* – inquiring conversation.

---

[81] Ibid., p. 267.
[82] Plato, *Symposium*, 216d–e; see also Juliusz Domański, *Philosophy, Theory or Way of Life? Controversies in Antiquity, the Middle Ages, and the Renaissance*, tr. Matthew Sharpe, Andrew B. Irvine, and Matteo Stettler (Leiden: Brill, 2024), 16, 98–105.

We observe a man who had friends or, even better, "followers," meaning others who took his example and followed it, or at least attempted to do so.

In the early third century CE, a writer named Diogenes Laertius put together a series of *Lives of Eminent Philosophers*.[83] He organized his work on what were called "successions" of followers (*diadochoi*, in Greek). He posited a leader of a "school" of thought and then set that school's leading exponents out in order. And when Diogenes narrated his biographies, the greater part of each was devoted, not to the arguments of the philosopher in question, but rather to his life: to the philosopher's friends and followers, to his witty sayings, to those characteristics that made the philosopher a unique human being – or one might say to those features that gave the philosopher an "exemplary" status. Especially in an era without the mass reproduction of writing, whom you affected in life mattered more than what sorts of written arguments you preserved. Someone who loved wisdom was one who shared that wisdom with fellow human beings.

The point? For the longest time, exemplary status counted as much as arguments, when it came to judging a philosopher's impact. This long-lasting way of thinking about philosophy was erased from the history of philosophy when it was set on its modern footing in the eighteenth century, when philosophy began to be conceived of as more "argument"-oriented and especially concerned with "epistemology," the technical term for the study of how we know things. But it is worth keeping in mind the older concept: How you lived your life, rather than only what you said, counted in others' evaluation of your worth as a philosopher.

This, then, was one major consequence of Plato's depiction of Socrates: In dialogues that were often as appealing for their literary qualities as for their logical argumentation, he set forth the example of Socrates as one to be understood, broadcast, and imitated. In so doing, Plato linked that image of Socrates, with all the older thinker's exemplary qualities, to philosophy in that word's original meaning: the love of wisdom. Philosophers, especially those who practice academic philosophy in institutions of higher learning, have not always held this image of philosophy as highly as they might have done, often valuing the logical arguments – also present in Plato, needless to say – more than the depictions of Socrates' character. Plato meant for his readers to see both.

The second consequence of Plato's approach to philosophy was, if anything, more meaningful over time. For he laid the groundwork for the

---

[83] Diogenes Laertius, *Lives of Eminent Philosophers*, 2 vols., ed. and tr. R. D. Hicks (Cambridge, MA: Harvard University Press, 2000–2005).

notion of a unique but universal humanity, one whose members – human beings – were distinctive, each one an individual, each having a share of his or her own development. "Share" is an important word here: For Plato as for his contemporaries – as in truth for most of us – the individual exists in a dense web of social interactions, in which debate and discussion accompany norms exemplified by the behavior of those around us.[84] Nonetheless the individual is still there, if nothing else than as the basis of legislation, the agent whose conduct, however much it may have been shaped by interactions, is held responsible for his or her actions.

For Plato, each human soul was an individual, for one thing. And while it is true that Plato posited, somewhat fancifully, reincarnation and cycles of rebirth, the key quality of the human soul was that it was not fixed in place. Following virtue, restraint, and positive development, one could improve one's soul. One could make it more like that of the gods. His mythmaking in *Phaedo* was undergirded by the assumption that believing in life after physical death also encouraged people to better themselves in their lives on earth. Socrates said that philosophy is nothing other than a preparation for death.[85] He and Plato meant that, with death, that one definitive inevitability, lying ever in front of you and representing your and everybody's final earthly destination, it was wise to behave in such a way that, after death, your behavior would be judged well, should there be something more than our all-too-brief lives on earth.

Plato's world was small, by our lights. It was he who characterized his fellow Mediterranean-dwelling contemporaries as "frogs around a pond." And, with the localism characteristic of his era, he easily (and without any question, really) identifies certain interlocutors not from Athens as *xenoi*, "foreigners," meaning not one of us – and this even for friends of his and of Socrates. So, given the assumptions of his day, we should not expect to hear from Plato the sorts of theories of human rights that emerged in the Enlightenment and led to the notion that all people had the "right" to life, liberty, and the pursuit of happiness. And indeed, in his *Republic* he makes no bones about the fact that there will be classes of people who rule, those who support the rulers, and those who are ruled.

Still, if Plato was far from enunciating human rights theories, he laid the groundwork for them in his theorizing about the soul. Behavior in one's physical life, in which all could engage, formed the basis of how one would

---

[84] See Christopher Gill, *Personality in Greek Epic, Tragedy, and Philosophy* (Oxford: Oxford University Press, 1996).
[85] Plato, *Phaedo*, 67e.

experience the afterlife. But behavior, as well, was regulated by society. Socrates' martyrdom, one that he willingly accepted, furthered the idea that society will function only if there are laws to which every person chooses to adhere. That assumption was based on the idea that we are, each of us, shapers of our own conduct and in charge of the choices we make. We are all part of that human family. And, to close, we will be productive members of that family only if we model our behavior on the right sorts of examples. Each person unique, each able to partake fruitfully of society, and each possessing something that all shared: a soul that could be shaped. These features worked in tandem, not all of them right away, to create certain foundational western attitudes toward the nature of humanity.

If Plato, on balance, stressed the universally shared elements of what it meant to be human, his student Aristotle pointed the way toward an appreciation of the diversity of human experience. It is to Aristotle that we now turn, to trace the next bend in the road, a road whose pathway Plato designed, and which successive thinkers planned, reoriented, and refitted over time.

4

ARISTOTLE

From Observation to Ethics

Aristotle's biography and the genre in which his writings are preserved can frame our thinking.[1] From a part of northern Greece called Stagira, Aristotle came to Athens in 367 BCE, when he was seventeen years old to study with Plato. Aristotle frequented Plato's Academy for twenty years, until Plato died in 347. At that point, a discussion over succession ensued: Who should become the new head of Plato's Academy? Among the three candidates – Aristotle and two of Plato's other pupils, Xenocrates and Speusippus – it was Speusippus who won the palm and took over leadership of the Academy.

It might have been because of the succession question at the Academy, or it may have been due to a worsening political climate in Athens, but in any case, Aristotle left Athens and began a period of travel that lasted twelve years. It was a fruitful time. Alongside his friend and colleague Theophrastus, Aristotle engaged in research, especially about the natural world, that shaped his philosophy decisively. That work alerted him to nature's diversity and humanity's place within it. Along the way, King Philip of Macedon invited Aristotle to serve as a tutor to his son Alexander, a young man who, after his short, tumultuous, and world-conquering life came to be known as Alexander the Great. Aristotle's experience with the young, hard-drinking, dominion-obsessed prince convinced Aristotle to turn away from politics. He returned to Athens probably in 335, when Macedonian succession passed from Philip to Alexander, and soon thereafter Phillip was assassinated.

---

[1] On Aristotle's biography, see Carlo Natali, *Aristotle: His Life and School* (Princeton: Princeton University Press, 2013). For literature on Aristotle, see also Jonathan Barnes, ed., *The Cambridge Companion to Aristotle* (Cambridge: Cambridge University Press, 1995); Ronald Polansky, ed., *The Cambridge Companion to Aristotle's Nicomachean Ethics* (Cambridge: Cambridge University Press, 2014); Christopher Shields, ed., *The Oxford Handbook of Aristotle* (Oxford: Oxford University Press, 2012).

Aristotle remained in Athens for an extensive period, founding and teaching at his own school, which was called the Lyceum.[2] Plato's "Academy" was so called because he had set it up in a grove dedicated to the memory of a Greek hero named "Hekademus." And Aristotle's Lyceum was also situated in a grove that other philosophers, the late Socrates included, had been known to frequent. Both were so successful that the words Academy and Lyceum remain in use today, powerful signifiers of education, culture, and institutional instruction, the one (Academy) referring to Plato, the other to Aristotle. Aristotle left Athens for the city of Chalcis in 323 BCE, dying there one year later of an unknown illness.

The second factor distinguishing Aristotle from Plato has to do with the genre of his written work. Genre has proved particularly important in how Aristotle has been interpreted over time. Both Plato and Aristotle lived in a time when there was no internet, no printed books, no way of preserving information except by memory and writing by hand. Accordingly, when we read their works, we need to focus not only on the information and arguments contained within them, but also on the form in which the work survives. In Plato's case, what we possess (aside from some letters) are dialogues, works that carry with them Plato's distinctive, lasting, beautiful Attic prose, along with his fine sense for literature. Given the practices of his era and the greater reliance on memory (from authors as well as readers), Plato likely composed his dialogues orally and had a scribe transcribe what he said. But each dialogue was a work of literary art, conceived of and delineated as such, over which Plato had final say.

In Aristotle's case, we are presented with a different form of writing. For what we have are, in essence, Aristotle's lecture notes. The main works by which we know Aristotle and his thinking originated in his lectures in the Lyceum. These include the *Nicomachean Ethics*, for example, or his *Metaphysics*, or his *Physics,* or all his works on language and logic. The treatises resulted either from Aristotle's own notes or from those of a devoted student, which Aristotle may later have reviewed and edited. Whereas Plato created individual works intended to be listened to and read as separate works of art, the origins of Aristotle's works lay in classroom instruction. This difference in genre represents one important key in interpreting the two thinkers. Moreover, Aristotle wrote dialogues like Plato's that have not survived, as well as other works intended for audiences outside of his school;

---

[2] See J. P. Lynch, *Aristotle's School: A Study of an Educational Institution* (Berkeley: University of California Press, 1972).

and Aristotle himself hints that Plato taught things in the Academy that were not always completely reflected in the Platonic dialogues.[3]

So, as we explore Aristotle and his differences from Plato, these two factors, biography and genre, must be kept in mind. As to biography, students sometimes seek to differentiate themselves from their mentors. We see this propensity in Aristotle. But his differences lie as much in the method he developed as they do in a search for distinction from his former teacher. There are, in truth, more similarities between the two thinkers than differences. Indeed, some of their purported differences in the eyes of later interpreters have to do with not sufficiently foregrounding that their works as we know them are in fundamentally different genres. But if there is one central difference, it has to do with the relative weight each thinker gives to unity and plurality.

The world as we see it presents us with difference – massive amounts of data in nature, in the everyday world around us, in the people we see and with whom we interact. Yet, we seem naturally to fit things into categories. We find unity in plurality, sometimes in ways that are well informed, other times less so. It is an ancient problem and one that is still with us today: How do we make sense of the plurality that surrounds us?

Plato and Aristotle work toward categorization in different ways. Plato's Forms represent the ultimate unities: each the perfect, unified exemplar for every individual thing, which in its actual, observable manifestation to us will be different. And yet, as Plato realized in some of his later dialogues, the reality of the world – its multiplicity, its plurality – makes it difficult to defend the theory of Forms. Perhaps we can say that there is a Form of the Good, or of the Beautiful, or of Justice, in which earthly things that are good, beautiful, or just participate. But what about dirt? Or mud, which seems to be a combination of different elements? Plato himself had raised these and other arguments against the theory of the Forms in his late dialogue *Parmenides*, attempting to offer rejoinders to the critiques along the way.[4] Still, the more one tries to defend the Forms in every instance, the

---

[3] See Aristotle, *Aristotlelis qui ferebantur librorum fragmenta*, ed. Valentin Rose (Stuttgart: Teubner, 1967) for what remains of Aristotle's dialogues and other fragmentary works; Aristotle, *Politics*, tr. H. Rackham (Cambridge, MA: Harvard University Press, 1932), p. 186, 1278b30, on his own writings; Aristotle, *Physics*, vol. 1, Books 1–4, tr. P. H. Wicksteed and F. M. Cornford (Cambridge, MA: Harvard University Press, 1957), pp. 288–289, 209b15, on Plato's "unwritten doctrines."

[4] Plato, *Parmenides*, 129a–130e, in Plato, *Cratylus, Parmenides, Greater Hippias, Lesser Hippias*, eds. and trs. Harold North Fowler (Cambridge, Mass.: Harvard University Press, 1939), pp. 206–213.

more confusing and, importantly, removed from everyday reality things seem to become. One falls into an ever-deepening rabbit hole of contradictions, logical somersaults, and tormented verbiage, so much so that one risks losing sight of the search for wisdom.

For Aristotle, keeping language close to observable reality became a central concern, as did stating and outlining his method of inquiry. These two imperatives guide his approach in the work that is the subject of this and the next chapter: his *Nicomachean Ethics*. We will see how Aristotle calibrates his language to the subject at hand and in so doing gave all his future readers a set of methods they could use to delineate different domains of knowledge. We will also see that when it came to ethics, Aristotle possessed a basic, foundational assumption: observation of those around us forms the basis of ethical inquiry. Put another way, Aristotle accounted for different styles of life and calibrated his thinking accordingly.

Here is how the *Nicomachean Ethics* begins: "Every craft and every method of inquiry and likewise every action and deliberate choice seems to aim at some good; that is why they correctly declare that the good is 'that which all seek.'"[5] Aristotle frames his project, doing so around a specific concern: ethics. By "good" (the Greek is *agathon*), he means something like a goal. Things have goals toward which they are moving, or which represent a kind of final result. Aristotle clarifies: "But since there are many sorts of actions and of crafts and sciences, their ends are many as well. For health is the end of medicine, a ship of shipbuilding, victory of generalship, and wealth of household management."[6] Some arts fall under the categories of other, more all-embracing arts. Bridle-making falls under the art of horsemanship, which itself falls under the art of military matters, which in turn falls under strategy,

---

[5] Aristotle, *Nicomachean Ethics*, tr. C. D. C. Reeve (Indianapolis: Hackett, 2014), 1094a, p. 2. For the Greek text, see Aristotle, *Ethica Nicomachea*, ed. Ingram Bywater (Oxford: Oxford University Press, 1894). In a vast literature, see Julia Annas, *The Morality of Happiness* (Oxford: Oxford University Press, 1995), pp. 27–132; Edith Hall, *Aristotle's Way: How Ancient Wisdom Can Change Your Life* (New York: Penguin, 2019); Gabriel Richardson Lear, *Happy Lives and the Highest Good: An Essay on Aristotle's* Nicomachean Ethics (Princeton: Princeton University Press, 2004); Alasdair MacIntyre, *After Virtue: A Study in Moral Theory*, 3rd ed. (Notre Dame: University of Notre Dame Press, 2007), esp. 146–164; Amélie Oksenberg Rorty, ed., *Essays on Aristotle's Ethics* (Berkeley: University of California Press, 1981); and for two excellent general introductions to Aristotle, see G. E. R. Lloyd, *Aristotle: The Growth and Structure of His Thought* (Cambridge: Cambridge University Press, 1968); and John Sellars, *Aristotle: Understanding the World's Greatest Philosopher* (London: Penguin, 2023).

[6] Aristotle, *Nicomachean Ethics*, 1094a, p. 2.

and so on. The result is that there are "master" arts, which in effect subsume those under them.

What, then, is the best of all of these for human beings? "Politics," Aristotle declares. The Greek word for "politics" is *politikê*. It derives from the word *polis*: "state," or "city," or better, "city-state," which should be considered something in between a city and a country.[7] Small though these ancient cities were by modern standards, they considered themselves to be independent political units; they had distributed authority in their institutions; and they were surely one key ingredient in what one scholar has termed a period of Greek "efflorescence."[8] *Politikê* is the art of the city-state: the practices and rituals, doctrines and laws, with which a city is furnished. If it did not sound anachronistic, we might use the translation "political science" for *politikê*. How the city is arranged, what sorts of skills and arts should be practiced by different groups of people therein, and how people lived within it: These were the concerns. Aristotle characterizes his high regard for the city and life within it in this way: "For even if the good is the same for an individual and for a city, that of a city is evidently a greater and, at any rate, a more complete good to acquire and preserve."[9] Then he says something that can take a reader aback, in what has been a rather sedate discussion: "For though it is worthwhile to attain the end merely for one man, it is nobler and more godlike to attain it for a people or for city-states."[10] "More godlike." The Greek is *theioteron*, which can also mean "more divine." Here as elsewhere, Aristotle unremittingly thinks in terms of hierarchies, categories that are greater or lesser than each other. But there is little greater, he seems to say, than people living in community.

He states the parameters of the subject under discussion and offers a general rule as to how one should proceed in learned discourse: "Our discussion will be adequate if it has as much clarity as the subject matter admits; for precision is not to be sought for alike in all discussion, any more than in all the products of the crafts."[11] We observe a strong consciousness in Aristotle of disciplinary separateness. He sees the world as articulated in categories which, when they fall into the different realms that philosophy covers, manifest themselves as disciplines. Each area of inquiry will have its own subject matter, and each subject matter can be delineated, investigated, and understood with different levels of precision.

---

[7] See Ma, *Polis*.
[8] Josiah Ober, *The Rise and Fall of Classical Greece* (Princeton: Princeton University Press, 2015), esp. 1–19.
[9] Ibid., 1094b, p. 3.   [10] Ibid., tr. modified.   [11] Ibid., tr. modified.

And politics and ethics admit of great variety. Things that are noble or just seem so variegated that they may be thought to exist "by conventional law alone, and not by nature."[12] Actions that people consider good will change according to time and place. Even things people consider beneficial, like courage or wealth, are variable since people have been undone by excess in those realms. When it comes to the work at hand, we must be content "to indicate the truth roughly and in outline."[13] We are in a realm where precision will not be possible in the same way as it is in other fields. Aristotle has outlined guardrails for the subject at hand, which is ethics. He adds one more bit, which is that, since the subject matter deals with human actions, those with more experience in life will be better judges, whereas those who are young will not. Aristotle, whom we should consider here as a professor beginning a course, has digressed though in a necessary way. It is as if he is saying to students: you may want certainties of the sort you find in other fields. Here, in the realm of human behavior, things are trickier.

It is now time to zero in on the object of the discussion, which has to do with the highest aims of *politike* and ultimately "the highest of all goods that can be achieved by action."[14] Here, Aristotle introduces one of his most lasting concepts: happiness. Aristotle says that everyone, no matter their status, considers happiness the highest good. People "identify living well and doing well" with happiness.[15] Point taken. However, people are so different that they offer varied answers to the question of what happiness is. Some say it is pleasure, some wealth, some honor, and in any case the same person might give varying answers according to the situation: You might identify happiness with health when you are sick, with wealth when you are poor, and so on. Human variability is such that it would seem folly to produce one definition of happiness.

The question becomes: Is there a higher good that causes the goodness of the things people normally consider good (like wealth, health, honor, and so on)? To those who have encountered Plato, this sentiment might sound familiar. But Aristotle doesn't name whom he has in mind here and outlines another set of distinctions. These distinctions align happiness less with individual goods and more with three different ways of living one's life. There is the life of pleasure, which many believe manifests happiness. Aristotle means hedonism here, to greater or lesser extent. One reason for its appeal to common people, he suggests, is that people of great wealth and

---

[12] Ibid.   [13] Ibid.   [14] Ibid., 1095a, p. 4, tr. modified.   [15] Ibid.

power seem to live that life – think today of celebrities posting a swanky vacation on social media. Then there is the political life, whose success can be measured by honors achieved. But this too seems superficial, since honors depend as much on the giver of the honors as on the receiver, and Aristotle wants to orient his discussion around self-sufficiency. Finally, there is the life of contemplation, a style of life to be considered later, he says.

Now, however, Aristotle needs to return to that question at which he had earlier gestured: whether there exists some sort of universal good. It is a difficult discussion to have, Aristotle says, because "those who introduced the Forms were friends of ours."[16] By "friends" Aristotle means Plato, a name he does not need to mention to his listeners, but whose powerful imprint on Aristotle's intellectual community a modern reader easily senses. What to do? We must proceed: "Yet it would seem better, perhaps, and something we should do, at any rate when the preservation of the truth is at stake, to confute even what is properly our own, most of all because we are philosophers. For while we love both our friends and the truth, it is a pious thing to accord greater honor to the truth."[17] Nowhere is it more evident that Aristotle's works as we now have them were originally lectures than in this passage and its immediate context.

As to the context, one senses a lecturer hemming and hawing before arriving at a topic he must cover but that he knows is controversial. As to the passage itself, it enfolds several elements, all of which teach us much about Aristotle. The phrase "most of all because we are philosophers," for instance, points to the ongoing ancient effort – one that has never ended and is with us today – to define just what a philosopher is. What does it mean to be a "lover of wisdom?" Here Aristotle identifies it with absolute respect for the truth, even at the cost of departing from the ideas and opinions of friends, or, here, from one friend in particular, Plato. For it is Plato's signature theory of the Forms that Aristotle foregrounds. It was the theory that tied it all together for Plato, the theory, indeed, that made it possible for him to posit an eternal reality above and better than our own, one that superintended mortal life. On it, Plato built his theories and myths suggesting that human souls were immortal. On it, Plato had constructed his theory of knowledge, in which he suggested that when we learn something, we are really "remembering" what we had once known when we inhabited the realm of the Forms as a pure soul, but which we forgot as we traveled downward into our frail bodies, with their error-prone senses

---

[16] Ibid., 1096a.   [17] Ibid.

and irrational passions. When it came to Plato, the theory of the Forms grounded everything.

Aristotle's presentation leads one to sense that like many students he wanted to do something different from what his teacher had done, desired to add something meaningful to his mentor's work, perhaps even to supersede him. Yet, there is a stronger sense that this break with what Plato had taught was difficult for Aristotle, representing a move he did not want initially to make but one that became necessary, as his observation-oriented thinking evolved.

Aristotle looked out at the world and tried at every turn to ensure that the language he employed to describe it accorded with what he observed. When it came to ethics, he sought to match his language to the diversity of human experience and to our widely varying assumptions about what is "good." He found it impossible to believe that there could be only one Form of the Good, diversely expressed as good things in the world tend to be.

When Aristotle says that it is a pious thing to honor the truth above our friends, he is pointing to something like good faith in the immediate context – being an honest broker. And he means something more. The word he employs in Greek is *hosion*, an adjective that means "pious" and that also connotes something divine, imbued with the favor of the gods, and worth honoring. Tossed off as the sentence may seem to be (as sentences in lectures often are), the word and the sentiment behind it represent a way to find order, in the most literal sense: ordering things in their relative importance. There can be no doubt that we must care for the friends whom we love, the friends – Aristotle is saying – from whom we have learned so much. But seeking the truth is more important, even if it means arguing against the cornerstone of your friend's philosophy, as here in the case of the Forms.

Aristotle offers a clue to his thinking and to the way he views the world. Among arguments against the Forms, one stands out, and it concerns the Form of the Good: "Further, if of the things that are in accord with one **idea** there is also one **science**, then of all goods there would also be some one science."[18] The word "idea" is *idea* in Greek, and it is one of the words used to refer to a Form. The word "science" is in Greek *epistêmê*, a word that can denote a skill, can mean "knowledge," and (as here) can point to a very specialized type of knowledge, such as that which a "science" represents. As one interpreter has put it, *epistêmê* signifies "a body of knowledge about some subject, organized into a system of *proofs* or *demonstrations*."[19]

---

[18] Ibid., tr. modified.
[19] Smith, "Logic," in *Cambridge Companion to Aristotle*, 27–65, at 47 (emphasis is Smith's).

On the one hand, we would not want to be anachronistic in using that word, science. Aristotle and all his contemporaries lived in a very premodern world: no industrialization, no germ theory of disease, no telescopes, no possibility of the level of exactitude in measurement that our current conceptions regarding science entail. Importantly, there was also no institutionalized scientific community such as we are accustomed to today. Absent were the iterative processes of modern science, as theories drawn from evidence emerge, are made public, and then are studied, judged by peers, and evaluated, both for their achievements in the scientific community and for their benefits for humankind. Aristotle's world, two and half millennia ago, was small compared to our own, even as ours will likely seem quite meager when looked at from a similar temporal distance in the future.

On the other hand, Aristotle's conception that there must be one "science" for every "idea" foreshadows how we think about scholarship and, indeed, science, in more general terms. Classification comes to the fore. When Aristotle uses the word *epistêmê*, or science, the vision is one of different scholarly disciplines, each with its own object or purpose, meaning that each discipline will have its own subject matter, its own experts and, indeed, its own scholars, whose cumulative work will have a history of its own. Here, in the *Nicomachean Ethics*, Aristotle states that he wants to examine what Plato and the Platonists thought regarding ethics. But he is not concerned with Plato alone. In the beginnings of other treatises of his, he surveys what prior thinkers had thought regarding the problem at hand.

Aristotle's basic presumption is that, as you are getting ready to lay out your own thinking, the responsible thing to do is to understand your predecessors, their arguments, and their contributions, even if you wind up disagreeing with them in the end. Part of what he is doing is a performance, of course, a way of showing students in person how they should conduct themselves when engaging in scholarly inquiry. If we knew more than we did about Aristotle's exoteric works – the mostly lost dialogues he produced for literary consumption – then our sense of him might be different. But we have what we have. And posterity decided early on that it would be his redacted lecture notes, rather than his dialogues, that we would have available.[20] So, we are faced with a conscientious man, who wishes to be as comprehensive as possible in his explanations of any scholarly

---

[20] See Paul Moraux, *Die Aristotelismus bei den Griechen: von Andronikos bis Alexander von Aphrodisias*, 3 vols. (Berlin: De Gruyter, 1973–2001); Jonathan Barnes, "Roman Aristotle," in Jonathan Barnes and Miriam Griffin, eds., *Philosophia Togata II* (Oxford: Clarendon, 1999), 1–69.

matter, a comprehensiveness that includes his predecessors as well as any contingencies he might be able to imagine.

When it comes to ethics, the object is achieving something Aristotle calls *eudaimonia*. This word is traditionally translated as "happiness," and it is as good a translation as any, provided we divest that word from some of our modern associations and look, instead, toward what it meant for Aristotle.[21] The word is a combination of two different roots. The first is *eu*, which means "well." The second is a word that will ring familiar to those who have studied Plato: *daimôn*. It was a diminutive of this word (*daimonion*) that Socrates employed to refer to the conscience-like "divine sign" he would receive when considering a major ethical question: a reminder of something beyond him that was warning him not to do something unwise or unethical. The word *daimôn* signals divinity and can indicate a god or goddess, or a slightly inferior, semi-divinity, or something like the souls of figures from a bygone era, now so far back in time that they assume a divine patina, of sorts.[22] Accordingly, *eudaimonia*, this word that Aristotle uses to signify the goal of human life, means something like being "well-blessed," or "fortunate and living with the favor of the gods," or most simply, "flourishing." To be happy is to flourish, to reach your potential, to live in the best way possible. But what might that entail?

Answering this question requires more reflection on what it is that makes us human and what, indeed, distinguishes us from other forms of life. Life is common to plants, Aristotle states, and life and perception are shared by all sorts of animals. So, determining what is the "good" for humankind entails something deeper than life alone. Aristotle offers the following definition, with a key term highlighted:

> The human good is activity of soul in accord with **virtue**, and if there are several virtues, in conformity with the best and the most complete. But one must add, 'in a complete life'. For one swallow does not make a spring, nor does one day; nor, similarly, does one day or a short time make someone blessed and happy.[23]

The word translated as "virtue" here is *aretê* in Greek. It is often also translated as "excellence." Aristotle devotes a good part of the *Ethics* to these "excellences" or "virtues," which we will explore soon. Before that,

---

[21] See Terrence H. Irwin, "Conceptions of Happiness in the *Nicomachean Ethics*," in *The Oxford Handbook of Aristotle*, 495–528; and C. D. C. Reeve, "Beginning and Ending with Eudaimonia," in *The Cambridge Companion to Aristotle's* Nicomachean Ethics, 14–33.
[22] Homer, *Il.*, 1.122; Plut., 2.415a; Hesiod, *Op.*, 122.
[23] Aristotle, *Nicomachean Ethics*, 1098a15, tr. modified.

however, Aristotle's notion about "a complete life" calls out for comment. It indicates two aspects of his thought, having to do with both divinity and language, that seem hidden at first view but then, when glimpsed once, seem to pervade everything he writes.

The immediate question is: Why write a book about ethics, living in the world, and human conduct, and indeed, why write about "happiness" or "flourishing," when you cannot really tell if someone is happy, or has flourished, until he or she has died? The answer lies with the fact that the questions Aristotle raises, the examples he offers, and the occasional solutions he proffers, all have to do with life as lived. Aristotle later makes a distinction between "happiness," that is, *eudaimonia*, and things that are praised. Praise is awarded to different kinds of excellences, or virtues, which means that people tend to praise good and noble acts. An athlete achieves some milestone, and we praise him; somebody performs a courageous act, and we consider that act worthy of praise. And so on.

And yet, there remains a kind of unknowability regarding *eudaimonia*: "We never praise happiness [*eudaimonia*] as we praise justice, but call it blessed, since it is a more divine and better thing."[24] The first of those two hidden factors comes into play. Aristotle believes – really believes – in the existence of the divine. He does not do so in the same way as Plato, who adumbrates western Christian mentalities when it comes to rewards and punishments that the divine awards based on human conduct in life. But superintending almost everything Aristotle writes is the idea that there are things that may not be knowable in the ways that we normally know things and that some of these things have to do with divinity. Empirical as Aristotle's method is, understanding him and his thinking in their integrity means recognizing that, like Plato, Aristotle believes that divinity exists and stands above human endeavors. In this respect, "happiness" partakes of the divine, and is accordingly somewhat mysterious in nature. It is a "starting point," a "cause of what is good," and "something estimable and divine."[25] Plato and Aristotle, the two real founders of western philosophy, shared several assumptions, perhaps the most prominent of which is that there exist areas of inquiry that transcend the material, observable world, and that what we can know – and even knowledge as such – has different grades of certainty.

The second element has to do with language. Aristotle's careful lectures often circle back on themselves, restating and recasting things earlier said (as lecturers do). Much of Aristotle's work on different topics concerns how

---

[24] Ibid., 1101b25.   [25] Ibid., 1102a1.

to talk about the subject at hand. This notion – the limits of language – is one reason Aristotle is so careful to highlight that the study of ethics cannot result in the same sort of certainty as found in other areas. As much as he is talking about ethics, he is also talking about "how to talk about ethics."

To digress briefly, in another of his works, a minor treatise entitled *On the Progression of Animals*, Aristotle discusses how different animals move.[26] The treatise is shot through with finely articulated observations of different animals in motion: how birds, frogs, horses, and so on move about. But at the beginning, Aristotle says that we must delineate the different dimensions of motion which, he says, are six: up and down, forward and reverse, and right and left.[27] Later, Aristotle accounts for the varied ways that different animals move, focusing on the structure of their limbs, whether they even have limbs (as snakes do not), their gills (if they are fish), and so on. He bases his account on observation – done, as in his other natural philosophical works, at a level of exactitude that impresses even today. So, in one respect, his treatise *On the Progression of Animals* surely counts as a forerunner of the sorts of observational practices that we associate with modern science. Stepping back, it is also apparent that, in his meticulous attention to motion, Aristotle is talking about how to talk about motion. Aristotle's philosophical works, such as we have them, possess a language dimension that is worth noticing. He articulates various subject matters in his treatises with such clarity that they became the bases of the liberal arts, as these were studied in the High Middle Ages. But they also possess a sense of the limits of language, of how far language can get us when we are considering the world in all its complexity.

Nowhere is this more evident – to close this digression – than in the *Nicomachean Ethics*. Aristotle has arrived at a definition of happiness that works; accordingly, he states the purpose of investigating ethics as subject matter:

> Since happiness is an activity of the soul in accord with complete virtue, we must investigate virtue; for perhaps we shall thus get a better theoretical grasp of happiness. The true student of politics, too, is thought to have studied this above all things; for he wishes to make his fellow citizens good and obedient to the laws.[28]

---

[26] Aristotle, *On the Progression of Animals*, in Aristotle, *Parts of Animals, Movement of Animals, Progression of Animals*, ed. and tr. A. L. Peck and E. S. Forster (Cambridge, MA: Harvard University Press, 1961), pp. 484–541.
[27] Ibid., 705a, 490–491; similar language in *Physics*, 4.1, 208b.
[28] Aristotle, *Nicomachean Ethics*, 1102a5, tr. modified, cf. Ross tr.

To take the last first, one ultimate purpose of studying ethics is that it leads to an understanding of life in the city-state (the *polis*) and, more specifically, in how one encourages good citizenship. A lot of that enterprise will include identifying virtue. "Happiness," or *eudaimonia*, "is an activity of the soul in accordance with complete virtue."

"Activity" and "complete" are important words here. "Activity," in Greek, is *energeia*, whose range of meanings include, in addition to "activity": "action," "operation," and "performance." And remember, Aristotle is saying that happiness is an activity of the soul, specifically, and an activity, to boot, that is in accordance with **complete** excellence, or virtue. The word "complete" is an adjective, *teleia*, whose root is the noun *telos*: "end," or "final point." To be considered happy, a person must be observed as having displayed virtue in a way that is "complete."

Even now, arriving as we have at an early point in Aristotle's *Nicomachean Ethics*, we note that he sees virtue as connected with action or, better, with practice. To be good means to do good things repeatedly. Also, achieving happiness is most profoundly an action "of the soul." Accordingly, we can observe another area in which there are more similarities with Plato than might otherwise first appear. Aristotle is saying that there is a discrete part of every individual that is uniquely his or hers and that is, in some subtle sense, not only material. Aristotle does not commit to the notion that each individual human soul is immortal, in such a way that it would preserve its unique nature. But there is something unique that belongs to each person, something that he or she can fashion through action. It is in Aristotle's conception of the virtues that we can see this notion come most powerfully to life.

What, then, is virtue? We can look at how Aristotle classifies virtues, and we can also examine how he discusses them in themselves. As to classification, there are intellectual virtues as well as moral virtues. Virtues that have to do with high-level intellectual capacity, of the sort that we gain and improve upon through education and experience, are intellectual virtues. These virtues include craftsmanship, prudence, understanding, knowledge, and wisdom. Virtues that have to do with a person's character are moral virtues, which include things like generosity, or temperance.[29]

There are two closely intertwined ways of understanding virtue. First, there is a term, *hexis*, that Aristotle employs to describe virtue. This word has a range of meanings, centered around the ideas of "habit," "capacity," and

---

[29] Ibid., 1103a.

"disposition." Most closely, the word implies action and repetition. Take the virtue of courage. You may be born with the capacity to be courageous. But you won't be able to be described as courageous – as a person possessing the virtue of courage – without performing courageous acts. Moreover, you'll need to perform those courageous acts repeatedly (once won't be enough) and, even more, you'll need to do so in such a way that you understand what you are doing:

> For the things we must learn before we can do, we learn by doing. For example, we become builders by building and lyre-players by playing the lyre; so too we become just by doing just acts, temperate by doing temperate acts, courageous by doing courageous acts.[30]

Again, we see the importance of practice. Aristotle highlights the connection of his current discussion with politics, arguing that "legislators make citizens good by forming habits in them; this is to say, this is the wish of every legislator; and those who do not do it well miss their mark, and it is in this respect that a good constitution differs from a bad one."[31] People become who they are in their interactions with other people. Doing things that are just and thereby making yourself into a just person: This happens in the context of interacting with others.

The aim of ethics is to make people good.[32] So, Aristotle moves to actions, reminding his audience that this examination will be less exact than others: "for things in the sphere of action and matters regarding what is good for us have no fixed identity."[33]

This reflection leads Aristotle to the second way that he describes and understands virtues: as "means," or middle points between extreme states. Though he does not put it this way, what follows is essentially an explication of an old Greek proverb, once considered so important that it graced the exterior of the temple of Apollo: *mêden agan*, or "nothing too much," meaning that moderation was to be sought in most things.[34] Things like virtue are "naturally ruined by deficiency and excess."[35] Take courage, for example, a virtue if ever there was one. Someone who "avoids and fears everything and endures nothing becomes cowardly, whereas someone who fears nothing at all and goes to face everything becomes rash."[36] Becoming courageous and, accordingly, possessing the virtue of courage, will mean

---

[30] Ibid., 1103a33–1103b1, tr. modified.   [31] Ibid., 1103b2–5, tr. modified.
[32] Ibid., 1103b28.   [33] Ibid., 1104a4, tr. modified.
[34] Pausanias, *Description of Greece*, 5 vols., ed. and tr. W. H. S. Jones (Cambridge, MA: Harvard University Press, 1918–1935), 10.24.1, vol. 4, pp. 506–507.
[35] Aristotle, *Nicomachean Ethics*, 1104a10.   [36] Ibid., 1104a20.

behaving in such a way that the behavior one exhibits represents a mean between cowardice and foolhardiness.

Aristotle's action-oriented mindset involves choice: "Virtue, then, is a state concerned with choice, lying in a mean relative to us, one determined by reason and the one by which a practically-wise person would define it."[37] You will repeatedly make choices in life. To do so in a virtuous manner will mean making choices in line with your capacities in a way that is moderate and guided by reason.

Knowing what is virtuous also depends on doing things that a person possessing "practical wisdom" would determine are virtuous. The word Aristotle employs to designate the "practically-wise person" is, in Greek, *phronimos*, a substantive adjective related to the Greek word *phronêsis*, which in turn means practical wisdom or, in an older but still valuable translation, "prudence." This word represents a virtue, arguably the key virtue for Aristotle. Because of its capaciousness, it is worth spending some time fleshing out what Aristotle means by *phronêsis* and how it is connected to some other key virtues. For in his expositions, Aristotle offers a portrait of what a good life looks like. Of what does a good life consist? What are the people like who seem to live a good life? How do they behave and evolve? For Aristotle's answers to these questions, we can turn to our next chapter.

---

[37] Ibid., 1106b35–1107a1, tr. modified.

5

THE SHAPE OF THE GOOD LIFE

Virtue, Friendship, and Contemplation in Aristotle

ARISTOTLE'S VIEWS ABOUT WHAT CONSTITUTES A GOOD LIFE emerge most clearly when we seek not to impose our current, sometimes unarticulated assumptions onto what he sets forth. And if there is one assumption that can becloud the way we understand Aristotle, it is the egocentrism common in our current society. Aristotle takes for granted that human beings are social creatures, who relate to each other in different ways. Accordingly, when he offers descriptions of virtues, he is writing and thinking most fundamentally about examples. The characteristics he delineates as virtuous are those that people generally perceive to be virtuous. From generosity, to magnanimity, to justice, to prudence and finally to friendship, Aristotle uses observation and description to get where he wants to go.

We can start with generosity, about which Aristotle says:

> It seems to be the mean with regard to wealth; for the generous person is praised not in matters of warfare, or those in which a temperate person is praised, or again in legal judgments, but rather where giving or getting wealth are concerned – most of all the giving of it.[1]

Note the phrase "the generous person is praised." This phrase, like much else in the *Nicomachean Ethics*, asserts its perspective as observational. We see – so the notion goes – that the person we describe as "generous" gains praise from those who are watching that person using wealth. The presumption is that, interconnected as we all are, we observe each other's behavior. We look to each other as models, and we tend to find consensus on who someone is by how that person behaves.

The specific virtue in this instance (being generous with one's wealth) fits into a larger framework: "Now actions done according to virtue are noble

---

[1] Aristotle, *Nicomachean Ethics*, tr. Reeve, 1119b20, tr. modified.

and are done for the sake of the noble."[2] Here Aristotle is making a connection between virtue and what was translated here as "the noble." But the word in Greek, *kalos*, also means "beautiful." Yet, this usage is quite different from Plato's notion of the "beautiful," which he saw as a Form, independent of matter, existing above and separate from the material, human world in which we find ourselves, and as something in which earthly beauty – whether beautiful people or beautiful actions – participates.

For Aristotle, by contrast, the "noble" or the "beautiful" represent something like a consensus view of what each word implies. He goes on: "A generous person will give for the sake of the noble, and he will do so rightly, for he will give to the right people, the right amounts, and at the right time, and so on for all the other thing that giving in the right way entails."[3] There can be no final determination of what, precisely, constitutes "right" here (the right people, the right amounts, and the right time), since that determination will always be situational. What might be the right amount today might not be so tomorrow, since tomorrow you might have less money to give away for some reason, in which case you could not give in such a way that didn't reduce your own circumstances grievously. Those who seem like the "right" people might not seem so right if you discover tomorrow that they are nefarious in some fashion, even if, today, they present all appearance of perfect respectability. As ever with Aristotle, we see a drive toward completion: You can only know if the action is done in the "right" way once it has been completed. Aristotle cannot prescribe what you should or shouldn't do in a specific sense. And, with respect to his approach to ethical questions (here, what does "generosity" mean), one example could never be enough. One only really knows what generosity is by generalizing many instances of appropriately "generous" behavior, a process that will always be somewhat incomplete. We return, accordingly, to language. For when he offers his descriptions of what being a "generous" person is like, Aristotle is saying to his students: This is what we talk about when we talk about generosity. This is the conversation, or *logos*, or process of reasoning: We survey the world as we know it for examples, gather those examples as best we can, and from that gathering make general statements.

The same goes for another key virtue, magnanimity. It is one of a suite of virtues that are interconnected, in the sense that good people tend to have all of them. In this instance, a look at the Greek word for magnanimity is appropriate, for in its elegance it tells us much of what we need to know.

---

[2] Ibid., 1120a23, my tr.   [3] Ibid., 1120a23–25, tr. modified.

The word is *megalopsychia*. It combines two roots, the adjective *megala*, which means "great" in all the senses of that word, and *psyche*, which means "soul." A clumsy but accurate translation would be "great-souled-ness," and it would get across what Aristotle really means by the word. What he has in mind is the quality a person with a great soul possesses. There is a merging together of greatness with an appropriate consciousness of one's status and responsibilities: "Now a magnanimous man seems to be someone who thinks himself worthy of great things and is worthy of them. For whoever goes beyond what he deserves is silly, but no one who is in accord with virtue is silly or without reason."[4]

A portrait emerges as Aristotle sketches the magnanimous man. The magnanimous man will gain a lot of worldly honors, but he will deserve them. He "must be good."[5] He will likely be the recipient of goods of fortune, meaning he will be well born and with a good heritage, or possessed of wealth or power. But he will know how to comport himself, without going to excess, even though given his status he could easily do so. The magnanimous man likes to confer benefits but not receive them. He asks for nothing and is willing to give help readily. To those of a lower station, he will behave with moderation, not lording his status over them. Also, "He must be open in his hate and in his love, for to conceal one's feelings is a mark of timidity, and he must care more for truth than for what people will think, and he must speak and act openly."[6] He will not gossip, nor will he talk overmuch about himself. He will "possess beautiful and profitless things rather than profitable and useful ones, for this is more proper to a character that suffices unto itself." Finally, "a slow step is thought proper to the magnanimous man, a deep voice, and a level utterance. For the man who concerns himself energetically about few things is not likely to be hurried."[7]

What we have here, essentially, is a portrait of an aristocrat. Aristotle's language reveals his assumptions. He believes there is a structure to the world and accordingly a structure to society, however much he might insist that ethics exists in the realm of real life, with its inevitable changes according to time and circumstance. Here, with his example of the magnanimous person, one of these structural assumptions emerges, which is that society will have higher and lower orders, inevitably, and that to be "magnanimous" one needs, in general, to belong to the higher orders. Infamously, in his *Politics*, Aristotle set forth the notion that, even as there were those who were natural rulers, there were also those who were naturally to be ruled and indeed, to

---

[4] Ibid., 1123b1–4, tr. modified.   [5] Ibid., 1124a29.   [6] Ibid., 1124b25, tr. modified.
[7] Ibid., 1125a10–15, tr. modified.

be enslaved.[8] Here we see a thinker fully embedded in the terrible conventions of his time. Moreover, if we look ahead to later justifications for the practice of human enslavement, we can mark Aristotle's notion as pernicious, since it was later used as a justification for that practice.[9]

To return to his thinking on magnanimity, we see another assumption, or rather a blind spot, which is that Aristotle's basic set of examples – like Plato's and in truth like many of the thinkers who have for better and at times for worse shaped western thought – excludes about half of all people: women. There will be more to say about this unfortunate but none the less true tendency later. Here, it is enough to say that we need to read with sagacity. Parts of Aristotle's thinking on magnanimity can be readapted to our own age and extended to all people, by focusing on the kinds of qualities that we value today as elements of magnanimity. In a historical sense, however, the class assumptions remain when it comes to magnanimity and, indeed, they pervade Aristotle's thought. He is better thought of as an observer rather than a prescriber; and what he sees around him are order and hierarchies: order, in the sense that there is an order in nature whose outlines are sometimes hidden but which a philosopher must seek to uncover; hierarchies, in the sense that things seem to be arranged, in general, in such a way that certain inferior things seem to depend on other superior things. It is one of the disquieting aspects of his thought that people fit neatly into that overriding view of the world. In the most neutral way, we can say that Aristotle observes classes that exist in the world and records them. For him, someone considered magnanimous will likely possess other virtues, such as one we have seen, generosity, and one to which we can now turn: justice.

Justice warrants special treatment among the moral virtues. It has many elements. Aristotle again fleshes out its nature by observation and categorization. Overridingly, one thing is true about justice: It is eminently social, a virtue and condition that exists only in a human context, one where there are laws, agreed-upon norms, and, in short, society. Aristotle calls justice a "complete virtue," since "someone who possesses it can use his virtue in relation to another person and not solely with regard to himself."[10] Justice, like other virtues, is fundamentally social and finds expression in interaction with others.

---

[8] Aristotle, *Politics*, 1252a30; see also Fred D. Miller, *Nature, Justice and Rights in Aristotle's Politics* (Oxford: Oxford University Press, 1997), 108–109.

[9] See Edith Hall, Richard Alston, and Justine McConnell, eds., *Ancient Slavery and Abolition: From Hobbes to Hollywood* (Oxford: Oxford University Press, 2011), and especially therein S. Sara Monoson, "Recollecting Aristotle: Pro-Slavery Thought in Antebellum America and the Argument of *Politics* Book I," pp. 247–278.

[10] Aristotle, *Nicomachean Ethics*, 1129b30.

One way to understand justice is to think about the different sorts of injustice that people can commit and that in general occur. You could, for example, commit adultery with the intention of defrauding the person with whom you are engaging in adultery. In this case, you would be deemed unjust. Or you could commit adultery owing simply to unrestrained passion. In that case you would rightly be deemed intemperate, but not unjust. In general terms, there will be agreement in society as to what is and is not just, an agreement that will find its fullest expression in the law:

> In practice, most acts commanded by law are those prescribed from the point of view of virtue taken as a whole; for the law asks us to practice every virtue and forbids us to practice any vice. And the things that tend to produce virtue taken as a whole are those of the acts prescribed by the law which have been prescribed with a view to education for the common good.[11]

By "in practice" (*schedon* in Greek, which can also mean "more or less," "approximately," and so on – it is an adverb lessening exactitude), Aristotle means that the law is an indicator of how a society deems virtuous acts to be virtuous. Law thus represents a kind of encyclopedia of ethics shorn of extended reasoning but one that nevertheless sums up a society's morals. It will not work all the time. When it comes to education of the individual and the kind of education that will make the individual good, "we must determine later whether this is the function of the political art or another; for being a good man is presumably not in every case the same as being a good citizen."[12] Parenthetically, in his *Politics*, Aristotle discusses citizenship, stressing that someone who is morally good may not always be termed a good citizen, since the latter – in some states – implies direct involvement in government.[13] He should not be understood here as suggesting that in some circumstances a "good" person will disobey the law. He is, yet again, simply observing how different states operate and noting how different definitions of citizenship will include different sorts of people under their purview.

Aristotle also likens justice to proportion. Someone who acts unjustly has too much of what is good, someone treated unjustly has too little.[14] That is one way to think about justice: a quality shared by people who possess what

---

[11] Ibid., 1130b25, tr. modified.   [12] Ibid., 1130b29, tr. modified.
[13] Aristotle, *Politics*, bk. 3, 1276b33–1277a5; cf. Miller, *Nature, Justice and Rights in Aristotle's Politics*, 143–190.
[14] Aristotle, *Nicomachean Ethics*, 1131b20.

they deserve, no less and no more. They do not grasp greedily for more than that to which they are entitled.

Transactions matter as well. In this respect, "what is just in transactions ... is a sort of equality ... and the injustice a sort of inequality."[15] Aristotle means that there will be cases when someone will have taken something unjustly from someone else. Here as elsewhere Aristotle reverts to the law, arguing that the "judge tries to equalize things by means of the penalty," meaning you pay restitution to the person against whom you have committed a crime. All in all, "the just is intermediate between a sort of gain and a sort of loss, namely those losses which are involuntary, consisting in having an equal amount before and after the transaction."[16] Aristotle does not mean here that all people would have equal amounts of all things. Instead, in cases where an injustice has been committed, the implementation of justice will entail restitution for the person against whom the injustice was committed, so that he or she can return to a state of possessing "equal" to what he or she possessed before being treated unjustly.

As to justice as a virtue, the person who possesses it will do what is just by choice, giving to others and reserving for himself what is fair.[17] Justice, distribution, reciprocity: These matters, for Aristotle, are enshrined primarily in law and can exist only among people whose relations are governed by law.[18] Different though Plato and Aristotle are, here is one concern they share: a respect for the rule of law as a shared mechanism by which to regulate human desires. Indeed, both Plato and Aristotle recognized an important vice as being all-too-human, that of greed, or *pleonexia* in Greek, which means "wanting ever more" – more than your fair share, more than you might have earned, more than others, often for no other reason than that you see others and want what they have. *Pleonexia* is the foundation of injustice when we find it in society.[19] Accordingly, we establish laws, and we entrust their implementation to officials designed to safeguard those laws. The real concern is raising people so that they act in accordance with virtue. A society must find ways to develop its members' inborn capacities for various virtues and see that they develop them from potentiality into actuality. All the virtues, however diversely considered they are, are like that in certain ways: One will only manifest them fully if one

---

[15] Ibid., 1132b30 tr. modified. [16] Ibid, 1132b18, tr. modified. [17] Ibid., 1134a3.
[18] Ibid., 1134a25.
[19] See Plato, *Republic*, 349b–c; *Laws*, 875b–c (pp. 272–273); Aristotle, *Nicomachean Ethics*, 1129b1; *Politics*, 1302a31–34 (pp. 378–379).

conditions oneself to do so, a process in which the customs, habits, and morals of one's society have a meaningful role to play.

The individual, too, has a role to play. A notable moment occurs in the *Nicomachean Ethics* when Aristotle addresses the problem of individual character and, for want of a better term, the nature of the individual will. It has to do with why people do things that they know are wrong. Aristotle writes:

> Men think that acting unjustly is in their power, and therefore that being just is easy. But it is not. To have sex with someone's wife, to wound someone, to deliver a bribe, is easy and in our power. But to do them because of a certain disposition of character is neither easy nor in our power.[20]

Choice comes to the fore. You can choose to commit adultery or bribery, or you can choose not to do so. But your disposition will come into play. You may know these actions are wrong but engage in them anyway. Similarly, you may know that the law forbids certain things, but there are then further subtleties less easy to understand: how to act, for example, to achieve justice. The law, in its generality, cannot explain or even definitively shape human character in such a way that a person will always do the right thing.

Later, Aristotle discusses the vice of incontinence, meaning a lack of self-control. He brings up a notion he attributes to Socrates, who held "that there is no such thing as incontinence."[21] The idea was that no one acts against what they believe to be best. When they do, it is out of ignorance. There is evidence that Socrates and Plato held something like this view. In Plato's dialogue *Protagoras*, Socrates (the character) is discussing a wise predecessor named Simonides, and in fleshing out his opinions says: "I am fairly sure of this, that none of the wise men considers that anybody ever errs willingly or willingly does base and evil deeds; they are well aware that all who do base and evil things do them unwillingly."[22] The word for "err," here, is derived from the Greek verb *hamartanein*, which at its most basic level means "to miss the mark," as an archer with an arrow might do. But it also means "to make a mistake" and, in some respects, "to sin" or "to engage in conduct marked by vice." And the word for "willingly" derives from the Greek word *hekôn*, which implies action under one's own control. The point that Plato and Socrates are making and that Aristotle reports is this: If you truly knew what good conduct entailed, that is the conduct in which

---

[20] Ibid., 1137a10, tr. modified.   [21] Ibid, 1145b25.
[22] Plato, *Protagoras*, 345e, in Plato, *Laches, Protagoras, Meno, Euthydemus*, ed. and tr. W. R. M. Lamb (Cambridge, MA: Harvard University Press, 1924), pp. 92–257, at pp. 206–207.

you would engage. When people do bad things, it is because they simply do not know that those things are bad. They do not do them "willingly." Here, Aristotle spends a bit of time arguing against the strict Socratic view that "no one errs willingly." But he mostly talks about different varieties of "opinion" versus "knowledge," or "weak" versus "strong" beliefs, all of which can inflect what a person chooses to do, whether that conduct is virtuous or viceful. Aristotle, essentially, is fitting the discussion into his overall intellectual architecture of the virtues. But after Aristotle, the nature of wrongdoing and sin proved to be one of the most transformative questions related to ethics and the nature of the human person. It took centuries to come to fruition, but when it did, the western world was never the same, as we shall see in succeeding chapters.

For now, we can return to Aristotle's views regarding virtues. Thus far, Aristotle's views on the "moral virtues" have come to the fore. These virtues – generosity, magnanimity, and justice – are conditioned by upbringing and custom to be learned, accepted as a matter of course, and propagated. They relate to "morals" in that broad sense. There are also "intellectual virtues," virtues that must include the human intellect and its powers of reasoning to be effective. Aristotle believed the human soul had different parts, of which the intellect was one, hence the distinction. The most important intellectual virtue is the Greek *phronêsis*, commonly translated now as "practical wisdom" and traditionally as "prudence" (thanks to the Latin *prudentia*).[23]

Prudence forms part of an ensemble of virtues practiced using reason, by deliberating and making choices that involve affirmations and denials. Another of these virtues is "craft" or "art," the Greek for which is *technê* (from which our word "technical" derives). In the case of *technê*, it represents a "state concerned with making, involving true reasoning."[24] To have "art" means you can do a thing for which you possess the art (blacksmithing, say). The other two are *epistêmê* ("knowledge" of things that cannot be otherwise) and *nous* ("reasoning" or "rational intuition").

Prudence is the most important virtue because it is regulatory. When Aristotle had discussed the moral virtues and notion of the "mean" – that moral virtues represent a mean between extremes – he had said that the

---

[23] Aristotle counterposes *phronêsis* – in his discussion in the *Nicomachean Ethics*, Book 6 – with another virtue, *sophia*, which we have encountered before: "wisdom." It stands higher on a scale of virtues. For it is with "wisdom" that one gains knowledge, or *episteme*. To put it another way, possessing wisdom means one will also possess demonstrable knowledge.
[24] Aristotle, *Nicomachean Ethics*, 1140a20.

"mean" was "defined by reason and as a prudent man would determine it."[25] There is a strong sense of personal exemplarity: To know how to do certain things one needs to watch the people who are doing those things. "We will understand prudence only if we consider whom we describe as prudent."[26] Prudent people deliberate well about what is good for them, but in the broadest possible way. They deliberate about the kinds of things that lead to "living well," meaning, to the "good life."[27] Prudence, accordingly, is not knowledge, since knowledge must be about things that, in the final analysis, cannot be otherwise. One acquires prudence through experience, combining an ability to deliberate well about matters that are good, not only for the moment, but also over a longer time horizon; not only for the person him- or herself, but also – in whatever context the deliberation occurs – for people in general.

Moreover, prudence concerns action in the world.[28] It is linked to political wisdom, though it is not the same, since life presents choices beyond the political. It is a necessary counterpart to the moral virtues. For the moral virtues represent something that can and should be done well – being courageous, for example – and prudence will guide the choices that lead to acting courageous in a proper way, veering away from the extremes of cowardice and rashness. Prudence allows one to determine context for one's actions. Finally, it is proper to older people, Aristotle suggests, saying that one cannot find a person who is both young and prudent.

For Aristotle, the purpose of ethics is to make people better. It is no surprise that, after he offers some exhaustive arguments about the virtues, he moves to a discussion of friendship. "No one would choose to live without friends, even if he had all the other good things."[29] Even wealthy and powerful people seem to need friends. The reason can bring a modern reader up short: "For what benefit is there once the opportunity to be a benefactor – which occurs most and is most praiseworthy when it is toward friends – is removed?"[30] Why have wealth and power, in other words, if you cannot use them to help your friends? And of course, you need friends to help you guard your prosperity, since "the greater it is, the more exposed it is to risk."[31] The fact that this is how Aristotle begins his discussion of friendship reminds us that he lived in a time when personal, local connections mattered greatly, in what seem to us today like very small communities. In this context, it was expected that if you were wealthy one of the first things to which you would turn your attention was helping your friends

---

[25] Ibid., 1106. [26] Ibid., 1140a25. [27] Ibid. [28] Ibid., 1141b22.
[29] Ibid., 1155a5. [30] Ibid., tr. modified. [31] Ibid., tr. modified.

by engaging in the sorts of behaviors that would spread the wealth around. Today, it can be read as the corrupting effects of wealth and power. In Aristotle's day, it seemed more natural, part of the long (and in some ways still with us) premodern tradition of reciprocal gift-giving.[32]

But there are other, more productive ways in which Aristotle thinks about friendship, intimately connected to virtue as it is. Friendship, most powerfully, has to do with what Aristotle calls *philia*, in Greek, a word that means "love," but with some different resonances than those found in modern English usage. *Philia* encompasses affection, ties that bind, and reciprocal admiration. People "love" things that are good and pleasant, Aristotle says, a sentiment that pervades his thinking on friendship. He brings his realist's sensibility into the discussion of this central pillar of how human beings deal with each other, how they organize themselves, and, indeed, how they experience joy in social settings. He recognizes that friendships are complicated and that people become "friends" for different reasons.

Some people become friends out of utility. "They love each other because of some good which they get from each other."[33] Think of the many "friends" politicians tend to have. Those friendships exist because of benefits each partner will receive. Others become friends because of pleasure, meaning that one might like someone not for their character but because they are pleasant to be around.[34] You like to be around certain people because you find them funny, diverting – your interactions with them are pleasant. In both cases – people who like other friends because they may prove useful or because they find their company pleasant – Aristotle describes the friendships as incidental and one-way. Those sorts of friendships are easily dissolved, if for some reason the friends change in character, if they cease to be "pleasant or useful." What is "useful" always changes, of course. If the utility goes away, so does the friendship. I was your friend when you were trying to help me get elected. Now, after my election bid has failed and I have moved on to other things, there is no reason to continue the relationship. This sort of utility-based friendship exists mostly among older people, Aristotle says, since they are more inclined to value the useful over the pleasant. The young, conversely, aim more toward pleasure, so that they will be the ones – if we are speaking still of one-way friendships – who incline more in that pleasure-oriented direction. Aristotle believes that

---

[32] Marcel Mauss, *The Gift: The Form and Reason for Exchange in Archaic Societies*, tr. W. D. Halls (New York: Norton, 1990).
[33] Aristotle, *Nicomachean Ethics*, 1156a10, tr. modified.   [34] Ibid.

the young live under the sway of emotion. They look to what is right in front of them and are less inclined to think about the longer term.

People gather, and they associate in pairs and groups, members of which are called "friends." Still, it doesn't seem like enough has been said, as if the discussion of friendship has not yet been fully addressed. Accordingly, Aristotle moves to another level. To understand him, a close look at his language is warranted. After discussing these utility-oriented friendships, Aristotle writes (with some key words highlighted): "**Perfect friendship** is that of people who are **good** and who are alike in virtue. Given that they are good, they wish good things for each other, and they are in themselves good."[35] For "friendship" (just by way of reminding ourselves) Aristotle uses the word *philia*, whose basic meaning is "love."

The resonance of this word, *philia*, falls somewhere between the modern English words "friendship" and "love." The latter is too intense for what Aristotle has in mind and the former, "friendship," may be just a bit too anodyne. It is also meaningful that Aristotle uses the adjective "complete" here, which in Greek is *teleia*. That word, as one can see, shares the *tel-* root with the word *telos* – "end" or "goal" or "completion." This usage reminds us of Aristotle's difference from Plato. Aristotle is not saying that *philia* is something mystical – that, for example, two friends are "participating" in a "Form" of Beauty when they take delight in each other's company. Instead, like much else in Aristotle's thinking, the word "complete" implies that there are states of potentiality and actuality in all things, even friendship. At one end of a scale, there is the incomplete sort of friendship he has mentioned, unions that occur for utility or pleasure. At the other, "complete" end, there is a fully realized friendship between two virtuous people. These people are "good" in the sense that each has become aware of his or her capacity to be virtuous. Over time, they engage in behaviors that bring that potentially virtuous state to actuality by repeatedly doing good things and engaging in good behaviors. They are "alike in virtue," meaning that they have developed their virtue in this way, and as such they match, not as if they were two halves of a previously unrequited whole (as Plato had described lovers in his dialogue the *Symposium*), but rather as two people, discrete individuals, who care for each other in an unselfish way.

Selflessness has a role to play in Aristotle's vision. About these "complete" friends, he says that "those wishing good things for their friends, for the sake of their friends, are friends in the greatest degree."[36] Each friend "is good,

---

[35] Ibid., 1156b6, my tr. [36] Ibid., 1156b9–1156b10, my tr.

plainly, to the [other] friend" – "plainly," meaning without any qualification.[37] These sorts of friendships are rare, and they take time to create. Finally, in these complete friendships, friends get the same sorts of things from each other. In an ideal framework, then, this complete friendship stands at the top of a hierarchy of human interaction: virtuous people interacting with other virtuous people.

Aristotle, for the most part, is very grounded, less inclined than was Plato to look toward ideal worlds. But there was one realm, when it comes to ethics and its associated question of what constitutes the best life, where an ideal vision emerged in full force, reminding us that, for all of Aristotle's differences from Plato, they shared some baseline commitments. This moment comes in the last Book of the *Nicomachean Ethics*.

Happiness, Aristotle reiterates, is an activity pursued for the sake of itself and, in so far as possible, self-sufficiently and in line with virtue. What, then, is the best style of life? It will be a life of virtue, rather than of empty amusement, a serious life, rather than one full of laughter. Of all the elements of which we are composed – desire, emotions, intellect – it is intellect which we deem the highest. About "intellect," Aristotle manifests some uncertainty regarding its status.[38] Are we ruled by intellect? Is intellect itself "divine or only the most divine element in us?"[39] Whatever the answers to those questions, complete happiness will consist in activity of the intellect in accordance with the virtue that is proper to intellect.

We are in the realm, we recall, of the "best life" – of discerning what it is, what it will be about, and what parts of us play a role in achieving it. When we talk about "best," there can be nothing better than the divine. Clearly, that is where we want to be: near the divine, taking part in it in so far as we can. And of all our parts and out of all the things we do, our intellect is closest to being divine. Aristotle shies away from declaring that it is divine, suggesting (with his use of the word "whether") that it might be. Concerned as he is with language, that is as far as he will go.

Why might the life of the intellect be the best? It is self-sufficient, for one thing. A person who possesses any of the other virtues needs other people around to practice those virtues. "The just person," Aristotle says, "needs people towards whom and with whom he will act justly," and so on.[40] The

---

[37] Ibid., 1156b25.
[38] Cf. J. L. Ackrill, "Aristotle on Eudaimonia," in Amélie Oksenberg, Rorty, ed., *Essays on Aristotle's Ethics* (Berkeley: University of California Press, 1981), 15–33; and Thomas Nagel, "Aristotle on Eudaimonia," in *Essays on Aristotle's Ethics*, 7–14.
[39] Aristotle, *Nicomachean Ethics*, 1177a15.   [40] Ibid., 1177a30, tr. modified.

wise man, however, can engage in contemplation by himself, and he can do so more effectively as he grows wiser. Aristotle nods to the fact that teamwork can help in the enterprise of knowledge, writing that the wise man can perhaps better contemplate truth "if he has co-workers; but all the same, he is the most self-sufficient."[41] It is a slightly odd note in the massive, multipart symphony that Aristotle's work represents.

Several of his other works, especially those devoted to natural philosophy (in which subjects like physics and biology are present – in their ancient forms, of course) reflect Aristotle's use of teams of researchers. This tendency is especially prominent in his biological work, parts of which, observation heavy as they were, could not have been completed without teamwork. Moreover, in most of his major works, he offers an accounting, usually at the beginning, of what other authors and thinkers before him had proposed on the topic at hand. He can be credited, rightly, with anticipating the modern scholarly habit of the "literature review," citing and explaining the views of predecessors in the field. He believes that the production of human knowledge is a cumulative enterprise that builds on itself – a notion that takes for granted the idea that there will be "co-workers" with whom one collaborates. In other words, most of what Aristotle endorses extends his postulate in the *Nicomachean Ethics* that human beings are social creatures and that, when it comes to knowledge, the foundation of authentic wisdom, it will be a team effort.

But then there is this one lonely but meaningful moment in the *Nicomachean Ethics*, wherein it is clear that there is a part of us, the contemplative part and, we should emphasize, the best part, that will need to be alone to flourish most fully. It is worth listening carefully to Aristotle to understand why this is the case:

> If intellect is divine, then, in comparison with man, the life according to it is divine in comparison with human life. But we must not follow those who advise us, being men, to think of comparison with human things and, being mortal, of mortal things. Instead, we must, in so far as we can, make ourselves immortal and do everything we can to live in accordance with the best thing in us. For even if it is small in bulk, all the more so does it surpass everything in power and worth. This would seem, too, to be each man himself, since it is the authoritative and better part of him. It would be strange then, if he were to choose not the life of himself but that of something else.[42]

---

[41] Ibid., 1177a33.   [42] Ibid., 1177b30, tr. modified.

We must "make ourselves immortal," Aristotle says, preceding that statement (in Greek as in our translation above) with the qualifier, "in so far as we can." There is something in us that is best – our intellect and our consequent capacity for contemplation. It is "small in bulk," meaning that, of all the things that make up a human being, the intellect occupies a small space but an outsized one, when it comes to its "power" (*dynamis*, in Greek) and "worth" (*timiotês*, which can also mean "dignity" and "honorableness"). Then, somewhat awkwardly in Greek as well as in English, Aristotle says, "this would seem to be each man himself" (an expression which, reading him broadly, we should extend to read "each man and woman him- or herself"). The awkwardness arises from the fact that there is no clear antecedent to the word "this" (*touto* in Greek). Aristotle is referring to the whole enterprise at which he has just hinted – the intellect, its capacity for contemplation, and the fact that through it we can *athanatizein* – "become immortal." He is almost delightfully vague on whether this whole "becoming immortal" trajectory is really, truly possible, interlarding his language with a professor's qualifiers – "it would seem," "perhaps," "in so far as we can," and so on.

Aristotle offers one more rapturous defense of the intellect, a defense rooted in what is often called the "theory of natural place."[43] More usually associated with the physical universe, the notion is that things in the world have a proper place and that, when matters are working as they should, those things wind up in that place. Aristotle, for instance, thinks that the earth is immobile, spherical, and at the center of the physical universe. Physical things fall naturally toward the center, toward their natural place, which is how (what we would term) gravity works in Aristotle's view. Aristotle's account has been superseded by better observations and hence better physics. But it serves to illustrate his teleological belief system: There are states of potentiality, wherein things are or should be moving toward a certain end, and states of actuality, where things have reached a point of completion.

When it comes to the life of contemplation as the best life, Aristotle puts it this way: "that which is proper to each thing is by nature best and most pleasant for each thing; for man, therefore, the life according to intellect is best and most pleasant since intellect more than anything else is man." Again, for "man" let us understand "humanity." Aristotle is saying that the quality that most distinguishes us as human beings is the capacity to think and to do so discursively and at length. Animals do not share this quality,

---

[43] Cf. Helen S. Lang, *The Order of Nature in Aristotle's Physics: Place and the Elements* (Cambridge: Cambridge University Press, 1998).

even if they seem here and there to make rudimentary decisions about things. It is high-level contemplation that makes us who we are in our most developed and complete state. Aristotle, always so empirical, allows himself this one small moment in the *Nicomachean Ethics* to entertain the notion that it is this capacity by which we can "become immortal" because, of course, it is in this respect that we are – or can become – most like the gods.

Aristotle cannot remain long at those elevated heights. He begins to qualify what he has said and to admit that most people will not be able to share in this state: "Happiest, but in a secondary way, is the life in accord with the other virtue, since the activities in accord with it are human."[44] What he means here are the other virtues he has outlined: "Just actions, brave actions, and other actions that we do in accord with the virtues and we do in relation to each other in contracts, services and in every sort of action and in feelings as well ... And all of these seem to be human."[45] One senses a hierarchy emerging. Atop the hierarchy is contemplation. Then there is behavior in society, according to virtue. This behavior arises from a person's character, which emerges after being formed by education, an education that will consider a person's inborn capacities and emotions. We are connected: to each other, by social bonds; to the world in which we live, by our senses, our perception, in short, our bodies.

Before we take our leave from Aristotle, we need to focus on his portrayal of divinity in the *Nicomachean Ethics*. Human happiness can only be "complete" when it is characterized by contemplation. Why might this be the case? Here is Aristotle, with two key words highlighted: "We assume the gods to be **blessed** and **happy** in the greatest degree."[46] For happy, the adjective used is related to the noun, *eudaimonia* – "happiness," "flourishing" – around which the whole *Nicomachean Ethics* turns. It indicates being in a complete state, where there is no more potential to fulfill, where you have developed all your capacities most fully, and where the question whether you are flourishing has been answered affirmatively and in a self-evident way.

Then there is the word "blessed," or *makarios* in Greek, in its basic adjectival form. There are different uses of the word in Greek texts that even by Aristotle's day were classics. Homer's *Odyssey* presents one. In that work, Homer told the tale of the shrewd hero Odysseus (known in the Latin tradition later as Ulysses). Odysseus, the king of the Greek state of Ithaca and a participant and hero in the Trojan War, fought with his fellow Greeks

[44] Ibid., 1178a10.   [45] Ibid., tr. modified.   [46] Ibid., 1178b10, my tr.

against the Trojans. When the war ended, Odysseus found himself far from his home, Ithaca. The *Odyssey* recounts the ten-year journey back to Ithaca on the part of Odysseus and his comrades. Full of adventures, stunning character portraits, and instances of exemplary conduct good and bad, it was lodged in the consciousnesses of Greeks, almost scriptural in the way it was repeated and studied, its episodes mined for lessons, examples, and admonitory precepts.

One of these episodes narrated Odysseus's interactions with Circe, an enchantress, or even a witch. Highly knowledgeable when it came to herbs, medicines, and other sorts of drug-like substances, she lived isolated on an island, in a large home in the middle of the woods. In their wanderings, Odysseus and his companions had come upon her island. Some remained on board their boat (Odysseus was among this number), others disembarked to engage in the feast to which Circe had invited Odysseus and his crew. As they were served their food, however, the men were turned into swine. Or rather, all but one of them, Eurylochus. This faithful friend of Odysseus had suspected something was wrong and managed to extricate himself from the group, staying back as Circe serenaded the men.

Odysseus, hearing from Eurylochus what had gone on with his men, took the warning, allowed Eurylochus to stay on the boat, and proceeded to the island. Along the way he was met by the god Hermes, who gave Odysseus an herb potent enough to ward off (Hermes said) what Circe was about to do: drug Odysseus's food and make him suffer the same fate as his friends. She would try to harm him as she had the others. Hermes advised Odysseus that he must draw his sword and rush at her, as if he intended to kill her. Fearful, she will offer to take Odysseus to bed with her. Hermes tells Odysseus he must accept this offer and sleep with her, though not before persuading the witch-goddess to swear "a great oath on the **blessed**," an oath, that is, to the gods, that would bind her not to harm Odysseus then or in the future.[47] This he did, convincing her further to liberate his men who had been turned into swine. He and the rest of his companions stayed with Circe for a year before departing. Here the word "blessed" is used to signal divinity pure and simple. So, this was one background from which Aristotle wrote when he said that we assume the gods to be both "blessed" and "happy" in the highest degree. It is a way of indicating divinity, one that Aristotle uses comparatively, however, assuming that one can be blessed in a higher or lesser degree and that the gods are most blessed.

---

[47] Homer, *Odyssey*, 2 vols., ed. and tr. A. T. Murray, rev. by George E. Dimsock (Cambridge, MA: Harvard University Press, 1995), vol. 1, bk. 10, l.299, p. 380, my tr.

Another usage of the word occurred in the work of a poet, Hesiod, who flourished around the same time as Homer. In his poetic *Works and Days*, Hesiod set forth a scheme, in which there had been five ages of man that Zeus had fostered. There was an original "golden race of mortal men," who lived in the time of Cronos, one of the Titans.[48] Eventually they died out and were covered over by earth, even as they lived on as spirits, roaming the earth cloaked in mist, giving advice, and sometimes protecting people. Thereafter came another race, this time of silver, who were debauched in their conduct, refusing to honor the Olympian gods. They were stricken from the earth, eventually, and are "called **blessed** mortals under the earth," to whom some honor is still owed.[49] Thereafter came a terrible race of mortals, warlike, who employed bronze instruments of battle, destroying each other and eventually coming to an end. Like the others covered over by earth, in their post-mortal existence, they are not worthy of honor in any way. Fourth, there emerged a race of demi-gods, the race "before our own."[50] Among them were participants in the Trojan war, wherein "death's end enshrouded some of them."[51] For others of this generation Zeus provided "habitations far from men."[52] These people "live untouched by sorrow in the islands of the **blessed** along the shore of deep-eddying Ocean . . ."[53] Finally, there is the fifth age, that in which we live now, "indeed a race of iron," whose members suffer never-ending toil and who will, eventually, receive their comeuppance from the gods after fighting and arguing among themselves over small matters.[54]

How do Hesiod's opinions help us understand Aristotle's view on divinity? Hesiod is writing from the "present," looking back on a semi-mythical past, when there were Golden, Silver, and Bronze Ages. The old days were grander, sometimes better, filled with people greater in their appetites and achievements, both good and ill, than are we. Of Hesiod's two instances of the word "blessed," the first designates the shades – the ghosts – of the people of the Silver Age, who despite their decadence were still grand enough that honor is owed to them. Then there is the other usage, in the expression "islands of the blessed," a locution that designates an almost impossible distance from us, a "far-away-ness" that demarcates our lived experience, with all its challenges and triumphs, loves and enmities, feasts

---

[48] Hesiod, *Works and Days*, in Hesiod, *Theogony, Works and Days, Testimonia*, 2 vols., ed. and tr. Glenn W. Most (Cambridge, MA: Harvard University Press, 2018), pp. 86–155, at 1.109, p. 94, my tr.
[49] Ibid., 1.141, p. 98.   [50] Ibid., 1.160, pp. 100–101.   [51] Ibid., l. 165, p. 100, my tr.
[52] Ibid., 1.167, p. 100, my tr.   [53] Ibid., 1.171, p. 100 my tr.
[54] Ibid., 1.176, p. 102, my tr.

and famines, states of war and periods of peace. Somewhere, there is a place – the islands of the blessed – where these vagaries do not occur, where life is tranquil, and where all can flourish. Those who inhabit these islands form part of that fourth "race," demi-gods, who share properties of mortals and immortals, human and divine. And it is here where we see the most meaningful connections to Aristotle's considerations.

After Aristotle postulates that the gods must be among the most blessed, he moves on to describe what that status entails and more specifically, how we might conceive of the gods. He asks: "What sort of actions must we assign to them? Just ones? Won't they appear ridiculous if they engage in transactions, return deposits, and so on?"[55] Should we assign acts of bravery to the gods? How about acts of generosity? Wouldn't it be strange if "gods" had money? We cannot describe them as "temperate," since we cannot assume that gods have blameworthy appetites. Ultimately, the more we talk about ways of conceiving and practicing virtue that are essentially human in their parameters, "everything to do with action is petty and unworthy of the gods."[56] All of that may be true. And yet, about the gods, "everyone supposes them to be living, and hence in activity..."[57] Part of living, being real, is tied up intimately with action.

Here, then, is Aristotle's question: "if you take away action from a living being, and more so production, what is left but contemplation?"[58] For "action," Aristotle uses the Greek verb *prattein*, related to our word "practice." For "production" he employs the infinitive *poiein*, which in its most literal sense means "to make" or "making" or as translated here, "production." These words relate to what Aristotle conceives of as human production and activity. But there is another kind of activity in which the gods engage, the only one, really, in which they – being gods – can engage: contemplation. As Aristotle puts it: "Therefore the **activity** of **God**, which surpasses all others in blessedness, will be contemplative. The activity of humans, then, that is most like it will most bear the stamp of happiness."[59] The word for "activity" here is *energeia* in Greek, a word that enfolds the noun *ergon*, which means "work," and a word that signified being in a state of working – "being-at-work," if you will. Moreover, here, Aristotle does not refer to "gods" but to "God," implying that there was a realm of thinking in which he postulated a divine absolute, a divinity that possessed a Oneness. We should not think of his designation as a personal God, but rather as a linguistic consequence of the human capacity to project the idea

---

[55] Aristotle, *Nicomachean Ethics*, 1178b10. [56] Ibid., 1178b15–20. [57] Ibid.
[58] Ibid., 1178b20, tr. modified. [59] Ibid., 1178b22–24, tr. modified.

of the infinite and the absolute into logical space. "Contemplation" is the most divine thing there is, the activity that characterizes "God." The more we approach that activity, the closer our activity comes to the divine.

This issue – God – emerged as the most important and transformative concept in the history of western thought. How to characterize this being? What were its capacities? How far did its vision and purview extend, especially when human beings came into the picture? These questions and more animated the discussions carried out by early Christians, even as they enfolded the traces of an idea present in both Plato and Aristotle. From Aristotle, the precision of thought and the propensity to conceive of reality in a logically hierarchical way led to a rational assumption that there must be something supreme: We speak of some things being "better" than other things. But if, somewhere, somehow, there is no "best," then our everyday language becomes meaningless. From Plato, his "Form of the Good" generated a powerful idea: that there was a goodness that superseded and superintended our own. Plato privileged the immaterial world – what we cannot see, feel, and touch in the everyday – to the material world in which we live our daily lives. This too was meaningful.

That hierarchy (immaterial is better than material) served as a model of how to conceive of human life. But it was an incomplete model, one that was not realized in full for hundreds of years for one principal reason. The gulf between us and divinity, between our human world and the immaterial, seemed so great as to be unbridgeable. One figure served as the bridge, a bridge that, as it grew and took shape, became something more like an edifice, one with many rooms, with corridors occasionally leading nowhere and, most importantly, with a capacity to grow and change according to the environment. The figure in question, of course, is Jesus Christ. As we shall see, his life and, as important, what people said about his life thereafter, were the building blocks of this new edifice. Behind Christianity stood Judaism and the rise of Roman power, to which we now turn.

6

STRANDS IN THE FABRIC

Judaism, Hellenistic Thought, Rome

To understand Jesus and the spread of the Jesus movement, we need to step back and consider two elements of supreme importance: Judaism and Rome. Jesus was Jewish, of course, as were his initial disciples. Behind him were centuries of Jewish tradition, belief, folkways, and tensions, all of which had a shaping effect on his life and how he saw the world and framed it for his followers. As to Rome, the centuries between Aristotle's death in 322 BCE and Jesus' birth in 4 BCE saw powerful political changes in the Mediterranean world, changes that marked the rise of Rome to a position of unparalleled power. Moreover, Roman thinkers had at their disposal the Hellenistic schools of philosophy – Skepticism, Stoicism, and Epicureanism, all of which, when joined together with Platonism and Aristotelianism, produced new ways of thinking about the world.

Much of western philosophy took root and spread owing to Christianity's reach and to how Christianity adopted and adapted ancient philosophical ideas, especially those of Plato. Moreover, Christianity did so in such a way that those ideas came to be understood by large swaths of people, including those who could neither read nor write. What were these ideas? In some respect individual human beings have a fundamental, inherent equality, whatever their social status, because each possesses a unique soul. There is an immaterial world that somehow superintends our daily material world, a place where things are better than what we experience. Divinity as such should not be conceived of as like humanity, even as human beings strive to reach divinity and may possess a divine spark. There will be rewards and punishments after death for the righteous and the wicked. These frameworks formed the backbone of much Christian thinking, even as their roots in Plato signaled their deep and originally non-Christian origins.

Similarly, there was so much in Jewish thought as background to early Christianity that it is more accurate to name Christianity as an outgrowth of

Judaism. Jesus was Jewish and was seen by his contemporaries as Jewish.[1] Moreover, Judaism itself interacted deeply and productively with Hellenic and eventually Roman intellectual traditions.[2] The legacies of Judaism became part of Christianity's fabric, as sources of positive thinking, of contestation and reaction, and sometimes of violent and damaging prejudices whose lasting effects are with us today.

It is worth reiterating that this book is about western thought and its majority cultures. It is about how ideas traveled through time, shaping mentalities and in turn being reshaped by every successive generation. And it is also about something a bit more, something we can term "monumentality." In modern English, when we hear the term "monument," what comes to mind is usually a building of some sort, or a statue erected as a form of remembrance. But the Latin word *monumentum* bears deeper meanings, all of them centered on memory. When the ancient Roman poet Horace referred to his work as a "monument more lasting than bronze," he meant that he was proud of his work, believing that its reputation would endure even beyond the lifespan of bronze statuary.[3] Not all the works one will encounter in this book are "monumental" in that sense. That is, not all became threads in the rich, dense texture of Western intellectual life. Surely, however, the Book of Isaiah did.

Isaiah as a book of the Old Testament cannot do justice to ancient Judaism in all its variety and history. But for late ancient and medieval Christian thinkers it served as a key link in the chain connecting their new religion to Judaism. Christian adoption of Judaic themes led to many things, erasures among them. One term that is often used is "supersessionism," the idea that Christianity "superseded" Judaism, fulfilling and completing the many themes adumbrated by the older religion. If we cast a critical eye on this notion, as we surely should, it becomes obvious that over time Christians

---

[1] For different perspectives, see Paula Fredriksen, *From Jesus to Christ: The Origins of the New Testament Images of Jesus*, 2nd ed. (New Haven: Yale University Press, 2000); E. P. Sanders, *Jesus and Judaism* (Minneapolis: Fortress Press, 1985); Geza Vermes, *Jesus the Jew: A Historian's Reading of the Gospels* (Minneapolis: Fortress Press, 1973); Geza Vermes, *Jesus and the World of Judaism* (Minneapolis: Fortress Press, 1983); Geza Vermes, *The Religion of Jesus the Jew* (Minneapolis: Fortress, 1993).

[2] See Anthony J. Saldarini, with Amy-Jill Levine, "Jewish Responses to Greek and Roman Cultures, 332 BCE to 200 CE," in Bruce Chilton, Howard Clark Kee, Eric M. Meyers, John Rogerson, Amy-Jill Levine, and Anthony J. Saldarini, *The Cambridge Companion to the Bible*, 2nd ed. (Cambridge: Cambridge and New York, 2012), 327–480.

[3] Horace, *Carmina*, 3.30: "monumentum aere perennius." See R. G. M. Nisbet and Niall Rudd, *A Commentary on Horace: Odes Book III* (Oxford: Oxford University Press, 2004), pp. 364–378, esp. pp. 364–367.

took from the Jewish heritage selectively. Christians sometimes suggested concomitantly that Judaism was incomplete, and that Christianity represented the necessary perfection of a process that could only come to fruition with Jesus Christ's coming into the world as a salvific sacrifice, as one who came to earth as both God and human being to redeem the sins of humankind. Christians, having been led by the crucified Christ to the new covenant (promised in Isaiah and in Jeremiah 31:31–32), became "the true spiritual Israel," as one second-century CE writer, Justin Martyr, put it.[4] In this sense, Jewish people came to be seen by some as left behind, and more, as stubbornly sticking to a now outdated set of religious practices whose incompleteness was made ever more obvious as Christianity grew into western Europe's majority religion. A long history of seeing Jewish people as the "other" thus only grew more intense and focused during the Middle Ages.[5] It is important to acknowledge this fact, to recognize that alongside Christian adoption of Jewish ideas, there was another side that came out over the centuries, a side that sometimes served to exclude, rather than embrace, members of the founding faith of the west. Of course, violence and prejudice cannot simplistically be ascribed to any religion. Violence and prejudice form part of who we are as human beings when we are at our worst, part of the "clash within" us, reflecting the two natures we possess: one tolerant, open, and courageous; the other exclusionary, closed-minded, and weak.[6] In focusing on what the Christian majority in the European Middle Ages came to believe – how its members constructed their worldview – one does not need to endorse their prejudices or more importantly, suggest that their religion was the only cause of their flaws, or most meaningfully, to suggest implicitly or explicitly that their flaws should be the only thing that defines them. It was all part of a larger picture, one that was complicated, messy, and as such profoundly human.

---

[4] Justin Martyr, *Dialogue with Trypho*, tr. Thomas B. Falls, in *The Fathers of the Church* (Washington, DC: The Catholic University of America Press, 1948), 6: 141–366, at 165.

[5] See David Nirenberg, *Anti-Judaism: The Western Tradition* (New York: Norton, 2013); David Nirenberg, *Communities of Violence: Persecution of Minorities in the Middle Ages* (Princeton: Princeton University Press, 1998). The tendency continued even into modern scholarship on ancient Judaism and Christianity, with a reckoning only occurring after World War II; see Andrew S. Jacobs, "The Lion and the Lamb: Reconsidering Jewish-Christian Relations in Antiquity," in Adam H. Becker and Annette Yoshiko Reed, eds., *The Ways that Never Parted: Jews and Christians in Late Antiquity and the Early Middle Ages* (Tübingen: Mohr, 2003), 95–118.

[6] See Martha Nussbaum, *The Clash Within: Democracy, Religious Violence, and India's Future* (Cambridge, MA: Harvard University Press, 2007).

Isaiah contains many elements Christian thinkers prized. The foreshadowing of a coming savior born of a Virgin (Isa 7:14); themes of justice, fairness, and mercy; a future messiah who would suffer. These themes resonated in the Christian era, took hold among leaders of the early Christian world, and became part of Christianity's fabric. The Book of Isaiah is at once fascinating, difficult, and of its time and place – or rather, of its times and places. For like a lot of biblical literature, Isaiah shows that authorship is something difficult to disentangle. It is worth focusing on what scholars currently think about the question of the authorship of Isaiah, even as it will be equally meaningful to focus on certain themes within it that served as sources of inspiration and reflection for Christians in the centuries after Christ.

It is generally agreed that the Book of Isaiah, which comprises sixty-six chapters, can be divided into three sections. Proto-Isaiah includes chapters 1–39 and dates from roughly the time of the Prophet Isaiah in the late eighth century BCE. Deutero-Isaiah, or "Second" Isaiah (chapters 40–55), dates to the sixth century BCE. And finally, Trito- (or "third") Isaiah, comprising chapters 56–66, includes material largely from the fifth century BCE. Given this diversity, Isaiah is a complex book, rich in literary forms such as songs, poems, and invective, and thoroughly deserving of the vast amount of scholarship it has received. This scholarship has emphasized both the complexities involved in authorship and the importance of editorial and textual work over the centuries during which the canonical version of the Bible came into being.[7] Simply put, Isaiah is a complicated work whose form as we have it is the result of many hands. But, for western thinkers in the medieval Latin tradition, it seemed a work that, despite its surface heterogeneity, possessed an internal unity that needed to be discovered through never-ending interpretation.[8] The result is that the Book of Isaiah represents one meaningful way to see how western thinkers understood the multiplicitous Jewish heritage that, along with the Hellenic and Roman traditions, formed the basis of western thinking.

How readers have perceived the Bible over time mattered intensely for the history of western philosophy. The Bible comprised the Hebrew Bible (or *Tanakh*), most of which Christians came to know as the Old Testament, and the "New Testament," that is, the books of the Bible that covered the life of Christ (the Gospels), the Acts of the Apostles, the Letters of Saint Paul and others, and the Book of Revelation.

---

[7] For recent scholarship, see Lena-Sofia Tiemeyer, ed., *The Oxford Handbook of Isaiah* (Oxford: Oxford University Press, 2020); and Christopher B. Hays, ed., *The Cambridge Companion to the Book of Isaiah* (Cambridge: Cambridge University Press, 2024).

[8] See Anni Maria Laato, "Isaiah in Latin," in Tiemeyer, *Oxford Handbook of Isaiah*, 489–503.

The Bible became a lot more than the sum of its parts for the medieval Christians who incorporated Ancient Greek and Roman thinking into their own philosophizing. It became a touchstone for ethics, with the life of Christ serving as the most important set of examples to be imitated. But there were countless other episodes in the Bible that served as "exemplary," meaning as sets of examples, some of which were thought worthy of imitation, others as sources of conduct to be avoided. The Bible also served as a principal lens through which to observe humanity's place in world history. A later thinker we shall meet, Augustine of Hippo (354–430 CE), embraced a view of history different from his ancient forebears. Whereas one ancient model was cyclical – governments and empires rose, they fell, they rose again, and so on – in Augustine's vision, history had a direction and, notionally, an eventual end, an end in which God's justice would finally reign supreme. The Bible served as a commanding source for this vision: prophecy became teleology, which led to a new view of history.

As to the Book of Isaiah, it supplied a remarkably adaptable style of thinking and writing for Christians.[9] Correspondences between what was written in Isaiah and what Jesus said and did – and then, what later writers said about him – did not need to be exact. Instead, Christians had a way of thinking about the world that, through repetition and echoes in other parts of scripture, fostered deeper patterns of mental adherence. At its outset Christianity was Jewish – the earliest followers of Christ considered themselves Jews. Judaism and Christianity indeed developed into separate religions with different grounding assumptions. But their linking needs to be emphasized if we are to comprehend how premodern western philosophers understood their intellectual world. One Christian thinker, Saint Jerome, considered Isaiah so important that he suggested Isaiah was "more of an evangelist than a prophet."[10] Some Christians considered the Book of Isaiah a "fifth Gospel," its words echoed by Christ himself on numerous occasions. Four ways of thinking about the world and humanity's place in it stand out. These relate to: the nature of God, the nature of justice, the nature of humanity, and the nature of time. These Jewish inheritances shaped Christian thinking and mentalities, providing the "Judeo" in "Judeo-Christian."

---

[9] See John F. A. Sawyer, *The Fifth Gospel: Isaiah in the History of Christianity* (Cambridge: Cambridge University Press, 1996).

[10] Jerome, "Prologus" to translation of Isaiah, in Robert Weber, ed., *Biblia Sacra iuxta Vulgatam versionem*, 2nd ed., 2 vols. (Stuttgart: Württembergische Bibelanstalt, 1975), 2: 1096: "non tam propheta dicendus est quam evangelista."

As to God, it is the creativity, fundamental unity, and untranslatability that stand out. The first line of the first book of what Christians came to know as the Old Testament runs as follows: "In the beginning God created heaven and earth" (Gen 1:1).[11] The book of Genesis – hauntingly, poetically – goes on to describe the rest of God's creation in short order, all the way up to the creation of human beings. In Isaiah we read: "And now, O Lord, thou art our father, and we are clay: and thou art our maker, and we all are the works of thy hands" (Isa 64:8). God is a creator, the ultimate answer to the question: How did we get here? Underneath the relative simplicity of creation accounts lay a future history of unending interpretation, whether that interpretation involved squaring Genesis's account with ancient philosophers' thinking, or understanding further just what God's attributes were.

The attributes are meaningful. What sort of God was this? Certainly not like those of the ancient Greek pantheon, whose gods were often immoderate in their behavior and frequently immersed in conduct that could only be described as viceful – as Plato had warned. No, the God of the ancient Jews – the God that became the Christian God – was different. First, he was all-powerful, able to create from nothing. Second, he was just. This is to say that he often used his power to intervene in the world when injustices occurred. But what was "justice" in this context? It is worth looking in depth at a passage from Isaiah:

> Woe to you that call evil good, and good evil: that put darkness for light, and light for darkness: that put bitter for sweet, and sweet for bitter. Woe to you that are wise in your own eyes, and prudent in your own conceits. Woe to you that are mighty to drink wine, and stout men at drunkenness. That justify the wicked for gifts, and take away the justice of the just from him. Therefore as the tongue of the fire devoureth the stubble, and the heat of the flame consumeth it: so shall their root be as ashes, and their bud shall go up as dust: for they have cast away the law of the Lord of hosts, and have blasphemed the word of the Holy One of Israel. Therefore is the wrath of the Lord kindled against his people, and he hath stretched out his hand upon them, and struck them: and the mountains were troubled, and their carcasses became as dung in the midst of the streets. For all this his anger is not turned away, but his hand is stretched out still. (Isa 5:20–25)

Certain themes emerge. First there is, as often, exemplarity. Here we see negative examples, people who are immoderate in their consumption of

---

[11] I am intentionally using the term "Old Testament," since this is how medieval Christians saw things; in this locution, I echo the reasoning of John Barton in his remarkable *A History of the Bible: The Story of the World's Most Influential Book* (New York: Viking, 2019).

wine, who valorize evil men for personal benefit (for "gifts"), and who accordingly allow the wicked to escape justice.[12] In Isaiah and many other places in the Old Testament, the prophets presented vigorous, robust self-criticism. This aspect of Jewish tradition served as one of the foundations of Jesus' identity and arguably one of the most important threads in the development of modern western classical liberalism's densely woven fabric.[13] Ancient Jewish prophets criticized unjust or misguided rulers, often highlighting their lack of care for the disadvantaged (Isa 10:1–2; Amos 4:1; Mic 3:1–3). And they criticized their own polities as well (Isa 1:2–4; Jer 5:1–3; Ezek 22:23–31).

Moreover, as we see in the above quotation, there is a concern for justice as well as a strong prediction that it will be meted out. There will be consequences, fearful ones, and God will be their author. He will "strike" his people – descendants, ultimately, of the very people he created – when they so deserve. His "anger" will last. To an extent, this is what justice means. People know through observation what sorts of habits and conduct are just. They will face comeuppance when they transgress those standards, some of which will be explicit in law, others of which will be implicit and visible only when their boundaries have been transgressed.

God's power stands out, as he serves both as an absolute standard of justice and, importantly, as the one and only God. This is a god who says (again, in Isaiah), "I am the first and the last, besides me there is no God" (Isa 44:6). More: "Is there a God beside me, a maker, whom I have not known?" (Isa 44:8). God is protective of his status as "maker," that is, as creator. And God is just a little bit angry at the idea that people could even imagine other gods. In fact, "the makers of idols are all of them nothing, and their best beloved things shall not profit them ... for the makers are men: they shall all assemble together, they shall stand and fear, and shall be confounded together" (Isa 44:9–11). There is a strong distinction drawn between God and human beings. Human beings can do things like make idols, but those idols do not substitute for the real thing, God alone. Throughout the Old Testament, in fact, there are numerous prohibitions, imprecations, and warnings against "graven images" (Lev 26:1; Deut 4:16, 4:23, 5:8, 7:5, 7:25, 27:15). The implication is that human life, though created by God, is strictly separated

---

[12] See Theodore J. Lewis, *The Origin and Character of God: Ancient Israelite Religion through the Lens of Divinity* (Oxford: Oxford University Press, 2020), p. 537.

[13] See Yoram Hazony, *The Philosophy of Hebrew Scripture* (Cambridge: Cambridge University Press, 2012); Eric Nelson, *The Hebrew Republic: Jewish Sources and the Transformation of European Political Thought* (Cambridge, MA: Harvard University Press, 2010).

from God himself. Though there are passages in the Old Testament that speak of humanity being created in the "image and likeness" of God (Gen 1:26, 27; 5:1; 9:6), the God of the Old Testament still possessed a nature that was exclusively divine, and thus fundamentally separate from humanity. In Isaiah we read (Isa 55:8–9): "For my thoughts are not your thoughts, nor your ways my ways, saith the Lord. As the heavens are exalted above the earth, so are my ways exalted above your ways, and my thoughts above your thoughts."

Still, there are connections between God and human beings, especially when it comes to salvation. Nowhere can we see these more clearly than in a chapter in Isaiah (Isa 49) that medieval Christians saw as prefiguring Christianity. Isaiah, the prophet, takes on the identity of a future savior, identifying himself with Israel and accordingly, Israel with humanity at large. This tension – between Israel as representing the Jews as a separate community and Israel as representing something more – is present in Isaiah. The ambiguity allows readers to choose how to interpret. On what sorts of things should a reader lay emphasis? How and why might one fill gaps in the written text? "It is a small thing" – says God, through the prophet – "that thou shouldst be my servant to raise up the tribes of Jacob, and to convert the dregs of Israel. Behold I have given thee to be the light of the Gentiles, that thou mayst be my salvation even to the farthest part of the earth" (Isa 49:6). What could this mean? First, clearly, that it was not enough to care only for the "tribes of Jacob" and the "dregs" of Israel ("dregs" in the Douay-Rheims translation means here "what has been left behind," something like a remnant or residue).

More simply, Isaiah is saying that God told him that caring only for the Jewish community was not enough and that he should be a "light to the Gentiles." This God, Isaiah suggested, would be appealing to many:

> Many people shall come and say Come let us go, up to the mountain of the Lord to the house of the God of Jacob, that he may teach us his ways and that we may walk in his paths. He shall judge between the nations and shall arbitrate for many peoples; they shall beat their swords into plowshares, and their spears into pruning hooks; nation shall not lift up sword against nation. (Isa 2:2–4)

The message is a universalizing one, and the promise is peace among people. What had been a god only for one group of people was, instead, the one God who ruled over all. People will recognize this centrality: "They shall come from far away, they shall bring gold and frankincense" (Isa 60:4–6).

If all of this sounds to a reader like doctrines associated with Christianity (which we will examine in more depth in the following chapters), that is because Christians adopted these ideas, reading Isaiah as foreshadowing their beliefs. And the foundations are there in Isaiah and in other Old Testament books. What, after all, were Christians to make of passages like "Therefore the Lord himself shall give you a sign. Behold a virgin shall conceive, and bear a son, and his name shall be called Emmanuel" (Isa 7:14); or Isaiah 61:1: "The spirit of the Lord is upon me, because the Lord hath anointed me, he hath sent me to preach to the meek, to heal the contrite of heart ..."; or Isaiah 9:68: "For a child is born to us, and a son is given to us, and the government is upon his shoulder: and his name shall be called, Wonderful, Counsellor, God the Mighty, the Father of the world to come, the Prince of Peace"? Or finally, there is the following emotion-laden passage, which all saw as prefiguring the life of Christ and its salvific purpose:

> Despised, and the most abject of men, a man of sorrows, and acquainted with infirmity: and his look was as it were hidden and despised, whereupon we esteemed him not. Surely he hath borne our infirmities and carried our sorrows: and we have thought him as it were a leper, and as one struck by God and afflicted. But he was wounded for our iniquities, he was bruised for our sins: the chastisement of our peace was upon him, and by his bruises we are healed. (Isaiah 53:3–5)

As noted, the Book of Isaiah is large and comprises different discrete parts, not all of which (historically speaking) were written at the same time. And it is true that the Book as such possesses some significant unities of themes, which "testify to methodical editorial activity," as one scholar has put it.[14] This is to say that at some point there were editors of the text who may have added elements here and there to bring some of those unities out across its three discrete parts. Still, most Christians later saw the text as prefiguring Jesus Christ's ascent and his soteriological function, that is, that despite his divine nature Jesus came to earth as an embodied human being to take on the weight of human sin and to save humanity (*soter*, in Greek, means "savior.") The Lord is said to "open the eyes of the blind, and bring forth the prisoner out of prison, and them that sit in darkness out of the prison house" (Isa 42:6–8). For later Christian scholars who wrestled to reconcile Judeo-Christian thinking with the pagan philosophical heritage, a passage like this, so reminiscent of Plato and his myth of the cave, could not but induce them to see essential unities in thinking and, to boot, to create "classics" of their own – as we shall see.

---

[14] See Uwe Becker, "The Book of Isaiah: Its Composition History," in Tiemeyer, *The Oxford Handbook of Isaiah*, 37–56, at 38.

There was one more major facet that Judaism contributed to the mental formation of western thinkers: a teleological sense of time. Put differently, God was acting through history and time. One of the most important ideas in this regard came from the Book of Jeremiah, when God foreshadows a new "covenant" with the Jewish people: "Behold the days shall come, saith the Lord, and I will make a new covenant with the house of Israel and with the house of Juda, not according to the covenant which I made with their fathers, in the day that I took them by the hand to bring them out of the land of Egypt: the covenant which they made void, and I had dominion over them..." (Jer 31:31–33). The word "covenant" (the Hebrew *b'rit*, translated into Greek as *diatheke*) came to mean "testament," and it was thus that Christians came eventually to call their scripture the New Testament. Jesus' arrival, his deeds, and what people eventually came to believe about him made many think that the Jesus movement represented this "new" covenant which God had signaled to his people. It happened in time, and history, and it denoted change. Time would go on, and there would be other ways that God would intervene in the world.

Take a passage like this one from Isaiah: "On that day the Lord will punish the host of heaven in heaven, and on earth the kings of the earth ... Then the moon will be abashed, and the sun ashamed; for the Lord of hosts will reign on Mount Zion and in Jerusalem, and before his elders he will manifest his glory" (Isa 24: 21, 23). The implication is that God is watching over things and will at some point in the future act decisively – in this case to punish the wicked and to make his presence felt. As we shall see, the Christian thinker Augustine contributed compellingly to the idea that history itself had a direction. But it was already there in Jewish thinking, in the ever more insistent hopes expressed in Isaiah and elsewhere, that someday a Messiah would come, that justice would reign, and that God would come close to human beings.[15] Judaism, then, gave to western thinkers a unitary conception of a creator God, who was just and all powerful, along with glimmerings of a God concerned with human salvation (*human* salvation, not just salvation for one specific group).

Still, it took another ancient element (along with the Hellenic and Jewish heritages) to set the stage. This was the legacy of Rome. For our purposes, four aspects need to be highlighted: the sense of power that Rome fostered, a capacious sensibility regarding philosophy, the Greek heritage as refracted

---

[15] See Annette Yoshiko Reed, "Messianism between Judaism and Christianity," in Michael L. Morgan and Steven Weitzman, eds., *Rethinking the Messianic Idea in Judaism* (Bloomington: Indiana University Press, 2014), 23–62.

through Rome, and the importance of the Latin language. And to do so, two other "monumental" authors need to be considered, however incompletely: Virgil and Cicero.

There can be no better place to begin a discussion of Rome than with a few lines written by the poet Virgil at what we now think of as the beginnings of the Roman Empire, in his magnificent work, *The Aeneid*. The *Aeneid* tells the story of the founding of Rome with a focus on the hero Aeneas. Aeneas, a Trojan, was a refugee from the Trojan War, an epic conflict between Greece and Troy, in which Greece had won. We'll get to the lines momentarily, but to set them in context, we need to think about the background of the *Aeneid*.

The ancient Greek poet Homer served as Virgil's predecessor and model for the *Aeneid*.[16] Homer recounted the story of the Trojan war in two Greek epics. The *Iliad* told of the war. Alongside action-filled battle scenes, there were countless examples of heroism and courage, numerous interventions of the gods into human affairs, and memorable literary devices that subsequently became part of the western literary imagination. Of the latter one such example is the "ekphrasis" of the Shield of Achilles.[17] "Ekphrasis" signifies the detailed verbal description of something visual, a painting, or a sculpture, for example – or in this case a shield, one that was fashioned by the god Hephaestus for the Greek hero Achilles. Homer's description of the relief work on the shield goes into detail – there are the constellations, images of cities fortunate and less so, and people doing various things, from fighting and dancing to running and celebrating. It is a beautiful episode, and one among many in which the poet Homer uses extensive visual description to convey deeper ideas. It is no surprise that Virgil, in his *Aeneid*, included a similar *ekphrasis*, this time of a shield that Vulcan made for the hero Aeneas, on which were depicted (in "detail unable to be told") Rome's future triumphs, ending with the ascendancy of Augustus himself.[18] Another such device was the *katabasis*, which represents a descent into the underworld,

---

[16] See Alessandro Barchiesi, *Homeric Effects in Vergil's Narrative*, tr. Ilaria Marchesi and Matt Fox (Princeton: Princeton University Press, 2015); Georg Nicolaus Knauer, *Die 'Aeneis' und Homer: Studien zur poetischen Technik Vergils mit Listen der Homerzitate in der 'Aeneis'* (Göttingen: Vandenhoek and Ruprecht, 1964).

[17] Homer, *Iliad*, 2 vols., ed. and tr. A. T. Murray and William F. Wyatt (Cambridge, MA: Harvard University Press, 1985) 18: 478–608 (vol. 2, pp. 322–333).

[18] Virgil, *Aeneid*, in Virgil, *Eclogues, Georgics, Aeneid*, 2 vols., ed. and tr. H. R. Fairclough and G. P. Goold (Cambridge, MA: Harvard University Press, 1999) 8: 625–731, at l. 625 (vol., 2, p.104): "et clipei non enarrabile textum."

such as Aeneas engages in the passage we shall examine and such as Homer had his hero Odysseus undertake in Book 11 of the *Odyssey*. Later, the "Harrowing of Hell" – the idea rooted (somewhat tenuously) in Scripture whereby Christ descends into the underworld to preach in a messianic fashion – also took part of this tradition.[19]

If the *Iliad* told of war, the *Odyssey* recounted the story of the return home to Greece of Odysseus, a "complicated man," as he is introduced at the poem's beginning.[20] Wily and clever, Odysseus and his colleagues go on a long journey to return home to Ithaca, the Greek city he was from, after the war. Along the way, he experiences remarkable adventures, encounters mythical creatures, and showcases his gift for trickery. The story of his defeat of the Cyclops, his lengthy affair with the magical woman Calypso, and other memorable incidents marked the *Odyssey* and remained part of the literature of the west.

Homer's epics were by Virgil's era acknowledged masterpieces, sources of history and myth, and "classics," if anything ever deserved that word. Vergil's *Aeneid* was like the two Homeric epics combined into one. The first half (Books 1–6) resembled the *Odyssey*, in that they told of Aeneas's wanderings after the Trojans were defeated. There, as Odysseus does in the *Odyssey*, so too does the hero Aeneas encounter adventures of all sorts in his wanderings. The *Aeneid*'s second half, Books 6–12, told of the battles Aeneas fought, a story that culminates with Aeneas violently killing a rival and setting the stage for the foundation of Rome. In this martial sense, this part of the *Aeneid* was like the *Iliad*. Full of literary devices, common myths, and lessons large and small, the *Iliad*, *Odyssey*, and *Aeneid* allowed Greeks and Romans to tell their own stories to themselves, to create narratives of great variety but unified literary power.

Here is the passage in question from the *Aeneid*, which occurs toward the end of book six, that is, toward the end of the epic's first half:

> Others will forge bronzes that breathe with greater gentility, (this indeed I believe); out of marble they will portray faces that seem alive, they will be better public speakers, with a pointer they will trace out the motions of the heavens and narrate how the stars rise. You, Roman, remember to rule

---

[19] See Matt 12:40, Acts 2:31, Eph 4:9, 1 Pet 4:6. Later Christian thinkers developed these New Testament hints into a fuller story; see Matthew R. Anderson, "The Curious Voyage of Christ: *Katábasis*, *Anábasis*, and the New Testament," *Les Études classiques* 83 (2015), 385–396, esp. 387–389.
[20] To use Emily Wilson's translation of the word *polytropos*, in Homer, *Odyssey*, tr. Emily Wilson (New York: Norton: 2018) 1: 1.

peoples with power (these will be your arts), to bestow morality upon peace, to spare the conquered, and to war down the proud.[21]

The immediate context is this: Aeneas has been permitted to enter the Underworld, a place where shades of the dead reside. He sees the brutal fates of those who were evil in life, hearing their groaning and seeing their punishments, and eventually he is allowed access to Elysium, a place of peace and beauty, where the blessed reside. There he meets his deceased father, Anchises, whose shade speaks and offers Aeneas a lengthy prognostication of Rome's fate. Though the city is yet to be founded, Anchises tells Aeneas the roles that its early heroes will play. They will emerge from Aeneas's eventual descendants, and they – and the Romans – will develop an ethos that guides their behavior. Idealized in the passage cited above, this ethos validated raw power, admitted of a capacious sense of philosophy, respected the achievements of Greek predecessors, and developed the Latin language into a peerless instrument of oratory and literature.

Take the quotation's final three lines:

tu regere imperio populos, Romane, memento
(hae tibi erunt artes), pacique imponere morem,
parcere subiectis et debellare superbos.

Translated as follows:

You, Roman, remember to rule peoples with power
(These will be your arts), to bestow morality upon peace,
To spare the conquered and to war down the proud.

Remember to rule over people with "power," the Latin word for which is *imperium*, a word often also translated as "empire." Romans, the character Anchises is telling his son, are made to rule. The ways of ruling will be their "arts" – *artes* in Latin, from the singular word *ars*, which has within it a sense of craftsmanship and skill. The assumption is that rule will be natural for Romans, and the prediction, here, in this moment of deep literary prehistory, is that Romans will develop those skills over time, year by year, decade by decade, century by century – and, of course, conquest by conquest.

Virgil was writing as Rome's first "emperor," the way we understand that term, was ruling. This was Caesar Augustus (63 BCE–14 CE, emperor from

---

[21] Virgil, *Aeneid*, 6: 847–853 (vol. 1, p. 592): "excudent alii spirantia mollius aera / (credo equidem), vivos ducent de marmore vultus, / orabunt causas melius, caelique meatus / describent radio et surgentia sidera dicent: / tu regere imperio populos, Romane, memento / (hae tibi erunt artes), pacique imponere morem, / parcere subiectis et debellare superbos."

27 BCE–14 CE). By that era, Rome's dominion had grown greatly, including lands from Spain to northern France, parts of North Africa to Greece and what is now Turkey, and more. Augustus augmented Rome's dominion, stretching it to Egypt, even as he increased Rome's territory northward and eastward. What began, historically, as the province of a small tribe on the banks of the Tiber River, had become a large and complicated empire. Idealized above in Virgil's language are the qualities that Romans – in the best versions of themselves – were thought to possess. Disciplined, they did not hesitate to use military force. Upon conquering vast territories, the hope was to include the conquered in the growing empire. The Romans would "spare" these conquered peoples but also "war them down" if they refused to go along with the new "morality" that Rome bestowed.

As an image of Rome and Roman conduct, this quotation captures not only Rome's idealized self-conception, but also how Rome was perceived by the countless many who learned Virgil's poetry by heart in the Middle Ages. And it was not just an image. Jesus was born into the Roman empire, as Luke's Gospel declares: "And it came to pass, that in those days there went out a decree from Caesar Augustus, that the whole world should be enrolled" (Luke 2:1). Joseph, Mary's husband, traveled with Mary out of Nazareth into the Roman province of Judea, to be registered. Luke claims, that is, that Augustus ordered a census (which he did, even if the dating and other aspects of Luke's account are problematic) and that it happened just as Jesus was born.[22] Immediately thereafter in Luke, one reads some of the New Testament's most memorable lines: shepherds who were standing watch had their night interrupted by an Angel, who said, "behold, I bring you tidings of great joy, that shall be to all the people; for this day, is born to you, a Saviour, who is Christ the Lord, in the City of David" (Luke 2:10–11). This linkage – between Rome's sweeping imperial power and the birth of a child later considered a savior to all mankind – remained potent throughout the Middle Ages.

Beyond what seems a coincidence of Jesus' birth happening in the reign of Augustus, there remains the fact of Roman power. In the centuries after

---

[22] Scholars have long noted problems in Luke's account. When Roman censuses were taken, it was incumbent on residents to return to their current (rather than ancestral) residence, so that Joseph's return to Judea would not have been necessitated by the census. And the account in Matthew (Matt 2:1–23) differs in important ways. The point here, of course, has to do with the cultural memory that Luke's account engendered. See Robert Cargill, *The Cities that Built the Bible* (New York: HarperOne, 2016); Sabine R. Huebner, *Papyri and the Social World of the New Testament* (Cambridge: Cambridge University Press, 2019), pp. 31–50.

Augustus, Rome expanded more, reaching northward into Britain. As it did, Romans often incorporated conquered enemies into the empire, offering various benefits in return for peaceful acquiescence. And in 212 CE, Emperor Caracalla offered citizenship to all freeborn citizens throughout the empire.[23] Some of this political largesse was gestural, and of course, more citizens meant more tax revenues. And it does not take more than common sense to remember that Roman ways did not match those of modern tastes. Many people were still not eligible for citizenship, and the Romans were inhumanly merciless when they deemed it necessary, using war and slaughter to achieve their aims. But the universalizing idea of Roman power – its origins, its growth, and its uses – remained in the minds of medieval Europeans.

Early in the *Aeneid*, Virgil brings the god Jupiter forward – the supreme god of the Romans and their equivalent to the Greek Zeus. Jupiter makes a series of predictions regarding the founding of Rome, with references to Romulus's role and to other parts of early Roman history. These and other aspects of Rome's mythical early history Virgil includes – here as later in the *Aeneid* – as a means of creating and solidifying cultural and historical memory for the Romans. All who read the *Aeneid* were exposed to this solidified cultural memory and all – whatever their individual perspectives – would have had the various myths, characters, and trajectories in their minds henceforth.

The trajectory that Jupiter predicts is meaningful. In Latin: *His ego nec metas rerum nec tempora pono; imperium sine fine dedi*; in English: "For these Romans I set no limits of space or time; I have given them empire without end."[24] The word translated here as "empire" is the Latin word we encountered above, *imperium*. It is a word that signified, in its most basic meaning, "power," as in the "power to command." Roman military figures were routinely given *imperium*, as they went out to far-flung provinces of the ever-expanding empire, there to defeat enemies and come back in triumph or die trying. An *imperator* was one who held this sort of power, a power understood as temporary in most cases. That is, one would possess it for a limited time and then give it up again when the need had passed. The idea was that Rome was a republic, a form of society where power was shared. But with

---

[23] See Arnaud Besson, *Constitutio antoniniana: L'universalisation de la citoyenneté romaine au 3e siècle* (Basel: Schwabe Verlag, 2020); Alex Imrie, *The Antonine Constitution: An Edict for the Caracallan Empire* (Leiden: Brill, 2018); Myles Lavan and Clifford Ando, eds., *Roman and Local Citizenship in the Long Second Century CE* (Oxford: Oxford University Press, 2021).

[24] Virgil, *Aeneid*, 1: 278–279 (vol. 1, p. 280), my tr.

Augustus, something changed. He kept imperial power, after triumphing over his various political rivals, and though he was careful about how he wielded his power, there was no doubt that he was firmly in charge.

As Jesus was born, in other words, a new model was emerging for Roman and state power: hierarchical, with a unitary figure at the top, and intended and understood to have few if any limits at all. For Christianity, two consequences emerged: First, the Church itself over time took on that hierarchical model, along with the expansionist propensities Rome had modeled. The expansive tendencies played themselves out in variegated ways throughout the empire, especially on the frontiers.[25] But that Roman model remained meaningful as the western church grew and centered itself in Rome. Second, the undeniable power of the Romans also fostered a sense that there were two worlds, one secular, which needed to be respected and understood as such, even as the other world was greater and more important. Christ says in the gospel of Matthew (22:21) that one should "render therefore unto Caesar the things that are Caesar's and to God the things that are God's." This notion of a separation between the world we live in now, with its own political and financial conditions, and another one, different in fundamental quality and tenor, endured. Later, in the thought of Augustine, it became fundamental, as we shall see.

If Virgil's quotation above provides insight into Roman power and its reputation, it also helps us understand another fundamental aspect of the Romans: their respect for Greek culture. Recall the words with which the quotation began:

> Others will forge bronzes that breathe with greater gentility, (This indeed I believe); out of marble they will portray faces that seem alive, They will be better public speakers, With a pointer, they will trace out the motions of the heavens and narrate how the stars rise.

"Others," "They" – the unnamed referents here are the Greeks. By Virgil's era they were understood as having done foundational work in culture of all sorts: figurative art, literature in all its manifestations from epic (Homer) to theater (Aeschylus, Sophocles, Euripides), and all forms of philosophy, which included what we now consider the study of the natural sciences, alongside logic, ethics, politics, and metaphysics. The names of Plato and Aristotle were revered. Their philosophical outlooks, along with those of the Hellenistic schools of philosophy – Skeptics, Stoics, and Epicureans – were

---

[25] See Peter Brown, *The Rise of Western Christendom: Triumph and Diversity, A.D. 200–1000*, 10th anniversary rev. ed. (London: Wiley-Blackwell, 2013), pp. 145–188.

known to Roman elites, as we shall see. The Roman poet Horace said that anyone desiring to excel should "turn the pages of Greek books night and day," meaning that any well-educated Roman should know the Greek heritage.[26]

But as the quotation from the *Aeneid* above hints, and as the work of Roman thinker Cicero makes clear, the Romans by and large believed there were limits to the place of philosophy, even as they cultivated a broad understanding of what philosophy was and could be. Again, we can recur to a few carefully chosen passages, here from Cicero, that can serve as a springboard for understanding Roman attitudes toward philosophy that eventually permeated medieval western European Christian thinking.

Who was Cicero?[27] First, he was an orator. This is to say that he had been schooled in rhetoric and philosophy and that his skills as a speaker and orator became the foundation of his career. He served as an advocate – a lawyer, basically – for many people, and he also held numerous public offices in the Roman republic. In his work we sense the waning of the republic, with its strong, elective legislative institutions (the senate especially) and the waxing of strongmen such as Julius Caesar and eventually Octavian – who would become Caesar Augustus. Through all the travails of Cicero's active, political life, he adhered to the study of philosophy as a kind of refuge, writing extensively on politics, on theories of knowledge, and most especially on ethics. Cicero was one of those highly educated Romans who was bilingual in his native tongue, Latin, as well as Greek (he spent significant time in Greece, studying philosophy in its universally agreed-upon home).[28]

---

[26] Horace, *Ars poetica* ll. 268–269 in Horace, *Satires, Epistles and Ars Poetica*, ed. and tr. H. Rushton Fairclough (Cambridge, MA: Harvard University Press, 1991), p. 472, my tr.: "Vos exemplaria Graeca / nocturna uersate manu, uersate diurna." See also Caroline Bishop, *Cicero, Greek Learning, and the Making of a Roman Classic* (Oxford: Oxford University Press, 2018).

[27] For literature, see Jed W. Atkins and Thomas Bénatouïl, eds., *The Cambridge Companion to Cicero's Philosophy* (Cambridge: Cambridge University Press, 2022); Gian Biagio Conte, *Latin Literature: A History*, tr. Joseph B. Solodow, rev. by Don Fowler and Glenn W. Most (Baltimore: Johns Hopkins University Press, 1994), pp. 175–208; Catherine Steel, ed., *The Cambridge Companion to Cicero* (Cambridge: Cambridge University Press, 2013); Laurel Fulkerson and Jeffrey Tatum, *A History of Latin Literature: From Its Beginnings to the Age of Augustus* (Cambridge: Cambridge University Press, 2024), pp. 94–104, 141–144; Claudia Moatti, *The Birth of Critical Thinking in Republican Rome*, tr. Janet Lloyd (Cambridge: Cambridge University Press, 2015); Claudia Moatti, "Cicero's Philosophical Writing in Its Intellectual Context," in *The Cambridge Companion to Cicero's Philosophy*, 7–24; J. G. F. Powell, ed., *Cicero the Philosopher: Twelve Papers* (Oxford: Oxford University Press, 1995).

[28] See Michel Dubuisson, "Le grec à Rome à l'époque de Cicéron: Extension et qualité du bilinguisme," *Annales: Histoire, Sciences Sociales* 47 (1992), 187–206.

Cicero's philosophical works, written late in life, run the gamut of subject matters. Still ethics was most prominent.[29] And they all share another quality: deep respect for the Greek heritage.

Cicero's signal achievement was to translate, culturally, Greek philosophical ideas to his Roman compatriots.[30] Through him, Romans (and his later, western readers) learned about Plato and Aristotle, of course, and the various ideas and theories they propounded. Cicero also engaged seriously with the Hellenistic schools of philosophy. These are important enough that it is worth opening a parenthesis to discuss them.[31]

After the death of Alexander the Great in 323 BCE, Greek culture spread in many areas formerly dominated by the Persian Empire, during what historians have traditionally called the "Hellenistic" period. This epoch ended in 31 BCE, when Octavian (later to become Emperor Augustus) defeated Mark Antony and Cleopatra at the Battle of Actium. Egypt fell, the last of the "Hellenistic" kingdoms – those reigns established by Alexander's successors. With the long benefit of hindsight, we can see Octavian's triumph as the beginning of the Roman Empire. During the Hellenistic period, from the Balkans to Turkey, from Egypt to Italy, Greek philosophy spread, with three "schools" rising as especially meaningful: Skepticism, Stoicism, and Epicureanism. Cicero appreciated the importance of the Hellenistic schools, attracted by their general focus on ethics and the care of the individual soul, along with the relative cosmopolitanism they adopted, recognizing that their growing, changing world included what we would today call different cultures.

Philosophical skepticism was one of these schools.[32] Skeptical thinkers faced the question of how to find criteria of truth and certain knowledge when there is so much uncertainty in the world – from our unreliable

---

[29] See Malcolm Schofield, "Writing Philosophy," in *The Cambridge Companion to Cicero*, 73–87.
[30] See Carlos Lévy, "Cicero and the Creation of a Latin Philosophical Vocabulary," in *The Cambridge Companion to Cicero's Philosophy*, 71–87.
[31] See Kelly Arenson, *The Routledge Handbook of Hellenistic Philosophy* (New York: 2020); Paul Oskar Kristeller, *Greek Philosophers of the Hellenistic Age*, tr. Gregory Woods (New York: Columbia University Press, 1993); A. A. Long and David Sedley, eds., *The Hellenistic Philosophers*, 2 vols. (Cambridge: Cambridge University Press, 1987); John Sellars, *Hellenistic Philosophy* (Oxford: Oxford University Press, 2018); R. W. Sharples, *Stoics, Epicureans and Sceptics: An Introduction to Hellenistic Philosophy* (London: Routledge, 1996).
[32] See Richard Bett, ed., *The Cambridge Companion to Scepticism* (Cambridge: Cambridge University Press, 2010); Tobias Reinhardt, "Cicero's Academic Skepticism," in *The Cambridge Companion to Cicero's Philosophy*, 103–119; Brad Inwood and Jaap Mansfeld, eds., *Assent and Argument: Studies in Cicero's Academic Books* (Leiden: Brill, 1997).

senses, which often fail us, to the general complexity by which we are surrounded. For any "dogmatic" claim – by which they meant a strong opinion, held to be outside the realm of argument – one could usually find an opposing claim that was equivalent in its effect. Faced with that complexity, "Pyrrhonian" skeptics advocated for a style of life that included a "suspension of judgment" (called *epochê* in Greek), which would if practiced correctly lead to what they called *ataraxia*, or "tranquility of mind."[33] "Academic" skeptics (so named because skeptical thinkers for a time led Plato's Academy) went so far as to reject the notion that one could agree even on a criterion of truth – that is, that thing by which one can tell if something is true or false. In his *Academica*, Cicero profiled these and other skeptical concerns.[34]

Cicero deeply respected another Hellenistic school of philosophy, Stoicism.[35] Spanning the fourth to the first centuries BCE, Stoic thinkers such as Zeno of Citium, Chrysippus of Soli, Panaetius of Rhodes, and Posidonius of Apamea cultivated a coherent philosophical outlook that Cicero appreciated. They believed that the world was divinely ordered by reason, and that one could discover certain truths using reason. The concept of *logos* as a rational principle governing the cosmos found resonance in early Christian thought, most notably in the Gospel of John, where Christ is identified with the *logos*: "In the beginning was the Word [*logos*], and the Word was with God, and the Word was God" (John 1:1). Employing the term *logos*, the author of the Gospel of John appropriated a Stoic philosophical concept to articulate a Christian theological truth, emphasizing both the rationality and divinity of Christ. Scholars have noted that this deliberate usage reflects the broader Hellenistic intellectual milieu in which early Christian thought developed.[36]

---

[33] See Sextus Empiricus, *Outlines of Pyrrhonism*, tr. R. G. Bury (Cambridge, MA: Harvard University Press, 1933), 1.4.8, pp. 6–7 and in general, bk. 1, pp. 2–149; "Pyrrhonian" derives from an early skeptical thinker, Pyrrho of Elis, on whom see Richard Bett, *Pyrrho, His Antecedents, and His Legacy* (Oxford: Oxford University Press, 2003).

[34] See Cicero, *Academica* in Cicero, *On the Nature of the Gods. Academica*, ed. and tr. Horace Rackham (Cambridge, MA: Harvard University Press, 1933).

[35] See John Sellars, *Lessons in Stoicism: What Ancient Philosophers Teach Us About How to Live* (London: Penguin, 2019); John Sellars, *The Art of Living: The Stoics on the Nature and Function of Philosophy*, 2nd ed. (London: Duckworth, 2009); John Sellars, ed., *The Routledge Handbook of the Stoic Tradition* (London: Routledge, 2016).

[36] See John Dillon, "Logos and Trinity: Pattern of Platonist Influence on Early Christianity," in Godfrey Vesey, ed., *The Philosophy in Christianity* (Cambridge: Cambridge University Press, 1989), 1–13; Marian Hillar, *From Logos to Trinity: The Evolution of Religious Beliefs from Pythagoras to Tertullian* (Cambridge: Cambridge University Press, 2012).

Stoics also emphasized duty and action in the world, and for Cicero their cultivation of traditional virtues was something that formed the bedrock of his outlook. Later thinkers took similar inspiration reading Cicero's work. Here too, Cicero saw the deeper messages behind the Stoics' seemingly severe, "virtue is its own reward" ethos: Stoicism (like the thinking behind the other Hellenistic schools) was intended to rid the person's soul of disturbance, as if it were an illness. As he wrote: "Understand this clearly: there will be no end to wretchedness if the soul is not cured, and this is something that cannot happen without philosophy."[37] After Cicero, as we shall see in a later chapter, Stoic thinking possessed parallels to Christianity.

Finally, Cicero also transmitted to his Roman contemporaries the teachings of the philosophical school known as Epicureanism.[38] Adherents of this school of philosophy often emphasized the pleasure principle, by which they meant that pleasure served as a motivating factor in most if not all of what people did. More profoundly, they stressed that pleasure meant having your desires satisfied. Accordingly, the fewer desires you had, the more easily you could have pleasure. In one respect, all three Hellenistic schools of philosophy underscored something like that idea. There was a great emphasis placed on self-control: the idea that we should train ourselves in such a way as to control our impulses, desires, and other seemingly irrational aspects of how we behave.[39] It was only in that fashion that we could live a "happy" life, that is, a life of *eudaimonia*, as Aristotle had put it, a word that really means "flourishing." How could we flourish in the world as it is? The Hellenistic thinkers dear to Cicero all considered this question in one way or another, even as they advocated for different styles of life.

It is worth commenting on the Ciceronian work from which we drew the quotation above ("there will be no end to wretchedness if the soul is not cured"). Titled the *Tusculan Disputations*, it is a dialogue. In it, Cicero avails himself of the verbal arguments of different philosophical schools, to discuss certain questions: How might one overcome a fear of death and how might

---

[37] Cicero, *Tusculan Disputations*, ed. and tr. J. E. King (Cambridge, MA: Harvard University Press, 1945), 3.6.13, pp. 240–241, my tr.: "Illud quidem sic habeto, nisi sanatus animus sit, quod sine philosophia fieri non potest, finem miseriarum nullum fore."

[38] See John Sellars, *The Fourfold Remedy: Epicurus and the Art of Happiness* (London: Penguin, 2021).

[39] See Long and Sedley, *The Hellenistic Philosophers*; Martha Nussbaum, *The Therapy of Desire: Theory and Practice in Hellenistic Ethics*, 2nd ed. (Princeton: Princeton University Press, 2013); Sharples, *Stoics, Epicureans and Sceptics*; Sellars, *Hellenistic Philosophy*.

one bear pain? How could one come to understand that grief is an emotion that can be moderated and that other sometimes-damaging emotions can be controlled? And then there is virtue, which if practiced correctly (as Cicero argues in the final book of the *Tusculan Disputations*), is something self-sufficient that can help the virtuous person be happy despite life's travails. Both the genre and the book's contemporaneity are meaningful. As to the genre, the *Tusculan Disputations*, like other Ciceronian dialogues, manifests a certain mood: slow and deliberative, allowing extended conversation to take place among friends (even when they disagree), and self-conscious of the need for an appealing style. Cicero went so far as to tell his dedicatee that he always believed philosophy in its most complete form treated important problems with "fullness and beauty."[40] Speaking of the dedicatee (in this case Cicero's friend, the senator Marcus Junius Brutus), the very fact that there was a dedicatee reminds us that this work was part of a real conversation between two people, wherein Cicero, knowing he had a willing partner in his friend Brutus, would have expected a response, further discussion, and so on.

Cicero had clear aims for the *Tusculan Disputations* as a written work. He tells us so at the outset, stressing that he wished to make philosophy available in Latin (rather than Greek) to his Latin-reading contemporaries, who – he says – have "shown more wisdom than the Greeks" in the areas that matter most: morals, the household economy, and war. And here he means the Greeks of his own time and recent centuries, rather than the classical Greeks, whom he holds in much higher regard. Indeed, when it comes to the kinds of virtues that make the Romans who they are: "Where has such seriousness, such firmness, such steadiness, greatness of soul, honesty, loyalty, where has such outstanding strength in every field been found in any of mankind to justify comparison with our ancestors?"[41] Cicero signals these qualities as most important, and he does so in conversation with a friend. In the text, there will be detailed arguments to come, of course, but Cicero's framing stands out.

Meaningful as well is Cicero's *De officiis*, or *On Duties*. It is not that Cicero doesn't cover more technically sophisticated forms of Greek philosophy in his other works, for he does do that. And, read against the

---

[40] Cicero, *Tusculan Disputations*, 1.7, pp. 10–11, my tr.: "Hanc enim perfectam philosophiam semper iudicavi, quae de maximis quaestionibus copiose posset ornateque dicere..."

[41] Cicero, *Tusculan Disputations*, 1.1.2, pp. 4–5, tr. modified: "Quae enim tanta gravitas, quae tanta constantia, magnitudo animi, probitas, fides, quae tam excellens in omni genere virtus in ullis fuit, ut sit cum maioribus nostris comparanda?"

circumstances under which Cicero wrote it – a republic collapsing under civil war – it is a work that reveals much about Cicero's attitudes toward the politics of his day.[42] But the *De officiis* is one of those monumental works that far outlived its author. It sums up the worldview that Cicero embodied and that – for many after him in the medieval west – came to stand for "the Romans," as I have been using that term here.[43] It is a locution that obviously cannot cover the actual, historical Romans in all their cultural multiplicity. Rather, it denotes what they came to stand for in cultural memory. Through it we can see a respect for philosophy at large alongside a sense that lived ethics was, quite simply, more important than other branches of philosophy.

Cicero addresses the work to his son, also named Cicero, who had himself been studying philosophy. Cicero asks: "Who would dare be called a philosopher without handing down lessons regarding duty?"[44] Philosophers don't just think and write, they teach; and the most important thing they teach is ethics. Later, he adds, "while the whole field of philosophy is fruitful and productive and no part of it is barren and waste, still no part is richer or more fruitful than that which deals with moral duties; for from these are derived the rules for leading a consistent and moral life."[45]

The message is this: Nothing is more important or meaningful than ethics as manifested in the world of everyday choices. Moreover, in *De officiis*, Cicero presents us with one attestation (among many ancient ones) that philosophy could and should be conceived broadly. Take what he writes to his son in the preface to book two: "Although my books have aroused in not a few men the desire not only to read but to write, yet I sometimes fear that what we term philosophy is distasteful to certain wealthy gentlemen, and

---

[42] See A. A. Long, "Cicero's Politics in his *De officiis*," in Long's *From Epicurus to Epictetus: Studies in Hellenistic and Roman Philosophy* (Oxford: Oxford University Press, 2006), 307–334.

[43] Long, "Cicero's Politics," at 309, usefully describes "Roman ideology" with the words "*virtus* [virtue or excellence], *dignitas* [worthiness or merit], *honestas* [honor or reputation], *splendor* [honor, especially as publicly displayed], *decus* [moral dignity], [and] *laus* [renown or esteem] and *gloria* [justified fame]." Together these represented a kind of code for Romans, one nowhere more fully displayed than in *De officiis*.

[44] Cicero, *De off.*, 1.5: "Atque haec quidem quaestio communis est omnium philosophorum; quis est enim, qui nullis officii praeceptis tradendis philosophum se audeat dicere?" Tr. altered.

[45] Ibid., 3.5: "Sed cum tota philosophia, mi Cicero, frugifera et fructuosa nec ulla pars eius inculta et deserta sit, tum nullus feracior in ea locus est nec uberiorquam de officiis, a quibus constanter honesteque vivendi praecepta ducuntur."

they wonder why I devote so much time and attention to it."[46] Admittedly, Cicero goes on, he has faced difficult political woes of late. And yet, all things considered, he cannot help but think that it is wisdom that is most important:

> What is better for a human being, what more worthy of human nature? Those who seek after it are called philosophers; and philosophy is nothing else, translating into our idiom, than the 'love of wisdom'. Wisdom, moreover, as the word has been defined by the philosophers of old, is 'the knowledge of things human and divine and of the causes by which those things are controlled'.[47]

Yet again, we come face to face with a fact: Cicero, like many other ancients, would have understood that philosophy as a scholarly discipline possessed many branches, often specialized – and necessarily so. But when push came to shove, the basic definition of philosophy as "the love of wisdom" came up, over and over, not as a trite locution or merely lexical indication, but rather as a clarion call for their contemporaries and hoped-for successors, urging posterity never to forget both the breadth that the search for human wisdom entailed, and the need to relate the precepts one studied and elaborated to everyday human life. It is precisely this for which Cicero (in another work) singles Socrates out, writing that while early philosophers busied themselves with astronomy, "Socrates on the other hand was the first to call philosophy down from the heavens and set it in the world of cities and homes, compelling it to ask questions about life, morals, and things that have to do with good and evil..."[48] No one would suggest that philosophy should not concern itself with technical matters or important, if recondite, issues related to the natural world. But the idea that philosophy – and philosophers – should always remember to ask questions that relate to everyday human life: This was paramount to Cicero.

---

[46] Ibid., 2.2: "Quamquam enim libri nostri complures non modo ad legendi, sed etiam ad scribendi studium excitaverunt, tamen interdum vereor, ne quibusdam bonis viris philosophiae nomen sit invisum mirenturque in ea tantum me operae et temporis ponere."

[47] Ibid., 2.5: "Quid enim est, per deos, optabilius sapientia, quid praestantius, quid homini melius, quid homine dignius? Hanc igitur qui expetunt, philosophi nominantur, nec quicquam aliud est philosophia, si interpretari velis, praeter studium sapientiae. Sapientia autem est, ut a veteribus philosophis definitum est, rerum divinarum et humanarum causarumque, quibus eae res continentur, scientia; cuius studium qui vituperat, haud sane intellego, quidnam sit, quod laudandum putet." Tr. modified.

[48] Cicero, *Tusculan Disputations*, ed. and tr. J. E. King (Cambridge, MA: Harvard University Press, 1945), 5: 10–11, pp. 434–435: "Socrates autem primus philosophiam devocavit e caelo et in urbibus collocavit et in domus etiam introduxit et coëgit de vita et moribus rebusque bonis et malis quaerere..." Tr. modified.

There are many implications to this idea, none more important than the need for breadth and custodianship. Who "owns" philosophy in this broad sense? Is it for everyone? Is it only for those who read and write? Only for socioeconomic elites? Even in Cicero's day, when it came to philosophy as lived, there were custodians and there was an audience. Just what the size of that audience was or could be, remained an open question, one the Jesus movement answered in certain decisive ways — a process about which we will have more to say in the following chapters.

There is one more reason Cicero and Rome deserve our attention, a reason related to custodianship, to be sure, but broader and deeper, when it comes to western European intellectual life. This is the importance of the Latin language. By the fifth century CE, Latin became the language of western intellectual life, used for scripture, liturgy, and other matters pertinent to the Church, and for education. Even in its native varieties, Latin was diverse over the geographies in which it was spoken, and elsewhere it always intermingled with local vernaculars.[49] One seventh-century grammarian, Virgil of Toulouse, characterized Latin as "vast" and "abundant" and "like an immeasurable ocean," and he was not wrong.[50] But there was a time when it was no longer spoken in the home, by parents to children, in something like its normal written form. Even as Latin ceased to exist as a native language, a process that occurred gradually (and in a geographically differentiated fashion) but was complete by the end of the Early Middle Ages, Latin remained the language of scholarship and intellectual activity. From schools run by clerics in the Early Middle Ages to universities (the dominant educational institutions of the High Middle Ages and beyond), Latin was the language used for education.[51] In the Italian Renaissance — or "rebirth," in the term's most literal signification — one of the most important things that Italian Renaissance thinkers wanted

---

[49] See J. N. Adams, *The Regional Diversification of Latin, 200 BC–AD 600* (Cambridge: Cambridge University Press, 2007); and Alex Mullen and George Woudhuysen, eds., *Languages and Communities in the Late-Roman and Post-Imperial Western Provinces* (Oxford: Oxford University Press, 2023).

[50] Virgilius Maro Grammaticus, *Epitomi ed epistole*, ed. Giovanni Polara (Naples: Liguori, 1979), *Epistulae* 2.119–122: "tam multa sit et copiosa latinitatis totius regio et ut ita dicam pelagus inmensum..." cit. in Carin Ruff, "Latin as an Acquired Language," in Ralph Hexter and David Townsend, eds., *The Oxford Handbook of Medieval Latin Literature* (Oxford: Oxford University Press, 2012), 46–62, at 57.

[51] See Einar Löfstedt, *Late Latin* (Oslo: Aschehoug and Co., 1959), esp. 1–10; Helmut Lüdtke, *Der Ursprung der romanischen Sprachen: Eine Geschichte der sprachlichen Kommunikation* (Kiel: Westensee-Verlag, 2009); Roger Wright, *Late Latin and Early Romance in Spain and Carolingian France* (Liverpool: Francis Cairns, 1982).

to see "reborn" was the Latin language of Roman antiquity, and more precisely that of Cicero.[52]

Cicero's mastery of the language was acknowledged early on by writers who themselves became "classics." The great encyclopedist and statesman, Pliny the Elder (23–79 CE), celebrated Cicero for being the first to win a laurel wreath for his prowess in oratory (as opposed to poetry, the normal route to laureation) and said of Cicero that he was the "parent of eloquence and of the literature of Latium."[53]

Another first-century CE luminary, Quintilian (35–100 CE), spoke of Cicero with reverence, arguing that "Cicero" should stand not only for the man himself but also for eloquence writ large, and that he should be considered the exemplar for all who strove for the best: "Let us fix our eyes on him, let him be the model we set before ourselves."[54] What Quintilian has to say is meaningful enough that we should pause with him for a moment. Born in a region of what is now northeastern Spain, Quintilian was one of many young men drawn to Rome. He studied there and became proficient in Latin, so much so that he eventually opened his own school of rhetoric, counting among his students none other than Pliny the Elder's nephew, Pliny the Younger. Quintilian authored the most famous educational treatise of Roman antiquity, called *Institutio oratoria*, or *The Education of an Orator*, in which he set forth the basic ideas, theories, techniques, and facts needed for the first-rate oratorical education of a young man, from boyhood to adulthood.

---

[52] See Christopher S. Celenza, *The Lost Italian Renaissance: Humanists, Historians, and Latin's Legacy* (Baltimore: Johns Hopkins University Press, 2004); Tore Janson, *A Natural History of Latin* (Oxford: Oxford University Press, 2004), 145–148; Jürgen Leonhardt, *Latin: Story of a World Language*, tr. Kenneth Kronenberg (Cambridge, MA: Harvard University Press, 2013); Françoise Waquet, *Latin, or The Empire of a Sign*, tr. John Howe (London: Verso, 2001); Keith Sidwell, "Classical Latin, Medieval Latin, Neo-Latin," in Sarah Knight and Stefan Tilg, eds., *The Oxford Handbook of Neo-Latin* (Oxford: Oxford University Press, 2015), 13–26; Ronald G. Witt, *"In the Footsteps of the Ancients": The Origins of Humanism from Lovato to Bruni* (Leiden: Brill, 2000).

[53] Pliny the Elder, *Natural History*, 37 books in 10 vols., ed. and tr. Horace Rackham (Cambridge, MA: Harvard University Press 1942), 7: 117 (vol., 2, pp. 582–583): "primus in toga triumphum linguaeque lauream merite, et facundiae Latiarumque litterarum parens." Tr. modified.

[54] See Quintilian, *The Orator's Education*, 5 vols., ed. and tr. Donald A. Russell (Cambridge, MA: Harvard University Press, 2002), 10.1.109–113 (vol. 4, pp. 310–313), at sec. 112: "Quare non inmerito ab hominibus aetatis suae regnare in iudiciis dictus est, apud posteros vero id consecutus ut Cicero iam non hominis nomen sed eloquentiae habeatur. Hunc igitur spectemus, hoc propositum nobis sit exemplum, ille se profecisse sciat cui Cicero valde placebit."

"Oratorical" and "young man" are terms that draw attention. First, as to "oratorical": much of ancient higher education was rhetorical education, or rather, excellence in rhetoric was the pinnacle, the goal for which primary and secondary education prepared the student.[55] In a society where success often depended on being able to persuade one's peers, talent in public speaking was paramount. But for Quintilian, and for the best thinkers in rhetoric, this pursuit was not to be an empty one, designed only to persuade. It was a moral enterprise, wedding together the practicality that public actors needed to possess, with the ethical foundation required of a person of good character. Indeed, in his *Institutio*, Quintilian describes the person he would hope to mold through this project of education as a *vir bonus dicendi peritus*, or a "good man well-skilled in the art of speaking."[56] "Well-skilled," or *peritus*, means that the student will have been instructed in different branches of learning as well as in the technical aspects of rhetoric: how to structure a speech, how to gauge the mood and expectations of an audience, how to adorn one's speaking with artful yet persuasive references, and so on. Cicero himself wrote technical work in this regard, and Quintilian was adding to it.[57] "Good" means something like what Cicero outlines in his moral philosophical works, the *De officiis* included: a person who takes his duties and obligations seriously, who treats others with respect, who values justice and generosity, and who is generally moderate in outlook and modest in comportment. This is what Quintilian pointed to, when he said that Cicero should be considered to stand for eloquence itself. By "eloquence" Quintilian meant not only smoothness of speech and discourse, but also proficiency in human activity informed by wisdom – in short, philosophy in its more ample meaning.[58]

To return to the "young man" locution, there is inevitably a gender-related phenomenon, when it comes to Quintilian, to "the Romans" in general, and to the Latinate culture they represented and fostered. As the Latin language developed in its classic phase – when we can take Cicero in

---

[55] See W. Martin Bloomer, ed., *A Companion to Ancient Education* (Oxford: Wiley Blackwell, 2015); Stanley F. Bonner, *Education in Ancient Rome: From the Elder Cato to the Younger Pliny* (Berkeley: University of California Press, 1977); Anthony Corbeill, "Rhetorical Education in Cicero's Youth," in James M. May, ed., *Brill's Companion to Cicero: Oratory and Rhetoric* (Leiden: Brill, 2002), 23–48; Fulkerson and Tatum, *A History of Latin Literature*, 75–109; Henri Irenée Marrou, *A History of Education in Antiquity*, tr. George Lamb (Madison: University of Wisconsin Press, 1956), pp. 194–205, 284–291.
[56] Quintilian, *The Orator's Education*, 12.1.1 (vol. 5, pp. 196–197), echoing Cato the Elder.
[57] See John Dugan, "Cicero's Rhetorical Theory," in Steel, ed., *The Cambridge Companion to Cicero*, 25–40.
[58] Cf. Gary Remer, "Philosophy, Rhetoric, and Politics," in *The Cambridge Companion to Cicero's Philosophy*, 200–214.

prose and Virgil in poetry as the key exemplars – it carried with it a deeply interwoven strand of idealized masculinity. The language reflects martial and Stoic virtues, even as it employs feminine and feminizing words derogatively. A prominent scholar of the ancient Latin language, Joseph Farrell, has commented: "In Latin culture women play the role of the linguistic Other."[59] The associations that the Latin language fostered can be seen, for one example, in a very common verb, *effeminare*, which at its roots means "to make womanly" but has the extended meaning of "dishonoring" or "disgracing" or "enervating" someone or something by improper – read, unmanly – conduct. Moreover, the oratorical function of the language was precisely that, oratorical, so that it was used in fundamentally public situations from which women were customarily excluded. And as Farrell has remarked, there was no Roman Sappho, that is, no female poet among ancient Latin writers who occupied in antiquity the same canonical space as Sappho had for the Greeks.[60]

Two phenomena are worth observing. First, as to the ancient Romans themselves, their own societal norms surely contributed to this exclusion of women, even as scholarship in the last forty years has corrected the record when possible, not only by finding hitherto unnoticed instances of women's agency and women's writing in the ancient past, but also by reconsidering how to talk about certain disciplines in a more unrestricted fashion than customary, philosophy included. As a result, the contributions of women become visible and where possible accessible.[61] Second, social and cultural memories, even – perhaps especially – those that rest on difficult-to-discern foundations, retain an awful lot of power. And the acculturated sense that Latin represented the Romans and that Roman virtues were "masculine" virtues, remained, buttressed by the Latin language and its later uses in the Middle Ages and Renaissance.

Finally, Latin was and remained an instrument, a linguistic tool that every major western medieval thinker we shall meet employed. It was a language so

---

[59] Joseph Farrell, *Latin Language and Latin Culture: From Ancient to Modern Times* (Cambridge: Cambridge University Press, 2001), p. 83.
[60] Ibid., 52–58.
[61] See, for example, Raffaella Cribiore, *Gymnastics of the Mind: Greek Education in Hellenistic and Roman Egypt* (Princeton: Princeton University Press, 2001), pp. 74–101; Bartolo A. Natoli, Angela Pitts, and Judith P. Hallett, *Ancient Women Writers of Greece and Rome* (New York: Routledge, 2022); Katharine R. O'Reilly and Caterina Pellò, eds., *Ancient Women Philosophers: Recovered Ideas and New Perspectives* (Cambridge: Cambridge University Press, 2023); Jan R. Stenger, *Education in Late Antiquity: Challenges, Dynamism, and Reinterpretation, 300–550 CE* (Oxford: Oxford University Press, 2022), pp. 99–140.

deeply embedded in medieval education that it would have scarcely been possible to think certain concepts in a language other than Latin. And in Christian late antiquity, as we shall see, thinkers like Augustine developed the Latin language, made it their own, and created classics that became part of the fabric of medieval life. By then, however, that is, by Augustine's era in the late fourth and early fifth centuries of the common era, much Latin writing was bound up with Christianity, to whose beginnings we now turn.

7

CHRISTIANITY

Jesus' life and what was said about him after his death shaped subsequent centuries in ways too numerous to count. A Jew from Galilee, in what is today northern Israel, he was born into humble circumstances, grew up, and attracted followers drawn to his teaching, preaching, and the style of life he advocated. In addition to his early followers, Jesus garnered attention from two groups. First, there were traditional community leaders, some of whom resented his newfound popularity and disagreed with his preaching. Second, there were the Roman authorities, who saw his preaching and the loyalty he inspired as potentially revolutionary and subversive. After his crucifixion by Pontius Pilate in approximately 30 CE, elements of his message, stories about his life, and evolving interpretations about what he said and did all became part of the fabric of western thought.

For our purposes, what matters most is how he was seen by later premodern thinkers, who had recourse to the New Testament but who obviously did not have access to modern philological scholarship.[1] Accordingly, it is close reading of New Testament accounts that will help us paint the portrait of Jesus as exemplar. By the same token, reading these accounts as later premodern readers might have done will help flesh out how "Jesus as exemplar" fits the model of a philosopher in the traditional sense – someone who sought a wise way of life, who had followers, and whose doctrines lived on after him.

---

[1] Valuable perspectives in Bart D. Ehrman, *How Jesus Became God: The Exaltation of a Jewish Preacher from Galilee* (San Francisco: Harper One, 2014); Robyn Faith Walsh, *The Origins of Early Christian Literature: Contextualizing the New Testament within Greco-Roman Literary Culture* (Cambridge: Cambridge University Press, 2021); Paula Fredriksen, *From Jesus to Christ: The Origins of the New Testament Images of Jesus*, 2nd ed. (New Haven: Yale University Press, 2000); and the indispensable Diarmad MacCulloch, *Christianity: The First Three Thousand Years* (New York, Penguin, 2011).

As to Jesus' message, one of the most salient and seemingly paradoxical elements has to do with how, though preaching humility, he gained authority. To understand this aspect of the story, a turn to the Bible is needed. Of the four Gospels – Matthew, Mark, Luke, and John – the first three are known as the "synoptic" gospels: They include many of the same narratives about Christ's life, sometimes in the same wording.[2] It is likely that all of the Gospel writers were educated and familiar with Greco-Roman literary conventions of various sorts, so that the narratives at times seem stylized, sharing family resemblances to other contemporary forms of exemplary life-writing.[3]

Scholars consider Mark to be the earliest, dating from around 70 CE.[4] Matthew and Luke draw on both Mark and on another source that preserved many of Jesus's sayings (this source has been known as "Q," short for the German word "Quelle," or "source").[5] So, we can turn to Mark first, remaining aware that for late ancient and medieval readers the distinctions that scholars draw today (regarding authorship, relative importance of each Gospel, etc.) were not self-evident.[6] The Gospel of Mark skips Jesus' childhood and begins with him mature, attracting apostles, and teaching. We learn that Jesus, after drawing to himself a few apostles, went to Caparnaum (a small village on the Sea of Galilee), "and straightway on the Sabbath day he entered into the synagogue and taught" (Mark 1:21). The reaction to his preaching was noteworthy: "they were astonished at his teaching, for he taught them as one that had authority, and not as the scribes" (Mark 1:22). There are three key words in that last passage: "teaching," "authority," and "scribes." To understand them we need to think about both the language and the genre in which the Gospel of Mark was recorded.

---

[2] See David Laird Dungan, *A History of the Synoptic Problem: The Canon, the Text, the Composition, and the Interpretation of the Gospels* (New Haven: Yale University Press, 1999).
[3] See Walsh, *The Origins of Early Christian Literature*.
[4] See William R. Telford, *The Theology of the Gospel of Mark* (Cambridge: Cambridge University Press, 1999), pp. 9–15.
[5] John S. Kloppenburg, *The Formation of Q* (Philadelphia: Fortress Press, 1987). See James M. Robinson, Paul Hoffmann, John S. Kloppenborg, and Milton C. Moreland, eds., *The Critical Edition of Q: Synopsis Including the Gospels of Matthew and Luke, Mark and Thomas with English, German, and French Translations of Q and Thomas* (Minneapolis: Fortress Press; Leuven: Peeters, 2000).
[6] St. Augustine, for example, whom we will meet later, considered Mark to be "an attendant and epitomizer" of Matthew; see Augustine, *De consensu evangelistarum*, ed. Franz Weinrich, Corpus Scriptorum Ecclesiasticorum Latinorum, 43 (Vienna: Tempsky, 1904), 1.2.4: "Marcus eum [sc. Matthaeum] subsecutus tamquam pedisequus et breviator eius videtur."

First, as to the language of the New Testament: Though multilingual like others in his region among Aramaic, Hebrew, and Greek, Jesus likely spoke mostly – to the apostles, as he preached, and in everyday life – in Aramaic, a language that had become the common language of the Jewish community (replacing spoken Hebrew) in the part of the Middle East where the action takes place.[7] The Gospels, however, were written in Greek, and a specific variety of Greek at that: *koinê* or "common" Greek, meaning that the Gospels are written, not in the high-flown prose of Plato, but rather in a language close to the way Greek was spoken. Alongside Aramaic, Greek was also spoken as a kind of market language, even as it was the language of written record. Jesus spoke simply to his followers, in sentences and parables that could be easily understood, even if they concealed deeper meanings. The New Testament's Greek reflects that simplicity. As to the Gospel of Mark, scholars have dated it to thirty to forty years after Jesus's death.

As to its genre, it is an *euangelion*, a Greek word that reflects a combination of two elements: *eu*, a prefix that means "well" or "good," and *angelos*, which at its root means "messenger" or "announcer" and would later mean "angel." An *euangelion* refers to a genre that "announces good or great tidings" or "good news." A reader of Greek in that era might not first have thought of religion when seeing the title *euangelion* and might have considered instead that the written work under examination promised to reveal something extraordinary. Jesus' behavior did seem extraordinary. Recorded decades after his death though they were, the gospels' accounts of his life reflected the impact he had on his contemporaries and, as importantly, how his way of life survived him and became part of the cultural memory of early Christians.

To return to the three words, "teaching," "authority," and "scribes," the word for teaching in Greek is *didachê*, a noun related to the verb, *didaskein*: "to teach." It covers what we mean when we use the word "teaching." But it is precisely because it is a normal concept that Jesus' actions stood out in the context of the synagogue in Capernaum, the small fishing village whose customs seemed a matter of course to its inhabitants. Jesus was not the sort of person who should have been teaching. But he did, and in such a way that he gained *exousia*, a Greek word that connotes "authority," "power," and even a kind of control in some contexts. One ancient usage, in a text by

---

[7] Cf. John C. Poirier, "The Linguistic Situation in Jewish Palestine in Late Antiquity," *Journal of Greco-Roman Christianity and Judaism* 4 (2007), 55–134; and Seth Schwartz, "Language, Power, and Identity in Ancient Palestine," *Past and Present* 148 (1995), 3–47.

Plato, as it happens, signifies control over the wealth and goods needed for a society to flourish.[8] So, Jesus' acquisition of authority by speaking was momentous. He was unknown to the town and to those who might normally have spoken in and frequented the local synagogues. More notably, he taught as if he had authority and did so in a way that was unlike the scribes.

"Scribe," in Greek, is *grammateus*. A reader will notice the root, *gramma*, or "letter" (as in "letter of the alphabet"), which is at the basis of our word "grammar," cluing us in to the fact that the word has to do with writing. More meaningfully, it has to do with writing, reading, and texts that were to be studied, mastered, and used in making pronouncements. Sometimes these were legal and, in this environment, related to Jewish law. Other times, these pronouncements had to do with diverse matters, from the scholarly to the public. That *gramma* root, expanded into the noun *grammateus*, or "scribe," signifies here a class of people whose members were empowered to pronounce, to teach, and to do so publicly. Scribes possessed that special type of authority that comes to people who can read and write in a society in which very few can.[9] A "scribe" was a scholar, writer, and reader all in one and as such was unlikely to take kindly to members outside of that class who intervened. Yet this is precisely what Jesus did: he entered a place and context where he did not belong and by force of his presence captured the attention of the locals, along the way teaching his new disciples in such a way that they were "astonished." Usurping the authority of a professional class was one of the ways Jesus was remembered.[10]

Jesus also gained authority by doing things perceived as miraculous.[11] In the Gospel of Mark, immediately after the just-cited passage and in the same synagogue, Jesus was addressed by a man possessed by an "unclean

---

[8] Plato, *Laws*, ed. and tr. Richard Bury (Cambridge, MA: Harvard University Press, 1926), 828d (vol. 2, p. 126).

[9] On literacy, see Mary Beard, ed., *Literacy in the Roman World* (Ann Arbor: University of Michigan Press, 1991); William V. Harris, *Ancient Literacy* (Cambridge, MA: Harvard University Press, 1989); William Johnson, "Toward a Sociology of Reading in Classical Antiquity," *American Journal of Philology* 121 (2000), 593–627.

[10] H. Gregory Snyder, *Teachers and Texts in the Ancient World* (London: Routledge, 2000), p. 165.

[11] See Barry L. Blackburn, "The Miracles of Jesus," in Graham H. Twelftree, ed., *The Cambridge Companion to Miracles* (Cambridge: Cambridge University Press, 2011), 113–130; Andrew J. Kelley, "Miracles, Jesus, and Identity: A History of Research Regarding Jesus and Miracles with Special Attention to the Gospel of Mark," *Currents in Biblical Research* 13 (2014), 82–106; H. Van der Loos, *The Miracles of Jesus* (Leiden: Brill, 1968). For sources pertaining to the ancient context, see Wendy Cotter, ed., *Miracles in Greco-Roman Antiquity: A Sourcebook for the Study of New Testament Miracle Stories* (London:

spirit" (Mark 1:23). Jesus spoke directly to the spirit, telling it to leave the man, in a way that had an obvious effect on both the spirit and the man: "And the unclean spirit, tearing him and crying out with a loud voice, went out of him" (Mark 1:26). All were struck with wonder: "What thing is this? What is this new doctrine? For with power he commandeth even the unclean spirits, and they obey him" (Mark 1:27). Jesus' power was validated by the experience of the crowd who observed him. Again, we see the word *didachê*, "teaching," translated here as "doctrine." Jesus' words, which seemed to observers to be a "new doctrine," merged with his unusual behavior into something "astonishing" to those who encountered him. It is no surprise that his reputation spread "forthwith into all the country of Galilee" (Mark 1:28). Thereafter, in Mark's account, Jesus continues to perform healing miracles, curing people of leprosy and other ailments (Mark 2:1–12; 3:1–11; 5:1–43; 6:56; 7:24–37).

Jesus also flouted social conventions in favor of a new and more explicit model of the role of the healer and teacher. He sat down to eat with "publicans" (tax collectors held in low repute) and sinners. Thereupon "Pharisees" – strict observers of law and social convention who held their own sanctity in high repute – and "scribes" asked Jesus' disciples: "Why doth your master eat and drink with publicans and sinners?" Jesus, hearing this question, replied: "They that are well have no need of a physician, but they that are sick. For I came not to call the just, but sinners" (Mark 2:17). Jesus' disciples began to abandon certain customs, like fasting on prescribed days. When Pharisees questioned this break from well-established ritual, Jesus stressed the newness of what he was doing, saying: "But new wine must be put into new bottles" (Mark 2:22). He meant that since he was a new kind of spiritual leader, the old customs did not apply.

The more Jesus engaged in the work of healing, the more his reputation grew. He and his disciples were followed by many, among whom were people who needed healing. One group, people possessed of evil spirits, followed him and perceiving his sanctity, "fell down before him" (Mark 3:11). Astonished, they said, "Thou art the son of God." The crowd's

---

Routledge, 1999). There is a rich literature on healing miracles, see Austin Busch, George D. Chryssides, Gregor Etzelmüller, Eric Eve, Daniel Frank, Lee M. Jefferson, Melanie Köhlmoos, Lidija Novakovic, Aaron D. Panken, Celia E. Rothenberg, W. Barnes Tatum, David Thomas, and Annette Weissenrieder, "Healing Miracles," in Dale C. Allison, Jr., Christine Helmer, Volker Leppin, Choon-Leong Seow, Hermann Spieckermann, Barry Dov Walfish, and Eric J. Ziolkowski, eds., *Encyclopedia of the Bible and Its Reception*, 29 vols. to date (Berlin: De Gruyter, 2009-), vol. 11: coll. 474–502; and Amanda Porterfield, *Healing in the History of Christianity* (Oxford: Oxford University Press, 2005), esp. 20–41.

recognition of Jesus' presumed divinity increased his followers' loyalty. He selected twelve men to follow him, bade them come up onto a mountain, so that the group could bond more closely, then sent them out thenceforth to preach. Thereupon, "he gave them power to heal sicknesses and cast out devils" and renamed some: Simon became Peter, for instance (Mark 3:16). Jesus still faced accusations, this time, that he was casting out devils by the devil's power. But he refuted such claims, and when his family came looking for him, he said: "Behold: my mother and my brethren. For whosoever shall do the will of God, he is my brother and my sister and my mother" (Mark 3:34). Jesus stated, obviously, that humanity was a kind of family and, in his humility, invited all to join him in doing the "will of God."

As to humility, that trait too emerged in the way Jesus preached. Jesus went to the seaside, where he was followed by many: "And he taught them many things in parables..." These stories, humble in their evocations of everyday middle eastern daily life, often agrarian in character, served as a signature. They possessed a surface meaning but then, too, a deeper significance. Memorably, he said: "Hear ye, behold: the sower went out to sow" (Mark 4:3). As the sower sowed his seeds,

> some fell by the wayside, and the birds of the air came and ate it up. And other some fell upon stony ground, where it had not much earth, and it shot up immediately, because it had no depth of earth. And when the sun was risen, it was scorched, and because it had no root, it withered away. And some fell among thorns; and the thorns grew up, and choked it, and it yielded no fruit. And some fell upon good ground, and brought forth fruit that grew up, and increased and yielded, one thirty, another sixty, and another a hundred.

Jesus finished the parable saying: "He that hath ears to hear, let him hear" (Mark 4:4–9).

This parable, now so well-known that it seems part of a common heritage, appears in all three synoptic gospels. (Matt 13:1–23; Mark 4:1–20; Luke 8:4–15). That fact tells us that Jesus' custom of preaching by telling stories was something he did so regularly that it became part of how people remembered him. This specific parable offered an explanation about the point of these stories, sometimes seemingly enigmatic on the surface but full of deeper meaning on further contemplation. In this case, he was preaching to a large crowd, saying "he that hath ears to hear, let him hear." When his twelve disciples asked him about this new custom of preaching in parables, he responded: "To you it is given to know the mystery of the kingdom of

God. But to them that are without, all things are done in parables" (Mark 4:11). Jesus created a community of insiders, even as he informed his disciples that people were uneven in their perceptions. Accordingly, he gave the disciples a focused mission: They must be like the sower, spreading the word of God – which is what the seed represented – as far and wide as possible.

The different conditions of the ground represented a typology of different sorts of people. Some could not be reached (like the seed that fell by the wayside). Others, like the stony ground, might be receptive, even enthusiastic, but at the first sign of stress might give up the Word, just as the fledgling plants were scorched when they first saw the sun. Still others, like the ground covered with thorns (which we can think of as weeds), might be receptive to the message. But just as the thorns crowded out the healthy plantings, so too would immorality, luxury, and other vices crowd out the real message of love that Jesus, with the "word," sought to impart. Finally, there are those truly receptive, in whom the word once planted will grow, albeit in different degrees, just as the seed that fell in healthy ground grew in thirty, and sixty, and a hundred measures according to where it landed. This message accounts for human difference, and it offers a challenge to those preachers who would follow Jesus and his exhortations.

The Word – in the Greek, the expression we encounter is *logos*, that capacious and important word in Plato, which meant everything from "reasoned, logical argument" to "reciprocally reinforcing conversation." Here, in the humble Greek of the New Testament, it acquired another, deeper layer of meaning. The "word" both reflected and led to divinity. On one hand, it pointed to how God arrived at humanity – a stand-in for the divine presence, one that, though adumbrated in Jewish scripture of the Hellenistic era, could only be complete when Jesus' presence on earth, as both God and human being, was realized.[12] *Logos* also served as a stand-in for a series of messages Jesus wanted to impart. Finally, these divine messages emerged from two connected philosophical impulses. First, there were words and storytelling, in which that broad meaning of *logos* took on its fullest potential, connected as it was to the second aspect: style of life, in which Jesus's actions matched his words. As one might say today, he didn't just talk the talk, he walked the walk.

But the talk was important, and to understand what was most meaningful about the lessons Jesus imparted and the way he did so, we can turn to what can be seen as a manifesto concerning how to live in the new way he was

---

[12] See, e.g., Wis 9.1–2; John 1:1–8.

proposing: the Sermon on the Mount, which occupies three important chapters toward the beginning of the Gospel of Matthew.[13] In other contexts, Jesus preached on the seashore, from a boat and to an ever-growing audience. In this case, instead, he preached on a mountain to his disciples only, having traveled there when the gathering crowds seemed to become too much and when, so we can infer, he realized he needed to impart a new way of life to these followers, given how central they would be in spreading his message.

Simple on the surface, his discourse concealed layers of complexity that, over time, could be revealed by different interpretations in diverse contexts. On the surface, there is no doubt what Jesus considered central: humility. The Sermon on the Mount begins with a series of short sentences that have become known as the "beatitudes," a word that derives from the Latin word *beatus*, which means "blessed." As we shall see, though the New Testament was written in Greek, it gained a long-lasting life after it was translated into Latin, the language that became the language of learning, politics, and diplomacy in Europe. In this case, the Beatitudes acquired their name for a simple reason. Each one of them begins with the word "blessed."

They are as follows:

Blessed are the poor in spirit, for theirs is the kingdom of heaven. Blessed are the meek, for they shall inherit the land. Blessed are they that mourn, for they shall be comforted. Blessed are they that hunger and thirst after justice, for they shall have their fill. Blessed are the merciful, for they shall obtain mercy. Blessed are the clean of heart, for they shall see God. Blessed are the peacemakers, for they shall be called the children of God. Blessed are they that suffer persecution for justice's sake, for theirs is the kingdom of heaven.

Those are the first nine, and then there is the final one, followed by an exhortation: "Blessed are you when men shall revile you and persecute you and shall say that all is evil against you untruly for my sake. Be glad, for your reward is very great in heaven" (Matt 5:3–12).

It would be difficult to overestimate the power and importance of the Beatitudes. They represent an ethos that is at once understated and humble, revolutionary and bold, hortatory and spirited. As to the humility, Jesus preaches respect for those who did not traditionally sit at the top of normally

---

[13] Cf. W. D. Davies, *The Sermon on the Mount* (Cambridge: Cambridge University Press, 1966); and William C. Mattison III, *The Sermon on the Mount and Moral Theology: A Virtue Perspective* (Cambridge: Cambridge University Press, 2017).

accepted social and political hierarchies. There is also an imagined social cohesion different from the models in play at the time. Jesus lived at a time when slavery was widespread and when many assumptions that we take for granted were absent. The most central of these assumptions is aspirational: that every person, by virtue of nothing more than being a person, has an inherent value and dignity. It is an aspiration, needless to comment, that has been realized very imperfectly in the western world, and that in many parts of the world today does not seem self-evident to people as an inherent good. But if the idea – of equality among people – exists at all in western thought, it has quite a bit to do with the Christian assumption that even the lowest on the usual social and economic hierarchies deserve respect and dignity and that they "count" in the ways that matter most.

Another way to say this is that all persons count equally in the eyes of God, even if they are not treated as equals here on earth. Accordingly, the next question is: How does this form of religion – the form that Jesus, embryonically but powerfully, is advocating here – interact with society and politics? Here are two of the Beatitudes, which we can set next to each other. First: "Blessed are they that hunger and thirst after justice, for they shall have their fill." Here, justice seems to be a good thing, something for which one should "hunger and thirst." Then: "Blessed are they that suffer persecution for justice's sake, for theirs is the kingdom of heaven." In this case, justice seems more ambivalent. Why would people who have been persecuted for justice's sake be "blessed," if justice is a good thing? How do we reconcile those two statements? Or are they two ways of saying the same thing? Perhaps Jesus is saying that "those who hunger and thirst after justice" will "have their fill" only after their human lives have ended, when they enter what he elsewhere in the beatitudes calls the "kingdom of heaven." And when he says that those who "suffer persecution" for the sake of "justice" are blessed, he means "justice" as it is conceived in human legal systems, rather than the universal, divine justice adumbrated in the earlier Beatitude.

More simply, is Jesus, in his evocation of a larger superintending power, advocating that those who follow him be connected only marginally, or incidentally, to worldly politics? Is the "justice" that reigns in human affairs – the justice of laws and courts – only a figment of human creation, whereas real justice is that which reigns in the kingdom of heaven?

One can find different answers to those questions. But one thing should be clear, even from the beginning of the Sermon on the Mount: The notion of a more powerful, more important, more permanent, and ultimately more real world when compared to our earthly one, reminds us of

Plato. Jesus' evocations of two types of justice here cannot help but remind us of Platonic Forms. The "justice" for which those who "hunger and thirst" will be blessed and of which they will "have their fill," if only eventually, seems like a Form: an ultimate, pure reality, something of which anything we find in our world will only be an imperfect copy, even if it has the same name.

Here it is worth pausing for a moment to talk about ideas. How are they formed? How do they travel across space and time? How do they become part of "cultural memory," meaning part of the inherited memory of groups of people, who may not, indeed, know the original source of what they have come to believe, but adhere to it none the less?[14] If Jesus seems to be echoing Plato's conception of an immaterial realm greater than our own that also superintends our earthly realm, that is precisely how we should see it: as an echo. On the one hand, it is true that there was a "Hellenizing" of Jewish culture from roughly 300 BCE–100 CE, as the Greek language gained popularity in ancient Palestine and other ancient Jewish communities, and as Jewish thinkers creatively appropriated Greek educational techniques and styles of thought.[15] On the other, even if Jesus may never have read Plato's work or even heard of Plato, ideas, once enunciated, can take on a life of their own. In truth, they can sometimes have even more power when and if they are voiced in a context different from their original entry into the world.

We should keep this thought in mind as we go forward, since this question of transmission will come up again and again. The idea of this specific sort of immaterial world emerges in Plato's writings. It is an immaterial world that is not just a land of the shades, where ghosts of past heroes reside, as in Homer, but a place where divinity holds all that is good and eternal in custodianship and moreover, where eternal versions of good things serve as aspirational models for what transpires on earth. Still, the question of "who said it first" is less important than how the conversation plays itself out in different contexts. And, to return to the Sermon on the Mount, the context in Jesus' day was such as to create the beginnings of a momentous social movement that took centuries to solidify but that finds its clarion call at the end of the Beatitudes.

---

[14] See Aleida Assmann, "Memory, Individual and Collective," in Robert E. Goodin and Charles Tilly, eds., *The Oxford Handbook of Contextual Political Analysis* (Oxford: Oxford University Press, 2006), 210–224.

[15] Cf. Erich Gruen, *Heritage and Hellenism: The Reinvention of Jewish Tradition* (Berkeley: University of California Press, 1998); and Martin Hengel, *Judaism and Hellenism: Studies in their Encounter in Palestine during the Hellenistic Period*, 2 vols. (Philadelphia: Fortress, 1972).

For it is here where Jesus says to his twelve disciples: "Blessed are you when men shall revile you and persecute you and shall say that all is evil against you untruly for my sake. Be glad, for your reward is very great in heaven." He is giving them a mission. He is saying that even he, who is divine, will not be sufficient to promulgate his message, that he needs their help and that, for their efforts, they may indeed be reviled. He is trying to inspire them, and he is promising that they will have a reward – again, perhaps not in this world but in that to come.

Here too, one observes an echo of something noted in Plato and the vision of philosophy he propounded. When we think of intellectual history – the history of philosophy broadly conceived – we think of written texts. These, of course, represent our evidence. They are what we possess to make sense of thinkers of the past. But these texts often signal that, in the moment, there was more in play than only the written words that have chanced to survive. In this case, what was in play was this: how to judge success. And success meant not only having the best arguments but also amassing followers, people who had faith in your message and were willing, indeed eager, to model their lives on your own. One observed this tendency in Plato's work, where Socrates seemed such a powerful life model. It is present again here in the New Testament, where alongside the messages Jesus chose to transmit in parables and preaching, his way of life served also as a model.

One part of that model had to do with what Jesus said, another with what he did. As to what he said, the Sermon on Mount continued after the somewhat revolutionary beatitudes. Jesus exhorted his disciples to embrace a life that had one element at its core: purity. Some who heard his early preaching ventured the critique that he was a revolutionary, that he was trying to disturb established law. To this, Jesus responded: "Do not think that I am come to destroy the law or the prophets. I am not come to destroy, but to fulfill" (Matt 5:17). He advocates a new and different version of the law, again employing a comparison to the "scribes": "except your justice exceed that of the scribes and of the Pharisees, you shall not enter into the kingdom of heaven" (Matt 5:20). What he means is that, though the "scribes and Pharisees" seek to preserve written culture inviolate, doing so will not be enough. Instead, a new way of life must be sought, one in which the spirit as well as the letter of the law reigns supreme.

As to the law, Jesus refers first to the Ten Commandments, those pillars of Jewish law that appear twice in the Old Testament. First, they are enunciated in the Book of Exodus, after Genesis the second book of the Hebrew Bible, which tells of the sons of Israel, who, led by the prophet Moses, escape their enslavement by the Egyptian king (Exod 20:1–17). They appear again in the Book of Deuteronomy, a book that outlines Jewish law in many matters (Deut 5:6–21). The Ten Commandments were foundational, and Jesus, in his Sermon on the Mount, seeks to explicate them beyond their literal sense.

He focuses first on a prominent one, familiar to all: "You have heard that it was said to them of old, 'Thou shalt not kill, and whoever shall kill shall be in danger of the judgment'" (Matt 5:21). What does this commandment mean, however, if we penetrate its deeper meaning? Jesus says: "But I say to you that whosoever is angry with his brother shall be in danger of the judgment ... and whosoever shall say, 'Thou fool.' shall be in danger of hell fire" (Matt 5:22). It is not enough, in other words, to follow the law's literal prescription not to kill. Instead, one must look to the commandment's deeper meaning: As members of the human family, made in God's image, we owe each other a duty of care. To perform that duty, we need to train and shape our inner selves accordingly. That deeper meaning is something Jesus in his Sermon looked to flesh out even more, as he moved away from the Ten Commandments and toward other aspects of the Jewish law, aspects which, again, had been set forth in Exodus.

For example, Jesus says, in a passage that is worth quoting at length:

> You have heard that it hath been said, 'An eye for an eye, a tooth for a tooth'. But I say to you not to resist evil, but if any man strike thee on thy right cheek, turn to him the other also. And if any man will go to law with thee and take away thy coat, let him have thy cloak also. And whoever shall force thee to go one mile, go with him other two. Give to him that asketh of thee, and from him that would borrow of thee turn not away. (Matt 5:38–42)

In the Book of Exodus, soon after Moses promulgated the Ten Commandments, he enunciated a series of other laws, designed to give the Jewish community social cohesion, boundaries, and norms. One set concerns personal injuries. For instance: "He that striketh a man with a will to kill him, shall be put to death" (Exod 21:12); or: "He that curseth his father or mother, shall die the death" (Exod 21:17); or: "If two men quarrel, and one strike a woman with child, and she miscarry indeed, but live herself: he shall be answerable for so much damage as the woman's husband may require, and as arbiters shall award," meaning the offender will need to compensate the family for the lost child. "But," the discussion goes on, "if her death ensue thereupon" – that is, if the woman whom the offender has struck should herself die – then, "he shall render life for life" (Exod 21:22–23). Then there occurs the phraseology to which Jesus will later allude: "eye for eye, tooth for tooth, hand for hand, foot for foot, burning for burning, wound for wound, stripe for stripe" (Exod 21: 24–25). It is a stark vision, one in which justice means, essentially, retribution in kind.

The vision that Jesus promulgated, instead, was rooted in a different style of life, one that drew focus away from the law as a form of binding a society together, and toward the individual. When Jesus says to turn the other cheek, he is urging one to focus on oneself, on one's own reactions. However a law may be written, understood, and realized in society, it does not in itself reflect the pure goodness that God represents and that human beings are called – in this new view – to mirror in the world. We are individuals, Jesus is saying, who are bound to each other not by the law's letter but by its spirit, not by acts of retribution but by acts of kindness and charity. He says you should love not only your neighbors but your enemies as well. To love only your neighbors would be to do as the rest of society does. You must treat all with the same sort of respect and dignity. Why? "Be you therefore perfect, as also your heavenly Father is perfect" (Matt 5:48). In Greek, the word for "perfect" is *teleoi*, based on the noun *telos* – meaning "end" or "goal" or "point of completion." Aspiring to be a good person in this newly defined way is to become complete and to lack nothing, mirroring (incompletely of course) how God lacks nothing.

Jesus' focus on the shaping of one's own personal character continues as he addresses his followers on the mountain. He says: "Take heed that you do not your justice before men to be seen by them; otherwise you shall not have a reward of your Father, who is in heaven" (Matt 6:1). Thus begins a discourse on the behavior of the individual, revealing an attitude toward law and custom that is unusual, and veering again toward the inner intention of the doer rather than outwardly recognized behavior. For instance, if one gives alms, then "sound not a trumpet before thee as the hypocrites do in the synagogues and in the streets, that they may be honored by men" (Matt 6:2). When you perform acts of charity, in other words, keep them secret, "and thy Father, who seeth in secret, will repay thee" (Matt 6:3). The notion is that God sees all things, including those that the rest of the world cannot – including those things deep inside one's individual consciousness. Shaping that individual consciousness becomes paramount.

One way to think about religion is as a collection of rituals in which people engage, practices they carry out, often in each other's presence.[16]

---

[16] See Emile Durkheim, "Religion and Ritual," in Emile Durkheim, *Selected Writings*, ed. and tr. Anthony Giddens (Cambridge: Cambridge University Press, 1972), 219–238; Jack Goody, "Religion and Ritual: The Definitional Problem," *British Journal of Sociology* 12

They do so both to worship and – looked at from a sociological point of view – to solidify the bonds among the members of the community, indeed, to create a community by shared, regularly repeated rituals that then become part of that community's collective memory. Jesus, however, is advocating something different. It is not that he is denying that religion has a public, performative aspect. Rather, he is saying that the private, inward-facing, individual part is more important. Take what he says about prayer: "But thou, when thou shalt pray, enter into thy chamber, and having shut the door pray to thy Father in secret, and thy Father, who seeth in secret, will reward thee" (Matt 6:6). He adds that you should not say much, as do the "heathens" (by which he means simply those pagans who pray to multiple gods), believing that the more loudly they pray, the more they will be heard. There is no need to do so, since "your Father knoweth what you stand in need of before you ask him." Here we see, weaving its way into the fabric of Christianity, the notion that God is omniscient: that he knows all things – including things specifically about you. Accordingly, as you pray, you should consider that He knows your "thoughts afar off," as the Psalm had it (Ps 139:3).

The Sermon on the Mount contains similar qualifications when it comes to rituals. Fasting, for instance, is part of the landscape. But, when you fast, "be not as the hypocrites" (Matt 6:16). They – the "hypocrites" (a term that could also signify "stage actors") – want everyone to know they are fasting. Jesus recommends presenting yourself as if you were not fasting, because "thy Father, who seeth in secret, will reward thee" (Matt 6:18). Again, we are presented with a vision of a God who is omniscient in an absolute sense, so much so that He knows one's true intentions.

Having created this foundation, Jesus builds on it. He constructs an edifice representing the human person, whose building blocks are values bound to seem contrarian. More meaningfully, these values laid the groundwork for a broad introduction to society of a rarified, ancient set of practices: asceticism. That word comes from the Greek, *askêsis*, which meant everything from "practice," "training," or "exercises," to "adornment," to "way of life." It came later to designate the practices of Christian desert-dwelling monks and other holy men, whose long periods in the wilderness served to train their spirits and bring them closer, so they hoped, to God. Gradually some of these ascetics gained status, seen by their contemporaries as holy and worthy

(1961), 142–164; Marcel Mauss, *Oeuvres, 4 vols., vol. 1: Les fonctions sociales du sacré* (Paris: Éditions de Minuit, 1968).

of respect.[17] Jesus himself spent forty days in the wilderness doing the same thing. What is notable here in the Sermon on the Mount, however, is the way he offers a coherent vision for why behaviors of that sort could be justified, extreme though they might seem to be.

Jesus says, for instance, that "no man can serve two masters" and more specifically that no man can "serve God and Mammon." The latter word, "Mammon," is an English word that derives from a Latin word (that comes from a Greek word, that was originally taken over from Aramaic), and that means one thing: wealth. Jesus is saying that, though most people will be inclined to pursue wealth and its associated goods, his followers instead should reject that pursuit: "Therefore I say to you: be not solicitous for your life, what you shall eat, nor for your body, what you shall put on. Is not the life more than the meat, and the body more than the raiment?" (Matt 6:25). Birds are beautiful and free, they do not sow seeds or reap harvests, or store things up in barns, and yet: "your heavenly Father feedeth them" (Matt 6:26). Care not for the sort of food you will eat or the clothes you will wear. Instead, "See ye first the kingdom of God and his justice, and all these things shall be added unto you" (Matt 6:33). A follower of Christ must be willing to reject the customs with which he or she is surrounded and be confident, instead, that a deeper, more meaningful life is to be found in service of, and in search of, God. Note the language: "his justice" and "all these things." Jesus spent a fair amount of the Sermon on the Mount suggesting that what passes for justice in society is often far from true justice. He does that here as well, suggesting that "his justice" – God's justice – represents justice in its authentic form. And he implies the same sort of thing when it comes to wealth and worldly goods, with the language of "all these things." He means that real, authentic wealth will come to you if you embrace his vision of God, religion, and the individual.

The Sermon on the Mount finally contains a form of wisdom familiar in antiquity, expressed as it was in pithy sentences, aphoristic in their style, meaningful in their messages. The statements are familiar, since they have become proverbial: "Judge not, that you may not be judged," "ask, and it shall be given you; seek, and you shall find," "all things therefore whatsoever

---

[17] See Peter Brown, "Holy Men," in Averil Cameron, Bryan Ward-Perkins, and Michael Whitby, eds., *The Cambridge Ancient History, Vol. 14: Late Antiquity: Empire and Successors* (Cambridge: Cambridge University Press, 2001), 781–810; Garth Fowden, *The Egyptian Hermes: A Historical Approach to the Late Pagan Mind* (Princeton: Princeton University Press, 1993); William Harmless S. J., *Desert Christians: An Introduction to the Literature of Early Monasticism* (Oxford: Oxford University Press, 2004); John Wortley, *An Introduction to the Desert Fathers* (Cambridge: Cambridge University Press, 2019).

you would that men should do to you, do you also to them," "beware of false prophets who come to you in the clothing of sheep, for inward they are ravening wolves" (Matt 7:1–15). Codes for living well and according to Jesus' model, they represented pithy portraits of who he was. In that sense, they served as reminders of Jesus for his followers. The style of these aphorisms allowed them to recall the short message in question, even as the sayings permitted one to reenter the world he created, with both his preaching and his life.

Among the four Gospels the fullest account of Jesus's life is that of Luke, a gospel that begins in the form of a letter and, notably, stresses that it relies on eyewitnesses.[18] Luke presents his account as both credible and comprehensive, moving from before Jesus' birth (when Luke tells of the birth of John the Baptist and John's preaching) to Jesus' death and resurrection. Luke relates things about Jesus and his broader story that run counter to the way most people experience reality. John, for example, was born to an elderly couple, Zachary and Elizabeth, who had reconciled themselves to infertility. And yet, to Zachary, a priest who was performing his priestly duties, there comes an angel foretelling the birth of John, who, the angel declares, "shall be filled with the Holy Ghost even from his mother's womb" (Luke 1:15). The same angel, Gabriel, "was sent from God into a city of Galilee called Nazareth, to a virgin espoused to a man whose name was Joseph, of the house of David; and the virgin's name was Mary" (Luke 1:27). Gabriel said to her: "Hail, Mary, full of grace, the Lord is with thee; blessed art thou among women" (Luke 1:28). The angel brought her the news that she would bear a child. Disturbed, she asked how this was to happen, since "I know not man," meaning she had never had sexual intercourse. The angel responded that the holy spirit would come upon her, and that "the Holy which shall be born of thee shall be called the Son of God" (Luke 1:35). The angel mentioned the case of Elizabeth, Mary's cousin, an example that convinced Mary that what was happening was part of God's "word," meaning the newly unfolding plan in which, even if she did not understand it as such, she believed.

From the beginning, then, Jesus' arrival was surrounded by miraculous events: occurrences that simply did not happen during everyday life. Later, the fact that Jesus was born during the reign of the Roman emperor

---

[18] On Luke, see John T. Squires, "The Gospel According to Luke," in Bruce Chilton, Howard Clark Kee, Eric M. Meyers, John Rogerson, Amy-Jill Levine, and Anthony J. Saldarini, eds., *The Cambridge Companion to the Bible* (Cambridge: Cambridge University Press, 2021), 177–198.

Augustus came to seem evidence of a divine plan. The Gospels differ on this aspect, but the chronology broadly speaking is there, something that later medieval thinkers could not help but noting.[19]

Jesus' birth – like the circumstances surrounding his conception – also seemed miraculous. Luke tells of three shepherds, who, watching over their flocks by night, were visited by an angel of the Lord, who came surrounded by great brightness and caused them to fear. The angel put their minds at ease, however, saying: "I bring you tidings of great joy that shall be to all the people, for this day is born to you a savior, who is Christ the Lord, in the city of David" (Luke 2:10–11). They were to know who this savior was by finding "the infant wrapped in swaddling clothes and laid in a manger" (Luke 2:12). The shepherds made their way to Bethlehem, finding the child with his parents in a manger. Astounded, they returned, praising God.

A series of themes emerges. This child, the angel had foretold, would be and become known as the Son of God, in other words, someone of great importance. And yet, his birth was humble, as was his family. This would be one theme: A person of low socioeconomic status could and would rise to do great things.

As the child grew, he began to reveal his unusual status to his parents, Mary and Joseph. Once, they went to a religious festival in Jerusalem, along with their kin. On their way home to Nazareth, they realized that Jesus, then twelve years old, was not with them. They returned to Jerusalem, only to find him seated among learned men in temple, discoursing with them in such a way that "all that heard him were astonished at his wisdom and his answers." (Luke 2:47). When Mary and Joseph asked the twelve-year old child why he had absented himself and worried them, he replied: "How is it that you sought me? Did you not know I must be about my Father's business?" (Luke 2:49). Their reaction is unknown, but Luke says that "they understood not a word he spoke to them," meaning that they were by then likely quite aware of the special nature of the child they were raising (Luke 2:50).

Special though he was, his own city did not see him that way, driving him out of town as his profile rose. Jesus, recognizing what was occurring, said that "no prophet is accepted in his own country" (Luke 4:24). He left, healing people as he traveled, his reputation growing. More miracles ensued: He persuaded fishermen who believed there were no fish to be caught to lower their nets once more. When they pulled up the nets, a multitude of

---

[19] The accounts in Luke (Luke 2: 10–11, which refers to Augustus's census) and Matthew (Matt 2:1–23) differ. See Chapter 5, n.13.

fish were contained therein, leading to their astonishment and admiration of Jesus. (Luke 5:1–11). Later, he had sent out his apostles to preach and they, following him into the wilderness were subsequently joined by a crowd of five thousand people. The apostles asked Jesus to send the crowd away, so that its members could go back to their homes for food. The apostles then said they had only five loaves of bread and two fish, so that it would be impossible for them to feed such a large group. Jesus, instead, blessed the bread and fish, and there was thereafter enough to feed everyone, with more to spare.

By this point, Jesus and his followers realized unequivocally that he was special, marked for a meaningful, possibly world-changing destiny. This impression was solidified when Jesus took three of his trusted disciples up onto "a mountain to pray." But this was to be no ordinary gathering, for while Jesus was praying, "the shape of his countenance was altered, and his raiment became white and glittering, and behold: two men were talking with him" (Luke 9: 29–30). These, as it happened, were the ancient prophets, Moses and Elijah, who spoke with Jesus about the death he would suffer. A cloud emerged, and from it boomed a voice that said: "This is my beloved son; hear him" (Luke 9:35). As Luke's narrative proceeds, it gains strength from moments like these. Jesus appears miraculous and, here, specially favored by God – a status both validated by witnesses and connected to authoritative members of Jewish tradition, as Moses and Elijah surely were.

Jesus gained more followers, deputizing seventy-two disciples to carry out his word, disciples who, armed with their faith, could cure people, cast out demons from those possessed by them, and preach a message that was becoming ever more urgent. The message was increasingly apocalyptic: "the Kingdom of God is at hand," Jesus commanded the disciples to say to those listeners who stubbornly refused to believe (Luke 10:11). And more: "he that heareth you, heareth me, and he that despiseth you despiseth me. And he that despiseth me despiseth him that sent me" (Luke 10:16). The idea was that you needed to take sides now, you could not keep going the way you had, you needed to choose. If you did choose, what awaited was something like absolute equality.

For example, as he was among his newly empowered seventy-two disciples, Jesus was approached by a lawyer who asked what he must do "to possess eternal life" (Luke 10: 25). Jesus asked the lawyer what the law suggested – Jewish law, drawn from Hebrew scripture and its interpretations – and the lawyer responded that one must love the Lord God completely and must love "thy neighbor as thyself" (Luke 10:27). Jesus confirmed what the lawyer had said, but the lawyer, still unsatisfied, asked: "And who is my neighbor?" (Luke 10:29).

In response, Jesus told what has become known as the story of the good Samaritan. In this tale, a man traveling from Jerusalem to Jericho was set upon by robbers, "who also stripped him, and having wounded him went away, leaving him half dead'" (Luke 10:30). As the man lay there, a passing priest saw the wounded man, and kept going. Then, a Levite (a descendant of the tribe of Levi, part of a distinct kin group), saw the man and did the same: passed him by, despite seeing him, and did nothing. Finally, third in the story, a Samaritan arrived at the scene. Samaritans too represented a kin group, one on which Jesus' audience did not look fondly. Instead of observing the wounded victim and moving on, the Samaritan stopped and cared for the afflicted man, binding up his wounds and transporting him to an inn. The Samaritan, before he left the inn the next day, gave the innkeeper money to cover the costs of room and board. The Samaritan then promised the innkeeper that, should the cost exceed the sum he had given, he would pay the innkeeper upon his return.

Jesus asked the lawyer who had begun the conversation: "Which of these three in thy opinion was neighbor to him that fell among the robbers?" (Luke 10:36). The lawyer responded: "He that shewed mercy to him" (Luke 10:37). Jesus said, "Go, and do thou in like manner," meaning on one level: Go out into the world, look into the eyes of those who are suffering, and help them generously.

On another level, however, that parable meant something more. The bonds and rivalries among long-dead groups of kin in a premodern society are hard to recreate and understand today. But Jesus' mention of the "Samaritan" would have spurred an immediate reaction, an emotional one, existing below the surface of conscious articulation (and thus even more powerful): These are not "our kind of people." That the story's hero was a Samaritan would have violated the audience's expectations, making Jesus' main and most important message here clear: Your worth in the eyes of God does not have to do with your origin, your kin group, your wealth, or any other customarily important mark of societal status. Instead, your worth and status in this new dispensation will have to do with your actions and the way that you follow the exemplary sorts of self-sacrificing conduct that Jesus's life represented. This exemplar has to do with humility and respect for all persons, regardless of status.

However, there is another side to Luke's narrative, one that is present to varying degrees in all the synoptic gospels. This other side reflects a moral militancy, one that has to do with leaving behind one social order and following another. As the life of Jesus proceeds, this side comes to the fore as well. Like the image of a charitable, humble Jesus, this side also became part of his legacy and indeed part of the genetics of Christianity. Jesus continued, for example, to accuse the Pharisees and other upstanding societal figures of hypocrisy, of valuing rank and ceremony over a purer and more authentic religiosity. Once, when certain Pharisees grumbled that Jesus had not, as was customary, washed his hands before entering temple, he replied that they cared about cleaning the outside of the "cup and of the platter," even as their "inside is full of rapine and iniquity" (Luke 11:39). He continued: "Woe to you Pharisees, because you love the uppermost seats in the synagogues and salutations in the marketplace" (Luke 11:43).

As Jesus continued to level such accusations in public contexts, resentment arose among those "leading citizen" types of people. Luke relates that they were "lying in wait for him and seeking to catch something out of his mouth, that they might accuse him" (Luke 11:54). As Jesus was earning followers, he was also gaining enemies. In one respect, alongside his gentleness and humility, Jesus emerged as a kind of scourge of the establishment. If you cared too much about what could seem empty ritual, he would call you out in public contexts. If you cared overmuch about your own wealth, or clothes, or food, he would remind you that those things were transitory.

Jesus added new and deeper levels to this critique, advocating not only that people abandon insalubrious and uncharitable habits and rituals. He also urged those who heard his message to follow him, even at the cost of separating themselves from their own families. Take this startling statement that Luke reports. Jesus begins with a question:

> Think ye that I am come to give peace on earth? I tell you no, but separation; for there shall be from henceforth five in one house divided; three against two and two against three shall be divided: the father against the son and the son against his father, the mother against the daughter and the daughter against the mother, the mother-in-law against her daughter-in-law and the daughter-in-law against her mother-in-law. (Luke 12:51–53)

Jesus, in short, was demanding that his followers separate themselves from everything: their immediate and extended families, their broader kin groups, and all their customary assumptions. This set of demands, once translated into actual human action, would represent a different, quite new way of life, especially so in the kin-based, premodern world in which Jesus and his followers were living. Imagine: choose me over your father, mother, brothers, and sisters. Choose something that you cannot necessarily see – a world of justice, the full version of which will be known to you only when you die – over the perks and customs, the easy familiarities, and the unspoken habits with which you and yours have structured your lives.

Jesus told another interesting parable, one so dramatic, cogent, and meaningful, that it has entered the lexicon of everyday life: that of the prodigal son. There was a man who had two sons. One asked his father to have his portion of his inheritance early. The father agreed, and the son, rather than using the sum responsibly, went abroad and wasted his wealth by "living riotously" (Luke 15:13). A famine arose and, with no wealth left, the son found a citizen there who allowed him to work on a farm, feeding the pigs. The son became so hungry that he was willing to eat the corn husks with which he was feeding the pigs. He had hit bottom. At one point, the son asked himself: "how many hired servants in my father's house have plenty of bread, and I here perish with hunger?" (Luke 15:17). Humbled and ashamed, he determined to go back home. He would offer to be one of his father's servants, since the son believed he had no further title to be called a son, given his shameful behavior. But upon his return his father saw his prodigal son from a distance and the father, overjoyed, greeted and hugged the wayward young man. The son requested indeed to be nothing more than a servant. But his father told his household to bring fine clothes for his son, to put a ring on his hand and shoes on his feet and to kill a fatted calf, so that they might all feast upon it and make merry (Luke 15:20–23). There was a reason for all this, the father said, "because this my son was dead and is come to life again; he was lost and is found" (Luke 15:24). His father was so overjoyed at seeing his son, in other words, that he forgot all possible offense and wanted only to celebrate.

Then, however, Jesus' parable turns to the elder son – the son who had faithfully and dutifully stayed behind. When the elder son heard all the merrymaking, he asked one of the household servants what was transpiring and was told the story about the fatted calf. These events angered the elder son, who remained outside, refusing to go in and celebrate with his father, brother, and kin. His father, seeing this unwillingness, went outside to try to convince his elder son to come in and join the festivities. The elder son replied angrily: "for so many years do I serve thee, and I have never transgressed thy commandment, and yet thou hast never given me a kid [i.e., a goat] to make merry with my friends" (Luke 15:29). He complained that his father, despite his younger brother's poor behavior, was – seemingly unfairly – celebrating that wayward brother. His father responded: "Son, thou art always with me, and all I have is thine. But it was fit that we should make merry and be glad, for this thy brother was dead and is come to life again; he was lost and is found" (Luke 15:32). Jesus ends the parable there, offering no further explanation.

What is one to make of this story? On the one hand, the father's deeply rooted, unambiguous, unconditional love for his prodigal son mirrors God's love, as Jesus was trying to define it: not an epiphenomenon of human action, contingent on the good things you did or didn't do, but always present, a gift for which you need only humbly, repentantly, to ask and which, accordingly, you would receive. On the other hand, there is a sense that all people, whatever their status, are equally worthy of this love, no matter who they are or what they have done. The normal hierarchies do not apply in this new dispensation, a new world that was bound to disturb those whose place in the hierarchy seemed to grant them special privileges.

Luke's narrative shows Jesus evincing an awareness that he will need to suffer. His function as he began to define it was to be the "son of man." That locution would have had messianic connotations to his Jewish audience, recalling as it does the Old Testament's Book of Daniel (7:13), where it signifies someone glimpsed in a vision who had divine authority. And the phrase also signaled that Jesus wished to be seen as a representative of all humanity. Consequently, though he will be like a light for the world, "first he must suffer many things and be rejected by this generation" (Luke 17:25). Jesus saw himself as revealing hitherto unknown things to the world and, with his ever more insistent, increasingly angry preaching, as a messenger of unpalatable truths. He recalled Old Testament examples of God wreaking vengeance on an ungrateful, impious populace. The destruction caused by the flood that Noah and his chosen ones escaped in the ark; the fate of the viceful city of Sodom, where "it rained fire and brimstone and destroyed them all": these examples from the distant past served to structure his thinking in the present and, more meaningfully, to predict the final judgment to come: "Whoever shall seek to save his life shall lose it, and whosoever shall lose it shall preserve it ... Two men shall be in the field; the one shall be taken, and the other shall be left" (Luke 17:35). Something was coming, some sort of momentous event in which the hand of God would appear – and act – within the world. Somehow, Jesus himself would be involved.

He presented himself sometimes as the Son of Man in the present. Other times he referred to a moment when the Son of Man would come, ready to judge and to sort people out based on their conduct. After another parable, for example, one that focused on the conduct of an unjust judge who despite his lack of ethics finally listened and responded to a widow seeking justice, Jesus asked: "And will not God revenge his elect that cry to him day and night and have patience in their regard? I say to you: He will quickly avenge them. But when the Son of Man cometh, shall he find, think you, faith on earth?" (Luke 18:7–8). This brief quotation contains elements that became part of the Christian tradition and, indeed, sources of debate and controversy over time. Note that Jesus mentions the "elect." The Greek original, *eklektikoi*, means the "chosen." But how did – or would – God choose the "chosen"? Has He done so already – meaning, has your fate already been decided and are you already either one of those chosen or one of those who will be left behind? Or would God instead choose to save people based on their conduct on earth? Could your actions contribute to your own salvation or damnation? In the Gospels, one can find evidence for both positions. But debate over this choice – whether you are already saved or damned or whether you can do things in this life to earn salvation – became a central thread in "Christianity's rich texture over time. Here, in the Gospels, there is little by way of resolution to this evergreen question concerning human free will. But the debate never ended.

Jesus, in any case, cleverly wavered between presenting an image of rebellion against societal institutions and respecting custom. At one point, he entered the temple in Jerusalem and threw people out who seemed to be selling and buying things there, accusing them of having turned the house of God into a "den of thieves." He subsequently stayed in the temple and taught, to the consternation of the "chief priests and scribes," who along with other societal leaders sought his destruction, befuddled and angered as they were at Jesus' presence and unusual way of interacting (Luke 19:45–48). Soon thereafter, the "chief priests and scribes," still against him, sent spies to try to entrap Jesus. These spies asked him publicly, since he rejected common customs and taught "the way of God in truth," whether it was lawful for them "to give tribute to Caesar." By this they meant doing things like paying taxes and fulfilling any other financial obligations they had to the Roman emperor, under whose governance they were all living by then. Jesus understood the trap that they were trying to lay and responded by asking them to show him a coin and tell them whose image and inscription they saw on the coin. They responded that they saw the image and inscription of "Caesar," that is, the current emperor. Hearing this, Jesus said: "Render therefore the things that are Caesar's unto Caesar and to God the things that are God's" (Luke 19:24–25). This response was enough to shut down the two troublesome interlocutors. In the life of Jesus too it showed yet another side of Jesus that the authors of the Gospels wanted to memorialize: Jesus as a savvy, clever protagonist among the people of his day, who was aware enough of how the world worked to know that he would need occasionally to respond to men such as those who tried to ensnare him.[20]

The notion that one should "render unto Caesar" the things that are Caesar's suggested something more: that there were two worlds, two communities to which one could owe allegiance. The first was the one of taxes and financial obligations, contracts and agreements, basic political practices that defined everyday life. The other was more important but harder to define. This was the kingdom of God, a place one wanted eventually to go. To get there, one might have to leave behind family, spurn normal customs, welcome into one's life people with whom one would not normally associate: the poor, the infirm, the helpless.

These two visions stood, and stand, uneasily together. It was and is hard to know where to draw the lines: Where and when, that is, one should conform to normal societal dictates and "render unto Caesar" and when, on the other hand, one should stand apart from those normal practices for the sake of a higher good. Often, people come to know how and where to draw these lines only under the direction and influence of a leader who inspires them and whom they are willing to follow. It is this type of leader that Jesus proved to be, inspiring and hectoring, charismatic and angry, alive to the day-to-day problems of his world yet looking ever upward, outward, away from life on earth. He left behind him tales of miracles performed, a life lived in service of the lowest on earth, and of course, a movement that outlasted him and came to shape the western world. Jesus' death and the subsequent memorialization of his life, its meaning, and especially, how later generations interpreted him in the immediate centuries after his death: These elements are worth treatments of their own.

---

[20] See Walsh, *The Origins of Early Christian Literature*, 170–194, for parallels to other "subversive lives," that is, exemplary ancient biographies designed to showcase cleverness.

8

THE DEATH OF CHRIST

THE WAY SOMEONE LIVES – HABITS, MORALS, WAYS OF speaking – forms part of how we remember them. Yet an integral part of living, for all of us who walk the earth, is dying. No one who has seen a loved one perish can forget the experience. As groups of people gather and remember a beloved person they have lost, that person's death becomes part of the group's social memory. What led up to the death, how it occurred, how the beloved person reacted to death's final inevitability – if indeed it was not a sudden death: All this remains with us, becoming part of the stories we tell ourselves about that person after he or she has left us. Jesus Christ's life and death shared the same characteristics. Even as the end of his life was dramatic, laden with cruelty, pathos, and high emotion, the memory of his life and death as recorded in the Gospels shaped his followers' lives for centuries thereafter.

Toward the end of his life, Jesus' dealings with his contemporaries grew increasingly heated, as his predictions about the future emerged. Once, in the temple, an old woman of few means gave a very small gift, even as rich men ostentatiously "cast their gifts into the treasury" (Luke 21:1). About this woman's humble gift, Jesus said, "this poor widow hath cast in more than they all," since she had given, proportionally, more of her own resources (Luke 21:3). Still, some commented on the temple, noting that it was "adorned with goodly stones and gifts," suggesting as they did that the temple was admirable. To this Jesus responded: "these things which you see, the days will come in which there shall not be left a stone upon a stone that shall not be thrown down" (Luke 21:6). When his followers asked him to explain what he meant, Jesus launched into an extended declaration prophesying suffering and dark times that would occur of necessity. In that prophecy, the guiding assumption was that his followers would lose him.

Jesus said: "many will come in my name, saying: I am he and the time is at hand. Go ye not therefore after them" (Luke 21:8). He was beginning to suggest that after his death there would come a moment when he would return but that many in the intervening time would try to claim his legacy. And in that intervening time there would surely be disasters. There would be wars: "Nation shall rise against nations, and kingdom against kingdom" (Luke 21:10). There would be earthquakes, pestilences, and famines. There would be "terrors from heaven: and there shall be great signs" (Luke 21:11). Jesus was giving his followers a set of predictions, a way of registering seemingly negative phenomena and most importantly, a template with which to interpret the world. Since earliest human history, religion and myth had provided such a template. Jesus now offered a way of interpreting not only natural matters but also wars and other humanly created actions: They were part of a divine plan, or rather, part of God's plan – not a plan of "gods" but of the one God, unitary, all-knowing, all-powerful, and supremely good.

He also gave his followers a new way to interpret suffering, namely, their suffering, which would come before all the variously foreshadowed natural disasters: "they will lay their hands upon you and persecute you, delivering you up to the synagogues and into prisons, dragging you before kings and governors for my name's sake, and it shall happen unto you for a testimony" (Luke 21:12). That last word, "testimony," is, in Greek: *martyrion*. And that indeed is the root meaning of the word "martyr": "testimony," or "witness." Jesus was telling his followers that there would come a time when they would be asked why they followed him. When that moment occurred, they should not think about how to answer, "for I will give you a mouth and wisdom which all your adversaries will not be able to resist and to gainsay" (Luke 21:15). They should prepare, too, to be betrayed even by members of their own families and kin. Ominously, he said: "some of you they will put to death" (Luke 21:16). And yet, Jesus continues addressing his followers present and future: as you suffer, you will "possess your souls" (Luke 21:18).

Having declared that his followers would suffer as martyrs and be witnesses to truths society would not always be ready to countenance, Jesus also predicted a dramatic, final battle: "And when you shall see Jerusalem compassed about with an army, then know that the desolation thereof is at hand" (Luke 21:20). This epochal war represents the "days of vengeance," when "Jerusalem shall be trodden down by the Gentiles," a time when "there shall be signs in the sun and in the moon and in the stars, and upon the earth distress of nations by reason of the confusion of the roaring of the sea and of the waves, men withering away for fear and expectation of what shall come upon the whole world" (Luke 21:22, 24–26). It was then, when the greatest destruction was at hand, that "they shall see the Son of Man coming in a cloud with great power and majesty" (Luke 21:27). What should the followers do? "But when these things come to pass, look up, and lift up your heads, because your redemption is at hand" (Luke 21:28).

This, then, was the narrative that both his followers and then the countless many who would for centuries read these gospel accounts would face: One would pass through periods of suffering and would need during that suffering to stay true to the cause, faithful that when called upon to bear witness, God would offer inspiration to act correctly. One would witness gathering storms in the world, literal as well as metaphorical. One would be present when wars occurred, including one final one, during which all the impulses toward vengeance that people possess would be violently realized. Many would die. At the end of this final battle, the Son of Man would return, offering redemption.

This prophetic template proved useful and, indeed, evergreen for Christians, who would always need to answer a series of questions, asked in different forms and in varied contexts.[1] Whom, first of all, did Jesus have in mind? He is addressing people in the second person, that is, "you." But who was that? Contemporary listeners only? Future followers? If the latter, how long did that future extend? How long would one have to wait before the end? And, given that the end would be accompanied by signs and symbols, how much latitude did one have when explaining the latest flood, or earthquake, or famine, or pestilence? When should one interpret one of these occurrences as part of a divine plan, and when not? And who got to do so? These and associated queries framed how people later remembered and interpreted Jesus and all he did and said, sparking ever renewable debates about prophecy, apocalypse, and redemption.[2]

Another way Jesus was remembered was through his death: the events that led up to it, the dramatic way he died, and what happened thereafter.

---

[1] See Niels Christian Hvidt, *Christian Prophecy: The Post-Biblical Tradition* (Cambridge: Cambridge University Press, 2007).

[2] See Norman Cohn, *The Pursuit of the Millennium: Revolutionary Millenarians and Mystical Anarchists of the Middle Ages* (Oxford: Oxford University Press, 1970); Paula Fredriksen, *Ancient Christianities: The First Five Hundred Years* (Princeton: Princeton University Press, 2024), pp. 90–124; Matthew Gabriele, *Between Prophecy and Apocalypse: The Burden of Sacred Time and the Making of History in Early Medieval Europe* (Oxford: Oxford University Press, 2024), esp. 19–46; Bernard McGinn, *Visions of the End: Apocalyptic Traditions in the Middle Ages*, 2nd ed. (New York: Columbia University Press, 1998); Bernard McGinn, John J. Collins, and Stephen J. Stein, eds., *The Continuum History of Apocalypticism* (New York: Continuum, 2003); James T. Palmer, *The Apocalypse in the Early Middle Ages* (Cambridge: Cambridge University Press, 2014); James T. Palmer and Matthew Gabriele, eds., *Apocalypse and Reform from Late Antiquity to the Middle Ages* (New York: Routledge, 2018).

As to the events, two noteworthy incidents began Jesus' inevitable progress toward death: a betrayal and a shared meal, both elemental aspects of the human condition. His twelve disciples included among their number Judas Iscariot. "Satan entered into Judas," Luke tells us, who thereupon went to the various "chief priests and magistrates" who were eager to see Jesus killed. Judas discussed with these figures how he might betray Jesus, and accepted money to do so. Soon thereafter came the "day of the unleavened bread," the feast day – Passover – when a lamb was eaten. Jesus instructed his followers where he wanted to share this meal with them. Then, as Luke relates it, Jesus spoke as follows, with words that resounded for millennia:

> And taking bread, he gave thanks and brake and gave to them, saying: this is my body, which is given for you. Do this for a commemoration of me. In like manner, the chalice also, after he had supped, saying: this is the chalice, the new testament in my blood, which shall be shed for you. (Luke 22:19–20)

These words, repeated at every liturgy of the Eucharist, offered the most poignant distillation from Jesus himself of what his soon-to-come death would come to represent: a redemptive sacrifice suffered for the sake of all humanity.

Before that, however, Luke's narrative presents Jesus as enduring a death both painful and humiliating. Jesus was arrested, and according to Luke: "they blindfolded him and smote his face," continuing thereafter to mock and to harm him. They then brought him before Pontius Pilate, the prefect of the Roman Province of Judea. Before Pilate they laid a mixture of potent and false accusations: "we have found this man perverting our nation and forbidding to give tribute to Caesar and saying that he is Christ the King" (Luke 23:2). Perverting our nation: The Jews as a community lived with their own rituals and customs, laws and norms, all at that time under the umbrella of Roman rule. The accusers were saying that Jesus was subverting that separateness. In his insistence on newness and his implicit and at times explicit lack of respect for Jewish custom and law, he was in effect turning Jewish practice upside down, "perverting" it, as it were. There is then a lie, intended to persuade Pilate, the Roman governor, that Jesus was problematic, to the effect that he had been telling them not to give tribute to Caesar, when Jesus said explicitly that they should indeed do so, giving unto Caesar what is Caesar's. And finally, there is the accusation that Jesus was suggesting he was "Christ the King." As to "Christ," the word means "anointed," meaning that Jesus believed himself to be the anointed Son of God, as did his followers.

As to "King," there is an episode in his life story that Luke does not cover but that Matthew did. It occurred after he was born, when Magi, "wise men" from the east, came to visit (Matt 2:2–12). When they arrived, Matthew reports, they asked: "Where is he that is born king of the Jews? For we have seen his star in the east and are come to adore him" (Matt 2:2). The reaction to this question is telling: "And King Herod hearing this was troubled, and all Jerusalem with him" (Matt 2:3). It should be said that Matthew does not specify how many wise men arrived. One common assumption has been three, since he does state that they offered three gifts, gold, frankincense, and myrrh. Matthew does not report either where precisely they visited the infant Jesus, saying only that they went into a "house" (*oikia*, in Greek). The artistic legacy of splendidly dressed, royal, wise visitors from the east visiting baby Jesus in a manger, surrounded by animals, is thus a mixing together of different traditions regarding Jesus' birth. On the one hand, there is the Christ of Luke, unprivileged and poor, whom humble shepherds came to visit and by whom they were astonished. On the other, we have Matthew's version: the omen-attended birth of a figure so momentously important that a star signaled to far-away observers that they must go visit, and more, that they intuited from their observance of the star that this baby was not only important, but also a "king."

Matthew reports that "King Herod hearing this was troubled," as was "all Jerusalem," which we can take to be "official" Jerusalem – the magistrates, scribes, and all others who would fear being displaced by some new and different form of power. In Matthew's version, Herod – who was the king of Judea, a province under Roman rule in which Jerusalem was central – even attempted to enlist the wise men, asking them to let him know when they had found the child, in the hopes, Herod said, "that I also may come and adore him" (Matt 2:8). But when the wise men experienced the presence of Jesus during their visit, they abandoned that plan. Having learned in a dream that "they should not return to Herod," they went home to their original land by a different route (Matt 2:12).

When Herod realized that the wise men did not carry out his plan, he became enraged. So intent was he on eliminating the seeming threat Jesus posed that Herod caused all the male children in Bethlehem who were under two years old to be murdered. Jesus, Mary, and Joseph had left by that point, since Joseph had received notice – from an angel, who came to him in a dream – that there would be violence. The massacre of the innocent children occurred and soon thereafter, Herod died. An angel came yet again to Joseph recommending that he and his family return "to the land of Israel," which Joseph did. When he realized it was ruled by

Herod's son, Joseph left (again advised in a dream) and went into the city of Nazareth, in Galilee, which at the time was not part of the same Roman province and thus would not be subject to the rule of Herod's son. That city, though fertile, was at the time held in low repute by elite Jewish leaders. Joseph's adoption of that city thus had an added resonance, one made louder by the ending of the chapter, in which Matthew says that the choice to have Jesus grow up in Nazareth resulted in "what was said by the prophets" being fulfilled: "He shall be called a Nazarene" (Matt 2:23). Though that phrase is nowhere found in the Old Testament prophets, it is nonetheless noteworthy that Matthew singles out humble Nazareth as the place where Jesus would be raised. Jesus, even from birth, was attended by a reputation commensurate to his future status.

And there is one more element that needs highlighting, something that in the propulsive narrative passes in the blink of an eye: the slaughter of the innocents, as Herod's mass child-murder has become known. This episode formed part of the narrative of Jesus' life, linking that life and all it entailed to sacrificial death. There were, then, these two versions of his life that merged: one, omen-attended, where Jesus's importance in history was recognized immediately on his birth by the ruling class; the other, wherein his divinity was revealed more gradually. Each, however, ended in a great, final, redemptive sacrifice.

Returning to Luke, we witness what has come down to us as the "passion," derived from the Latin word *passio*, which means "bearing" or "suffering." And in Jesus' last days, quite a bit of suffering ensued. The notion, recall, was that Jesus was "perverting the nation" and claiming to be "king." When the crowd brought him before Pontius Pilate, the Roman prefect could find no severe fault with Jesus. Pilate asked Jesus: "Art thou the king of the Jews?" Jesus answered: "Thou sayest it," meaning "I will not say so myself." Pilate sent Jesus to Galilee, where Herod (a later Herod) had jurisdiction, since Pilate had heard about Jesus' birth in that region. Herod and his cohort interrogated Jesus, with Jesus staying silent and offering no response. Mocking him, they sent him back to Pilate, who in turn called together the "chief priests and magistrates" and telling him that he found "no cause" against Jesus when it came to the things of which they had accused him. Pilate communicated that he intended to release Jesus, but the crowd was having none of it: "Crucify him! Crucify him!" they cried. Again, Pilate resisted, asking "why, what evil hath this man done?" Once more, the crowd clamored for Jesus' crucifixion, whereupon Pilate, his resistance to the crowd's demand worn down, did indeed "deliver" Jesus "up to their will" (Luke 23:25).

So, Jesus was led to Calvary, a mountain also known as Golgotha, "skull mountain," in Aramaic, outside the walls of the city of Jerusalem. Two other prisoners were to be crucified that day, with one situated to Jesus' right, another to his left. About the crowd's actions, Jesus declared in an open prayer: "Father, forgive them, for they know not what they do" (Luke 23:34). The horrible events that unfolded showed humanity at its worst. Unwilling to let the execution simply occur, the crowd, attracted by spectacle, mocked Jesus; Roman soldiers taunted him as he hung; and a derisive sign was attached to Jesus' cross above his head, saying in Greek, Latin, and Hebrew, "This is the king of the Jews" (Luke 23:39). As Jesus died, he said, "Father into thy hands I commend my spirit" (Luke 23:46). Thereafter, a Roman centurion who was present remarked: "Indeed this was a just man" (Luke 23:47).

Thus far, in his account of the Passion, Luke presents readers with a story that, for all its symbolic resonances, is painfully human: the unjust execution of an innocent man, accompanied by suffering and intensified by the crowd's vicious behavior. Dramatic as it may seem, things like this had happened before and, sadly, remain part of the human experience.

Unquestionably, the story fueled the horrible, ever-renewable fires of anti-Jewish prejudice, since Jews were depicted here as the ones lobbying for Jesus' execution, even when the Roman authorities were willing to free him. It is one of the terrible ironies of history that the truth was probably closer to the reverse.[3] There can be no doubt that due to the style of his preaching and his counter-cultural way of life, Jesus made members of the "Temple establishment" deeply uncomfortable, some so much so that they may indeed have been in favor of his execution. But it was the Romans who held the statutory power to put Jesus to death and did so (and who customarily took extreme measures when movements appeared that seemed to threaten the Empire's political stability). And it is likely that when the synoptic Gospels were written decades after Jesus' death, the Christian community was distancing itself ever more from the Jewish community. Especially in the wake of the first major Jewish revolt against Rome (66–73 CE) and the Roman destruction of the Second Temple in Jerusalem by the Roman general Titus, this distancing may have recommended itself to Christian writers as prudential, even as it inflected the ways they portrayed Jews in the gospels. But because of the force of the Gospel narratives, "Christ-killer" henceforth became one among many horrible epithets

---

[3] MacCulloch, *Christianity*, 92–93.

launched against Jews – the original monotheists and the ones out of whose religious practices and scriptures Jesus' teaching grew.

After Jesus' death, the story took a different turn. We hear of a series of events that shaped perceptions of Jesus in the centuries after he walked the earth and that, indeed, have inflected Christianity for its entire existence, right up to the present day. At first, things proceeded normally, if poignantly. A mourner, Joseph of Arimathea, persuaded Pilate to release Jesus' body. Joseph wrapped Jesus' body "in fine linen and laid him in a sepulchre that was hewed in stone," meaning that it was sealed (Luke 23:53). Galilean women who had arrived saw the body laid out and returned with "spices and ointments," though because it was the day before Sabbath, they did not apply them (Luke 23:56). Thus far, what we see is a common human practice: mourning and honoring the dead with locally shared rituals that, in their nature, are most legible to their immediate community members. Luke was narrating a regular occurrence, as normal as an open-casket funeral might be today for some communities, or as would be the energetic funeral processions one sees in New Orleans. Each might seem exotic and different to outside communities, but inside the home community, the rituals make sense. So too here. Jesus died, and he was buried and mourned by those who admired him.

Then, however, a stranger set of circumstances emerged, one that was qualitatively different in genre and impact than any of Plato's deliberately fabulist, delightfully articulated myths about underworlds, afterlives, and so on. For here, in the New Testament – in Luke, whose account we are following here, as well as in the other three evangelists – Jesus is presented as really, truly dying, on the one hand, but then, on the other, really, truly coming back to life. There were antecedents to the idea that resurrection *could* occur in Jewish Old Testament tradition. In the Book of Daniel, the prophet says that "those who sleep in the dust of the earth shall awake," and in Isaiah we hear that "thy dead men shall live, my slain shall rise again."[4] And there are other hints along similar lines elsewhere: visions and predictions manifesting an idealized hope, or the one-off resurrections of dead people through the power of singularly gifted prophets who appealed to the Lord.[5] But Jesus' resurrection was of a different order altogether, a fulfillment of those older prophecies and a recasting of humanity's relation to divinity.

---

[4] Dan 12:2–3, Isa 26:19.
[5] Ezek 17:1–14; Job 19:25–2; Ps 15:10; Hos 6:1–2, 13:14; 1 Kgs 17:17–24.

Luke's narrative resumes with the women and their spices returning to the sepulcher to prepare the body. When they arrived, the stone placed to seal the sepulcher was gone, and as they entered, "they found not the body of Jesus Christ" (Luke 24:3). They were astonished at this situation and, as they stood there, what Luke describes as two men in white (or shining) apparel, appeared before them. Matthew's gospel instead describes an angel (one, not two), who had removed the stone. Mark's account postulates a "young man" in a white robe, and in John, there are two angels (Matt 28:2–3; Mark 16:5; John 20:12–13).

The different gospel accounts point to diverse perceptions of the details surrounding Jesus' death. But they agree on one thing: He was resurrected. Luke's account preserves a kind of mystery about the event. The two "men clad in white" (the angels, in other words), witnessing the women's anxiety, asked: "why seek you the living among the dead? He is not here but is risen" (Luke 24:5–6). The angels reminded the women that Jesus himself had said he would be "delivered into the hands of sinful men and crucified," to rise again three days later (Luke 24:7). The women left the sepulcher and told the gathered apostles what had transpired. They had trouble believing, thinking that what the women told them were "idle tales," though Peter, seeing the "linen cloths laid by themselves," departed, "wondering in himself at that which was come to pass." Two of the apostles left that day for a nearby town, Emmaus. On their way they were joined by Jesus himself, though they did not know it was Jesus. Along the way, he asked why they were sad. They responded with incredulity, asking whether he had heard of the momentous events that had occurred in Jerusalem concerning "Jesus of Nazareth," expressing disappointment that, though the third day had come, Jesus was nowhere to be seen (Luke 24:19). He responded to them that it had been thus prophesied and that they should be firm in their belief. By the time they arrived in Emmaus, it was late, so they invited him to stay with them. As they ate together, "he took bread," blessing it, breaking it, and giving it to them. And then, "their eyes were opened," and they recognized that this was indeed Jesus. And yet, all of a sudden, "he vanished out of their sight" (Luke 24:30–31). Filled with a newfound energy, they returned that very hour to Jerusalem and told the remaining apostles that "the Lord is risen indeed..." (Luke 24:34). They related what had happened, how the breaking of the bread made them recognize Jesus.

And then Jesus appeared. Once more, an anxiety overcame the assembled disciples, who believed he was a spirit. But he reassured them, asked them why they were troubled, and used his physical presence to show that he was before them: "See my hands and feet, that it is I myself. Handle and see, for a spirit hath not flesh and bones, as you see me to have" (Luke 24:39). He asked for food, which they gave him, and he ate. He spoke, and in so doing reminded them that he was there as fulfillment: "These are the words which I spoke when I was yet with you, that all things must needs be fulfilled which are written in the law of Moses and in the prophets and in the psalms concerning me" (Luke 24:44). He went on to say, oscillating now, and describing himself in the third person, that it accordingly "behooved Christ to suffer and to rise again from the dead, the third day" (Luke 24:46).

Thus far in Jesus' reappearance, he has reinforced the message that he was there as fulfillment of prophecies in the Old Testament that a redeemer would come. This connection between the Old Testament and the New began, accordingly, with Jesus himself and would later be developed in depth by Christians, as the Gospels took on the weight of scripture.

Then Jesus, again speaking of himself in the third person, reminded them "that penance and remission of sins should be preached in his name, unto all nations, beginning at Jerusalem" (Luke 24:47). Reinforcing the importance of this early group of followers, Jesus said: "And you are witnesses of these things" (Luke 24:48) They began to travel together, Jesus included, who accompanied them for a bit, "as far as Bethany," we are told. There, Jesus raised his hands and blessed the group. Luke's gospel ends: "And it came to pass, whilst he blessed them, that he departed from them and was carried up to heaven. And they adoring went back into Jerusalem with great joy. And they were continually in the temple praising and blessing God. Amen" (Luke 24: 51–53). The apostles were left satisfied, even as Jesus, physically, was gone for good. Thereafter, it would be up to the apostles and their followers to spread the word, and to do so, as Jesus recommended, "unto all nations." It is this story, of Christianity's growth and diffusion throughout the Mediterranean region and Europe, that served as the backbone to western intellectual history.

What you have read in the last two chapters is a narrative shaped by the canonical gospel sources that we have. As noted, they were written significantly after Jesus' life and death, and as such they represent a repository of aggregated memories. For centuries, there has been probing scholarship, sorting out which parts of that narrative can be verified – whether by archaeological remains, attestation of similar facts in other texts, or corroborating ancillary evidence (coins, inscriptions, and so on). Moreover, over the last two millennia countless authors have interpreted that narrative, revealing over time its complexity – a complexity that itself has led to very different interpretations of the very same biblical passages.

But as you have seen, there is an exemplary quality to the story of Jesus' life and death, the style of life he modeled, and the way he gathered a school of followers around him. Omens and signs, contestations and community-building, inspiration and disillusionment, crime and redemption, faith and betrayal, kindness and cruelty: These things are part of the human condition. For centuries, millions of people have had something like the narrative you just read in their minds. It was, and for many is, a narrative that has formed at least one set of basic mental building blocks, providing comfort in times of distress, wisdom in times of uncertainty – and sometimes, specious, decontextualized justifications for self-interested practices.

As we go forward, we will observe how that narrative was shaped and how parts of it were fashioned into durable aspects of Christian theology. We will also see how later figures developed their own thinking, their own philosophizing, and their own ways of being in the world, often in explicit, and almost always in implicit dialogue with Christianity. This narrative remained a fundamental part of the ongoing series of conversations that western thinking represents. To recount it without cynicism does not imply credulous acceptance, naïveté about sources, or ignorance of the later processes of canon formation that privileged the sources used here over other early gospels, some of which had different emphases. Recognizing the narrative's centrality, however, does evince respect for a tradition that has mattered deeply to significant numbers of people worldwide and to majorities in the nations and regions traditionally identified as western.

9

VESSEL OF ELECTION, LIGHT OF THE GENTILES

IN THE EARLY YEARS AFTER JESUS' DEATH, THE MEANING OF HIS life served as a source of debate and inspiration. There was no figure more important than Paul of Tarsus. His personal conversion served as a model in the centuries to come, even as his interpretations of Jesus' message shaped western intellectual history definitively.[1]

After the four gospels, the next book of the New Testament in its canonical ordering is the Acts of the Apostles, which records the activities and interactions of Jesus' earliest followers, including Paul. We will follow the account in Acts and then turn to three of Paul's letters, even though, chronologically, the authentic letters of Paul come first. Indeed, the seven letters that Paul himself is believed to have written represent the earliest major Christian writings that we possess, written only a few decades after Jesus' death and for the most part before the gospels. The letters accepted as authentic are: Romans, 1 and 2 Corinthians, Galatians, Philippians, 1 Thessalonians, and Philemon. Of the remaining six, Colossians, Ephesians, and 2 Thessalonians are disputed, meaning that some scholars believe they were written by followers of Paul and others believe that all or parts of them are authentic. The final three in the Pauline corpus (1 and 2 Timothy and Titus), are believed to have been written significantly later, again by self-identified followers of Paul.[2]

---

[1] See James D.G. Dunn, *The Cambridge Companion to St. Paul* (Cambridge: Cambridge University Press, 2006); Paula Fredriksen, *Paul: The Pagans' Apostle* (New Haven: Yale University Press, 2017); Bruce W. Longenecker, *The New Cambridge Companion to St. Paul* (Cambridge: Cambridge University Press, 2020).

[2] Arland J. Hultgren, "The Pastoral Epistles," in James D.G. Dunn, ed., *The Cambridge Companion to Saint Paul* (Cambridge: Cambridge University Press, 2003), 141–155, at 142–144.

Acts, however, is a continuance of the gospel of Luke.[3] There is a very old tradition suggesting that Luke authored both the eponymous Gospel and the Acts of the Apostles.[4] While modern scholarship does not identify the author of both texts as the Luke whom Paul mentions as a companion (Col 4:14), it is believed that the voice behind both texts is the same. So, again, Acts is later than Paul's seven authentic letters. Beginning with Acts makes sense, however. Its canonical ordering in the New Testament ensured that later thinkers encountered it directly after the fourth gospel. Moreover, Acts contains exemplary episodes regarding both Paul and the dynamics of the early stages of the Jesus movement.

One episode was especially important regarding Paul. His name in Hebrew was Saul, and he is referred to in this way in Acts (until his journeys take him out of Jerusalem, in Acts 13, when he is referred to as Paul). Like many, Saul harbored suspicion against the Jesus movement. Acts relates that once, as he was travelling to Damascus to find and root out any followers of Jesus, a "light from heaven" flashed at him, causing him to fall to the ground. (Acts 9:3-4). Saul's experience marked an important moment, one that stood out as a model thenceforth: The model was one of conversion and the undertone was that of God's power, whose interventions proved so meaningful that Saul went from a vehement persecutor of Christians to their most ardent defender, theorist, and intellectual architect.[5]

There was a story behind this conversion. The growing Jesus movement still faced skepticism, as the local community continued making the sort of charges that had been waged against Jesus himself. This time the accused was Stephen, whom the early community had named a deacon and whose function was to help distribute alms to widows, among other things. About him, "the ancients and the scribes" stirred up resentment and fear, bringing him "to the council" and setting up "false witnesses" against him, who said, "This man ceaseth not to speak words against the holy place and the law" (Acts 6:13). Stephen, in response, offered an oration that recapitulated the history of the Jews as told through the Hebrew Bible, recounting

---

[3] Mikael C. Parsons, "The Third Gospel and the Acts of the Apostles," in Patrick Gray, ed., *The Cambridge Companion to the New Testament* (Cambridge: Cambridge University Press, 2021), 134–154.

[4] Eusebius, *Ecclesiastical History*, 3.4.6; Irenaeus, *Adversus Haereses*, 3.14.1.

[5] See Karl F. Morrison, *Understanding Conversion* (Charlottesville: University of Virginia Press, 1992); Arthur Darby Nock, *Conversion: The Old and the New in Religion from Alexander the Great to Augustine of Hippo* (Oxford: Oxford University Press, 1933); Lewis R. Rambo and Charles E. Farhadian, eds., *The Oxford Handbook of Religious Conversion* (Oxford: Oxford University Press, 2014).

the story of Moses: how he saw the burning bush, heard God's voice, and led the Jews out of Egypt. Stephen also offered a selective version of their history, ending his tale by introducing Jesus and Jesus' appearance on the scene, and then accusing his listeners of having always treated their prophets poorly and of being stubborn and unwilling to accept change: "you always resist the Holy Ghost. As your father did, so do you also" (Acts 7:51). This harangue enraged the members of the Sanhedrin, who were keepers of tradition, arbiters of the law – in short, the establishment. Despite their anger, Stephen, "being full of the Holy Ghost, looking up steadfastly to heaven, saw the glory of God and Jesus standing on the right hand of God" (Acts 7:55). Stephen then declared precisely this – that he saw God and Jesus – whereupon his listeners, "crying out with a loud voice, stopped their ears and with one accord ran violently upon him" (Acts 7:56). They took him outside the city walls and stoned him to death. As Stephen was dying, he said, "Lord Jesus, receive my spirit," thereafter crying out right before his death, "Lord, lay not this sin to their charge." (Acts 7:58–59). Acts, chapter seven ends with the following sentence: "And Saul was consenting to his death."

Three things stand out. First, here as elsewhere in the New Testament, one observes a template for a narrative of supersession and the links of that narrative to antijudaism. Jesus was a new prophet, bringing a new message, one that superseded the laws and customs by which the Jewish community had considered itself bound. That is the idea, one that Jesus himself suggested many times. Here we see a follower proclaiming that idea and meaningfully, doing so in a public context – that of a court – weaving together a narrative that recapitulated Jewish history and then accused the Jews of stubbornness. This latter accusation forms the core of the second notable aspect of the story of Stephen, as recounted in Acts. Christianity – at that moment in history simply a breakaway sect of Judaism – defined itself not only as an innovative continuance to what came before, but also in opposition to it. As this narrative took hold – a centuries-long process – Jewish people came to be seen sometimes as simply stubborn, characterized as such in a blanket fashion, over and above their part in the Christian narrative. Other times, they have been seen as villainous "Christ-killers," who, despite the reticence of Pilate (the representative of Roman government), urged the crucifixion of Jesus.

Alongside the core Christian message, one of respect for the poor, the dignity of all persons regardless of their social or economic status, and a God interested in individuals and in justice for all, there would always be this other terrible aspect of the story: the Jews as villains, the Jews as "other."

It was a story on which the unscrupulous could – and sadly did – fasten many times in western history, with pogroms, ethnic cleansing, massacres, and other assorted and related crimes justified by these sorts of prejudices, whatever the more immediate sociopolitical causes might have been.[6]

Second, Stephen's story is an example of martyrdom. The Greek word *martys* means "witness," at its most basic level: someone who observes something. But it came to mean a witness to the truth, in this case represented by Jesus and his message, and also something more: someone who, thanks to this witnessing, sacrificed him- or herself on that very account. Unwilling to renounce the truth of what they have seen, faithful to the cause until the end, martyrs die professing their faith with their last breath.[7]

Third, Stephen's story serves as a key element in the conversion narrative of Paul, then called Saul, who was there at Stephen's brutal public execution. Saul formed part of the many who persecuted the early Christian community, thinking like other critics that this new religion would subvert custom. Those who stoned Stephen put down their extra garments at Saul's feet. And then, after Stephen's death and as the devout mourned Stephen, Saul "made havoc of the church, entering in from house to house, and dragging away men and women," putting them in prison, no less (Acts 8:3). Saul's conversion narrative arises directly out of the persecutions he carried out. Indeed, he was heading to the Syrian city of Damascus to do the same to any Christians he found in that city. He had asked for letters of introduction from the high priest in his home city, Jerusalem, so that, should he find any Christians in Damascus, he might bring them back to Jerusalem to imprison them.

It was then, as he was on the way to Damascus, that he saw that blinding light and heard a voice from heaven, asking him: "Saul, Saul, why persecutest thou me?" (Acts 9:4). Unsure of the voice addressing him, Saul asked "Who art thou, Lord?" And the voice responded: "I am Jesus whom thou persecutest" (Acts 9:4). Stunned and trembling, Saul asked: "Lord what wilt thou have me to do?" (Acts 9:6). The response? "Arise and go into the city; and there it shall be told thee what thou must do" (Acts 9:7). Saul had been traveling with a group, and they too were astounded since they heard a voice but saw no one. Saul got up and he could not see, so his fellow travelers led

---

[6] See David Nirenberg, *Anti-Judaism: The Western Tradition* (New York: Norton, 2013).
[7] See Paul Middleton, ed., *The Wiley Blackwell Companion to Christian Martyrdom* (London: Wiley, 2020).

him by the hand the rest of the way to Damascus. For three days, he remained blind.

Meanwhile, in Damascus, the Lord decided to speak directly to a disciple named Ananias, asking him to find Saul. Ananias answered with puzzlement, saying that he had heard "how much evil" Saul had done to Jesus' followers in Jerusalem. The Lord responded, telling Ananias to proceed nonetheless, and saying about Saul: "this man is to me a vessel of election to carry my name before the Gentiles and kings and the children of Israel" (Acts 9:15). Despite Saul's past behavior, God was choosing him to carry the new Christian message forward, and outward, to the "Gentiles," meaning pagan polytheists, largely Greek; to the "kings," meaning people of high station; and to the "children of Israel," meaning to the Jews. The newness of the Christian religion begins to emerge here.

The expression, "vessel of election," deserves to be foregrounded. Within it lies a central dilemma, one that would loom ever larger in the history of Christianity. Saul, clearly, had done things that were bad from the perspective of an adherent to the Jesus movement: He had persecuted Jesus' followers and was fully intent on persecuting more. But then, he arrives at a moment of personal crisis, one signaled by a sign: in this case the blazing light at Damascus accompanied by the voice of the Lord. His past conduct, which he chose freely, can be erased. God chooses him to be a *skeuos eklogés*, in Greek, or in the Latin Vulgate translation, which from the fifth century AD served as the dominant one in the West, a *vas electionis*. What does it mean to be a "vessel of election?" The word vessel can imply an inherent passivity. A vessel holds things, contains them, and it can also be a means to an end. Then there is "election," which in this case means something different from the everyday way we use that word in modern English. Here, in the narrative of Acts, it means "choice" or "choosing." Saul will be a vessel of God's choosing, the goal being to spread the new Christian message.

Ananias, the Damascan disciple, went to Saul as Jesus had asked him to do. "Brother Saul, the Lord Jesus hath sent me," Ananias said, so that "thou mayest receive thy sight and be filled with the Holy Ghost" (Acts 9:17). Straightaway, Saul was able to see, as "there fell from his eyes as it were scales..." (Acts 9:18). "Scales falling from one's eyes" has become a metaphor for sudden moments of clarity, all reaching back to this conversion experience of Saul. So stunned was he by the appearance of Jesus on the way to Damascus that he was rendered practically powerless. Then, when a disciple of Jesus transmitted that potent message to him, giving him back his sight, Saul arose a different man. He began to preach in synagogues that Jesus was the son of God (Acts 9:20).

One of Saul's tasks was to work with the "Gentiles," in this case meaning mostly Greeks and Romans, those polytheistic heirs of the intellectual world of Plato, Aristotle, and other philosophers. Accordingly, the next time Saul makes an appearance in the Acts of the Apostles it is beside another disciple, Barnabas, as they journey together to Cyprus, a Greek-speaking town. Saul, who from Acts 13:9 is called Paul, begins his work of preaching, sometimes accompanied by miracles. When in Lystra, for example, Paul met a man who was lame but who seemed to have faith. Paul said: "Stand upright on thy feet" (Acts 14:9). The man did so and was healed, to the astonishment of the locals. They cried out that the gods had come among them. They called Barnabas "Zeus" and Paul, "Hermes." Paul and Barnabas reassured the people that they were mortals, come only to preach the living God. Upon hearing this, the people, who were about to make sacrifices to Paul and Barnabas as if they were gods, refrained from doing so.

Their travels continued, winning them converts along the way. But there was occasional resistance. In the Macedonian city of Philippi, Paul, by then traveling with other disciples, was imprisoned. He and Silas, one of the disciples, prayed in prison, praising God in such a way that others imprisoned therein heard them. Then, "there was a great earthquake, so that the foundations of the prison were shaken" (Acts 16:26). The doors opened and everyone's chains came loose. A natural event, an earthquake, occurs at a propitious time, once again lending the narrative a divine patina. The episode sends the message that God is watching over his evangelists as they spread the good news of Jesus. Seeing this event and moved by it, Paul's jailers converted and were baptized. Thereafter, the magistrates who had ordered Paul's imprisonment set him free.

In Acts 13, when in Antioch, Paul and Barnabas relate what the Lord had said to them: "I have set thee to be the light of the Gentiles: that thou mayest be for salvation unto the utmost parts of the earth" (Acts 13:47). This notion was meaningful in at least two ways. First, it implies a universalism to the Church, one reason the Church in the early Christian centuries would come to use the name "Catholic," a word whose two Greek roots, *kata* and *holon*, mean "on the whole," or less literally, "universal."[8] This new message would be universal, worldwide, and apply to all people. This vision both shaped Paul's mission and was shaped by him, as we shall see.

---

[8] For the first usage of the term, around 107 CE, see Ignatius of Antioch, "Letter to the Smyrnaeans," 8.2, in Bart D. Ehrman, ed. and tr., *The Apostolic Fathers*, 2 vols. (Cambridge, MA: Harvard University Press, 2003), 1: 296–309, at 304–305.

Second, it meant that Paul and his cohort took their message to places where the reception would be uncertain, skeptical, and at times hostile. One such instance occurred when Paul traveled to Athens, the home of western philosophy, the place where both Plato and Aristotle had plied their trade, and a city whose inhabitants appreciated vigorous public debate. Paul's time in Athens, brief though it seems to have been, served as a meaningful example in the cultural memory of Christianity (Acts 17:16–34).

When he arrived, everywhere he looked Paul saw altars, statues, inscriptions, and other public monuments reflecting Greek polytheism. As Paul approached the task at hand (to preach the good news), he took an interesting tack. Instead of angrily railing at the Athenians, he used rhetoric – persuasion – to bring them along. One staple of rhetoric is a technique known by its Latin name, a *captatio benevolentiae* – "capturing the benevolence" of one's audience at the beginning of a speech. Like so much else in the early Christian story, this episode served as an "exemplary" background to later ways of engaging in philosophy.

After Paul saw the evidence of polytheism all around, he "disputed" not only in Athens' synagogues (to Jewish audiences) but also "in the marketplace, every day, with them that were there" (Acts 17:17). This type of thing was customary in Athens, as people would meet in the *agora* to discuss issues ranging from current events to weightier philosophical concerns. Acts tells us that members of two philosophical schools, the Epicureans and the Stoics, wondered publicly what this "sower of words" was trying to say. Was he, perhaps, setting forth "new gods"?

As to the two schools of philosophy, not much else is said in the Bible. But they are presented as if they are known quantities, their doctrines and opinions so well-understood that one needed only to name them, and a reader would grasp who they were and what they represented. The Epicureans held as axiomatic that pleasure (*hêdonê* in Greek) was the main principle and motivator in human life. We seek pleasure and avoid pain. But pleasure also meant having your desires satisfied; accordingly, the more you could reduce your desires, the more "pleasure" you would experience. They also believed in atomism, meaning that, in their view, all things, from rocks and plants to planets and stars, and – very importantly – people, were made of tiny, invisible and indivisible particles. These combined and recombined to form things in the universe. As to people, this meant that, when you were here on earth, living life, enjoying the fellowship of your friends, and so on, you were here. But after you died, you were gone. No Platonic – or by now Christian – afterlife with rewards and punishments, no immortal soul, and so on. And as to God and gods, it is not that the Epicureans denied their existence. The belief, instead, was that the divine did not care about us, about life on earth, about individual people. This belief, too, would have run into opposition among Christians, committed to the idea of a personal God so interested in our human redemption that he took on human form and suffered death for us. Unthinkable for Epicureans.

Stoics too did not believe in an activist, people-centered divinity. The gods might use human beings for their own ends, but we could do nothing about it. Instead, we could worry about things under our control: our own behavior, our virtue, our own society. For Stoics, duty represented the primary motivating impulse to life and to ethical action. Politically, where Epicureans were detached from the active life of politics, the Stoics participated. But both schools were guided by beliefs that stood at odds to the incipient Christian message that Paul was in Athens to spread. Again, while Acts tells us nothing more than that "Epicureans and Stoics" were curious as to Paul's preaching, it shows that they were a presence in Athens. They represented two sets of voices in the Athenian polyphony, in an Athens that was as much an ideal as a physical place: a vibrant, active, sometimes disputatious public culture and, in cultural memory, the heart of western thinking. It was here that Paul with his new message would sow powerful seeds.

The philosophers' curiosity about Paul and his message impelled them to bring him to the Areopagus, a hill north of the city center, where trials had once habitually taken place. They said to Paul: "For thou bringest in certain new things to our ears. We would know therefore what these things mean" (Acts 17:20). Paul responded with a short and delicately calibrated speech. It oscillated back and forth between praise and critique, using language – at least as Acts records it – that contains carefully chosen ambiguities. He began: "Ye men of Athens, I perceive that in all things you are too superstitious" (Acts 17:22).

The phrase, "too superstitious," renders the Greek comparative adjective, *deisidaimonesterous*, which can denote either excessive superstition or deep religious reverence, depending on the tone and context. The Latin Vulgate preserves this ambiguity somewhat in its translation: *superstitiosiores* (and it is worth noting that the English translation used in this book is the Douay-Rheims English translation, which relied on the Latin Vulgate). While often understood pejoratively, *superstitiosus* in Latin also carried a spectrum of meanings, from "given to superstition" to "overly scrupulous" when it comes to religious observance. This ambivalence shaped later interpretations, particularly among medieval readers who encountered the Vulgate and brought to it their own theological and cultural presuppositions. It also explains why modern translations, like the New International Version, read the lines more neutrally: "People of Athens! I see that in every way you are very religious."

Paul was, accordingly, using language in a subtle and rhetorically astute way. To later Christian readers, often predisposed to see Athens as a symbol of pagan error, his words might have seemed a rebuke. But to his original audience, he may have appeared to be offering praise, skillfully engaging their attention before introducing a new and unfamiliar conception of the divine. And though Paul's message was in many ways unprecedented, it still bore enough resonance with Greco-Roman religious sensibilities to invite serious consideration rather than outright dismissal.

After his polyvalent opening sentence, Paul continued in his direct address, saying: "passing by and seeing your idols, I found an altar on which was written, 'to the unknown God.' What therefore you worship without knowing it, I preach to you" (Acts 17:23). Again, one observes a casual but meaningful suggestion of commonality: An altar the Athenians had placed to an unknown god served as a foreshadowing of what Paul would now tell them about Jesus and his place in the divine economy. Paul stresses that God made all things and did not reside "in temples made with hands," meaning that, though we might worship in conventional, earthly ways, God stood over and beyond anything purely human. Finally, God did not need anything, "seeing as it is he who giveth to all life and breath and all things, and hath made of one all mankind to dwell upon the whole face of the earth . . ." (Acts 17:25–26). Up until now, this description of God could have resonated with ancient pagan descriptions, not so much in following them exactly, but in recapitulating and reframing two ideas that, by then, were part of people's thinking about the divine. The first was that there was a "creator." Plato had spoken of a "demiurge" in his dialogue *Timaeus*, a kind of great artisan who had fashioned the world and who was "always in existence and has no becoming."[9] Aristotle had spoken of a "prime mover," or as he put it in his *Metaphysics*, "that which, not having been moved, moves."[10] That there must, at some point, have been a creator of some sort was a familiar notion.

Second, there was the idea that this creator was unitary. In Plato, there had been hints here and there that there might be one supreme god and

---

[9] See Plato, *Timaeus*, in Plato, *Timaeus, Critias, Cleitophon, Menexenus, Epistles*, ed. and tr. R. G. Bury (Cambridge, MA: Harvard University Press, 1929), 28a (pp. 48–50).
[10] Aristotle, *Metaphysics*, 2 vols., ed. and tr. Hugh Tredennick (Cambridge, MA: Harvard University Press, 1933), 12.1072a (vol. 2, p. 146).

similarly in Aristotle.[11] Paul's Epicurean and Stoic listeners would not have been too surprised at what he had said thus far. There is something about our ability, as human beings, to project the notion of unity into logical space that inclines us to this sort of thing: oneness (as opposed to the plurality we see all around us) somehow lodges in our minds.

These two factors, creation and unity, were part of the Greek philosophical vocabulary. What was different was the way that Paul's God related to humanity. As noted earlier, Acts, where this speech appears, was written later than Paul's letters, which we shall encounter soon.[12] But the important factor here is cultural memory: how a community came to understand its own history. In this case, the early Christian community, whose self-image shaped western thinking decisively, eventually saw the New Testament as a kind of bedrock text, the authoritative font and origin of their own thinking.

As Paul's speech continues, we see how and why the Christian God came to be seen as different, radically so, from Greco-Roman conceptions. For Paul says that, in addition to God's having established all of humankind "as one," He also determined "that they should seek God, if happily they may feel after him or find him, although he be not far from every one of us" (Acts 17:27). Two factors stand out. First, God has made us in such a way, Paul suggests, that we are hard-wired to seek him (as we would say today). Second, God is "not far from every one of us." There was certainly a strand in Plato suggesting that we were inclined to reach the divine, provided we could strip ourselves of our bodily passions. But no ancient figure thought God – the one, unitary God which they had only inchoately theorized – was "close to us" as personal individuals in the way Paul is suggesting here.

Then Paul says, regarding God, "for in him we live and move and be, as some also of your own poets said: 'for we are also his offspring'" (Acts 17:28). As it happens, Paul is citing a Greek poet named Aratus, who flourished in the first half of the third century BCE and may even have been from Paul's hometown, Tarsus (today in Turkey). The one major work of Aratus that survives is a lengthy poem, *Phainomena* (*Appearances*, or *Visible Signs*), that set forth the universe's natural phenomena in elegant Greek. Paul's quotation comes from close to the beginning, where Aratus is praising Zeus "whom," the poet says, "we men never leave unspoken."[13] Aratus presents other

---

[11] See Plato, *Rep.*, 517b (vol. 2, p. 116), and Aristotle, *Metaphysics*, 12.1076a (vol. 2, p. 174).

[12] Cf. Paula Fredriksen, *From Jesus to Christ: The Origins of the New Testament Images of Jesus*, 2nd ed. (New Haven: Yale University Press, 2000), pp. 52–55.

[13] Aratus, *Phaenomena*, ed. and tr. Douglas Kidd (Cambridge: Cambridge University Press, 1997), pp. 72–73.

things about Zeus, hinting at how human beings should conceive of him: "Filled with Zeus are all highways and all meeting-places of people, filled are the sea and harbors; in all circumstances we are all dependent on Zeus."[14] Zeus, it is clear for Aratus, is everywhere. Aratus continues with the passage Paul has cited: "For we are all his children, and he benignly gives helpful signs to men..."[15] Aratus' point is to set the context for his poetic work, in which he goes on to discuss the heavens, constellations, and then eventually meteorological phenomena, all in a stately poetic hexameter. For Aratus, Zeus serves as a benevolent presence, ever-present if you know where to look for him. Aratus' Zeus, if not a personal god such as evolving Christianity was developing, nonetheless has planted signs and clues in nature, all toward the end of allowing human beings to work with nature – to know when and how to harvest, how to recognize different weather events, and so on.

For Paul, leaning in Aratus' direction served important functions. Paul does not name Aratus but suggests, to his Greek audience, that the thought comes from "your poets." Accordingly, his listeners on the Areopagus subtly could be attracted: If they recognized the quotation, they might consider themselves part of an in-group. If they did not, they would want to listen more avidly to Paul, who is "meeting them where they are," in our current parlance. Moreover, Paul is suggesting that the Greeks have – in their own way – also been drawn to the idea of a supreme being, a being who, in Aratus' telling at least, has a benevolent side. With his idea that "we are all his offspring" (offspring of God, that is) Paul has laid a foundation for the edifice he is building, an edifice that rises as he proceeds and one whose architectural contours take on a newness, one that is understated but no less noticeable, at least with the privilege of hindsight: "Being therefore the offspring of God, we must not suppose the divinity to be like unto gold or silver or stone, the graving of art and device of man" (Acts 17:29).

The message: Elaborate temples, altars, and idols, however luxurious and exotic they may be, will not reflect God's truth. One must jettison old attitudes and take on new ones. This newness, attractive and yet unnerving, comes through more clearly in what Paul next says: "And God indeed having winked at the times of ignorance, now declareth unto men that all should everywhere do penance" (Acts 17:30). Meaning, God has always been there, observing the way humanity has evolved over time. He has "winked at" – that is, he has seen but decided somewhat to overlook – the

[14] Ibid.   [15] Ibid.

many religious practices, both pagan and Jewish, which contravened his will. But matters have escalated of late. He decided to embody himself in another, new form, that of his son, Jesus, whom he sent to preach his message and then die sacrificially for us human beings – for our redemption and as a promise of things to come. One of those things will be a final and meaningful judgment of humanity, at a time in the future when God decides, a moment fundamentally unknown to us, try as we might to observe signs of his eventual return.

Accordingly, God now demands more, and God is decisively now not *a* god, but rather, God: a fundamentally unique being whom we must address, worship, and understand as such. Part of that worship and understanding is now to include "penance," as our translation has it. It is worth pausing for a moment to focus on this expression, "penance," and how it appears in the original Greek and then in the Latin translation, the latter of which became centrally important.

The word "penance" in the translation we are using is drawn from a Latin word, *paenitentia,* which means repentance in addition to penance. Within it, the word *paenitentia* carries another root word, *poena,* a word that has a range of meanings, including "compensation," "punishment," and "penalty." The Latin word *poenitentia,* accordingly, can possess a transactional, exchange-oriented, and legal sense. In that sense, the implication is that one can right a wrong by paying a debt, by suffering punishment, or by paying a penalty.

If we turn to the Greek expressions of the same passage, however, the resonance changes somewhat. For there, Paul uses the Greek word *metanoiein*. Within this word lies the root *nous,* which means "mind" or "state of mind" in Greek. Paul is saying that his listeners need to "change their minds" or "change their way of thinking." To be sure, it is still an urgent task, something demanded by God and now, through Paul – God's vessel of election – made manifest through preaching. The Greek concept calls for internal change on the part of the individual, whereas the Latin version can include outer validation; in Greek, it is about personal conversion, in Latin, it can connote paying a price for one's sins. It is the Latinate locution that wended its way through the Middle Ages. But that original Greek sentiment was always there too, even to readers of Latin, who could explicate and have explicated to them that wider meaning. This twofold sense provided an oscillation in Christianity and its long history, a kind of private–public dichotomy embracing both one's innermost self and the way one lives in the world.

Two noteworthy instances conclude Paul's episode on the Athenian Areopagus. First, Paul says that God has "appointed a day wherein he will judge the world in equity, by the man whom he hath appointed: giving faith to all, by raising him up from the dead" (Acts 17:31). As to the first part, that God would engage in judgment of humanity was likely unsurprising. Or at least one could say it was consonant with what Paul had earlier said. As to the second part, concerning "the man whom he hath appointed" (that is, Jesus), and the fact that God raised Jesus from the dead, here is what Acts reports as the reaction of the listeners: "And when they had heard of the resurrection of the dead, some indeed mocked. But others said: we will hear thee again on this matter" (Acts 17:32).[16]

About this latter passage one notes first that it is hard for people to believe that a dead person can be raised, bodily, back to life. Next, one observes a slight slippage in language. Paul, in his speech, says that God "raised him" – meaning Jesus – "up from the dead." But then in the very next sentence (which was mocked), the phrase is "the resurrection of the dead." Here as elsewhere, there is something worth remarking about the differences between the Greek version and the Latin translation. In Greek, the mocking listeners hear about the *anastasin nekrôn*, with the first word meaning "resurrection" and the second word meaning one of two things: "of the dead" or "from the dead." The word, *nekrôn*, is in what grammarians call the "genitive case," meaning that its ending is modified in such a way that the single word itself carries a meaning that, in English, we would need to express with one of two prepositions: either "of" or "from." In Latin however, the listeners hear of *resurrectionem mortuorum*. The first word, again, means "resurrection." But the second, also in the genitive plural, is less ambiguous than the Greek: in Latin it means "of the dead." Accordingly, in the Greek original you could read the sentence as indicating a "resurrection from [the company of] the dead," so that the statement might be referring to the case of Jesus alone: a one-off event, in which God raised *Jesus* from the dead, with no implication that this operation (raising a living person from the dead back into life) was in any way a normal state of affairs. The Latin phraseology, however, leaves open the idea that the "resurrection of the dead" could be made more general.

What then were the listeners mocking? Was it the idea that God had raised Jesus from the dead? Or was something deeper? Was Paul implying instead that there would come a time when everyone would be raised from the dead, their bodies somehow restored in defiance of all rationality, a miraculous moment that would mark a final time of judgment, to be

---

[16] On this passage, see N. Clayton Croy, "Hellenistic Philosophies and the Preaching of the Resurrection (Acts 17:18, 32)," *Novum Testamentum* 39 (1997), 21–39.

decided by God alone, adumbrated by his human voices, his "vessels," such as was Paul? This notion of the resurrection of the dead became part of Christianity, an important strand in its intricately woven texture. Here, we see how much these brief, humbly elegant words of the New Testament could be subject to almost endless interpretation over time.

Moreover, the same passage notes that not all listeners mocked the Apostle Paul, that there was a group who said they would "hear him again concerning this matter."[17] The author of Acts wants us to know that Paul was making headway, even in Athens, even in the very heart of ancient paganism. Indeed, the second important moment occurs directly following: "But certain men adhered to him and believed, among whom was also Dionysius the Areopagite and a woman named Damaris and others with them" (Acts 17:34). We have two names. There is Dionysius the Areopagite, one of the first Gentile converts to Christianity. The attribute, "the Areopagite," signifies that he was an habitué of the Areopagus, that part of Athens where trials had been held. Some five centuries later, a body of work emerged that fused together several ancient (largely Platonic) philosophical ideas with Christian notions. Though its origin was late, it was nonetheless attributed to Dionysius the Areopagite – this Dionysius, that is, the one in Acts, symbolically (if inaccurately) merging ancient Platonism with this dramatic moment of Paul's mission to the Gentiles. Then, of course, there is Damaris. She is only a name, mentioned only here and with no other identifying information. There have been countless hypotheses about who she might have been. For our purposes, what is important is that she was a woman, welcomed as all would be who believed, into Paul's evolving Christian community.

Acts chronicles much of the early Jesus movement's experiences, and in doing so it gives us an important window into Paul's work. Three of Paul's letters offer another lens through which we can view his activities and ideas.

First, from the perspective of Christian inclusivity, there is his letter to the Galatians, written between 48 and 55 CE, and directed to the community in Galatia, today a part of Turkey. Collectively, Paul's letters offer insight into the nature of his mission. In them, he tells the story of his own life and conversion; he reminds the various communities (often ones he has already visited) of the gospel and the need to set old ways aside and to embrace the new; he cajoles, corrects, lectures, and persuades, all toward the end of keeping already existing but still precarious local churches within the faith.

---

[17] Likely the Stoic listeners; see Croy, "Hellenistic Philosophies" for discussion.

The letter to the Galatians is no exception. After some autobiography, reminding them of his former life as a persecutor of Christians and conversion to a life of Christian evangelism, Paul moves to a discussion about the "law," meaning traditional Jewish law. He stresses that, in its time and context, the law was necessary: "It was set because of transgressions, until the seed came down ..." the "seed" being Jesus. The Law had served as a useful discipline, a way of keeping errant behaviors in check, of regulating society. And yet, the Law was also a kind of barrier: "But before the faith came, we were kept under the law shut up, unto that faith which was to be revealed" (Gal 3:23). In other words, the whole time under which communities lived under the Law, they were in some respects students needing that sort of discipline: "Wherefore the law was our pedagogue in Christ: that we might be justified by faith. But after the faith is come, we are no longer under a pedagogue" (Gal 3:24–25). The old teacher has departed, and a new one has come in its place: "For you are all the children of God, by faith in Jesus Christ" (Gal 3:26). If you accept the faith and accept baptism in Christ, you have become a member of the community. That is all you need.

And then, in a statement that is remarkable given the time and place of its utterance, Paul says: "There is neither Jew nor Greek; there is neither bond nor free; there is neither male nor female, for you are all one in Jesus Christ" (Gal 3:28). What Paul offers here is a radical equality of all persons. It is striking for at least three reasons. First, it would be difficult to imagine just how far-removed Paul's society was from that of most readers of this book. It was tribal, intensely so, and not in the way people talk today about the "tribalism" of politics. No, this was the real thing, the kind of world wherein, if you were somehow catapulted into this or that group of people whom you hitherto hadn't known, you had better make friends quickly, because there was no presumption of universal human rights. Second, the presumption of gender equality in Paul's statement is equally meaningful. Men and women were seen to have different roles and different relations to the public world of governance and politics. Here, Paul is positing a new realm in which those two differentiations of tribe and gender had less weight, in an idealized sense. Finally, it is worth looking toward the future when considering Paul's statement. He says, of course, that this equality he is promising is available to all who believe. One could argue that he is simply exchanging one tribe for another. But the truth is that what he says here remained part of the DNA of western culture. By the time of the European Enlightenment, the notion that all people are inherently equal, precisely because they are people, began finally to be woven into systems of law. It was and still is a startlingly imperfect project, as the existence of enslavement and the lack of female suffrage well into modern times demonstrate. In the United States of America, a country notionally founded on the idea that all people are equal, the extent of health, economic, and other disparities suffered by African Americans – in the long wake of the crime against humanity that was enslavement and the generational disadvantages that ensued – is so great as to make many cynical about the very idea.

But it is an idea that is also an ideal, an aspiration that, wedded to religion as it is here, with more concomitant emotional resonance than any legal system could ever have, was destined to grow: Every person, great or small, rich or poor, citizen or non-citizen shares in being human and as such possesses certain rights. This notion was far from being fully realized in Paul's day and, again, he suggests that it is available only to those who believe in Christ. But it is there nonetheless and worthy of note. Ideas have a way of migrating. They are written down once, in a certain context with their author's often unknowable inner intention as their core, but then they are subject to reinterpretation through rewriting and rethinking. That core idea – that all people are equal in principle – was powerful. Once it became available to many through Christianity, it had the freedom to evolve, to become secularized, to migrate out of the realm of religion and into that of politics, touching on conceptions of human rights, freedom of worship, and other topics, all of them milestones along a never-ending road to a more just society.[18]

If Galatians presents this notion of radical equality of all persons under God, Paul's Letter to the Romans offers a view of the nature of God. Again, the idea here lasted, was subject to endless reinterpretation, and represented a source of anxiety as well as hope. The Letter to the Romans is the first of Paul's letters in the canonical ordering of the New Testament (though scholars believe it was written later in his ministry). Its basic message is that salvation for human beings comes through their faith in Jesus Christ. But at its core there is a recognition that conceiving of God – one God, supreme above all – entails certain assumptions about just what, precisely, it means to be supreme, first, best. Paul does not articulate the problem in that way. Instead, he reaches back into Old Testament examples, stories with which many of his listeners would have been familiar, and which had some harsh messages embedded within them. The first is a passage from the Book of Malachi, the last of the Old Testament's prophetic books. It was a book of

---

[18] Cf. Larry Siedentop, *Inventing the Individual: The Origins of Western Liberalism* (Cambridge, MA: Harvard University Press, 2014); and Robert Louis Wilken, *Liberty in the Things of God: The Christian Origins of Religious Freedom* (New Haven: Yale University Press, 2019).

correction, one in which the unnamed prophet ("Malachi" means "my messenger" or "my angel" in Hebrew) was offering "tough love" to the Israelites in Jerusalem, wanting them to discipline themselves and correct their seemingly lax religiosity. One of its themes is God's justice, which can seem harsh and explicit but that – in the context of Malachi – highlights that God had favored the Israelites (the sons of Jacob) and not their neighbors, the people of Edom (the sons of Esau). Hence there occurs this line, spoken by the Lord through Malachi: "Jacob have I loved and Esau have I hated" (Mal 1:3). It is a line Paul quotes in full in his Letter to the Romans. The context is only somewhat similar, in that it is a moment when Paul the Apostle is urging the Romans to continue in their new faith.

The letter, accordingly, is a statement of faith and theology. Part of theology concerns the nature of God; and in this version, God makes choices. Earlier in the letter, Paul said that the individual Christian is saved by faith in Christ. Here, he is explaining God's sometimes inexplicable choices, repeating that quotation about Jacob and Esau, whereafter he writes: "what shall we say then? Is there injustice with God? God forbid" (Rom 9:14). Paul again echoes the Old Testament (in this case the Book of Exodus): "For he saith to Moses: I will have mercy on whom I will have mercy" (Rom 9:15, referring to Exod 33:19). In Exodus, Moses was in direct dialogue with God, who had indicated His favor toward Moses and his people, urging them to leave Egypt. For Paul, this quotation serves to highlight his conception of God, a conception that grows ever clearer as he moves on: "So then it is not of him that willeth nor of him that runneth but of God that sheweth mercy" (Rom 9:16). In other terms, God will choose whom to save, whom to exalt, whom to support. The things we do as individuals, like make choices ("will" things) or act in the world ("run" around, doing things in our everyday interactions) have no impact.

Paul offers another metaphor, a powerful and startling one. He begins by voicing a possible objection, in dialogue with a potential listener to his message: "Thou wilt therefore say to me, 'Why doth he then find fault? For who resisteth his will?'" (Rom 9:19). In other words, here I am believing in God, doing what I believe I am asked to do. Why would God find fault with me? To this query Paul says: "O man, who art thou that repliest against God? Shall the thing formed say to him that formed it, 'Why hast thou made me thus?' Or hath not the potter power over the clay of the same lump to make one vessel unto honor and another unto dishonor?" (Rom 9:21). In contrast to the language of Galatians, which can almost seem to adumbrate modern egalitarian human rights theories, here, instead, Paul's vision is stark, merciless, and lonely. The metaphor is that of a potter and clay. God is the potter, we are the clay. And though we are made from the same "lump," meaning the same basic matter, God will choose for reasons known only to him to save some, and damn others: to make of some people "vessels unto honor" and of others "unto dishonor." It is not really our place to know why this is so. It simply is, Paul suggests, existing as a kind of design feature of God. Paul does not put it this way, but his conception is linked to what we might call radical monotheism. If, that is, we can "think" a supreme being, that same being must, by virtue of being supreme, be in some ways fundamentally unlike us, better to such a degree that there will be a large and (in some fashion) unbridgeable gulf between us and it.

There were, then, these two polarities available early on in Christianity. First, a God filled with so much love directed at us, as human beings, that he took the form of one of us, embodied himself in a mystical way in his son, Jesus, and allowed Himself/His Son to be sacrificed for our redemption, to take on the weight of all of our sin – His cross being ever thereafter a symbol of burden, of sacrifice, of deliverance. This God is a personal God, filled with love, for every individual rich or poor, great or small, a God whose immense power is available to all equally, provided only that they believe.

Second, however, there is that other side of the divine calculus that recognizes the mental operation involved: projecting a unitary absolute into logical space and dealing with the consequences of that projection. This is a God whose ultimate intentions and reasons you can never really know, whose plan can only be hinted at, deduced from the flow of history and, more, from His attributes. For in addition to being omnipotent (able to do anything, with no limits), He is also omniscient, able to know everything there is to know, including your every action. In this latter respect He can see the past, the present, and the future, all as if it were an eternal present. Then, finally, He must also be good. His goodness is an inherent quality, an unquestioned part of God and, of course, the explanation as to why bad things sometimes happen to good people: It is part of God's plan, unknowable to us but part of the goodness that God progressively reveals to and through the world.

Paul's first Letter to the Corinthians can help us understand this mix: on the one hand, a God who can seem remote and inexplicable ("Jacob have I loved, Esau have I hated"), on the other, a God who is present for each and every individual, manifesting something unusual in the premodern world – a sympathy that crossed race ("neither Jew nor Greek"), class ("neither bond nor free"), and gender ("neither male nor female"). Biblical scholars believe that Paul likely wrote up to four letters to the Corinthians and that what we possess (the "first" and "second") letters represent a merging together of those multiple letters into two.

The first letter proved crucially important over time. Two key concepts emerge with power, if not always with complete clarity, owing to their mystical nature. The first is what in the Greek is termed *agapê* in the Latin Vulgate (the version known to the western European Middle Ages) as *caritas*, and in older English translations as "charity." It is often translated today as "love." Paul signals its importance when he writes: "If I speak with the tongues of men and of angels, and have not charity, I am become as sounding brass, or a tinkling cymbal" (1 Cor 13:1). Here we see the distinction between the outer person, who may be eloquent in public, as he or she appears in society, and the inner person, whose existence will be hollow if what he or she does is not animated by "charity."

For Paul, charity is in one respect divine, serving as a way for human beings to take the lessons of Christ's humility and manifest them in their own lives. But it is also very human and ethical in the basic Aristotelian sense: It takes effort and repeated practice to bring to fruition. It is worth taking a deeper look at Paul's language.

After the warning about being only a "tinkling cymbal" without charity, he makes two more statements noting that traditional markers of religiosity will not be enough: "And if I should have prophecy and should know all mysteries and all knowledge and if I should have all faith, so that I could remove mountains, and have not charity, I am nothing" (1 Cor 13:2). "Prophecies," "mysteries," and "knowledge": Paul is saying that the traditional attributes of a priestly class would not be enough to ensure righteousness without charity, thus emphasizing in a different key, themes that Jesus, with his frequent criticism of the "scribes" and "Pharisees," had set in motion. Paul goes on: "And if I should distribute all my goods to feed the poor and if I should deliver my body to be burned, and have not charity, it profiteth me nothing" (1 Cor 13:3).[19] Again, public acts, whether they are acts of alms, like giving money or food to the needy, or acts of spectacle, like martyrdom, will also not be enough without charity.

---

[19] The phrase "deliver my body to be burned" (*tradidero corpus meum ita ut ardeam*) follows the Vulgate and the majority reading in the Latin tradition (and accordingly the one that most medieval western readers encountered). Certain Greek manuscripts, however, read *hina kauchēsōmai* ("that I may boast"), a variant most modern critical editions prefer. Both readings convey an act of extreme self-surrender – whether martyrdom (to be burned) or ascetic heroism (boasting in one's sacrifice). Yet, Paul insists that even such acts, without charity (*agapē*), "profit nothing." See Bruce M. Metzger, *A Textual Commentary on the Greek New Testament*, 3rd ed. (Stuttgart: Deutsche Bibelgesellschaft, 1975), pp. 563–564; Nestle-Aland, *Novum Testamentum Graece*, 28th ed. (Stuttgart: Deutsche Bibelgesellschaft, 2012), apparatus at 1 Cor 13:3; Gordon D. Fee, *The First Epistle to the Corinthians*, rev. ed. (Grand Rapids: Eerdmans, 2014), pp. 696–701.

What then is this virtue of charity? Paul tells us, in a passage known from countless weddings. In doing so, he leads into some of the most meaningful lines of his oeuvre:

> Charity is patient, is kind. Charity envieth not, dealeth not perversely, is not puffed up, is not ambitious, seeketh not her own, is not provoked to anger, thinketh no evil, rejoiceth not in iniquity, but rejoiceth with the truth, beareth all things, believeth all things, hopeth all things, endureth all things. (1 Cor 13:4–8)

"Charity," or "love," is a virtue that is other-directed. Having it will make you cultivate the inner strength to resist common temptations, such as the temptation to envy others for what they have and you do not; to "dealing perversely," meaning taking unfair advantage over someone else; to excessive pride, so that you are not "puffed up"; to destructive ambition. Cultivating charity will allow you to avoid anger, thinking ill of others. It is, in short, "patient and kind," and it gives you the ability to endure.

In one sense, then, charity is highly personal, like Aristotle's basic and intuitive point regarding virtues. We all have capacities, but developing them in full takes education, self-discipline, and training. For Paul, charity is distinct from "hope" and "faith," both of which are virtues of their own. But it is charity that ties the virtues together because something deeper lies within it. Paul goes on: "Charity never falleth away, whether prophecies shall be made void or tongues shall cease or knowledge shall be destroyed" (1 Cor 13:8). One sees that there is a mystery at the heart of charity.

It is in one respect very personal and human, allowing people who have it to live with each other in peace. In his *Nicomachean Ethics*, Aristotle had said that *politikê* – "politics" and the study and practice thereof – was the most "authoritative" *epistêmê* ("science" or "branch of knowledge").[20] The reason was that, "to secure the good of one person only is better than nothing; but to secure the good of a nation or a state is a nobler and more divine achievement."[21] The study of the virtues in Aristotle's *Ethics*, geared in the first instance toward the development of the individual, was also directed toward the betterment of society at large. Individual flourishing would serve as the innermost concentric circle, radiating outward to society, to the *polis* at large. The *polis*, or "state" – its stability, its flourishing, and its ultimate

---

[20] Aristotle, *Nicomachean Ethics*, ed. and tr. Horace Rackham (Cambridge, MA: Harvard University Press, 1934), 1.2.1094a–b (pp. 4–5).

[21] Ibid., 1.2.1094b (p. 7).

harmony — served as the highest object of moral philosophy. Make people good, and the state will become good.

Paul's charity is to some extent like this. But in another respect, it is quite different. It represents a perdurable quality that will endure even when important "prophecies" are proven invalid by events, even when there are no people left with whom to interact in conversation ("when tongues shall cease"), and even when all the "knowledge" we may have built up passes away.

As to the end of the world, Paul begins to hint at it, mixing the fate of the individual with the hoped-for evolution of society: "For we know in part, and we prophesy in part. But when that which is perfect is come, that which is in part shall be done away" (1 Cor 13:9–10). Paul has suggested a teleology, a process of development wherein things are moving toward a final point. If in our current situation we "know in part," there will nonetheless come a time when "that which is perfect" will have arrived. And we should not be deceived by the English word "perfect." In Latin it is *perfectum* and in the original Greek, *teleion*. Both imply "completion," meaning that God has set a process in motion, one whose constituent parts are moving toward a goal but a goal that, importantly, we cannot see fully and clearly from our current vantage point.

The process is progress toward a goal. The metaphor is one of growth: "when I was a child, I spoke as a child, I thought as a child. But when I became a man, I put away the things of a child" (1 Cor 13:11). Paul speaks about himself in a way that makes him a stand-in for humanity at large, provided people take up the new faith. Things on which we used to focus will seem small, childish. What is to come, something we shall discover only after it matures, will be much greater, self-evident in its importance, and superior to anything we can imagine here on earth. We will encounter the face of God, that very same God who encodes in his mysterious being absolute, far-away Oneness and unifies it to each of us through love, a love that we are called upon to imitate in our own conduct.[22] As to the face of God: "For now we see through a glass, darkly, but then, face to face. Now I know in part. But then shall I know even as I am known" (1 Cor 13:12). This magnificent passage, reaching back as it does to Platonic themes and forward to our ever-evolving struggle with our human identity, deserves to be understood in full.

---

[22] Cf. how God is described in Exodus (33:20); although God spoke to Moses in a familiar fashion, He also told him: "Thou canst not see my face, for man shall not see me and live."

There are two key terms, "glass" and "darkly." As to "glass," the word in Greek is *esoptron*, which appears in the Latin Vulgate as *speculum*. Both words mean something like our modern term "mirror" or the less modern "looking glass." The "glass" of which Paul speaks shows us a reflection of a reality, rather than the reality itself (in Paul's day these "glasses" or mirrors were usually made of polished metal, contributing to the lack of clarity Paul is emphasizing). If there is one moment in the New Testament that serves as a vector for Platonic thinking entering the fabric of Christianity, this is it. Paul's sentiment reminds a reader of the *Republic*'s "cave" analogy, where the cave's inhabitants see only shadows of a bigger, better, brighter reality that for most of them exists outside their ken. But in terms of consequences and range, Paul's version was much more powerful, since it eventually reached millions upon millions of people in a way that Plato only rarely could: through the repetitive, ritualistic means of religion, a realm in which faith – binding, often unarticulated, emotional – holds more sway than either reasoned argument or fanciful myth.

Then there is the term "darkly," an adverbial rendering of two words: *en ainigmate* in Greek, and *in aenigmate* in Latin. At the root there is the word *aenigma*, or "enigma" in the most literal English rendering. One of the word's meanings, in both Greek and Latin, is "riddle": it encodes the possibility of trickery, of misplaced judgment, of being wrong about one's outward assumption. It also implies that you may need to work to figure out the riddle. It implies a state of uncertainty, a "darkness" that will lift only at some future time. As to what that time will be like, Paul says it will be a time when we see "face to face," which means that our face will see God's face. Paul says: "Now I know in part," meaning that, in his current, regular, very human life, he experiences a lack of completion. It is only "then" – at some future and undetermined time – when he will see face to face, that he will know "as he himself is known" (to paraphrase his first-person account), meaning that his eventual knowledge of God will be such as he has of himself, of his own existence. Writing in the first person as he does, Paul is nonetheless signaling to humanity that this is the fate people can and will have, should they choose to believe.

That notion of a future (but as of now unknown) time when things will become clearer remains a jewel with different facets. It is a commanding conception precisely because one can read so much into it. Jesus himself had foretold a future time of judgment, of course. Paul adds to the hints in Jesus' words, solidifying and fostering this anticipatory longing with thoughts on the idea of resurrection, doing so in the same first Letter to the Corinthians. Paul reiterates certain tenets of the gospel in his ongoing effort to define and reinforce the beliefs of this new community: "For I delivered unto you first of all, which I also received, how that Christ died for our sins according to the scriptures and that he was buried and that he rose again the third day according to the scriptures and that he was seen by Cephas and after that by the eleven." (1 Cor 15:3–5). One recalls that in Acts, when Paul was in Athens and preaching to the Greeks, the idea of Christ coming back from the dead had occasioned disbelief. Some of Paul's listeners had scoffed at that part of the tale, while others said they were willing to hear more, even if they did not completely assent to the idea.

And it is indeed a striking idea: that someone, once dead, could rise again and be seen by people and indeed that those witnesses would believe the person truly to have risen. It is one thing to hear about these sorts of occurrences in literature. In the *Odyssey*, for instance, Odysseus tells of offering a blood sacrifice to the dead, whereafter they arose to speak with him about various matters germane to his voyages.[23] But the case of Christ is different. It really happened, so the belief went.

Then, in Paul's preaching, a second step occurs, one that makes matters even more difficult to understand: People at large will also at some point be resurrected after death. Paul continues recounting the witnessing of Christ's resurrection, telling that, after Cephas and the eleven apostles (those that remained of the twelve, after Judas was expelled from their number for his treachery), there were others too who had seen the risen Christ including, Paul says, he himself. With the rhetorical power of his own and others' witnessing of Christ, Paul then asserts that resurrection of the dead must exist, since there were so many who observed Christ: "but if there be no resurrection of the dead, then Christ is not risen again" (1 Cor 15:13). There is a logical elision here: Christ of course was divine. Why should there be resurrection for those who are not divine, for those, in short, like us? Paul says: "And if Christ be not risen again, then is our preaching vain, and your faith is also vain." Even more, "Yea and we are found false witnesses of God, because we have given testimony against God that he hath raised up Christ, whom he hath not raised up if the dead rise not again." (1 Cor 15:14–15).

This new faith hinges on the idea of resurrection and on the link between Christ and humanity: "And if Christ be not risen again, your faith is vain, for you are yet in your sins." (1 Cor 15:16-17). What we learn is that humanity is incomplete, "still in its sins," meaning that human beings must await some future moment, when sins can be washed away and when, out of death, a

---

[23] Homer, *Odyssey*, 2 vols., ed. A. T. Murray and George E. Dimock (Cambridge, MA: Harvard University Press, 1998) bk. 11 (vol., 2, pp. 402–447).

new life will come. Paul explains rapturously: "But now Christ is risen from the dead, the firstfruits of them that sleep." (1 Cor 15:20). The "firstfruits." This charming term has resonances of farming and of premodern religious ritual, signifying the first produce of the year's harvest. In ancient communities they were offered to a religious leader, who served as conduit between the farmer, grateful that his harvest was a success, and divinity, without whose blessing the enterprise could not have succeeded.[24] Christ, in this analogy, seems akin to an offering, one whose directionality was deliberately ambiguous: on the one hand, from God to humanity, as God sent his son to the world as a human being to serve as a redemptive sacrifice for humanity's sins; on the other, from humanity to divinity, as Christ, in death part of those who "sleep," will newly rise up, the most important member of what will eventually be a long line of the resurrected. There will be an ordering to the process. Moreover, a sequence of events will ensue that will lead to destruction. The questions are: Of whom? And of what? Here is what Paul says, beginning with the ordering:

> But every one in his own order: the firstfruits, Christ; then they that are of Christ, who have believed in his coming. Afterwards the end, when he shall have delivered up the kingdom to God and the father, when he shall have brought to nought all principality and power and virtue. (1 Cor 15:23–24)

The sequence, then, is this: Christ, resurrected once (and now in that capacity serving as proof that the resurrection of the dead is a real possibility), will come back yet again, this time in the capacity of judge and vindicator. He will deliver the "kingdom" (*basileia* in Greek, and *regnum*, in Latin) to God, doing so after having "brought to nought" (meaning, destroyed) every "principality" and "power" and "virtue." These last three words all signify earthly, human power. Even the last word, "virtue" in our translation, is in the Greek original *dynamis* (where we get our word "dynamic"), a word that means "power," "might," "motion," "bodily strength," and "authority."

What this means is that politics, as we know it, will end at some point. The implications are powerful. For those who embrace this teaching, symbols of political authority will have less ultimate meaning than they otherwise might have done. Looked at under this lens, rulers who seem all powerful will pale in comparison to the power of Christ. And in this long perspective, seemingly "eternal" kingdoms will seem little more than temporary castles of sand. Recall that Aristotle, at the outset of his *Nicomachean Ethics*, said that *politikē* – "politics" or "the science of politics" – was the

---

[24] The term appears numerous times in the Old Testament; see e.g., Lev 23:10.

highest and most important of the branches of learning. It is not that after Paul no one believed anymore in politics and in the need to be careful and intentional about governance. But this notion – that there is, beyond us, a superintending world that we cannot now see and that is immeasurably more powerful than we, a world into which we will all someday be incorporated in some mystical but real fashion – can serve as a powerful destabilizing factor for human communities. It can undermine the legitimacy of a state in often unanticipated ways. If the seeds were sown in Plato's depictions of the world of the Forms, they took root much more meaningfully when they became the foundation of Christian belief.

Added to this otherworldliness, in Paul's vision, was a propensity toward apocalyptic thinking, a sense that there would be a final moment when everything as we now know it would end and something else be revealed. In the narrative, after Christ has come again to judge the living and the dead, "then," Paul says, "the Son also himself shall be subject to him that put all things under him, that God may be all in all." If this sounds a bit mystical, that is because it is. God will be "all in all." Does this mean that God – at whatever remove – will subsume everything he originally created into himself? Will all things become God, in some way? Paul does not say. But after him, these sorts of questions arise repeatedly in western thinking, nowhere more so than in the work of Saint Augustine, as we shall see.

As to Paul, he hints at this mystical process even more strongly, as the Letter to the Corinthians proceeds. It is a passage worth quoting in full:

> Behold: I tell you a mystery. We shall not all sleep, but we shall all be changed, in a moment, in the twinkling of an eye, at the last trumpet. For the trumpet shall sound, and the dead shall rise again incorruptible, and we shall be changed. For this corruptible must put on incorruption, and this mortal must put on immortality. And when this mortal hath put on immortality, then shall come to pass the saying that is written: 'death is swallowed up in victory'. O death, where is thy victory? O death, where is thy sting?
> (1 Cor 15:51–55, echoing and incorporating Isa 25:8 and Hos 13:14)

This passage, so meaningful for the history of Christianity, embeds within it the many interconnected factors that come into play, whenever one considers reading, writing, and scripture.

First, there is the interpretation of the passage itself. Paul is saying that even death, so seemingly final and permanent, will be vanquished. After we die, at some point, "we shall be changed" and we shall "put on immortality." The immortal soul will put on an immortal body. In Paul's own apocalyptic frame of reference, the emphasis falls less on a philosophical argument for the soul's innate qualities than on God's power to transform human beings for eternal life. Later Christian readers, however, understood this vision in ways that drew upon both Platonic and Aristotelian currents. From Plato came the conviction that each soul is unique and destined for immortality – an idea that, once absorbed into Christian teaching, spread far more widely than it ever could have if it had remained confined to formal schools of philosophers. At the same time, Aristotle's "hylomorphic" conception of the human being as a composite of body and soul provided a powerful framework for explaining resurrection.[25]

Christianity rejected Plato's doctrines of the pre-existence and reincarnation of souls; instead, it taught that each person comes into being as a unity of body and soul, created by God in time. The doctrine of resurrection, which Paul here proclaims – "this mortal must put on immortality" – thus came to mean that the dead would rise to an embodied existence transformed for eternity, with the righteous rewarded and the wicked punished forever.[26]

Had we world enough and time, there would be more to say about the Apostle Paul, the "light of the Gentiles" and the "vessel of election." The influence his writing exerted stands out. To understand it, we must leap forward several centuries to the intellectual world of late antiquity. There is no better lens through which to view these developments than a North African intellectual, teacher, and brilliant, searing writer named Augustine.

---

[25] Hylomorphism points to the notion that a thing is not a thing unless it is composed of matter (*hylê* in Greek) and form (*morphê*); it is a concept with a long history. See David Charles, ed., *The History of Hylomorphism: From Aristotle to Descartes* (Oxford: Oxford University Press, 2023).

[26] See Caroline Walker Bynum, *The Resurrection of the Body in Western Christianity, 200–1336* (New York: Columbia University Press, 1995); and Fernando Vidal, "Brains, Bodies, Selves, and Science: Anthropologies of Identity and the Resurrection of the Body," *Critical Inquiry* 28 (2002), 930–974.

10

AUGUSTINE, PLATONISM, AND CONVERSION

AUGUSTINE, BORN IN 354 CE INTO A BERBER FAMILY OF relative means in what is now Algeria, came of age in a tumultuous time.[1] By the time he died in 430, he had authored numerous works, none more important than his *Confessions*, a monument in the autobiographical tradition. It served as a model of personal conversion for many later Christians, a defining moment in the interpretation of the Christian God, and an elucidation of the human will and the limits of personal agency.[2] He also penned a work titled the *City of God* (the subject of Chapter 11), whose influence was immense in the west, shaping views of providence, of the destiny of humanity, and of history throughout the Middle Ages. To understand these works in context, the evolution of Christianity, the power and role of Rome, and the history of later Platonism all need to be foregrounded.

As to Christianity, by Augustine's maturity, certain aspects of the still evolving religion were coming into focus, even as much would have seemed precarious in the moment.[3] For one thing, there was the New Testament, in which Christians reposed belief. It was during Augustine's adult years that the twenty-seven books comprising the New Testament – the four Gospels, the Acts of the Apostles, the Letters of Paul and others, and the Book of

---

[1] See Peter Brown, *Augustine of Hippo*, 45th anniversary ed. (Berkeley: University of California Press, 2000); James J. O'Donnell, *Augustine: A New Biography* (New York: Ecco, 2005).

[2] For its western medieval influence, see Brian Stock, *After Augustine: The Meditative Reader and the Text* (Philadelphia: University of Pennsylvania Press, 2001).

[3] See Peter Brown, *The Rise of Western Christendom: Triumph and Diversity, A.D. 200–1000*, 10th anniversary rev. ed. (London: Wiley-Blackwell, 2013), pp. 1–122; Judith Herrin, *The Formation of Christendom* (Princeton: Princeton University Press, 1987), pp. 3–89; Hartmut Leppin, *The Early Christians: From the Beginnings to Constantine*, tr. Kathrin Luddecke (Cambridge: Cambridge University Press, 2023).

Revelation – came to be accepted by Christian leaders as a canon of scripture. Canon-making had been happening since at least the second century CE.[4] And there was a complicated history in the late fourth century, with a now mostly lost letter by an Alexandrian bishop serving (per later reports) as the first document in which those books were listed.[5] But during the Pontificate of Innocent I (Pope from 401–417), the twenty-seven books emerged as canonical, with Innocent himself writing a letter (in response to a query) listing them as such.[6] It is a striking fact, however, that it was only then that the process was complete. Those leading thinkers in the Church, among whom were people like Augustine, could not have known definitively that the process of scriptural canonization was complete. Christianity seemed then like a religion that needed protection, buttressing, and support. The new, accepted canon left out several earlier and now noncanonical writings, including gospel-like accounts that painted different pictures of Christianity and of the figure of Jesus.[7] In one, for example, the "Infancy Gospel of Thomas," a young Jesus vengefully curses a young boy who had bumped against him, killing the boy and in the process demonstrating miraculous power.[8] As this and other seemingly unnecessary works of scripture were finally excluded from the canon, it was now time to solidify

---

[4] See Bruce M. Metzger, *The Canon of the New Testament: Its Origin, Development, and Significance* (Oxford: Clarendon, 1997); David Trobisch, *The First Edition of the New Testament* (Oxford: Oxford University Press, 2000).

[5] Athanasius, "Thirty-Ninth Festal Letter," in Périclès-Pierre Joannou, *Fonti. Discipline Générale antique (IVe–IXe s.)*, 2 vols. (Rome: Grottaferrata, 1963), 2: 71–76, for what remains of the Greek version. There were also Coptic versions. See David Brakke, *Athanasius and the Politics of Asceticism* (Oxford: Clarendon, 1995), pp. 326–332; and David Brakke, "A New Fragment of Athanasius's Thirty-Ninth *Festal Letter*: Heresy, Apocrypha, and the Canon," *Harvard Theological Review* 103 (2010), 47–66.

[6] See Innocent I, "Letter" in Brooke F. Westcott, *A General Survey of the History of the Canon of the New Testament*, 5th ed. (Cambridge: Macmillan, 1881), 570–571; Joseph Verheyden, "The New Testament Canon," in James C. Paget, Joachim Schaper, et al., eds., *The New Cambridge History of the Bible, Vol. 1: From the Beginnings to 600*, part of *The New Cambridge History of the Bible*, 4 vols. (Cambridge: Cambridge University Press, 2013–2015), 1: 389–411.

[7] See Bart D. Ehrman, ed., *Lost Scriptures: Books that Did Not Make It into the New Testament* (New York: Oxford University Press, 2003); Bart D. Ehrman, *Lost Christianities: The Battles for Scripture and the Faiths We Never Knew* (New York: Oxford University Press, 2003); J. K. Elliott, ed. and tr., *The Apocryphal New Testament* (Oxford: Clarendon, 1993); Maurice Geerard, ed., *Clavis apocryphorum Novi Testamenti* (Turnhout: Brepols, 1992).

[8] See Thomas, "The Infancy Gospel of Thomas," 4.1–2, in J. K. Elliott, ed. and tr., *The Apocryphal New Testament*, (Oxford: Clarendon, 1993), 68–84, at 76; and Christopher A. Frilingos, *Jesus, Mary, and Joseph: Family Trouble in the Infancy Gospels* (Philadelphia: University of Pennsylvania Press, 2017).

the narratives that remained, to comment on them, to use them for inspiration, and to draw out their often-hidden meanings.

Before Augustine, Christianity developed a noteworthy relationship to philosophy.[9] In early Christian iconography, Jesus was sometimes depicted wearing the *pallium*, a cloak that served to denote a few things: first, that the wearer was a philosopher or other sort of intellectual; second, that the wearer had ties to the ancient Greek philosophical tradition; and third – especially important in the Roman context – that the wearer was *not* part of a suite of traditionally Roman identities and that he was setting himself apart.[10]

What does all this mean? In the first instance: Some of Jesus' early followers considered him a philosopher, seeing him as wise and as modeling a style of life that could be imitated. The early Christian era was no exception to the rule that different intellectual movements are often in competition with one another. So, for those early Christians who had an intellectual bent, associating Jesus (and themselves) with the traditional symbol of the philosophical life was a powerful signifier. For some, Christianity was becoming the "true philosophy" and Christians the "true philosophers."[11]

The Greek tradition in philosophy represented a rich symbolic field. No one could deny the centrality of Plato, Aristotle, and the other luminaries who had a shaping effect on philosophy. And yet, the word philosophy could sometimes be used in reproach, signifying spiritual barrenness, prideful

---

[9] See the studies in Mark Edwards, ed., *The Routledge Handbook of Early Christian Philosophy* (London: Routledge, 2021).

[10] See Corey Brennan, "Tertullian's *De pallio* and Roman Dress in North Africa," in Jonathan Edmondson and Alison Mary Keith, eds., *Roman Dress and the Fabrics of Roman Culture* (Toronto: University of Toronto Press, 2008), 257–270; Robin M. Jensen, "Visual Representations of Early Christian Teachers and of Christ as the True Philosopher," in H. Gregory Snyder., ed., *Christian Teachers in Second-Century Rome: Schools and Students in the Ancient City* (Leiden: Brill, 2020), 60–83; Michael Koortbojian, "The Double Identity of Roman Portrait Statues: Costumes and Their Symbolism at Rome," in Edmondson and Keith, *Roman Dress and the Fabrics,* 71–93; (Sister) Charles Murray, *Rebirth and Afterlife: A Study of the Transmutation of Some Pagan Imagery in Early Christian Art* (Oxford: British Archaeological Reports, 1981); Arthur Urbano, "'Dressing a Christian': The Philosopher's Mantle as Signifier of Pedagogical and Moral Authority," in *Studia patristica* 62 (2013), 213–229; Paul Zanker, *The Mask of Socrates: The Image of the Intellectual in Antiquity* (Berkeley: University of California Press, 1995), 289–307.

[11] Leppin, *The Early Christians,* 149–162; cf. Tertullian, writing around the year 210, *De pallio,* ed. and tr. Vincent Hunink (Amsterdam: Gieben, 2005), 6.2 (pp. 62–63): "Gaude, pallium, et exsulta! Melior iam te philosophia dignata est ex quo Christianum vestire coepisti." "Rejoice, pallium, and exult! A better philosophy has deigned you worthy, from the very moment you began dressing Christians." Tr. altered.

overinflation of self, and too much trust in the power of words at the expense of deeper truths. Paul had written (Col 2:8): "Beware lest any man cheat you by philosophy and vain deceit; according to the tradition of men, according to elements of the world, and not according to Christ." Some Christians would later dissociate themselves from philosophy and pagan thinking. The early Christian thinker Tertullian wrote, famously: "What has Athens to do with Jerusalem? What does the Academy have to do with the Church?"[12] He went on to say that Christians had no need to seek knowledge beyond Christ, no need to study anything beyond the Gospels.[13] These basic questions – How did Christianity and Christian thinking relate to different forms of ancient pagan thinking? What texts should one prioritize? – remained potent throughout late antiquity and beyond.

Yet, like Plato arguing against the sophists, Paul was emphasizing that those who claim for themselves the title of "wise" might not be so in reality. What seems like Christian foolishness, he writes elsewhere, is true wisdom (1 Cor 22–25). Christians taking upon themselves the mantle of the "true philosophers" meant that they were respecting those Pauline injunctions. It also meant that they believed Christianity could be understood as a way of life buttressed by certain beliefs and intellectual habits. In the late second century CE, for example, Melito, the Bishop of Sardis (in western Turkey today), wrote to none other than the Roman emperor and Stoic philosopher, Marcus Aurelius. Melito justified and urged Marcus to protect Christianity, or as Melito called it, "our philosophy," which emerged and flourished during the time of Augustus and thus became a good omen for the Roman Empire – "for from that time the power of the Romans became great and splendid."[14]

Marcus Aurelius, as noted, was a Stoic. The evolution of Stoicism, especially in the person of the notable Roman and contemporary of Saint Paul, Seneca, calls out for comment. Lactantius (250–325 CE, and one of Augustine's predecessors) believed that Seneca "could have become a true

---

[12] Tertullian, *De praescriptione hereticorum*, ed. Pierre de Labriolle and François Refoulé (Paris: Editions du Cerf, 1957), 7.9, pp. 16–18.

[13] Ibid., 7, l.37: "Nobis curiositate opus non est post christum iesum nec inquisitione post euangelium."

[14] Melito's work is lost but is quoted in Eusebius, *Ecclesiastical History*, 2 vols., ed. and tr. Kirsopp Lake (Cambridge, MA: Harvard University Press, 1926), 4.26 (vol. 2, pp. 386–393, at 388–389); see also Robert M. Grant, "Five Apologists and Marcus Aurelius," *Vigiliae Christianae* 42 (1988), 1–17, at 5–7.

worshipper of god, if only someone had shown God to him."[15] And one of Augustine's contemporaries, Saint Jerome, considered Seneca a Christian and believed in the authenticity of what we now know to be an apocryphal correspondence between Seneca and Saint Paul.[16]

Why did some Christians consider Seneca an ally? Seneca spoke of a unitary "God" as the "mind of the universe," and as one whose "magnitude is so great that nothing greater could be thought."[17] Like other Stoics he emphasized the value of the individual as self-sufficient, provided one cultivated the virtues correctly, a quality that resonated in the early Christian centuries as the Pauline propensity to see all human beings as equal in dignity and worth took hold. Seneca said things like *libera te primum metu mortis* – "first of all, free yourself from fear of death."[18] As early Christians came to see death as a portal to a new and better life (and as martyrs in the early Christian centuries came to seem heroes for defying the Roman authorities), sentiments like these resonated. And then, of course, there was the fact that, like Socrates, Seneca had gone to an unjust death willingly, forced as he was to commit suicide after he fell out with the emperor Nero, whom Seneca had faithfully served. He was, in short, another pagan who, though not a Christian, underwent the sort of sacrifice that Christ had exemplified perfectly, and who practiced what he preached, manifesting in his actions a style of life that could only be thought of as philosophical – a style lived by one ever in search of wisdom.

Philosophy was about finding the right, wise style of life. As the narrative of Christ's life and works grew in power and reach, his example served these ends. If, to be part of that project, one had to set oneself apart from evolving Roman traditions – as the *pallium* symbolically did – so be it. Adopting the philosophical mantle was a statement that Christianity had entered the disputatious, capacious, vigorously contested philosophical arena. Centuries of these sorts of interactions were behind Augustine as he came to maturity.

---

[15] Lactantius, *Divinae institutions*, 6.24.14: "[Seneca] potuit esse verus dei cultor." See Matthias Lahrmann, "Seneca the Philosopher," in Andreas Heil and Gregor Damschen, eds., *Brill's Companion to Seneca* (Leiden: Brill, 2013), 53–71, at 54.

[16] See Alfons Fürst, "*Epistulae Senecae ad Paulum et Pauli ad Senecam*," in Heil and Damschen, *Brill's Companion to Seneca*, 213–214.

[17] Seneca, *Natural Questions*, 7 books in 2 vols., ed. and tr. Thomas H. Corcoran (Cambridge, MA: Harvard University Press, 1971), 1.preface.13 (vol. 1, p. 10): "Quid est deus? Mens universi ... Sic demum magnitudo illi sua redditur, qua nihil maius cogitari potest, si solus est omnia, si opus suum et intra et extra tenet."

[18] Seneca, *Epistles*, 3 vols., ed. and tr. Richard M. Gummere (Cambridge, MA: Harvard University Press, 1917), Epistle 80, sec. 5 (vol. 2, p. 214).

As to Rome, different trajectories coalesced by Augustine's era. There were moments of history and, eventually, historical memory that came to signal power, weakness, and a promise yet to come. For one thing, there was the close association of Emperor Constantine – who ruled 306–337 CE – to Christianity.[19] As one might expect, this association had about it some legendary aspects, even as the reality was sometimes more prosaic.[20] As to legend, one of Augustine's patristic predecessors, Lactantius, told that on the night before one of Constantine's most important battles (that of the Milvian Bridge, in 312), he was advised in a dream to put the Greek letters "Chi" and "Rho" (the letters that begin the name of "Christ") on the shields of his men.[21] Another ancient Christian author, Eusebius, wrote that Constantine, upon marching into battle, saw a cross in the sky and the words, "with this sign, conquer."[22] Constantine's victory in battle solidified his belief in the power of Christianity. There were other accounts about his relationship to Christianity, two of which deserve mention: first, in 313, he and a co-ruler (the empire was divided) guaranteed freedom of worship to Christians and restored to them property seized by a previous ruler.[23] This official recognition of Christianity's legitimacy was meaningful, attaching itself as it did to the memory of Constantine thereafter. Second, he himself was reported to have converted to the new religion and been baptized on his deathbed.[24] Thereafter, in cultural memory, Constantine was tagged as "the first Christian Roman Emperor" and one who, to boot, buttressed Rome's status as a center of official Christianity.

It shouldn't surprise a reader that Constantine's engagement with Christianity was shaped by his social position – as a military leader, a savvy politician, and a person of his place and time. One of late antiquity's most eminent interpreters, Peter Brown, has written that "Constantine's 'conversion' was a very 'Roman' conversion. Worship of the Christian God had brought prosperity on himself and would being prosperity upon the Empire."[25] Constantine's embrace of Christianity, which unfolded in phases

---

[19] See Peter Heather, *Christendom: The Triumph of a Religion, AD 300–1300* (New York: Knopf, 2023), pp. 3–59.
[20] See Richard M. Price, "*In hoc signo vinces*: The Original Context of the Vision of Constantine," *Studies in Church History* 41 (2005), 1–10.
[21] Lactantius, *De mortibus persecutorum*, ed. and tr. J. L. Creed (Oxford: Clarendon, 1984), sec. 44 (pp. 62–63).
[22] Eusebius, *Life of Constantine*, tr. with introduction and commentary by Averil Cameron and Stuart G. Hall (Oxford: Clarendon, 1999), secs. 28–32 (pp. 80–82).
[23] Lactantius, *De mortibus persecutorum*, sec. 48 (pp. 68–73).
[24] Eusebius, *Life of Constantine*, secs. 61–62 (pp. 177–178).
[25] Brown, *The Rise of Western Christendom*, 61.

throughout his life, did not follow the Pauline model, familiar from the Acts of the Apostles where, as we have seen, Paul experienced a sudden, emotionally powerful moment on the way to Damascus – as if a switch had been flipped: One minute he was a skeptical persecutor of Christians, the next, he became one of Christianity's most ardent defenders, eloquent leaders, and effective shapers of belief. Constantine – the real, historical Constantine – followed a pattern unsurprising, given his political position and his situation as a Roman political actor immersed in Roman religious beliefs: If a new god served you and your state better, then that was the god to be preferred. But Constantine, as a powerful leader and as the specifically Roman Emperor, carried great symbolic weight for the subsequent Christian centuries.

The association of Rome with Christianity was complicated from the beginning. Paul had written his Letter to the Romans, Paul and the apostle Peter were believed martyred there, and Rome along with several other Mediterranean cities had early been a center of Christian practice. But Rome was always more than one among the many cities where this minority religion took root. It was a symbol – of politics, of conquest, and of empire – whose powerful political associations could not help but attach themselves to any mention of its name.[26] Even when the official seat of the empire was elsewhere (as it was at times — in Ravenna, in Milan, and Byzantium), the idea of power and empire was always linked to the city and its centuries-long legacy of political power. When Constantine allied himself to Christianity, with one of the key moments in his eventual embrace of Christ occurring in a battle at Rome, that symbolism mattered. It also held significance when a later emperor, Julian, decided to apostatize even though he had been raised a Christian.[27] He turned away from Christianity and, in the belief that the empire was losing power because it had lost its character, attempted to restore that character by reviving ancient pagan Roman religious practices. Along the way he suppressed and persecuted Christians. His rule as emperor lasted from 360–363. His imperial successors restored Christianity, with one of them, Theodosius I, fully embracing Christianity as defined in the Council of Nicaea (which Constantine had convened in 325) as the state

---

[26] See Claudia Bolgia, Rosamond McKitterick, and John Osborne, eds., *Rome across Time and Space: Cultural Transmission and the Exchange of Ideas, c.500–1400* (Cambridge: Cambridge University Press, 2011); Richard Jenkyns, ed., *The Legacy of Rome: A New Appraisal* (Oxford: Oxford University Press, 1992); Kenneth J. Pratt, "Rome as Eternal," *Journal of the History of Ideas* 26 (1965), 25–44.

[27] See Polymnia Athanassiadi, *Julian: An Intellectual Biography* (London: Routledge, 1981); Glenn W. Bowersock, *Julian the Apostate* (London: Duckworth, 1978); Stefan Rebenich and Hans-Ulrich Wiemer, eds., *A Companion to Julian the Apostate* (Leiden: Brill, 2020).

religion of the empire.[28] Theodosius ruled from 379–395 (379–394 as eastern emperor, 394–395 as sole emperor), during some of the key years in the life of Augustine, who, born in 354, came to maturity as this powerful and (by then) unusually long-lasting emperor linked the Christian faith to Rome.

Then there was Rome and its territories as a site of political power. At its height, Rome's dominion went north as far as England, stretched west to Spain, eastward to Syria and Mesopotamia and south across the Mediterranean to North Africa and Egypt. The Romans had expanded their power with care and intention, carrots and sticks, often offering benefits of citizenship to conquered peoples, even as they could be ruthless in suppressing revolt and dissent. Though there had been fall-off in Augustine's era, Rome – the symbolic idea of it – stood for empire, for aspirational power, and for military strength.

However, by Augustine's day the actual empire was under stress, the edges of its borders fraying. The process culminated in the first decade of the fifth century, when a Germanic tribe, the Visigoths, besieged Rome repeatedly, sacking the city mercilessly in 410. During one of the sieges, a telling moment transpired. Though the state religion was by then Christianity, there were still enough practitioners of Roman pagan rites – and still sufficient cultural memory of their presumed efficacy – that the suggestion was made to reinstate the rites and make sacrifices. The Bishop of Rome, Pope Innocent I, consented to this idea, provided they be enacted in private. Proponents claimed they would not work unless done publicly, and so the pagan Roman priests decided not to go forward.[29]

This episode reminds us that, to understand any historical moment, we need to put ourselves in the shoes of the protagonists. In this case, we need to forget for a moment that Christianity would later emerge triumphant.[30] It was still, then, precarious enough that even a bishop of Rome could countenance the idea that pagan rites might just work in gaining the favor of "gods," old and tired though they might be.

If, by Augustine's era, Christian leaders had just solidified what would count as scripture and Rome stood seemingly on a precipice, there was one

---

[28] See Mark Hebblewhite, *Theodosius and the Limits of Empire* (New York: Routledge, 2020).

[29] See Zosimus, *Historia nova*, ed. Johann Friedrich Reitemeier and Immanuel Bekker, Corpus scriptorum historiae byzantinae, 30 (Bonn: Weber, 1837), 5: 41; Eng. translation in Zosimus, *New History*, tr. Ronald T. Ridley (Leiden: Brill, 2017), p. 121. Cf. Thomas S. Burns, *Barbarians within the Gates of Rome* (Bloomington: Indiana University Press, 1994), p. 235; Henry Chadwick, *The Church in Ancient Society: From Galilee to Gregory the Great* (Oxford: Oxford University Press, 2001), pp. 509–510.

[30] Cf. Alan Cameron, *The Last Pagans of Rome* (Oxford: Oxford University Press, 2010).

more factor in place, an intellectual one, that shaped his environment: the evolution of Platonism. A signal figure appeared in the third century CE, Plotinus (203–270).[31] Born in Lycopolis (now in Egypt), Plotinus, after years of study, made his way to Rome, where he taught philosophy in Greek. Centuries had passed since Plato had walked the earth. But Plato's dialogues had emerged since then as a set of significant texts. By Plotinus' day, they were studied in a certain order, commented on, and used as a basis for further philosophizing. Plotinus did not write much until his fifties (as we learn from the biography penned by his student and admirer Porphyry), seeing philosophy as a living search for wisdom and not needing validation in writing.[32]

Eventually, however, Plotinus did write, spurred on by the demands of students. He produced a series of fifty-four short, lecture-length texts, which Porphyry (234–305 CE) edited and published in six "books," as the *Enneads* (a title taken from the Greek word for "nine," as each book contained nine treatises). Dense, difficult, and occasionally soaring in tone, the *Enneads* set forth a set of coherent ideas that, taken together, offered a kind of ontological architecture, even as they also pointed the way to a philosophical way of life.

As to ontology (or the study of being itself), Plotinus suggested that there was a hierarchy to being, with something called the One at the top. The One, for Plotinus, represented a hybrid between Plato's Form of the Good (that eternal, immaterial Form in which all the things that we understand as "good" participate somehow) and Aristotle's "prime mover," that first cause at which one would eventually arrive, if one went backward in a regression of causes (of causes, of causes, and so on). For Plotinus, the One was so great that it was beyond being, so that we could barely conceive of it and what it must be like. It did not think or act in any ordinary sense. Instead, the One was so full, so perfect, that it overflowed, leading down into the next ontological level, that of "mind" or "intellect."

---

[31] Plotinus, *Enneads*, 7 vols., ed. and tr. A. H. Armstrong (Cambridge, MA: Harvard University Press, 1966–1988); see Werner Beierwaltes, *Das wahre Selbst: Studien zu Plotins Begriff des Geistes und des Einen* (Frankfurt am Main: Klostermann, 2001); Lloyd P. Gerson, *Plotinus* (London: Routledge, 1994); Lloyd P. Gerson, ed., *The Cambridge Companion to Plotinus* (Cambridge: Cambridge University Press, 1996); Pierre Hadot, *Plotinus, or, the Simplicity of Vision*, tr. Michael Chase (Chicago: University of Chicago Press, 1993); Dominic J. O'Meara, *Plotinus: An Introduction to the Enneads* (Oxford: Oxford University Press, 1993); John Rist, *Plotinus: The Road to Reality* (Cambridge: Cambridge University Press, 1967).

[32] See Porphyry, "Life of Plotinus," in Plotinus, *Enneads*, 1: 2–87, at 13.

It is here, at the level of "mind," that Plato's Forms resided. These Forms provided differentiation of essence, representing the reason why, say, a tree is different from a fish, even though they both share life. From this level, there emerged "soul," the next step down on the ontological hierarchy and the place from which nature and all things physical finally emanate.

For Plotinus, human beings in their fashion descend from this hierarchy. We are embodied, a unity of matter and form. Matter represented evil. It was deprived of form and though it was at some remove created by the One, it also represented the primary obstacle in reaching the One. Though human beings have descended and become "enmattered," our souls were once pure and unencumbered by matter and so we are infused with a divine spark. We have something inside us that wants to return to the One, to "become like a God," in Plato's formulation, or in Aristotle's, to "put on immortality."[33] Plotinus weaved together concepts from Plato and Aristotle in this and other ways. And – based on his own experience and spiritual growth – he advocated the idea that human beings should actively engage in this search to return to the One, to develop and cultivate that internal spark by careful meditation.[34] His student Porphyry, who wrote an admiring biography, said that he saw Plotinus reach this state – a kind of ecstasy in which Plotinus experienced inner union with the One – only four times during their time together. In the same biography Porphyry says that he himself reached that state once.[35]

In one respect, this type of ascent to the One represented something common among late ancient intellectuals: the notion that one needed to cultivate self-control and to practice what was termed *askêsis*, a word that denotes "training" and "exercise."[36] As did many others, Plotinus believed that one could and should train oneself. In his case, the object of that training was to reach the One, eventually.

Yet, Plotinus inhabited a moment in the third century when a common assumption was developing regarding monotheism. That assumption is strange and different enough from common notions that it warrants comment. The strangeness – to modern ears – can be summed up by the expression scholars use to describe it: pagan monotheism. These two words do not sit comfortably next to each other in the common imagination. "Pagan" tends to imply the

---

[33] Plato, *Theaetetus*, 176b; Aristotle, *Nicomachean Ethics*, 1177b33.
[34] Hadot, *Plotinus, or, the Simplicity of Vision*, 25–27.
[35] Porphyry, "Life of Plotinus," sec. 23, pp. 69–71.
[36] See Pierre Hadot, *Philosophy as a Way of Life*, ed. Arnold I. Davidson, tr. M. Chase (Oxford and New York: Blackwell, 1995), pp. 128 and throughout.

polytheistic world of pagan religions, where one worshipped different gods for different purposes. Just so, "monotheism" implies a rigid adherence to the idea that there must be one god, absolutely speaking.

Plotinus' One, however, allows us a window onto that world, in the simple sense that the One would have been recognizable throughout the late ancient Mediterranean. It would not have been so, of course, in the precise ways that Plotinus described it. But the basic idea that there must, at some level, have been one supreme being, would have rung familiar. If you were an adherent of Roman religion, calling that supreme being Jupiter made sense; of Greek religion, Zeus. If you were in Egypt, you might have called it Amoun-Ra. It was, in short, a translatable concept, signaling that, even though one might worship this supreme being in different ways, there was still, in the end, only one of them.[37]

The Judeo-Christian tradition, however, was different, its monotheism more absolute. This was the God who had identified Himself to Moses in Exodus, saying "I am who am" and instructing Moses to tell the Israelites precisely that (Exod 3:14). This was the God who said: "You shall have no other gods before me," and who went on in dictating the Ten Commandments to say: "You shall not make for yourself an image in the form of anything in heaven above or on earth beneath or in the waters below. You shall not bow down to them or worship them; for I, the Lord your God, am a jealous God, punishing the children for the sins of the parents..." (Exod 20:2–5). The Judeo-Christian God was "one" not only in the sense of a necessary intellectual abstraction but also in an absolute sense.

This God, in short, was untranslatable, even as it shared the same sorts of properties with Plotinus' One, especially so as the late ancient centuries wore on. In Augustine's time, indeed, there was what amounted to a constant if often hostile conversation among pagans and Christians, a conversation whose volume rose precisely because they were, in effect, arguing over the same things. What was the nature of this supreme being? How did you reach

---

[37] See Jan Assmann, *Of God and Gods: Egypt, Israel, and the Rise of Monotheism* (Madison: University of Wisconsin Press, 2008); Jan Assmann, "Translating Gods: Religion as a Factor of Cultural (Un)Translatability," in Sanford Budick and Wolfgang Iser, eds., *The Translatability of Cultures: Figurations of the Space Between* (Stanford: Stanford University Press, 1996), 25–37; Polymnia Athanassiadi, *Mutations of Hellenism in Late Antiquity* (Farnham, Surrey: Ashgate, 2015); Polymnia Athanassiadi and Michael Frede, eds., *Pagan Monotheism in Late Antiquity* (Oxford: Oxford University Press, 1999); Stephen Mitchell, Peter Van Nuffelen, eds., *One God: Pagan Monotheism in the Roman Empire* (Cambridge and New York: Cambridge University Press, 2010); Stephen Mitchell and Peter van Nuffelen, eds., *Monotheism between Pagans and Christians in Late Antiquity* (Leuven: Peeters, 2010).

the supreme being? How did you access its powers or induce its presence on earth? What role did the individual play in those processes? And what sorts of roles could religious rituals play?

These latter two questions, concerning the power of individuals and the role of ritual, were especially prominent. In Plotinus' case, we observe a stark, lonely beauty to his thinking. He suggests that it is up to us, as individuals, who must look inside ourselves and find and activate the natural spark we have been given to ascend to the divine. Regarding the divine, he writes: "We cannot get there on foot ... You must not get ready a carriage, either, or a boat. Let all these things go, and do not look. Shut your eyes, and change to and awaken another way of seeing, which everyone has but few use."[38] Plotinus was saying that, if you train yourself well, you can shut out the world, so that your essence – your soul – can reach the divine and be unified to it. You didn't need external rituals, nor did you need organized structures, like priests or a church. You could do it on your own.

It is notable, however, that Porphyry only observed the master achieving that blissful state four times in their many years together. If the great Plotinus could only reach the divine rarely, what hope was there for the rest of us? For many in the late ancient Mediterranean environment, rituals and structures grew more important. Porphyry himself was ambivalent about all this, wanting on the one hand to be loyal to Plotinus' vision but seeing the power, on the other, of rituals.

A change occurred, however, in the next generation, in the work of Porphyry's student (and eventual antagonist) Iamblichus (245–325 CE). Iamblichus advocated a practice known as "theurgy." This word, *theiourgia*, in Greek, combines two roots: *theion*, which means "divine," and *ergon*, which means "work." The word accordingly means "doing divine work" or even "working the divine." To understand what he had in mind, and indeed, to comprehend how this conception had a counterpart in the evolution of Christian thinking, we can turn to what Iamblichus says regarding theurgy:

> Of the works of theurgy performed on any given occasion, some have a cause that is secret and superior to all rational explanation, others are like symbols [this word can also mean "passwords"], consecrated from all eternity to the higher beings, others preserve some other image, even as nature in its generative role imprints (upon things) visible shapes from invisible reason-principles...[39]

---

[38] Plotinus, *Enneads*, 1.6.8 (pp. 18–28).
[39] Iamblichus, *De mysteriis*, ed. Edouard des Places (Paris: Les Belles Lettres, 1966), 2.11; passage cit. and tr. in John Dillon, "Iamblichus' Defence of Theurgy: Some Reflections,"

We glean thus far that "works of theurgy" represent ritualistic behaviors that have a way of accessing divine power, power that the divine has given to the earthly world. Iamblichus goes on to say that theurgy represents the performance of "ineffable acts correctly performed, acts which are beyond all understanding, and by the power of unutterable symbols which are intelligible only to the gods."[40]

One is in the realm of behavior, ritual, and action, not reasoned argumentation. When Iamblichus speaks of "symbols," he means several things, all at once: signs, for example, that the divine has implanted in the universe, signs that one might discover on the inside of a rock when one broke it open, or in a certain plant. These types of natural phenomena he considered linked to supra-natural powers, the full rational understanding of which only the gods possessed. Then there is the notion of "ineffability," as when he speaks of "ineffable acts." Iamblichus is signaling that there are limits to language and, accordingly, limits to human rational argumentation. In the language of his ancient predecessors, he is saying that there are limits to *logos*, that capacious word that meant everything from "inquiring conversation" to "rational argument." *Logos* represented a skill and set of values that Socrates on his deathbed urged his young compatriots to preserve when he was gone, reminding them not to become *misologoi*, or "haters of *logos*," because if they did, they would then resemble *misanthropoi*, or "haters of their fellow men." The belief, in short, was that the verbal exercise of human reason could lead to discovery, progress, and harmony, provided it was exercised in a context of mutual, human understanding.

But the divine was markedly not human, and its far-off nature – far from us, with our finite senses and limited, all too human resources – had come to seem hard to reach. There was a gulf over which human reason could not leap. It was there even in Plato's more mystical passages about the Forms, heavily present in the thought of St. Paul, who had spoken of us, now, seeing only "through a glass, darkly," and certainly in Plotinus' One, which was so

---

The International Journal of the Platonic Tradition 1 (2007), 30–41, at 34; see also Crystal Addey, *Divination and Theurgy in Neoplatonism: Oracles of the Gods* (New York: Routledge, 2016), esp. 215–238; Henry J. Blumenthal and E. Gillian Clark, *The Divine Iamblichus: Philosopher and Man of Gods* (Bristol: Bristol Classical Press, 1993); John Dillon, "Iamblichus of Chalcis (circa 240–325AD)," *Aufstieg und Niedergang der römischen Welt*, 36.2 (1988), 862–909; Todd C. Krulak, "*Thusia* and Theurgy: Sacrificial Theory in Fourth- and Fifth-Century Platonism," *Classical Quarterly* 64 (2014), 353–382, esp. 355–360; Gregory Shaw, *Theurgy and the Soul: The Neoplatonism of Iamblichus* (University Park: Pennsylvania State University Press, 1995); and Ilinca Tanseanu-Döbler, *Theurgy in Late Antiquity: The Invention of a Ritual Tradition* (Göttingen: Vandenhoeck and Ruprecht, 2013), esp. 45–135.

[40] Iamblichus, *De mysteriis*, 2.11, tr. in Dillon, "Iamblichus' Defence," 37.

great it was beyond being and, accordingly, out of the reach of human reason – out of the reach of *logos*. Iamblichus saw clearly – in his pagan context – that there was a need for rituals. These rituals would guarantee that more than only a select few might reach union with the divine, even as the rituals would ensure that the divine presence could be experienced on earth. And of course, to do those things one needed mediators, people who knew the rituals, who could enact the "ineffable" behaviors, who could "work the divine." One needed something like priests.

It was precisely these concerns about the nature of God, the power of human beings to reach him, and the limits of human rational powers that Augustine faced. In his *Confessions*, he laid bare his deepest concerns along those lines, setting forth as he did so a paradigm for future Christians.

Augustine wrote his *Confessions* between 397 and 400, before the Roman Sack of 410 took place. But he was witness to the pressures under which Rome – both the city itself and the associated idea – suffered. He knew that the invasions and incursions and disturbances were ongoing and unlikely to come to any sudden halt. The world seemed to be growing old, and what was needed was a kind of manifesto for something new. In his *Confessions* and *City of God* Augustine provided just that. Together, these two works stand among the most important in western history, shaping narratives of conversion and perspectives on the place of humanity in the universe that were as profound as they were influential.

The primary importance of the *Confessions* lies in its moving account of Augustine's conversion, as he explored a variety of religious and philosophical perspectives and emerged, at the end, as a Christian. Along the way, he covered the nature of God, the associated problem of evil, and the place of books, speech, and written culture, revealing in that latter respect how deeply he and his cohort were invested in books and written debate as a means of defining and, hopefully, settling religious and philosophical problems. Lyrical, haunting, and suffused at every turn with references to scripture – the Psalms and Letters of St. Paul, most especially – the *Confessions* is a book that would have been strange to his contemporaries.

First, it was an autobiography, a genre of writing relatively rare in antiquity. There were precedents: lists of one's deeds, such as occur on the funerary inscriptions of ancient Egyptian leaders, or the *Res gestae divi Augusti*, a list of accomplishments of the Roman emperor Augustus, authored by the emperor himself.[41] The ancient Jewish historian Josephus

---

[41] Augustus, *Res gestae divi Augusti*, in Velleius Paterculus, *Compendium of Roman History* and Augustus, *Res gestae divi Augusti*, ed. and tr. Frederick W. Shipley (Cambridge, MA:

(37–100 CE), whose *Jewish War* and *Antiquities of the Jews* offered unparalleled insight into both Jewish resistance to Roman rule and Jewish custom and history, presented a short account of the facts of his life, as an appendix to his *Antiquities of the Jews*.[42] And a teacher of rhetoric named Libanius (314–392/3) wrote a narrative of his own life in Greek.[43] But Augustine's *Confessions* was a different sort of work entirely. The mentioned works gave accounts of people's lives, offering information on their background, education, and career, sometimes focusing on rivalries and score-settling, all with little introspectiveness.

Augustine, by contrast, focuses on himself, his weaknesses, and his evolution as he grows ever closer to God and, indeed, to Christianity. Rich with detail, his account of his life includes facts about his upbringing, his travels, and his studies. Augustine's form of address is what makes the *Confessions* most distinctive: It is addressed to God, so that the *Confessions* can be seen as an extended prayer, rich with autobiographical material though it is.[44] Augustine begins by alluding to the Psalms: "'Can any praise be worthy of the Lord's majesty? How magnificent his strength! How inscrutable his wisdom!'" (1.1, p. 21, referring to Ps 145:3).[45]

The fact that Augustine opens his *Confessions* with these scriptural quotations signals that the Psalms are and will remain one of the work's touchstones. Their notional authorship by King David, whose life Christians saw as a prefiguration of that of Christ, was significant, as was the fact that they represented an exemplary way to pray.[46] Augustine, like his learned Christian

---

Harvard University Press, 1924), 344–401. For the theme in general still valuable is Georg Misch, *Geschichte der Autobiographie*, 4 vols. (Bern: Francke, 1949–1969), vol. 1.

[42] See Josephus, *Life of Josephus*, ed. and tr. Steve Mason (Leiden: Brill, 2001), vol. 9 in *Flavius Josephus*, 10 vols. to date, ed. Steve Mason (Leiden: Brill, 2000–); and Pnina Stern, "Life of Josephus: The Autobiography of Flavius Josephus," *Journal for the Study of Judaism* 41 (2010), 63–93.

[43] Libanius, *Autobiography*, in Libanius, *Autobiography and Selected Letters*, 2 vols., ed. and tr. A. F. Norman (Cambridge, MA: Harvard University Press, 1992), 1: 52–337.

[44] Cf. Gary Wills, *Augustine's* Confessions: *A Biography* (Princeton: Princeton University Press, 2011).

[45] I will cite in the text with book, section, and page numbers from Saint Augustine, *Confessions*, tr. R. S. Pine-Coffin (New York: Penguin, 1961); for the Latin text see Augustine, *Confessions*, 3 vols., ed. and comm. James J. O'Donnell (Oxford: Oxford University Press, 2012).

[46] Scholars have of course advanced in their notion of the authorship of the Psalms. See William P. Brown, "The Psalms and Hebrew Poetry," in Stephen B. Chapman and Marvin A. Sweeney, eds., *The Cambridge Companion to the Hebrew Bible/Old Testament* (Cambridge: Cambridge University Press, 2016), 253–273, at 263–264. On early Christian interpretation of the Psalms, see Brian E. Daley, S.J. and Paul R. Kolbet, eds., *The Harp of Prophecy: Early Christian Interpretation of the Psalms* (Notre Dame: University of Notre Dame Press, 2015).

contemporaries, had the Psalms committed to memory. The result was that the Psalms, along with other key works, became a kind of architecture of the mind, a way to solidify points, to structure a conversation, and to ask questions. And in this case, the key question concerned the nature of God. The cited Psalm speaks of God as possessing majesty, strength, and inscrutability. God – omnipotent, omniscient, and good – represents a mystery, the central mystery for Augustine, and by extension for humanity.

Humanity comes immediately thereafter, as Augustine states: "man is one of your creatures, Lord, and his instinct is to praise you. He bears about him the mark of death, the sign of his own sin, to remind him that you 'thwart the proud'" (1.1, p. 21). Humanity is fallen. God stands above it, as creator and as eventual judge, as the final words – a quotation from the first letter of Peter in the New Testament (1 Pet 5:5) – reveal. Accordingly, Augustine continues, "our hearts find no peace until they rest in you" (1.1, p. 21, cf. 1 Pet 5:5).

We know, then, that we are programmed, as it were, both to praise God and to try to reach him, or better, to return to him. We have by our own fault become alienated from God. Our task in this life – and it is a monumental one – is to try to return to the God who created us, who loves us, but whose nature is often hidden. The problem? The world gets in the way with its pressures, social challenges, and chances for us to go off track. As Augustine narrates his life, from infancy onward, we receive a taste of what his own challenges were.

We learn, for instance, that his parents were ambitious for him, seeking out an education that was the best one could have. It is an education that in some respects will seem far more "theatrical" than one might imagine, for it was focused most of all one thing: the art of persuasion. Not so differently from Plato's day, the highly oral ancient culture of which Augustine took part meant that career success hinged on the ability to persuade one's fellow citizens. In Augustine's world, North African though he was, absolute fluency in literary and oratorical Latin was a must. Plato had said that inhabitants living around the Mediterranean Sea were like "frogs around a pond." By Augustine's era, that pond was controlled by Rome (now more as symbol than political power), but culturally conditioned nonetheless to prize excellent Latinity as a key virtue.

Accordingly, Augustine learned the classics.[47] He studied and loved Virgil's epic poem, the *Aeneid*, which told of the Trojan Aeneas, who, after

---

[47] See James J. O'Donnell, "Augustine's Classical Readings," *Recherches Augustiniennes* 15 (1980), 144–175; Harold Hagendahl, *Augustine and the Latin Classics*, 2 vols. (Gothenburg: Elander, 1967).

the Trojans were defeated by the Greeks in war, left and founded Rome.[48] In its first six books, it was a lot like Homer's *Odyssey*, a tale of wandering and adventures, of mythical creatures, of a descent into and a return from the underworld, and even of romantic entanglements. In its second half, Books 6–12, the *Aeneid* resembled Homer's *Iliad*, recounting war, heroism, and exemplary, battle-tested virtue and vice. Augustine was nourished on this poetic masterpiece, as were other educated people in the realm of Roman power. Studying the *Aeneid* allowed students to learn Latin vocabulary and grammar, of course. On top of that, it represented a culture and a series of reference points, to which one would habitually return in life, with quotations emerging practically unbidden to one's memory. In his *Confessions*, Augustine tells that, as a boy he "wept for Dido," the queen who lured a traveling (and married) Aeneas to her island, induced him to stay with her for a time amidst amatory pleasures, but then herself wept with disappointment as he left her, intent as he was on his journey (1.13, p. 34).

And yet, Augustine recounts, he also learned things that came to seem incongruous, such as about Jupiter (the Roman version of the Greek Zeus and, as such, the supreme god among the polytheistic pantheon of pagan gods): "Jupiter punishes the wicked with his thunderbolts and yet commits adultery himself. The two roles are quite incompatible" (1.16, p. 36). This objection – that a "god" should not be called a god, if he engages in immoral activity – had also been dear to Plato. Augustine is signaling that these stories about the gods were part of traditional education, that he like others imbibed them, as they studied Latin literary discourse. In the process they received a language equipping them to deal with the world.

It is a remarkable fact that, in his *Confessions*, Augustine succeeded in creating a new sort of Latin language. It was rhetorically appealing, borrowing from classical Latin much of the sentence structure and basic lexicon, even as he drew energy from the language of his own sermons.[49] Traditionally, someone with his education would have inserted classical examples and quotations into his text, perhaps drawing them from the *Aeneid*, perhaps from other memorized classics. Augustine created instead a literary masterpiece in which sacred scripture served that exemplary function. Later, evolving Christianity (high and low, institutional and popular) would sometimes turn Roman temples into Christian churches and

---

[48] See Sabine MacCormack, *The Shadows of Poetry: Vergil in the Mind of Augustine* (Berkeley: University of California Press, 1998).
[49] See Brown, *Augustine of Hippo*, 252–253.

celebrate Christian festivals at times when there had been pagan religious ones.[50] Augustine is one of the Christian thinkers who staked out the intellectual ground early on; here he adopts the habits of the educated – memorization of important texts with a concomitant insertion of quotations from those texts in one's own work – and "Christianizes" those habits. He was one of a small group of Latinate figures of his era who created a new kind of classic, fusing together the habits of one age with a set of texts appropriate for a new.

One of the problems with which he wrestled was the question of sin. Why do we do things that we know are wrong? What is it about our will that allows this sliding into sin to happen? As he looks back on his youth, Augustine recounts an episode that stuck with him throughout the years, one that in its simplicity renders it profound. When he was young (in his teenaged years) he committed a crime, a theft to be more precise. About it, he writes: "I was willing to steal, and steal I did, although I was not compelled by any lack..." (2.4, p. 47). He did so "only to enjoy the theft itself and the sin." He zeroes in on what he did:

> There was a pear-tree near our vineyard, loaded with fruit that was attractive neither to look at nor to taste. Late one night, a band of ruffians, myself included, went off to shake down the fruit and carry it away... We took away an enormous quantity of pears, not to eat them ourselves, but simply to throw them to the pigs. Perhaps we ate some of them, but our real pleasure consisted in doing something that was forbidden. (2.4, p. 47)

The elemental nature of this late ancient scene stands out: farms, pigs, pear trees, and young, boisterous boys, getting into trouble together, fueling each other with their mischief, daring each other to go further and finally committing an illegal act, as they took pears that did not belong to them.

There are two ways to look at Augustine's retrospective glance at this episode from his youth. One is to think about his personality, one side of which was intensely inward-looking. His narrative of this event (of which only the central part has been reported here) is long enough to indicate that he was still deeply bothered by his own behavior, even when writing decades later. He was a person hyper-conscious of his every wrong move, ever wondering if an omniscient God could forgive him of this and his many

---

[50] See Peter Brown, *The Cult of the Saints: Its Rise and Function in Latin Christianity*, 2nd ed. (Chicago: University of Chicago Press, 2015); Richard Krautheimer, *Rome: Portrait of a City, 312–1308* (Princeton: Princeton University Press, 1980), pp. 1–108; Feyo L. Schuddeboom, "The Conversion of Temples in Rome," *Journal of Late Antiquity* 10 (2017), 166–186.

other transgressions. And it is from this perspective that the second way emerges.

What are the attributes of God? This is to ask: What can we say about Him? For Augustine, God was one, first of all, a unity – and this despite the doctrine on the Trinity, expressed in the New Testament in Matthew (28:19). There Jesus told the apostles that they must go and "make disciples of all nations, baptizing them in the name of the Father, the Son, and the Holy Spirit." God as three-in-one is a difficult notion to understand logically, if one wants to preserve the unity of the one God. Some early Christians understood these three aspects as three "persons" of God. The Latin word *persona* (like its Greek equivalent, *prosopon*) means at its root a "mask," as in a theatrical mask that an actor might wear. Underneath he is still the same person, even if the mask facilitates his ability to tell different stories and to have different functions in the play. This composite notion soon seemed to go too far, however, as thinking was refined and as Christians sought to grasp how the Father, Son, and Holy Spirit could be both separate and one. During the early Christian centuries, the notion of the "person" (as in the three "persons" of the Trinity) was refined to mean that each person – the Father, Son, and Holy Spirit – were distinct but not separate in substance.

By Augustine's day the nature of the Trinity was well developed and doctrinally affirmed (at both the 325 Council of Nicaea and the 381 Council of Constantinople), even as how one might articulate it was not fully settled. Augustine helped that process along in his *On the Trinity*, where he laid out his opinions on the matter.[51] Just as the soul has memory, understanding, and will and remains one soul, so too does the Trinity preserve unity in separateness.[52] Or one might think of love: there is the one who loves (in this case God the Father), the one who is loved (Jesus or God the son, who stands in for humanity), and love itself (God the Holy Spirit).[53] The three aspects are separate, but they cannot exist without each other. They are all love, a love – Augustine implies – without which the cosmos would lack order, beauty, and goodness.

Parenthetically and as to the doctrine of the Trinity, it is better taken as an article of faith than a logically provable set of propositions. Indeed, in his *On the Trinity* and elsewhere Augustine suggested that there were limits to our

---

[51] See Augustine, *Sancti Aurelii Augustini De trinitate libri XV*, 2 vols., ed. W. J. Mountain (Turnhout: Brepols, 1968); for an English translation, see Augustine, *On the Trinity*, ed. Gareth B. Matthews, tr. Stephen McKenna (Cambridge: Cambridge University Press, 2012).
[52] Augustine, *On the Trinity*, 9.5, pp. 30–31.   [53] Ibid., 8.10, p. 22; 9.2, pp. 25–27.

understanding, bound by sense as that understanding often is.[54] To grasp the eternity, equality, and unity of the Trinity, "we must believe before we understand."[55] It is a great blessing to touch God with our mind, Augustine said in a sermon, "but to comprehend him entirely is impossible."[56] There were mysteries to God's nature, to be sure, so that an epistemic humility was always called for. That God was one, however, was a bedrock belief.

Next, Augustine considered God omnipotent, supremely Good, and omniscient. As to the first two matters: God – being God – could do anything he wished to do, with no limits. It was thus an enduring puzzle of a life of faith that things occur in the world that are bad, by any commonly understood human definition. Accordingly, the third concern – God's omniscience – came often to the fore. Regarding the bad things in the world, one could say that they are bad, indeed, to us in our limited human perspective and in our view of time. For God, however, time was something different: He saw all things, throughout all imaginable time, as if the past, present, and future coexisted in an eternal present. There would be reasons for the bad things, reasons that only God could really see and that human beings could never fully explain, at least with the power of human reason alone.

It was for these reasons that Augustine was so agitated by his own sinfulness, furnished as he was with a delicate and pensive psyche. This agitation runs through the *Confessions* before his conversion, even as the pear-tree episode serves as a stand-in for the whole, roiling problem of his consideration of sin.

As in many other matters, Paul stood at the forefront of this intellectual trajectory. In his Letter to the Romans, Paul had wrestled with sin and problem of the human will. He described there an "interior" and an "exterior" person. Paul uses himself as a stand-in for humanity, writing: "For that which I work, I understand not. For I do not that good which I will; but the evil which I hate, that I do" (Rom 7:15). Paul is saying: I don't know why I do what I do, and I do things I know and believe are wrong. He goes on:

> Now if I do that which I will not, it is no more that I do it, but sin that dwelleth in me. I find then a law, that when I have a will to do good, evil is present with me. For I am delighted with the law of God, according to

---

[54] Ibid., bk. 8, pp. 3–22.   [55] Ibid., 8.5, p. 12.
[56] Augustine, Sermon 117 in F. Dolbeau, "Le Sermon 117 d'Augustin sur l'ineffabilité de Dieu. Édition critique," *Revue bénédictine* 124 (2014), 213–253, at 231–232: "comprehendere autem omnino impossibile."

the inward man. But I see another law in my members, fighting against the law of my mind, and captivating me in the law of sin, that is in my members. (Rom 7:20–23)

Paul separates his "self" from his "will" – it is not "I" who do these evil things. Rather, the evil that he does is caused by the presence of evil in him. There is a law of God, which Paul knows to be good, of which he approves, and which he would like to follow. But then there is this other thing, a "law of sin," a law that resides in his "members." By this latter term Paul means his bodily members, which is to say his human physicality – and it is this, the body, that gets him into trouble.

An attentive reader will hear resonances, most especially of Plato, whose mistrust of the physical led him to postulate a higher reality, nonphysical and thus not subject to corruption and decay. And it will also remind one, closer to home – given that we are in Augustine's world – of Plotinus, who lived well after Paul, of course, but only a century before Augustine. So, it will come as no surprise that, as Augustine narrates his life and his eventual conversion, the self-directed course that he took was to go through the "works of the Platonists," only to land, forcefully, on Paul.

Although his mother Monica was a fervent Christian and had raised him as such, Augustine relates that he became an adept of Manichaeism, a sect so named after a Persian thinker named "Mani," who was active in the third century CE.[57] It is worthy of note that he inhabited the same century as Plotinus. Plotinus believed in the One, which sat above all things, indeed above all being, and was also identified with Plato's Form of the Good. Manichaeans believed, instead, that there were two, great cosmic principles, Good and Evil. They were at war with each other, and their theater of battle, in so far as it affected us, was here on earth. The Good was identified with light and immateriality; Evil, with darkness and matter. That cosmic struggle found a microcosmic mirror in every human being. Some, who had trained themselves, became "complete," and might renounce physical pleasures. They were considered holy and blessed. Yet again, it fell to very few to reach that state.

Augustine was never fully satisfied, ever wondering whether his sins were his fault or the fault of some outside force, Evil, for which he could incur no personal blame, but which affected him, nonetheless. He sought out famous Manichaean leaders, but upon meeting one of them was disappointed,

---

[57] See Michel Tardieu, *Manichaeism*, tr. M. B. DeBevoise (Urbana-Champaign: University of Illinois Press, 2008); and for Augustine's complex engagement, Jason BeDuhn, *Augustine's Manichaean Dilemma*, 2 vols. (Philadelphia: University of Pennsylvania Press, 2010–2013).

believing him to be shallow. As Augustine was getting ready to renounce Manichaeism, he was "still trying to discover the origin of evil" (7.7, p. 142). On his journey of self-discovery, he "turned to the books of the Platonists." By these, he meant Plotinus, most especially, along with works of Plotinus' student Porphyry, both of whose texts were circulating in Latin translation.[58] From these texts, Augustine learned much that harmonized with Christian scripture, so much so that in making this connection between Platonism and Christianity, Augustine cites extensively from the Gospel of John. The message is that the Platonists came close but not close enough to the truth. What he learned from the Platonists was that dualism would not work: there could not be a supremely good God who was battling an equally powerful Evil. God must be one, and He must be good.

There was one thing Augustine did not find reading Platonic texts, something on which everything hinged. In the books of the Platonists, he says, "I did not read that 'the Word was made flesh and came to dwell among us,'" citing the Gospel of John (John 1). He puts it this way (addressing God): "for you, evil does not exist, and not only for you but for the whole of your creation as well," meaning that, in some fashion, good resides in God and everything God has done, in all his creation (7.7, p. 148). Reflecting on his past beliefs, Augustine writes that "those who find fault with any part of your creation are bereft of reason, just as I was when I decried many of the things you had made." Augustine could not find fault with God, so instead he took refuge in "the theory of the two substances," that is, Good and Evil. He was making progress toward a mature belief and a mature faith, but he wasn't there yet. What he was lacking (to come to that one thing on which the whole project hinged) was Jesus Christ.

Augustine diagnoses the issue: "I thought of Christ, my Lord and Savior, as no more than a man of extraordinary wisdom, whom none could equal" (7.19, p. 152). The conundrum was even deeper: "by reading these books of the Platonists, I had been been prompted to look for truth as something incorporeal" (7.20, p. 154). These two statements, taken together, encapsulate the problem Augustine faced and the mystery he needed to solve. It can be expressed, finally, in a question: What was the exemplary value of Christ? Or better, how should one conceive of his various functions and attributes? Augustine began to realize that there was something missing in all his prior reading: "For how could I expect that the Platonist books would ever teach me charity?" (7.20, p. 154). What Augustine says needs to

---

[58] See Pier Franco Beatrice, "*Quosdam platonicorum libros*: The Platonic Readings of Augustine in Milan," *Vigiliae Christianae* 43 (1989), 248–281.

be highlighted: In his view, Christ was exemplary. There were three levels to this exemplarity.

First, just as for Plato the life of Socrates was exemplary, so too did Christ's human life provide ethical models. In Christ's case these included: countenancing and combating injustice; helping the less fortunate; and taking little notice of formal and established hierarchies and instead understanding people as individuals with their own dignity, whatever their economic or social station might have been. That was one level, and a common one at that, when it came to the often unarticulated but no less profound meaning of philosophy: the search to find a way of life that was wise and that was recognized as such by followers. Christ's life served as an example of a "wise man" that would have been culturally familiar.

Yet, for Augustine, there were deeper levels to this question regarding the value of the life of Christ. One had to do with the fact that, though he was God, he was "incarnated," meaning that Jesus took on human form, human "flesh." To return briefly to the Socratic analogy: Socrates was wise, and he was – as the interlocutor Phaedo says at the very end of that eponymous dialogue – "the best, and also the wisest, and the most upright" among men. But Socrates was no god. This new conception of Christ, however, represented a sea change, not so much in how it was originally articulated, but rather in how it was accepted.

If, on one level, Christ's deeds served a familiar exemplary function, on another, he was regarded as really divine. Christ claimed some divine attributes for himself, as his public career grew. He referred to himself as the Son of Man, emphasizing his universal humanity. But he also presented himself as the Son of God, during the trial at the Sanhedrin that led to his death, as related in the Gospel of Mark. After Jesus was silent about certain charges leveled against him, a dramatic moment occurred:

> Again the high priest asked him, and said to him: 'Art thou the Christ, the son of the blessed God'? And Jesus said to him: 'I am. And you shall see the Son of man sitting on the right hand of the power of God and coming with the clouds of heaven.' (Mark 14:61–62)

In its original context (that is, for those who wrote and read the early Gospels), this passage and others like it would have recalled Old Testament references, such as the prophecy in the Book of Daniel, where the prophet says, "I beheld therefore in the vision of the night, and lo, one like the son of man came with the clouds of heaven..." (Dan 7:13). Recapitulating, restating, and reinterpreting familiar matters of Jewish ritual and scripture in this new, still nascent Christian context: This sort of operation was normal for the writers of the New Testament. But texts do not belong to themselves once they are inscribed. People interpret them.

So, as time went by, Augustine, when asked by a friend named Laurentius to summarize some central principles of the Christian faith, wrote a short *Handbook*, modeled on the three most important Pauline virtues of faith, hope, and charity. About Jesus, Augustine had this to say:

> Accordingly Christ Jesus, the son of God, is both God and man. He was God before all ages, man in this our age ... the one son of God, and at the same time Son of Man; the one Son of Man, and at the same time son of God.[59]

What Jesus had proposed, sometimes obliquely, became for his followers an accepted fact: This human being, Jesus, was also divine and, moreover, not a god but, instead, God with all the untranslatable oneness that conception demanded. By Augustine's day, this mysterious oneness (both God and man, Father and Son) became an acknowledged truth for those who professed the Christian faith. Christ-as-example, thus, had far more reach and force than would have been possible within the Greek, pagan, socioreligious economy.

Jesus as ethical example, Jesus as God: to these two exemplary sides of Christ, there must be added a third when it comes to Augustine's views. This third side has to do with those three Pauline virtues on which Augustine based the structure of his *Handbook*. Paul had said that "now there remain faith, hope, and charity, these three. But the greatest of these is charity" (1 Cor 13:13). In the *Confessions*, as Augustine was narrating the final intellectual moves in his conversion, he had passed from the dualist teachings of the Manicheans (two roughly coequal principles, Good and Evil, fighting it out in the world, among people, on whose hearts this cosmic battlefield was etched), to the "Books of the Platonists" (absolute Oneness, so absolute that it stood above all humanly accessible reference points). Moreover, Augustine noted that, from his reading of Platonic works, he had been prompted to look for the truth "as something incorporeal" (7.20, p. 154). He felt that he was getting wiser, but: "I had now begun to wish to be thought wise. I was full of self-esteem..." (7.20, p. 154). Even as his opinion of himself rose, there was a major gap in his formation, as he indicates with a question: "For was I not without charity, which builds its

---

[59] Augustine, *Enchiridion de fide, spe et caritate*, ed. E. Evans, Corpus Christianorum, Series Latina, 46 (Turnhout: Brepols, 1969), 10: 35, (pp. 49–114, at p. 69): "proinde christus iesus, dei filius, est et deus et homo: deus ante omnia saecula, homo in nostro saeculo ... unus dei filius, idem que hominis filius; unus hominis filius, idem que dei filius; non duo filii dei, deus et homo, sed unus dei filius; deus sine initio, homo a certo initio, dominus noster iesus christus."

edifice on the firm foundation of humility, that is, on Jesus Christ?" And then, a further question: "But how could I expect that the Platonist books would ever teach me charity?" (7.20, p. 154).

What was missing, in other words, was the Christian virtue that Paul had said was most important: *agape*, "charity," or as it is more commonly translated today, "love." In the Gospel of John, soon before he is betrayed, Christ gives his disciples a "new commandment": that they should "love one another" (*agapate allelous*, in Greek) as he had loved them (John 13:34). Once more, there is a Socratic parallel. Socrates on the night before his death reminded his followers not to be "haters of conversation" (*misologoi*), since if they did, they would be like "haters of their fellow men" (*misanthropoi*).[60] In recognizing the centrality of *logos* – reasoned, inquiring conversation, necessarily enacted in human communities – they would recognize each other and accordingly the common humanity they shared with all. Again, however, the parallel is incomplete, since the love of which Christ spoke was fundamentally deeper than the Socratic example. Why?

Christ's exemplary status came precisely from his willing incarnation. That is, he opted to become a human being, despite being God and, accordingly, under no obligation to us, His creatures. He *chose* to take on human suffering, as a way of dramatizing and then redeeming original sin. What he did was nothing other than the ultimate act of *agape*, offering a lived example of a love that is fundamentally other-directed, so much so that – Augustine is suggesting – once one truly understands it, it cannot be forgotten, undone, or unlearned. Augustine foregrounds "charity" as simply unavailable in the pagan philosophical tradition. It guided much of his thinking, including how he read scripture.[61]

It is no surprise, then, where Augustine next turned, as he relates in a meaningful passage in the *Confessions*:

> So I seized eagerly upon the venerable writings inspired by your Holy Spirit, especially those of the Apostle Paul ... I began to read and discovered that whatever truth I had found in the Platonists was set down here as well, and with it there was praise for your grace bestowed. For Saint Paul teaches that he who sees ought not to boast as though what he sees, and even the power by which he sees 'had not come to him by gift.' (7.21, p. 155)

---

[60] Plato, *Phaedo*, 89c–d.
[61] Cf. Augustine, *De doctrina christiana*, ed. and tr. R. H. P. Green (Oxford: Clarendon, 1995), 15: 23 (pp. 156–157): when dealing in scripture with figurative language subject to different possible interpretations, one should keep reading (my tr.) "until one arrives at an interpretation that lands in the realm of charity" (*donec ad regnum caritatis interpretatio perducatur*).

Two factors in this passage stand out.

First, Augustine had finally found, not just more books, but rather the right books. He was a "book person," and like most intellectuals, he thrived when he had important texts to scrutinize, to examine, and to interpret. Having surveyed everything available to him in the non-Christian textual tradition, he found, finally, the texts that would work. Conversion stories exist at least in part to serve as examples to others.

This example, the Augustinian one, went on to do a lot of cultural work in the Christian intellectual tradition. It served as a way of integrating Platonism into Christianity – the intellectual equivalent of the early medieval practice of turning pagan temples into Christian churches. It provided validation to bookish people interested in and, increasingly, formed by scripture. Augustine became a "classic" and in so doing expanded and changed the range of acceptable literary language.

Augustine's example offered something else, something that, in truth, was not as clear-cut as the rest: This was the acceptance, fostered most powerfully by Paul, of what we can call a "strong" version of the idea of God's grace. The passage contains a citation within a citation, in the phrase: "had not come to him by gift." Augustine is alluding to Paul's first letter to the Corinthians: "For who distinguisheth thee? Or what hast thou that thou hast not received? And if thou hast received, why dost thou glory, as if thou hadst not received it?" (1 Cor 4:7). The idea is to encourage humility. Whatever advantages, skills, and benefits you have, remember, they are owed not to you but to God and, more specifically, to God's "gift" to you or, in other terms, to his "grace." If we conceive of God as an absolute unity which, despite being "one" is also infinite (in the sense of possessing infinite power and knowledge), consequences ensue. One of these is that, as we examine our lives and our surroundings, and as we try to understand our place in relation to God, we seem small. If He is infinite, we are finite. If He is eternal, we are time-bound. If He is all-knowing, we will always be limited, epistemologically speaking, to a fraction of all available knowledge on earth, let alone to the larger, universal knowledge to which God is privy. We are small, in other words, and this smallness can weigh heavily on a person.

So, the big question: Are we "free"? Are we free to make choices, to sin or not to sin, to commit crimes or to stay free of them? Our laws and institutions, surely, are predicated on the notion that we make choices and that, if we make the wrong ones, we will be punished for them. Accordingly, if we are "free," precisely what kind of freedom do we possess, given God's infinite nature?

This latter question roiled Augustine's heart. Even such a small matter as the youthful theft of pears (little more than a prank) haunted him. What is more, his sexual side bothered him as he proceeded through life. Even as he was ever more attracted to Christianity, he feared he could not give up his sexuality. It was as if he was fettered in chains. Once, as he was considering monasticism and the consequent celibacy it would impose, he prayed to God: "give me chastity, but not yet" (8.7, p. 169) His soul, he said, feared the "stanching of habit," as if to say that he understood on a deep psychological level how difficult it would be to change behavior to which he had long been habituated (8.7, p. 170). How on his own power could he do what he increasingly realized he needed to do?

Regarding the intense extended moment that preceded his final conversion, he wrote: "meanwhile I was beside myself with madness that would bring me sanity" (8.8, p. 171) He relates manic behavior, tearing his hair and weeping. Looking back – and to boot echoing Plotinus – he realized that, to arrive at inner peace, he "needed no chariot or ship" (8.8, p. 171). But, very much unlike Plotinus, Augustine came to believe that he needed help. It was not completely under his control to reach the peaceful state of faith in God that would lead him where he needed to go. He, like all of us, carried the burden of original sin or, as he put it, "the sin freely committed by Adam" (8.10, p. 173).

Augustine believed he needed God's direct intervention, which God could give him only if God so chose. Augustine needed grace. It came to him in the guise of a child. In the medieval tradition that followed him, the story Augustine related became a template for works of art and a way of memorializing his conversion.

As he was living with a companion named Alypius, Augustine used to retire to a small garden they shared. Beset by emotion, finding himself yet again in tears, Augustine's attention was captured, and he turned to a beautiful sound, the voice of a child in song: "Whether it was the voice of a boy or girl I cannot say, but again and again it repeated the refrain: 'take it and read, take it and read'" (8.12, p. 177). Take it and read: *tolle, lege*, in Latin. But what was he to read? Augustine was unaware if this was a children's game of some sort, or a habitual chant. And then he realized what was going on: "I stemmed my flood of tears" – remember, he was in a state of extreme emotional distress – "and stood up, telling myself that this could only be a divine command to open my book of Scripture and read the first passage on which my eyes should fall" (8.12, p. 177). He was reminded of the story of Antony – an early Christian monk – who had "happened to go into a church while the Gospel was being read" and had taken that happenstance as a divine message.

Augustine, accordingly, already conditioned by a conversion story that was part of Christian culture, and now himself emotionally ready to be overcome by the Lord, took the same path. This voice of a child was really God – in all His infinite majesty – singling out finite, fragile Augustine, pointing the way for him, a way whose direction was shaped by a book: Holy Scripture. Augustine opened the book which he had been reading: Paul's letters.

In silence he read the first passage on which his eyes fell: "Not in reveling and drunkenness, not in lust and wantonness, not in quarrels and rivalries. Rather, arm yourselves with the Lord Jesus Christ. Spend no more thought on nature and nature's appetites" (8.12, p. 178, citing Rom 13:13–14). It was a passage from Paul's Letter to the Romans, the very letter in which Paul confronts God's infinitely powerful nature.

Peace washed over Augustine. He shared what he had read with his companion, Alypius, who was himself on the verge of dedicating himself to Christ. Finally, Augustine informed Monica, his devout Christian mother, who had all the while been praying that he would finally convert. She rejoiced. Augustine addresses God: "You converted me to yourself, so that I no longer desired a wife or placed any hope in this world, but stood firmly upon the rule of faith, where you had shown me to her in a dream so many years before" (8.12, p. 178). His mother's prayers answered, Augustine considered his conversion complete.

The section of Paul's Letter to the Romans from which Augustine quotes happens to be embedded in a part of that Letter urging its readers to obey earthly law, since "there is no power but from God, and those that are, are ordained of God" (Rom 13:1). Paul is referring to human governance and humanly instituted laws, even as he is suggesting that such laws as do exist are there because, at some remove, God wants them to be so. In that same chapter, however, directly before Augustine's quotation, Paul hints at the instability, not so much of earthly law, but of the world as we know it, saying:

> Now is the hour for us to rise from sleep. For now our salvation is nearer than when we believed. The night has passed, and the day is at hand. Let us therefore cast off the works of darkness, and put on the armor of light. Let us walk honestly, as if in the day... (Rom 13:11–12)

And it is directly thereafter that the passage on which Augustine landed begins: "not in rioting and drunkenness," and so on.

Complexities abound in Paul's Letter to the Romans, and especially in the section under discussion. Obey humanly instituted governance, because it is part of God's providence, which encompasses many things unknowable to us, all of which must be good, since they derive from God. But also realize that, humanly instituted as that governance is, it is temporary when compared to God's eternity. Moreover, something new is coming: "Now our salvation is nearer" than we previously thought. Paul is obliquely signaling his belief, inherited from the Jewish messianic tradition and adumbrated by Jesus himself, that Jesus will come again, eventually to judge the living and the dead. And he is suggesting, as well, that the time is nearer than we might think: "the night has passed, and the day is at hand."

For Augustine, his quotation of Paul's Letter to the Romans in the *Confessions* is one among many citations of Paul. In itself, it is unsurprising. Augustine had identified Paul as especially important for his own spiritual growth. Encountering Paul, Augustine learned of a new way to read, as he gradually came to believe that many of the ideas found in the "Platonists" were more fully developed in Paul.

However, there is something more to the vision toward which Augustine gestures. For it is a sketch, inchoate in the *Confessions*, of a view of history that he went on to develop more robustly in his *City of God*. This vision signaled that history had a direction, that it was not an endlessly repeating cycle of powers rising and falling, and that in some way or another God was behind that directionality.

11

AUGUSTINE, THE *CITY OF GOD*, AND HISTORY

As Augustine was living in the North African city of Hippo, the city of Rome was sacked by foreign invaders in 410. Alaric, king of the invading Visigoths, besieged Rome, torched some central buildings, and pillaged the city, humbling the citizens of what had once been the actual, and not just symbolic, center of a world empire. Augustine became aware of people's reactions. Some believed the sack had occurred because Romans' worship of the pagan gods had waned, blaming the misfortune on their too-great adherence to "new" gods, or rather, to the Christian God.

Augustine wrote the *City of God* in part against this latter notion, that is, that Christianity was somehow not a valid religion and that the Christian God was not a powerful god.[1] He structured the work in twenty-two "books" (ranging, usually, from thirty to fifty pages in a modern edition). Late in life, he sent a letter to a correspondent suggesting how it was to be divided, if one were to bind the various "books" into "codex" format (the word "codex" signifies the basic "book" format as we know it today, with pages between two covers).[2] Since there were too many individual books to fit into one codex, Augustine said one could divide it into either two or five parts. He went into detail about the five-part division. In the first part (Books 1–5) he wrote against those who maintained that the worship of

---

[1] I will cite in the text using book, section, and page numbers from Augustine, *Concerning the City of God Against the Pagans*, tr. Henry Bettenson, with introduction by John O'Meara (London: Penguin, 2003); Latin text can be found in Augustine, *The City of God Against the Pagans*, 7 vols., ed. and tr. George E. McCracken, William Green, and others (Cambridge, MA: Harvard University Press, 1962–1972). For bibliography and important perspectives, see Gerard O'Daly, *Augustine's* City of God: *A Reader's Guide*, 2nd ed. (Oxford: Oxford University Press, 2020).

[2] Augustine, *Oeuvres de Saint Augustin, Lettres 1*–29**, Bibliothèque Augustinienne, 78 vols. to date, vol. 46B, ed. Johannes Divjak (Paris: Études Augustiniennes, 1987), let. 1a, pp. 54–59.

pagan gods could lead to happiness in this life. In part two (which covers Books 6–10), that trajectory continues, as he offers both genealogies of pagan worship practices (how they came about, what they are, and so on) and refutations of their efficacy. Part three (11–14) addresses creation, both that of the earth and that of humanity. Part four (15–18) considers more of human history up through Christ. Finally, part five (19–22) addresses the most pressing questions, including the highest good for humanity, the last judgment, and the resurrection.

To modern eyes, the *City of God* is a long work that can seem to meander and range across subjects hardly worthy of discussion, meaningful though these were to Augustine. To understand why it was so powerful and lasting, four topics come to the fore: Augustine's views of history, his opinions on the power of the pagan gods versus that of the Christian God, his statements concerning pagan philosophy, and his declarations on predestination.

The word "history" embeds many different senses. The Greek word *historia* possessed several meanings, but the basic one was "inquiry," usually done by observation. It could also connote a record of those observations and, indeed, a narrative account of events. There were some similar variabilities in the Latin tradition as well. But what is most difficult to grasp for modern readers is history's rhetorical nature in the premodern world. For the most part, one wrote history to persuade people by means of, and one read it to learn from, examples. They might be examples of conduct in battle, of a leader who exhibited virtue, or an enemy who exhibited vice. The notion was that one would learn what to imitate and what to avoid.[3]

But the theory of history was a different matter. Was history, for example, cyclical? The Greek historian Polybius (200–118 BCE) had developed the idea that history progressed through different types of rulership each of which had a good, and then a bad, manifestation. One began with "rule by one" (monarchy), a situation that was untheorized and simple: One man rose up to rule. One then moved to kingship – a state in which the institution of kingship exists as such. But then, eventually, that institution would be abused, and a tyranny would arise, with unjust rule provoking dissatisfaction. A society would then proceed to "aristocracy" (rule by the "best" or *aristoi*, in Greek), only to be supplanted by "oligarchy," or rule by the "few" (*oligoi*), who were concerned only with keeping power among their own

---

[3] See Matthew B. Roller, *Models from the Past in Roman Culture: A World of Exempla* (Cambridge: Cambridge University Press, 2018); and Christian Habicht, *Historiography: Ancient Medieval, and Modern*, 3rd ed. (Chicago: University of Chicago Press, 2007), pp. 1–66.

restricted numbers, without regard for the wishes and needs of society at large. Eventually, in reaction, a "democracy" would emerge, a positive rule by the "people" (*demos*), which would then turn into "ochlocracy," or rule by the "mob" (*ochlos*), in which chaos would eventually reign. Out of that roiling chaos would arise one strong ruler, and so the cycle would begin again.[4] Polybius recognized (as had Aristotle long before, in his *Politics*) that there were in general these three types of constitutions (rule by one, by the few, and by the many), and that they vacillated between good and bad forms. There was no sense of inevitability, that history was necessarily trending in one direction.

For Augustine, however, the sense of direction was important. He explains why in a preface, directed to his friend Marcellinus, who had asked for Augustine's help in explaining why Christianity should not be seen as a cause of Rome's weakening over time. Augustine writes that he is sending along a book:

> in which I have taken upon myself the task of defending the glorious City of God against those who prefer their own gods to the Founder of that City. I treat of it both as it exists in this world of time, a stranger among the ungodly, living by faith, and as it stands in the security of its everlasting seat. This security it now awaits in steadfast patience, until 'justice returns to judgment' [Augustine quotes Psalm 94:15], but it is to attain it hereafter in virtue of its ascendancy over its enemies, when the final victory is won, and peace established. The task is long and arduous; but God is our helper. (1.pref.3)

Several concepts stand out, none more so than the City of God. It is "glorious," according to Augustine, but it also clearly has enemies, "who prefer their own gods" to the one true God. It has a dimension that we can perceive and parameters within which we behave – it "exists in this world of time," as Augustine states. But there is something about the City of God that is different from any earthly city, ever. True, its members live in the everyday world. But they also live "by faith," a faith that allows them to understand, and to believe, that the City of God has an "everlasting seat." This is to say that the City of God has a dual aspect. In its time-bound, earthly instantiation, it may suffer defeats and seem less powerful than it is. In its eternal aspect, however, it is more powerful than any community the world has ever known. Eventually, the City of God will defeat its enemies,

---

[4] Polybius, *The Histories*, 6 vols., ed. and tr. W. R. Paton, F. W. Walbank, and Christian Habicht (Cambridge, MA: Cambridge University Press, 2010), 6.2.4 (vol. 2, pp. 298–301).

it will have a "final victory," it will, with God's help, achieve everlasting peace.

In the New Testament, in the book of Revelation, John of Patmos had written: "And I saw a new heaven and a new earth, for the first heaven and the first earth was passed away, and the sea is now no more" (Rev 21:1–4). John saw "the holy city, the new Jerusalem," come down from heaven, and he heard a loud voice announce the city as the "the tabernacle of God with men, and God himself with them shall be their God." God would be directly present to human beings, in other words, "with them" at this undetermined moment yet to come. This passage from Revelation joins any number of instances from scripture pointing to a divine order as set against the corrupt institutions of worldly power (and to the Christian community as the new Jerusalem), all of which went into Augustine's lasting conception.[5]

Also, by the "City of God," Augustine means to say that its citizens comprise the Church broadly conceived, what later thinkers in the Middle Ages would term the *congregatio fidelium*, or "congregation of the faithful."[6] The faithful are its citizens, and God is its ultimate ruler, however the earthly Church might arrange and govern itself at any given moment.

The consequences that might ensue from a view of this sort are easy to fathom. The world, with its numerous daily events, conflicts, ups and downs, is now to be interpreted providentially. Any defeat one suffers, as a citizen of the City of God, will take on a singular patina. An advantage of this view is that it can generate needed humility in life in general, and more specifically, in one's view of politics. A disadvantage: disengagement in politics might ensue.[7] If everything we do in our everyday world is part of a pilgrimage to the Eternal, then real-world instruments of carrying out Christ's message might not seem so urgent. For instance, as Paul had said, in God's eyes there were "neither Jew nor Greek, neither male nor female, neither bond nor free," so that everyone at a root sense is equal. Should we, then, be doing something to ameliorate the conditions of the poor and other disenfranchised people such as the enslaved? Or will that and other such possible, action-oriented missions seem less urgent in Augustine's larger, providential view of history and our place within it? One could say that, if the world is full of patent injustice, well, those who have suffered humbly

---

[5] E.g., Isa 2:2–4; 24–27; 60–66; Dan 2:44, 7:13–14, 2:27; John 18:36; Matt 5:14.
[6] See Brian Tierney, *Foundations of the Conciliar Theory* (Cambridge: Cambridge University Press, 1955, repr. 1968), pp. 41–46.
[7] Cf. Gabriele, *Between Prophecy and Apocalypse*, 37–46.

will eventually receive their reward ... just not here, not now. After all, didn't Christ also say that the poor will always be with us, that one should give unto Caesar what is Caesar's (Matt 22:21)? Didn't Paul enjoin the enslaved to obey their masters, even as he also urged masters to be benevolent toward those who were enslaved, since in God's view "there is no respect of persons," meaning that all are equal in God's eyes (Eph 6:5–9)? Does this providential view of history not only lead to quiescence but also validate existing forms of injustice?

Augustine's view of history did not create, nor did it resolve, the evergreen contrast between the merits of involvement in the rough-and-tumble world of politics and the contemplative retreat therefrom. Nor did it prevent the emergence of many different opinions and actions related to societal injustices. The power of his narrative lay instead in the idea of hope. One day, he is saying, we in the City of God will win. We don't know when it will happen, but victory will assuredly ensue, finally and irrevocably.

There were signs all over that the denizens of the other city, the City of Man, adhere to beliefs, habits, and assumptions about the world that are, in a word, wrong. Augustine is compelled to tell that story too, interwoven as it is with that of the City of God. Take the misplaced notion (of the denizens of the City of Man) that their gods are somehow better than the one, Christian God.

The 410 sack of Rome itself proved how wrong they are. In the City of Man – the earthly city in which we live our day to day lives – wars occur, conquerors rise, people and cities are vanquished. We know this, Augustine says, for "we have the records of many wars, both before the foundation of Rome and after its rise to power" (1.2, p. 7). The Sack represented just another instance of this type of earthly conflict. Yet, let our enemies read the history of those wars, "and then produce instances of the capture of any city by foreign enemies when those enemies spared any whom they found taking refuge in the temples of their gods" (1.2, p. 7). Let them find the case of any general ordering his men to spare any people that they found in a temple. Augustine relates cases known to all in which sacred space served as no guarantee that violence against an enemy would not ensue, such as when the Greeks, Diomedes and Ulysses, violated a Trojan temple and later, with their fellow Greeks, went on to win the Trojan War (1.2, p. 7).[8] When a city is sacked, all is lost, and the victors give no respect to the faith of the conquered.

---

[8] Augustine draws on Virgil, *Aeneid*, 2.502–558.

The 410 sack of Rome was different, however, as the conduct of the conquering invader, Alaric, king of the Visigoths, proved. Alaric was an adherent of what is known as "Arian" Christianity, so named after the Christian thinker Arius (256–336 CE), who had theorized that Christ, rather than being a coequal part of the Trinity, had been begotten in time by God, even if Christ too could be counted as God. As Augustine and others refined the doctrine of the Trinity (three coequal persons, all of them "God" but all three having separate identities), Arianism eventually faded, even as it was surely a recognizable strand among the many that were interwoven in early Christianity's rich and complicated fabric.[9]

In the event, in Rome in 410, though it was a different Christian sect from that practiced by most Roman Christians, it was still Christianity. Alaric, though a conqueror, had a soft spot for the religion, and he spared Romans who had retreated to Christian places of worship. This fact allows Augustine to engage in some rhetorical jujitsu. To those pagans who said the sack had occurred because Rome was not paying enough allegiance to its old gods, Augustine replied instead that it was the Christian God who had protected them when the sack occurred: "They were spared for Christ's sake, pagans though they were; yet they scorn to acknowledge this" (1.3, p. 9). But to make this sort of point stick, Augustine needed to go further. His first step was to situate the sack in the context of the City of Man – the regular world, which will always have wars, temporary injustices, and events of all sorts, events that will be pleasing to some, less so to others. His first step, in other words, was to understand the sack as part of his new view of history, wherein the City of Man will be the site of endless such events, even as the City of God would eventually triumph.

He required something else: to delegitimize the very idea of the pagan gods. He had to combat the notion that they were worthy of being called gods at all. It should be noted that Augustine has respect for the City of Man, in so far as it is embodied in Rome, with its storied history of conquest and empire. It is just that, before the birth of Christ, the Romans were unable to understand whose hand was moving them forward (that of God, in Augustine's view). After Christ, it was only empty superstition that kept them invested in the idea of their gods. And there is an important reason for their adherence to their superstitions:

> The most plausible explanation of all this is the suggestion that the gods were once human beings who received adulation from men who wished to have them as gods. Those men instituted rites and ceremonies in honor

---

[9] See Marilyn Dunn, *Arianism* (Leeds: ARC Humanities Press, 2021).

of each of their heroes, based on their personalities, their characters, their achievements, and their adventures. (7.18, p. 276)

The gods had originally been regular people, outstanding in what they did in life, to be sure, but not divine in the way we – Augustine is implying – now understand divinity. Naturally enough, the pagans had wanted to commemorate their heroes. As time went by, custom, habits, and accreted rituals simply added to the popularity of these "gods," a process abetted by "the fictions of the poets and helped by the seductive arts of the deceitful spirits" (7.18, p. 276).

"The fictions of the poets." "The seductive arts of the deceitful spirits." Much lies embedded in those two seemingly tossed off phrases. As to the fictions of the poets, this complaint went back to Plato, who in his *Republic* set the paradigm for all future discussion of this issue. A poet is only an imitator, like a painter, since the poet's works don't reflect truth and instead "indulge the senseless element in the soul."[10] What Plato meant was that poets deal with emotions, which can easily be swayed. And their work becomes even more problematic when they represent "gods" as possessing the same sorts of foibles as human beings.

As to the "seductive arts of the deceitful spirits," Augustine is referring here to demons. One of the many possible dividing lines between premodern and modern (admittedly terms that are always subject to the assumptions of the interpreter) is belief in the existence of demons.[11] These were considered real, physically existent beings, airy in nature and thus suitable to inhabit the ether. One of Augustine's early third-century predecessors, Minucius Felix, hearkened back to Plato's dialogue *Symposium*, writing that Plato had described there a "substance between mortal and immortal, that is, between body and spirit."[12] It was out of this substance that love arose; it

---

[10] Plato, *Rep.*, 605c, in Plato, *Republic*, 2 vols., ed. and tr. Chris Emlyn-Jones and William Preddy (Cambridge, MA: Harvard University Press, 2013), 2: 430–431.

[11] See Stuart Clark, *Thinking with Demons: The Idea of Witchcraft in Early Modern Europe* (Oxford: Oxford University Press, 1997); Lorraine Daston and Katherine Park, *Wonders and the Order of Nature: 1150–1750* (New York: Zone, 1998); Stephen Gaukroger, *The Collapse of Mechanism and the Rise of Sensibility. Science and the Shaping of Modernity, 1680–1760* (Oxford: Oxford University Press, 2010); Walter Stephens, *Demon Lovers: Witchcraft, Sex, and the Crisis of Belief* (Chicago: University of Chicago Press, 2002); Gregory D. Wiebe, *Fallen Angels in the Theology of Saint Augustine* (Oxford University Press, 2021).

[12] Minucius Felix, *Octavius*, in Tertullian, *Apology, De spectaculis*. Minucius Felix, *Octavius*, ed. and tr. T. R. Glover and Gerald H. Rendall (Cambridge, MA: Cambridge University Press, 1931), pp. 314–437, at sec. 26, pp. 396–397. Minucius refers to Plato, *Symposium*, 202d–203a, in Plato, *Lysis, Symposium, Phaedrus*, ed. and tr. Chris Emlyn-Jones and William Preddy (Cambridge, MA: Harvard University Press, 2022), pp. 244–247.

could enter people and shape their emotions (*adfectus fingere*). Demons are like this, according to Minucius. They lurk "under statues and consecrated images," they "inspire prophets," "haunt temples," and "are the authors of oracles wrapped for the most part in falsehood."[13] Demons can inhabit people and become the real movers behind all sorts of damaging behaviors, calling people "away from the true God and toward material things."[14]

In some respects, then, demons seemed to have abilities superior to ours. In Augustine's day (as in the era of Minucius), some thought that demons were the messengers of the gods and that one could even worship them, show them respect and, by means of magical hidden arts, employ them for one's own ends. All this Augustine wishes to combat, though tellingly he does not deny that demons exist. Instead, he says they need to be considered in their proper place. Many believe there are three categories of beings with a rational soul: "gods, men, and demons" (8.14, p. 318). They are situated as follows: "the gods have their abode in heaven; mankind lives on earth; demons dwell in the air" (8.14, p. 318). The mistake people make is in assuming that the relative worth of these three categories of being corresponds to their locations, thinking that the gods are superior to men and demons, while people "are set below gods and demons in respect of difference of merit as well as in the order of the physical elements" (8.14, p. 318). True, demons have certain characteristics that distinguish them, such as eternal life, which Augustine admits they "share with the gods" (8.16, p. 322). But those human beings who worship demons on that basis are also wrong – for demons do not possess eternal bliss. Accordingly, they have no right to be worshiped, "these animals of air, who only have reason so that they may be capable of wretchedness, and passions so that they may in fact be wretched, and eternity so that their wretchedness can have no end" (8.16, p. 322). We see here what a strange kind of borderland Augustine inhabits, where he must argue that there is only one God, even as he admits the existence of "gods" as well as beings, demons, who share some divine characteristics.

To understand demons, Augustine relies on the account given by an earlier North African thinker named Apuleius, who had outlined many of the characteristics demons were thought to possess. Their existence seemed a self-evident fact. And yet, as Augustine moves through and beyond his discussion of demons, he expands outward, offering more criticism of pagan practices and differentiating Christian rituals. Pagans worship their "gods,"

---

[13] Minucius Felix, *Octavius*, sec. 27, pp. 396–397, tr. modified.
[14] Ibid., sec. 27, pp. 398–399.

who were almost all originally regular people. So, in one respect, pagan worship is a cult of the dead. Christian respect for martyrs, however, is not the same thing: "we certainly honor the memory of our martyrs, as holy men of God, who have contended for the truth as far as the death of their bodies" (8.27, p. 340). Augustine is subtly countering the charge that, with the evolving Christian respect for, and rituals surrounding, their saints and martyrs, Christians were simply engaging in the same practices as had the pagans, though calling them by different names. In truth, there was something to that charge.

One of the reasons Christianity succeeded in the eventually Europe-encompassing way that it did in the early Middle Ages was this: Christians adopted, adapted, and transformed the apparatus of pagan religion, which included the sacred calendar and, meaningfully, sacred places. For one example, take the "Pantheon" in Rome, or "Temple to all the Gods," taken over and Christianized in the seventh century and dedicated to Mary but also to the "commemoration of the saints," as one contemporary observer reported.[15] It is a stone's throw from the Roman Church *Santa Maria Sopra Minerva*, or "Saint Mary on top of Minerva." This Church was created as such in the Early Middle Ages.[16] But it had once been the site of a temple dedicated to the Egyptian goddess Isis (worshipped by Romans as well). Having fallen into desuetude in late antiquity, it then became associated with the Roman goddess Minerva, whence it was known as "Saint Mary on top of Minerva." The church of San Clemente (a few blocks from the Colosseum in Rome) was built over a residential ancient apartment house that contained a small "Mithraeum," that is, a religious site dedicated to Mithras, the originally Persian god worshipped by many Romans.[17] There was a lot of this sort of thing, none of it representing simple acts of

---

[15] Paulus Diaconus, *Historia Langobardorum*, ed. Georg Waitz, Vol. 1 of *Monumenta Germaniae Historica, Scriptores rerum Langobardicarum et Italicarum saec. VI–IX* (Hannover: Hahn, 1878), 4.36, at p. 160.

[16] See Almuth Klein, "Santa Maria sopra Minerva," in Daniela Mondini, Carola Jäggi, and Peter Cornelius Claussen (eds.), *Die Kirchen der Stadt Rom im Mittelalter 1050–1300*, 4 vols. to date, vol. 4., Forschungen zur Kunstgeschichte und Christlichen Archäologie Band 23, Corpus Cosmatorum II, 4 (Stuttgart: Franz Steiner, 2020), 310–336, esp. 311–315; Richard Krautheimer, *Rome: Profile of a City, 312–1308* (Princeton: Princeton University Press, 2000), p. 252.

[17] See Leonard Boyle, OP, *A Short Guide to Saint Clement's, Rome* (Rome: Collegio San Clemente, 1989), pp. 8–9; Federico Guidobaldi, *San Clemente: Gli edifici romani, la basilica paleocristiana e le fasi altomedioevali* (Rome: Collegio San Clemente, 1992); Richard Krautheimer, *Corpus Basilicarum Christianarum Romae: The Early Christian Basilicas of Rome (IV–IX Centuries)*, 5 vols. (Vatican City: Pontificio istituto di archeologia cristiana, 1937–1977), 1: 117–136.

appropriation. It was just that people repurposed ancient sites (secular as well as sacred), as local religious, political, and social interests changed. "Christianization," in that sense, was a long, complex process, one that in distant hindsight may seem linear, but in the moment included contingency, negotiation, adaptation, and conflict.[18]

But Augustine's vision – of one God, in charge of one city, whose destiny would be manifested over time – included these sorts of practices as essential. One took aspects of ancient paganism that were helpful to Christianity, used them, and allowed that fateful story to unfold. In fact, if one looked carefully enough, it was apparent that God had foreshadowed to the ancient pagans the notion that Christ, the guarantor of eternal life, would come: "This mystery of eternal life has been made known by the ministry of angels from the very beginning of the human race. It was revealed to those who were fit to receive the knowledge by means of signs and symbols appropriate to the times" (7.32, p. 293). The Jews were among those chosen to receive these adumbrations, and it was out of their community that prophets emerged, who foretold the advent of Christ.

Among philosophers, too, there were those who had the right inklings. As part of his unfolding of the City of Man, Augustine offers a history of philosophy, in a way that had become standard: tracing the evolution of

---

[18] See Kim Bowes, *Private Worship, Public Values and Religious Change in Late Antiquity* (Cambridge: Cambridge University Press, 2008); Jan N. Bremmer, "How do We Explain the Quiet Demise of Graeco-Roman Religion? An Essay," *Numen* 68 (2021), 230–271; Peter Brown, *The Rise of Western Christendom: Triumph and Diversity, AD 200–1000*, rev. ed. (London: Wiley-Blackwell, 2013); Peter Brown, *Authority and the Sacred: Aspects of the Christianisation of the Roman World* (Cambridge: Cambridge University Press, 1997), esp. 1–26; Jean-Pierre Caillet, "La transformation en église d'édifices publics et de temples à la fin de l'antiquité," in Claude Lepelley, ed., *La fin de la cité antique et le début de la cité médiévale de la fin du IIIe siècle à l'avènement de Charlemagne* (Bari: Edipuglia, 1996), pp. 191–211; John R. Curran, *Pagan City and Christian Capital: Rome in the Fourth Century* (Oxford: Oxford University Press, 2002); Hendrick Dey, *The Making of Medieval Rome: A New Profile of the City, 400–1420* (Cambridge: Cambridge University Press, 2021), pp. 1–136; Federico Guidobaldi, "Chiese titolari di Roma nel tessuto urbano preesistente," in Philippe Pergola and Fabrizio Bisconti, eds., *Quaeritur inventus colitur: miscellanea in onore di padre Umberto Maria Fasola*, 2 vols. (Vatican City: Pontificio Istituto di Archeologia Cristiana, 1989), 1: 383–396; Johannes Hahn, Stephen Emmel, and Ulrich Gotter, eds., *From Temple to Church: Destruction and Renewal of Local Cultic Topography in Late Antiquity* (Leiden: Brill, 2008); Claire Sotinel, "La conversion des lieux de culte, métaphore de la conversion des populations," *Archives de sciences sociales des religions* 63 (2018), 29–48; Bryan Ward-Perkins, "Reconfiguring Sacred Space: From Pagan Shrines to Christian Churches," in Gunner Brands and Hans-Georg Severin, eds., *Die spätantike Stadt und ihre Christianisierung* (Wiesbaden: Reichert Verlag, 2002), 285–290; Edward J. Watts, *The Final Pagan Generation* (Berkeley: University of California Press, 2015).

schools of philosophy. The Platonists take pride of place, largely because of their conception of divinity: "They realized that nothing changeable can be in the supreme God; and therefore, in their search for the supreme God, they raised their eyes above all mutable souls and spirits" (8.6, p. 307). The Platonic conception of the Forms was important, since it led them to the idea of one God: "they saw that in every mutable being, the form which determines its being, its mode of being, and its nature, can only come from him who truly is, because he exists immutably" (8.6, p. 307). The fact that they intuited God's immutability led them to the notion "that God is the creator from whom all other beings derive, while he himself is uncreated and underivative" (7.6, p. 308).

This notion, that there was – indeed, that there must be – one supreme being served as the reference point. Among all the schools of ancient philosophers, it was the Platonists who had arrived there. And it is meaningful that Augustine consciously speaks of "the Platonists." He says what he means by this, referring to "modern" philosophers, and saying that they term themselves Platonists. He reveals whom he has in mind: "Among these modern philosophers the most highly esteemed of the Greeks are Plotinus, Iamblichus, and Porphyry, while Apuleius of Africa stands out as a notable Platonist, writing in both Greek and Latin" (8.12, p. 316). What we observe here is twofold.

First, there is the idea that it is legitimate to use the ancient pagan tradition.[19] Augustine believed that, despite the dangerous ideas that could be found there, one could and should be aware of pagan antiquity and its literary and philosophical legacy. Like the Israelites in the book of Exodus who took and repurposed Egyptian treasures, so too should Christians take for their own use the parts of the pagan tradition that serve their new and better cultural aims, doing so, "as it were, from owners who have no right to them."[20] One could discard what was bad, and use what was good, or – a kind of middle way – repurpose that ancient legacy, much as one did in the case of buildings. Perhaps the foundation still existed, but the edifice would look different and be put to different uses. As Basil of Caesarea, a fourth-century Greek predecessor of Augustine's, suggested when it came to ancient pagan literature, one should behave as do bees. Why? "For bees

---

[19] There was a deep patristic background to Augustine's views. See Monique Alexandre, "La culture grecque, servante de la foi," in Arnaud Perrot, ed., *Les chrétiens et l'hellénisme: identités religieuses et culture grecque dans l'Antiquité tardive* (Paris: Éditions Rue d'Ulm, 2012), 31–59.
[20] Augustine, *De doctrina christiana*, ed. and tr. R. P. H. Green (Oxford: Clarendon, 1995), 2: XL, 60, pp. 124–125; Exod 3:21–2, 12:35–36.

neither approach all flowers equally, nor in truth do they attempt to carry off entire those on which they alight, but taking only so much of them as is suitable for their work, they let the rest go untouched."[21] And in any case, Basil said, most ancient writers who have at least some reputation for wisdom did, in places, write well about virtue.[22]

Augustine took this tendency in a slightly different direction. On the one hand, simply by surveying so many of the pagan classics, he showed that one could use pagan literature with profit. On the other, he fit that literature into a new narrative, one with a beginning, middle, and end. True, one could not say definitively where one sat on that chronological continuum. But where one stood in terms of its progression could be known. And in this respect, there was no doubt. The new, Christian world stood ahead of that of the pagans.

Indeed, Christian preeminence shines – and this is the second notable point – even with respect to the best of the philosophers, the Platonists. At the heart of Augustine's judgment stands a question. As he puts it: "is it right to worship one God, or many?" (8.12, p. 315). And the answer, regarding Plato and the best of the ancient philosophers, was that they "thought it right to render worship to a plurality of gods" (8.12, p. 316). It is after this discussion that Augustine launches into his lengthy thoughts about demons. He becomes obsessed by the question, citing ancient texts and opinions on demons, poking holes in theories when he can, but still, inevitably, believing that demons do exist.

If we look beyond his details for a moment and return to that question as to whether it is right to worship one God or many, we can see what Augustine's real problem is: Either you embraced the real unity of the divine or you didn't. Even though Plato and his followers conceded that there was one supreme being above all things, they still could not liberate themselves from their old polytheistic habits. As much as Augustine, like most early Christians, echoed certain pagan rituals, ideas, and mental frameworks, on this question – the nature of Christian monotheism – he was consistent. There was only one truly supreme God. And God being God meant that He possessed all the needed attributes: omniscience, omnipotence, and (even though it may lie hidden from our limited, human, mortal sight) omnibenevolence.

Respect for absolute oneness conditions the final noteworthy feature of Augustine's thought in the *City of God*: his ideas on predestination. Accordingly, one other aspect of God's superior Oneness comes to the fore.

---

[21] See Basil, *The Letters*, 4 vols., ed. and tr. Roy J. Deferrari (Cambridge, MA: Harvard University Press, 1926–1934), 4: 378–435, at 491, tr. modified.
[22] Ibid., 4: 399.

He has a plan. This fact puts our own actions in a singular light. Take what Augustine says regarding God's view of humanity:

> God almighty, the supreme and supremely good creator of all beings, who assists and rewards good wills, while he abandons and condemns the bad (and yet he controls both good and bad) surely did not fail to have a plan whereby he might complete the fixed number of citizens predestined in his wisdom, even out of the condemned human race. (14.26, p. 591)

Already one observes a tension.

Augustine wants to signal that there are rewards and punishments in the divine social economy (God "assists and rewards good wills"). But in truth it is halfhearted, overshadowed practically to the point of invisibility, by the looming mountain of absolute unity. Augustine cannot resist mentioning that God "controls both good and bad," and that God "surely did not fail to have a plan" when it came to predestination. Augustine goes on regarding whom God chooses, why, and how:

> He does not now choose them for their merits, seeing that the whole mass of mankind has been condemned as it were in its infected root; he selects them by grace and shows the extent of his generosity to those who have been set free not only in his dealings with them but also in his treatment of those who have not been freed. (14.26, p. 592)

Humankind is "condemned" in its "infected root." Augustine is referring to the notion of original sin, committed by Adam in the Garden of Eden. There, affected by desire, Adam turned from God and accepted a life enmeshed with all the physicality by which we are surrounded: flourishing growth, but also physical decay and corruption; proliferation and destruction; sex and death. In that moment Adam stood in for all of us human beings whether we liked it or not. We are all affected by that first disobedience to the one true God.

It should be said that Augustine, if he was not totally unique in his embrace of this idea regarding Adam, did solidify it. It became part of Christian tradition after him.[23] The Apostle Paul, whom Augustine admired and with whom he felt the greatest spiritual kinship, had said sin entered the world "by one man" and "by sin death. And so death passed upon all men ..." (Rom 5:12). It was a way to explain why Christ had come and what his advent meant for humanity: "for if by the offence of one" – again of Adam – "many have died, much more the grace of God and the gift of

---

[23] See Stephen Greenblatt, *The Rise and Fall of Adam and Eve* (New York: Norton, 2017).

grace in one man, Jesus Christ, hath abounded unto many" (Rom 12:15). The idea was that people from Adam up through the time of Christ had been, in some respect, "dead" and that Christ – his life and sacrificial death for us human beings – provided life to humanity. Or as Paul had put it elsewhere: "for by a man came death, and by a man the resurrection of the dead" (1 Cor 15:22). There was something deeply sinful in humanity, but then there was that other thing too, something divine, incarnate in its best form as Christ and, somehow, available to us all.

Augustine, however, placed more emphasis on the stark part, on the sinfulness. Part of this emphasis was owed to his personality and his concern with his own sexuality. In his *Confessions*, as he moves toward his final conversion, what he needs to give up most of all is precisely sex, something that he had a lot of trouble doing. In the *City of God*, Augustine discusses human procreation. Had Adam not sinned, procreation could have occurred without the mad passions of lust:

> the sexual organs would have been brought into activity by the same bidding of the will as controlled the other organs. Then, without feeling the allurement of passion goading him on, the husband would have relaxed on his wife's bosom in tranquility of mind and with no impairment of his body's integrity. (14.29, p. 591)

Augustine sees the passion that accompanies human sexuality as a loss of self-control and thus as a violation of one's wholeness. After Adam, in short, we – as people in the multifaceted world – are irremediably out of control. Sexuality is a stand-in for all the other things we do that, in some respects, we know we should not do – in Augustine's view, of course.

Accordingly, we need God's grace if we have any hope of being elevated from the swampy human condition. In fact, God "has selected" some human beings with His grace, for reasons known to Him and Him alone. This choice, on God's part, also implies inevitably that, while He freely gives His grace to some, from others He withholds it, an antinomy that, to say the least, can seem disquieting if we are also to consider God omnibenevolent. Indeed, the tension there (between God's omnipotence and His omnibenevolence) is so starkly present that Augustine's justifications for this seemingly contradictory state of affairs makes for difficult reading. He writes:

> It follows that the actions of sinners, whether angels or men, cannot obstruct "the great works of God, carefully designed to fulfil all his decisions" [Augustine is quoting Ps 111:2] since in his providence and omnipotence he assigns to each his own gifts and knows how to turn to good account the good and the evil alike. (14.27, p. 592)

This is to say that not everyone gets God's grace but that, in the big picture, He turns even seemingly bad things into part of His providential, ultimately good plan. Augustine goes further in this train of thought, bringing no less than Satan into the picture:

> Hence the evil angel had been so condemned and so hardened in evil, as the fitting retribution for his first evil will, that he could no longer have a good will; but nothing prevented God from turning him to good use and allowing him to tempt the first man, who had been created upright, that is, with a good will. (14.27, p. 592)

The "evil angel" was "condemned," but his condemnation was a result of his own "first evil will." So, was it the evil angel's choice to allow his will to turn toward evil? Did God stand out of the way of that choice? If so, why? Augustine's thorny logic continues, as he tries to explain Adam's fall:

> For just as it is not in our power to live in this physical frame without the support of food, and yet it is in our power not to live in it at all (which is what happens to suicides), so it was not in man's power, even in paradise, to live a good life without the help of God, yet it was in his power to live an evil life; but then his happiness would not continue and a most just punishment would follow. Therefore, since God was well aware that man would fall as he did, was there any reason why he should not have allowed him to be tempted by the malice of the jealous angel? (14.27, pp. 592–593)

Adam could have chosen not to sin, but he did sin. God of course knew he would sin. So, it was legitimate for God ("good" God) to use the "jealous angel" (Satan) to tempt Adam, thus causing humanity's fall from grace, but also, providentially, allowing the drama of the City of God to unfold, with the advent of Christ and his exemplary life and death. It was all part of the plan.

These are difficult questions. Logical discourse can only go so far in answering them. Augustine himself, in his *Confessions*, had admitted that he found himself powerless at times to cease from sinning – whether the sin was the youthful prank of stealing pears or the later, graver, sexual loss of control in adulthood. What Augustine is saying, of course, is that it was only when he accepted God's grace that he was – meaning that he *felt* – "saved." But, again, why would a good God choose to save only some people and not others?

Wanting to do things to earn your salvation but realizing that anything you do is so small compared to God's infinite wisdom and goodness, that it could never measure up; understanding God as infinitely Good and attentive to individuals but realizing that the very idea of God makes him, to some extent, out of reach – at least out of reach of our limited human reason: These paradoxes have hovered over Christianity ever since. Augustine found a way to weave his version into Christian intellectual history, and moreover, into a vision of history that we can describe as a blind teleology. We know that, at some point, human history – or the "City of Man" – will end, when Christ the redeemer comes back, one more time, to judge the living and the dead. What we don't know is when. So, it winds up being up to us to figure out our place in this historical scheme. Some of us will, inevitably, think that we are driven by God to do things. These might be charitable works, acts of mercy, and other good things. But we might also believe that God is guiding us to wage wars, to commit acts of violence, to lose focus on the individuals with whom we interact, because we believe it is all part of "God's plan," a belief we nourish without the proof of reason but with the certainty of faith.

Augustine's powerful legacy encoded all of these seeming contradictions. He gave to his successors a model of personal transformation and a view of history whose shaping effects resonated throughout the Middle Ages and beyond.

12

ENDINGS AND NEW BEGINNINGS

Gregory the Great and Beyond

AUGUSTINE'S *CITY OF GOD* STANDS AS A MONUMENTAL WORK. Copied by hand many times, it quickly became a classic, circulating widely from the time after Augustine died in 430 through to the Italian Renaissance.[1] The year 430, as it happens, saw the city of his bishopric, Hippo Regius (today Annaba, in Algeria) besieged by the Vandals, an invading tribe from what is now Poland.[2] Augustine, consumed by a fever and reading penitential Psalms hung on the walls of his room, died in prayer, in the hope that the city would not fall.[3] But fall it did.[4] The Vandals went on to establish a kingdom that included that corner of North Africa, along with Sicily, Malta, and other locations. Later, in the year 533, Justinian, the Eastern Roman emperor (whose seat was in Constantinople) defeated the Vandal kingdom. The City of Man continued, in other words, with its wars and treacheries, violence and decay, conquests and defeats all part of its continuing evolution.

Yet now, as history happened, Christians had at their disposal a theory that accounted for change in a way that pagan theories did not. History was

---

[1] See Guy Claessens and Fabio della Schiava, eds., *Augustine and the Humanists: Reading the City of God from Petrarch to Poliziano* (Gent: Lisa, 2021); Michael M. Gorman, "A Survey of the Oldest Manuscripts of St. Augustine's 'De civitate Dei,'" *The Journal of Theological Studies* 33 (1982), 398–410. The transmission of Augustine's works through manuscripts can be seen in the monumental series, Manfred Oberleitner et al., *Die handschriftliche Überlieferung der Werke des heiligen Augustinus*, 9 vols. to date (Vienna: Böhlau, 1969–).

[2] See Christian Courtois, *Les vandales et l'Afrique* (Paris: Arts et Mètiers Graphiques, 1955); Andrew H. Merrills and Richard Miles, *The Vandals* (Oxford: Wiley-Blackwell, 2010); Roland Steinacher, *Die Vandalen: Aufstieg und Fall eines Barbarenreichs* (Stuttgart: Klett-Cotta, 2016).

[3] Possidius, *Sancti Augustini vita*, ed. and tr. Herbert T. Weiskotten (Princeton: Princeton University Press, 1919), pp. 140–145; see also Erika Hermanowicz, *Possidius of Calama: A Study of the North African Episcopate in the Age of Augustine* (Oxford: Oxford University Press, 2008), pp. 17–63.

[4] In 431. Steinacher, *Die Vandalen*, 99.

not cyclical, nor was it the progress of a blind fate, nor was it the manifestation on earth of a struggle between two notionally equal principles of good and evil, all of which were theories that pagan antiquity had prized.[5] Now, instead, one could posit the existence of a fundamentally good, all-powerful God, one whose power was broad enough that He could be interested in individual human beings and also in control of, literally, everything that exists. He was, in short, magnificent, better than anything we could imagine, and desirable.

This last factor, God's desirability, signals one final feature that marks the *City of God*. About it, one can say that it overflows with encyclopedic learning, so much so that Augustine seemed to have read and to have had meaningful opinions on almost everything. Yet the learning is there with a purpose and not for its own sake. The literature that Augustine quotes is all part of the rich pagan inheritance he and others like him possessed, where references – for example – to Virgil's *Aeneid* sprang unprompted to memory. One had studied that epic poem intensely, memorized much of it, and learned to use its characters as exemplars both positive and negative for one's own behavior. It had become a part of the furnishing of one's mind. Studying the *Aeneid* and other classics also taught one to read with depth and acuity. One came to understand both that the text had many levels of possible interpretation and that one's obligation as a reader was to parse those levels, extending their richness in a never-ending conversation. And of course, for Augustine and other early Christians, one employed those techniques most intensely in one's reading of the Bible.[6]

It is here where we can see the paradigm shift, both in Augustine's case and in that of other early Christian writers. To be sure, one engaged in a lot of book learning. But one did so with a goal, and that goal was to get closer to God. It represented a new model of joining learning to religion, invigorating monastic spirituality in the Middle Ages as countless monks and clerics read, studied, and learned Latin.[7] Though that language died out as a native

---

[5] Cf. Ronald H. Nash, *The Meaning of History* (Nashville: Broadman & Holman, 1998).
[6] See Henri de Lubac, *Exégèse médiévale: les quatre sens de l'Écriture*, 4 vols. (Paris: Aubier, 1959–1991; reedition, Clamecy: Desclée de Brouwer, 1993); English translation, Henri de Lubac, *Medieval Exegesis: The Four Senses of Scripture*, 3 vols., tr. Marc Sebanc and E. M. Macierowski (Grand Rapids: Eerdman's, 2009); Beryl Smalley, *The Study of the Bible in the Middle Ages*, 3rd ed. (Notre Dame: University of Notre Dame Press, 1964), pp. 1–36; Tarmo Toom, ed., *Patristic Theories of Biblical Interpretation: The Latin Fathers* (Cambridge: Cambridge University Press, 2016).
[7] See Jean Leclercq, O.S.B., *The Love of Learning and the Desire for God: A Study in Monastic Culture*, tr. Catharine Misrahi (Chicago: University of Chicago Press, 1982); and Pierre

language in the early Middle Ages, it nevertheless remained western Europe's language of learning.[8] Indeed, Latin and the Christian religion became intertwined. To learn Latin, one needed the pagan classics. But then, one had to take that learning and channel it correctly.

Later, in the High Middle Ages, an anonymous Latin rhyme emerged. Seemingly simple and direct, it was intended to help students memorize the information it contained, information pertinent for reading Scripture but derived, ultimately, from the multilayered sort of reading practiced by Augustine and other late ancient thinkers: *Littera gesta docet, quid credas allegoria; Moralis quid agas, quo tendas anagogia.*[9] We can translate and explicate as follows: "The letter teaches deeds" (meaning that there is a literal interpretation of a text – sometimes also called the "historical" sense – that you should notice, understand, and internalize); "the allegory teaches what you are to believe" (there is a creedal level to reading Scripture, one in which the truths of faith are contained); "the moral level teaches what you should do" (reading Scripture is an exemplary guide for life, just as the classics had once been – but now, there is the greatest exemplar of all, Jesus Christ, whose actions, words, and style of life become worthy of reflection and imitation); "the anagogical level teaches where you are going." "The anagogical level" is not an expression one encounters every day. The Latin word *anagogia* comes from two Greek roots: *ana-*, which means "upwards" and *-gog-*, deriving from the Greek verb *agô*, which signifies motion. The "anagogical" way of reading Scripture embeds within it the basic assumption that part of one's identity as a Christian is to want to "go upwards," to find one's way to God.[10] Augustine and other Christians inherited this idea from "the Platonists," as Augustine might say, even as Christians could also look back to Paul. His mystical, yet somehow crystal-clear idea was this: we "now" – during our human life, in what Augustine would call our pilgrimage through the City of Man – see God, heaven, and the divine "through a glass darkly."

Riché, *Education and Culture in the Barbarian West: Sixth through Eighth Centuries* (Columbia: University of South Carolina Press, 1976).
[8] See James Clackson and Geoffrey Horrocks, *The Blackwell History of the Latin Language* (Oxford: Blackwell, 2007), pp. 265–304; Tore Janson, *A Natural History of Latin* (Oxford: Oxford University Press, 2004), pp. 87–92; Jürgen Leonhardt, *Latin: The Story of a World Language* (Cambridge, MA: Harvard University Press, 2013).
[9] It is reported by Nicholas of Lyra in his note on Paul, *Galatians*, 4.24, explaining the word "allegory" in Paul's phrase, "Quae sunt per allegoriam dicta"; see Nicholas of Lyra, *Literal Commentary on Galatians*, ed. and tr. Edwin Arthur Neumann (Kalamazoo: Medieval Institute Publications, 2016), at Gal. 4:24, pp. 62–63; and De Lubac, *Exégèse médiévale*, 1: 23.
[10] De Lubac, *Exégèse médiévale*, 2: 621–682.

But "then" – when Jesus returns and when the City of God will be made manifest to all – we will see God "face to face." If reading scripture in the allegorical dimension taught the virtue of faith, and reading on the moral level inculcated charity, it was the anagogical level that led to the other important Pauline virtue, that of hope: Hope that what is visible by us here on earth now was a sign of something infinitely better.[11] It might be invisible to us at present, but it was nonetheless our aspiration, our goal, and our real mission. Learning writ large, and accordingly philosophy in most of its meanings, began to be inflected by this idea: We were here now, on earth, but our job was to find our way upwards, to God.

There is a tradition of referring to important early Christian writers as the "Church Fathers."[12] There were several Greek authors, and then there were the "Latin Fathers," of whom four stand out. The first three were roughly contemporary. In addition to Augustine, there was Ambrose (337–397), the bishop of Milan, about whom Augustine writes with affection and who was at least partially responsible for Augustine's conversion.[13] Then there was Jerome (347–420), whose voluminous writings were complemented by his work on Scripture.[14] By his day, Scripture had been translated into Latin. But the translations were uneven and there were different versions of scripture in circulation. Jerome was already quite expert in Greek, but he knew he also needed Hebrew to deal with the Old Testament. He moved to Jerusalem, and then to Bethlehem with the support of a patron, finishing first his version of the Latin New Testament (known as the Vulgate).[15] Then he learned Hebrew so that he could approach the Old Testament. Jerome's version of Scripture became the Bible western European medieval thinkers

---

[11] Ibid., 2: 623.
[12] See Hubertus R. Drobner, *The Fathers of the Church: A Comprehensive Introduction* (Peabody: Hendrickson, 2007); Johannes Quasten, *Patrology*, 4 vols. (Utrecht: Spectrum and Westminster, Maryland: Newman Press, 1959–1986); overview in Marcia L. Colish, *Medieval Foundations of the Western Intellectual Tradition* (New Haven: Yale University Press, 1997), pp. 16–41.
[13] See Drobner, *The Fathers*, 307–318; Neil B. McLynn, *Ambrose of Milan: Church and Court in a Christian Capital* (Berkeley: University of California Press, 1994); Boniface Ramsey, O.P., *Ambrose* (London: Routledge, 1997).
[14] See Frans van Liere, *An Introduction to the Medieval Bible* (Cambridge: Cambridge University Press, 2014), esp. 80–109. On Jerome see Drobner, *The Fathers*, 339–351; J. N. D. Kelly, *Jerome: His Life, Writings, and Controversies* (London: Duckworth, 1975); Stefan Rebenich, *Jerome* (London: Routledge, 2002); Megan Hale Williams, *The Monk and the Book: Jerome and the Making of Christian Scholarship* (Chicago: University of Chicago Press, 2006).
[15] This period in Jerome's life is attended by uncertainty; see Mateusz Fafinski, "The Ends of History? Jerome, Geruchia, and the Rhine Crossings," *Early Medieval Europe* 33 (2025), 71–93.

used. Ambrose, Augustine, and Jerome each held an important place in Christian history, present at just the time when Christianity was developing definitive practices, enunciating creeds, and beginning to elicit lasting trust in ruling elites.

The world of the fourth Latin Father, Gregory the Great (540–604), was a different one entirely.[16] By the time of his maturity, many "barbarian" invaders were barbarians no longer, now part of what was just beginning to seem like continental western Europe, not least owing to their embrace of Christianity. Franks, Visigoths, Lombards, Burgundians, and other tribes carved out realms in various western European regions, coexisting with the original populace (sometimes harmoniously, other times less so), often adopting and adapting Roman institutions for their own ends – and thereby forging new identities both local and regional.[17] The "Roman" emperor was Roman now only in name, since the imperial seat was in Constantinople. And Gregory combined two qualities that, together, made him a unique figure in the history of Christianity. First, he came from an old Roman clerical family accustomed to the habits, practices, and practicalities of governance. His grandfather was a Pope (Felix III, 483–492), and Gregory himself became Prefect of the City of Rome at a young age.[18] He was familiar with practical politics. Second, despite his immersion in this world, Gregory's commitment to Christianity engendered in him a profound sympathy with monasticism, so much so that, after his father died, he converted the family home into a monastery dedicated to Saint Andrew, whom Jesus had called first, along with Peter, to be a "fisher of men" (Matt 4:18–22; Mark 1:16–20).

So, when Gregory became Pope in 590, he was poised, not so much to change the trajectory of Christianity, but to accelerate the development of tendencies already in play. For one thing, the violence and wars of late

---

[16] For overviews, see Peter Brown, *The Rise of Western Christendom: Triumph and Diversity, AD 200–1000*, rev. ed. (London: Wiley-Blackwell, 2013); Henry Chadwick, *The Church in Ancient Society: From Galilee to Gregory the Great* (Oxford: Oxford University Press, 2001); on Gregory, see R. A. Markus, *Gregory the Great and His World* (Cambridge: Cambridge University Press, 1997); and Conrad Leyser, "The Memory of Gregory the Great and the Making of Latin Europe," in Kate Cooper and Conrad Leyser, eds., *Making Early Medieval Societies: Conflict and Belonging in the Latin West, 300–1200* (Cambridge: Cambridge University Press, 2016), 181–201, who emphasizes the difference between Gregory himself – his goals and aspirations in his own context – and the memory of his pontificate.

[17] Chris Wickham, *The Inheritance of Rome: A History of Europe from 400–1000* (New York: Penguin, 2009), esp. 76–202.

[18] Gregory, *Ep.* 4.2, in *Gregorii magni registrum epistularum*, 2 vols., ed. Dag Norberg (Turnhout: Brepols, 1982), 218–219, at 218, describing himself in the past: "ego quoque tunc urbanam praefecturam gerens..."; Brown, *The Rise of Western Christendom*, 199.

antiquity, along with ever-present cultural difference, had led to great heterogeneity across the now quite vast territories where Christianity had found a home. To be effective, Gregory realized, one needed new and invigorated missions, especially to places like England and Ireland, far off from Rome in both distance and culture.

Gregory chose an apt missionary to do this work, a Benedictine monk providentially named Augustine, who led a group of forty colleagues northward and eventually held the title of Archbishop of Canterbury. Gregory furnished Augustine with a book on *Pastoral Rule*, which served for him and countless others in the Middle Ages as a manual setting out the qualities a pastor should possess and the duties he should carry out.[19] The focus on self-examination in the book stands out: The pastor emerges a someone with sage-like qualities, an example to all of how to live a good and holy life. He would be "pure in thought" and always ready to balance the demands of his exterior duties with a fundamental interiority, since the pastor's inner temperament will inevitably affect the conduct and disposition of those in his charge.[20] A guide to the style of life needed to be a Church leader, Gregory's *Book of Pastoral Rule* is "philosophy as a way of life," if ever there was such a thing.

If the Church was to see itself as one, it needed similar practices, the paring down of different sects of Christianity, and a sense of unity. The missions helped over time to bring into the fold several previously disunited groups in the British Isles, along the way stimulating a wave of brilliant scholarship in Latin. Because Latin had become increasingly unfamiliar to many in Britain (after the Roman withdrawal in the fifth century) – and was almost entirely new to the Irish – it had to be learned from the ground up. In mastering Latin, Irish scholars became deeply invested in the study of grammar. As ever fewer native speakers of Latin existed in Europe, the Irish became some of the finest custodians of a new kind of Latin, one that drew its strength from books – from Latin literature, to be sure, but also from Latin versions of Scripture, emerging Christian liturgical ritual, and the writings of Church Fathers.[21]

---

[19] Gregory, *Règle pastorale*, 2 vols., ed. Bruno Judic, Floribert Rommel, and Charles Morel (Paris: Éditions du Cerf, 1992); English tr. Gregory, *The Book of Pastoral Rule*, tr. George E. Demacopoulos (Crestwood: St. Vladimir's Seminary Press, 2007); and see Gregory, *The Old English Pastoral Care*, ed. and tr. R. D. Fulk (Cambridge, MA: Harvard University Press, 2021), pp. 2–3, for a prefatory poem hinting that Augustine had the *Pastoral Care* with him.

[20] Gregory, *The Book*, 1.10, p. 53; 2.7, pp. 68–74.

[21] Brown, *The Rise of Western Christendom*, 232–266; David Stifter and Nora White, "Early Literacy and Multilingualism in Ireland and Britain," in Alex Mullen and George Woudhuysen, eds., *Languages and Communities in the Late-Roman and Post-Imperial Western Provinces* (Oxford: Oxford University Press, 2023), 203–235.

None of this is to say that Gregory somehow succeeded in making western European Christianity uniform. For centuries, there were diverse religious practices, recurrences to pagan worship traditions, and many other variances in practice and mentality.[22] It was a geographically vast society whose constituents were and would remain unconnected by modern information flows.[23] And Gregory himself was relatively tolerant of diverse local ritual practices, provided they existed under the umbrella of a larger unity.[24] But the work Gregory set in motion contributed meaningfully to this fact: for most western Europeans in the Middle Ages (those interested in philosophy in all its forms very much included), Christianity was central, differently complected as it might have been in any given moment or place.

An indefatigable writer, Gregory produced an astonishing amount of religious literature beyond his *Book on Pastoral Care*. His writings grew in importance centuries after his death, especially in the time of Charlemagne (d. 814), setting the stage for how Gregory was remembered by later eras.[25] He wrote a commentary on the Book of Job (known as the *Moral Reflections on Job*) – a seemingly strange choice to modern ears, but one that allowed him to situate the woes and troubles of human life in a larger context.[26] It was strikingly successful, with over 500 manuscripts of the work surviving. He wrote a series of dialogues, which among other things contained a biography of Saint Benedict, the real founder of western monasticism, that became the standard biography of that saint.[27] And his correspondence included well over 800 letters, which together offer a portrait of an energetic leader who never tired of spreading the Christian message, expanding the reach of the Church, and doing so with a view toward its notional universality.[28]

In his commentary on Job, we find a preface (in the form of a letter of dedication) that lays out the different ways of reading scripture:

---

[22] See the studies in Werner Verbeke, John Marenbon, and Carlos Steel, eds., *Paganism in the Middle Ages: Threat and Fascination* (Leuven: Leuven University Press, 2012).
[23] Cf. Brown, *The Rise of Western Christendom*, 413, 420, 466–467.
[24] Markus, *Gregory the Great and His World*, 72–75.
[25] See Lucia Castaldi, *La trasmissione dei testi latini del medioevo, Gregorius I Papa* (Florence: Edizioni del Galluzzo, 2013).
[26] Gregory, *Moralia in Job*, 3 vols., ed. Marcus Adriaen (Turnhout: Brepols, 1979–85); Gregory, *Moral Reflections on the Book of Job*, 5 vols., tr. Brian Kerns (Collegeville: Liturgical Press, 2014–2019).
[27] Gregory, *Dialogues*, 3 vols., ed. Adalbert de Vogüé and Paul Antin (Paris: Éditions du Cerf, 1978–1980); Gregory, *Dialogues*, tr. Odo Zimmerman (New York: Fathers of the Church, 1959).
[28] Gregory, *Gregorii magni registrum epistularum*; Gregory, *The Letters of Gregory the Great*, 3 vols., tr. John R. C. Martyn (Toronto: Pontifical Institute of Medieval Studies, 2004).

It should be known that we run through some passages with a literal interpretation, whereas we examine others by means of allegory in a figurative interpretation. Others we discuss using the tools of allegory alone to illustrate the moral sense. Finally, we examine some passages with greater care using all three ways. In this way, we first lay a foundation of literal meaning. Then, through the figurative meaning, we elevate the structure of the mind into a citadel of faith. Finally, using the moral interpretation, we clothe our building with an additional shading.[29]

What Gregory describes here is something like that fourfold division of reading noted above. He does not explicitly designate the "anagogical" sense, but it is there in spirit when he says that some passages need to be examined in even greater depth, using "all three ways." And in other places he suggests that the "allegorical" way of reading itself raises the soul up to God.[30] The message is: one reads scripture carefully. It is a treasury of inherent worth, from which numerous riches can be drawn, provided one treats it with care. This approach remained a given going forward.

Two more factors are noteworthy about this passage. First, Gregory repeats himself. Not exactly, of course, but he does say the same thing about the three ways of reading in two different places. This type of repetition may seem superfluous in a written work. But it signals something important. For Gregory, his writing arose out of teaching, and those who teach often repeat their most important points with slightly different inflections. They know well that their audience might not always be paying attention or may not understand something new the first time around. When it comes to what this little, seemingly odd but eventually typical practice meant for the future, it is this: Much of what we possess of medieval religious and philosophical thought is similar, rooted fundamentally in teaching and sharing. In Gregory's case, he was lecturing on the Book of Job to a monastic

---

[29] Gregory, *Moralia in Job*, 3 vols., ed. Marcus Adriaen (Turnhout: Brepols, 1979–1985), dedicatory Letter, 1: 1–7, at p. 4: "Sciendum vero est, quod quaedam historica expositione transcurrimus, et per allegoriam quaedam typica investigatione perscrutamur, quaedam per sola allegoricae moralitatis instrumenta discutimus, nonnulla autem per cuncta simul sollicitius exquirentes tripliciter indagamus. Nam primum quidem fundamenta historica ponimus; deinde per significationem typicam in arcem fidei fabricam mentis erigimus; ad extremam quoque per moralitatis gratiam, quasi superducto aedificium colore vestimus." See also Markus, *Gregory the Great and His World*, 46–47.

[30] See e.g., Gregory, *Expositiones in Canticum Canticorum, in librum primum Regum*, ed. Patricius Verbraken (Turnholt: Brepols, 1963), sec. 2, p. 3, where allegory is likened to a *machina* helping to lift one contemplatively: "Allegoria enim animae longe a deo positae quasi quandam machinam facit, ut per illam leuetur ad deum"; see Markus, *Gregory the Great and His World*, 47.

community in Constantinople (this was before he was Pope, when he was serving as a papal legate there).[31] The word "lecture" derives from the Latin *lectio*. And what that word means, at root, is "reading."

Benedict, the founder of western monasticism, had prescribed in his Rule that monks should "listen willingly to holy reading," that at every meal the monks were to sit in silence and listen to a reading, that they would hear a "reading" after the evening ritual of Vespers, and so on.[32] Reading scriptural and other holy texts – or rather, hearing them read aloud – was part of life in monastic communities.[33] And a leader would often (like Gregory) expound on those readings.

So, what Gregory did was read, out loud, the Book of Job, and comment on various passages he considered worthy of exposition. Listeners heard the story of Job, this good man whom God nonetheless afflicted with a series of travails. They also heard Gregory's explanations, some of which offered larger points of interpretation, others pointing simply to the meaning of this or that word. Gregory revised some of his remarks, dictating more on the parts he hadn't yet covered, and then redacted the whole so that the text flowed smoothly.[34] In its written form, this set of interventions turned into a "commentary" on the text of the Book of Job, which indeed is what Gregory's *Moralia in Job* represents.

We readers have Gregory's text. But we have lost the dynamics of the original, personal interaction, where Gregory might have shaded what he said with a facial expression, or verbal inflection, or slight change of mood. Later in his career when he was Pope, he gave homilies in Rome, including on the Old Testament Book of Ezechiel. He told the community that there was much in sacred scripture that he understood more fully when *coram fratribus meis* – "in the presence of my brothers."[35] He went on: "If there is

---

[31] Gregory was in Constantinople as a papal legate from 579 to 585/6; it was there that he began lecturing on Job. He later redacted and added to his lectures, though they still bore the imprint of their origins. See Drobner, *The Fathers*, 513, 517–518.

[32] Benedict of Nursia, *Regula Benedicti*, ed. Rudolph Hanslik, Regula Corpus Scriptorum Ecclesiasticorum Latinorum 75 (Vienna: Hoelder-Pinchler-Tempsky, 1960), 4:55: "Lectiones sanctas libenter audire"; 38:5; 42:5. For an accessible English translation, see Benedict, *The Rule of Saint Benedict*, tr. Carolinne White (New York: Penguin, 2008).

[33] Riché, *Education and Culture in the Barbarian West*, 100–124.

[34] Gregory, *Moral Reflections on the Book of Job*, "Letter to Leander," 1: 49–50; he outlines a similar process in his 602 Letter to John of Ravenna; see *Gregorii magni registrum epistularum*, 12.6, pp. 974–977, at 975.

[35] Gregory, *Homiliae in Ezechielem / Homélies sur Ézéchiel*, 2 vols., ed. and tr. Charles Morel, S.J. (Paris: Éditions du Cerf, 1990), 2.2., vol. 2, p. 93: "Scio enim quia plerumque multa in sacro eloquio, quae solus intelligere non potui, coram fratribus meis positus intellexi."

anything in this Prophet [Ezechiel] that I will have understood less than fully, it is owed to my own blindness. If there is anything I will have been able to understand suitably, it is by the divine gift of your venerable character."[36] Gregory's graciousness to his audience aside, we can note a type of information transfer. One's reading gave rise to speaking and sharing. The feedback one received solidified, challenged, and sometimes corrected one's own understanding. One's new understanding would then subsequently be reflected in the final written product.[37] The Middle Ages will be full of this kind of work, based fundamentally in a teaching or preaching environment, but then formalized, and fixed, on a page.

Returning to Gregory's *Moral Reflections on Job*, it is worth remarking that his was not the first commentary on an important text, of course. Commentary-writing was common among ancient thinkers from the Hellenistic period onward, and as a genre it was diverse and destined to last and grow in the Middle Ages.[38] To take just one example, Gregory's patristic predecessor, Origen (185–253 CE), though controversial in some areas, wrote countless biblical commentaries in Greek that by Gregory's day had been translated into Latin and were appreciated as exemplary interpretive approaches to scripture.[39]

The ancient practice of commentary was rooted in a twofold assumption. First, to think (to philosophize) creatively, one recurred to authoritative texts. In them resided truth, but it might be veiled. These authoritative texts needed meditation, focus, and explication to allow the truth to come to light. It was this that the commentator did in the work of exegesis. Second, this type of interpretation naturally entailed what we today might consider misunderstandings, moments when an interpreter went beyond what the text's limits, historical context, or semantic range might allow.[40] These creative misunderstandings may not have reflected the original author's intention, but they served as a wellspring of innovation, founding the work of interpretation in an authoritative text's grounded reality, even as one

---

[36] Ibid.: "Quidquid ergo in hoc propheta minus intellexero, meae caecitatis est; si quid vero intelligere apte potuero, ex divino munere vestrae venerationis est."

[37] Cf. the brilliant Raffaella Cribiore, *Listening to the Philosophers: Notes on Notes* (Ithaca: Cornell University Press, 2024).

[38] See Wilhelm Geerlings and Christian Schulze, eds., *Der Kommentar in Antike und Mittelalter*, 2 vols. (Leiden: Brill, 2002–2003).

[39] See Scott Bruce, "Origen Issues: The Reception of a Renegade Greek Theologian in Early Medieval Europe," *The Journal of Medieval Latin* 33 (2023), 267–303.

[40] See Pierre Hadot, *Études de philosophie ancienne* (Paris: Les Belles Lettres, 1998), pp. 3–11; and Pierre Force, "The Teeth of Time: Pierre Hadot on Meaning and Misunderstanding in the History of Ideas," *History and Theory* 50 (2011), 20–40.

moved to new horizons in one's interpretations. These new horizons were often related to contemporary needs, whether these were of a teacher in a classroom, a preacher in a congregated community, or even a lone thinker for whom an old text could serve new ends. Gregory can stand as a good example of how this ancient practice took root in the Christian world, to be continued thereafter, evolving according to context.

In the passage above (from his prefatory letter to the *Moral Reflections*), an attentive reader will have noted Gregory's architectural metaphor, tinged with martial imagery: "we first lay a foundation of literal meaning. Then, through the figurative meaning, we elevate the structure of the mind into a citadel of faith. Finally, using the moral interpretation, we clothe our building with an additional shading." Embedded in this theory of layered reading is a kind of plan for the Church, reflected in the act of reading as if seen in a magnifying mirror. First, a foundation is needed. This the Church now had in Gregory's day. The Canon of Scripture had been set since the early fifth century, the Nicene Creed since the early fourth.

But the foundation required broadening – a key reason Gregory dispatched missionaries. They would expand the base of the Church, creating a Christian analogue of Roman power: centralized in Rome, yet distributed in ways that mirrored Roman genius. Since at least the Antonine era of the second century CE, the Romans had shown extraordinary capacity to integrate ever larger and more geographically diverse populations. Conquered groups could become citizens, and after the 212 "Antonine Constitution," all free men in the empire were granted citizenship. There were ever more people who considered themselves part of Rome, as both an idea and a reality.[41]

Gregory's metaphor reflects this dual structure, at both the personal and the institutional level. For the individual believer, the "foundation" was literal understanding: grasping the names, places, and facts of Scripture. On that foundation, one could raise a figurative citadel – a fortress of faith defended by allegorical insight. Similarly, the Church needed a wide base of believers, a stable infrastructure, and the ability to defend itself. No longer a fragile counterculture preaching only Christ's humility, the Church under Gregory was a growing institution, one that had to build with strength, consolidate its presence, and endure. Even if Gregory believed the end times

---

[41] See Arnaud Besson, *Constitutio Antoniniana: l'universalisation de la citoyenneté romaine au 3e siècle* (Basel: Schwabe Verlag, 2020); Alex Imrie, *The Antonine Constitution* (Leiden: Brill, 2018); Myles Lavan and Clifford Ando, eds., *Roman and Local Citizenship in the Long Second Century CE* (Oxford: Oxford University Press, 2022); and the discussion in Chapter 5 here.

were near (as did many other Christians), the truth was that no one knew when Christ would return and the final judgment ensue.[42] Until then, strength was necessary, a strength both defensive and welcoming, able to protect the faithful and open its gates to newcomers.

Finally, there was the "moral interpretation," through which "we clothe our building with an additional shading." For the individual, this meant that Christianity (by means of the study of its Scripture and sacred texts) would have an ethics of its own for both the individual and society. Not only would individuals be strengthened. They would also possess a new kind of eloquence, a Christian eloquence, such as Augustine and others had adumbrated. For example, we have examined in a prior chapter the great Roman orator and philosopher Cicero's book, *De officiis*, or *On Duties*. It was a Stoic-inflected guide to how citizens might live well and ethically, fulfilling their public duties and remaining true to their conscience. Ambrose, one of those Latin Church Fathers, writing roughly four centuries later, produced an *On Duties* of his own.[43] He modeled it on Cicero's structure and echoed Cicero's Latin, but Ambrose oriented his *On Duties* toward the clergy, the leading citizens of the Church.[44]

Gregory lived in a different world from that of Augustine, Ambrose, and Jerome. By Gregory's day, those three had become new classics for the Church, authors whose writing was redolent of a long-gone antiquity, a time when there were many native speakers of Latin, when the dream of a secular Roman Empire was fading, perhaps, but still somehow able to be imagined. By Gregory's era, figurative art was changing. Practitioners were beginning to move from depicting individuals in a realistic way (prizing the use of perspective and naturalism) to more symbolic representations. Just as the "language" of art was changing, so too did the language of the Church need to adapt.

Gregory suggests as much when he described the register of his language in the preface to his *Moralia in Job*: "Please don't expect a great deal of verbal eloquence as you read through the work, since God's word restrains frivolous and empty babbling, and it is forbidden to plant trees in God's temple

---

[42] On Gregory's expectation of the end times see Leyser, "The Memory of Gregory the Great," and Markus, *Gregory the Great and His World*, 51–67.

[43] Ambrose, *De officiis*, ed. and tr. Ivor J. Davidson, 2 vols. (Oxford: Oxford University Press, 2001).

[44] See Ivor J. Davidson, "Chapter 3: Model," in Ambrose, *De officiis*, 1: 6–19; and O. Hiltbrunner, "Die Schrift 'De officiis ministrorum' des hl. Ambrosius und ihr ciceronisches Vorbild," *Gymnasium* 71 (1964), 174–189.

[here he alludes to Deuteronomy 16:21]."[45] There are three messages. First, Gregory is exculpating himself for any lack of the sort of elegance a classically minded reader might expect. This work will not be expressed in the Latin of Cicero or even, for that matter, in that of the earlier Fathers. He could have written in a high style, given his education.[46] But it was the content, not the form, that was important, even as he was writing for audiences in search of "spiritual health."[47] This is to say, second, that he was writing to be understood, knowing that much of what he wrote would be read aloud; so there was an interest in keeping things clear and simple.[48] Third, this type of writing will imitate the humble style of Scripture. Writing becomes an exercise that recapitulates the Scripture it is designed to explicate.

Gregory goes on: "I have refused to be subservient to the kind of art of speaking that the masters of superficial instruction impart."[49] Recall that Augustine in his early years earned his bread as a teacher of eloquence. That is, he was a professional rhetorician whose livelihood had depended on his ability to master, and then to teach, the "art of speaking," before he adopted the conviction that it was an empty art, designed to sway opinion but not to improve people or, eventually, to get them closer to God. Here again, we observe the power of this centuries-long conversation that Plato had begun: The surfaces of things, what we see and hear and the things by which we are customarily persuaded, come to seem false and poor stand-ins for the truth.

Gregory continues: "As even the contents of this letter make clear, I do not avoid the clashing of 'm' sounds [meaning, I have not paid excessive attention to proper spelling]; I don't shun the disorder of 'barbarism,' and I disregard word order, usage, and even the government of prepositions, since I consider it quite unworthy to limit the words of the heavenly oracle to the rules of Donatus."[50] Gregory's use of the word "barbarism" and the name "Donatus" stand out. As to barbarism, the word (*barbarismus* in Latin)

---

[45] Gregory, *Moralia in Job*, sec. 5, p. 7: "Quaeso autem ut huius operis dicta percurrens, in his uerborum folia non requiras, quia per sacra eloquia ab eorum tractatoribus infructuosae loquacitatis leuitas studiose compescitur, dum in templo Dei nemus plantari prohibetur."

[46] Riché, *Education and Culture in the Barbarian West*, 145–152.

[47] Brown, *The Rise of Western Christendom*, 238.

[48] Cf. Michel Banniard, *Viva voce: Communication écrite et communication orale du IVe au IXe siècle en occident latin* (Paris: Institut des études augustiniennes, 1992).

[49] Gregory, *Moralia in Job*, sec. 5, p. 7: "Unde et ipsam loquendi artem, quam magisteria disciplinae exterioris insinuant, seruare despexi."

[50] Ibid.: "Nam sicut huius quoque epistolae tenor enuntiat, non metacismi collisionem fugio, non barbarismi confusionem deuito, situs modosque etiam et prepositionum casus seruare contemno, quia indignum uehementer existimo, ut uerba caelestis oraculi restringam sub regulis Donati."

comes from the Greek word *barbaros*, or "barbarian" in literally translated English. It was an onomatopoeic word that ancient Greeks had invented to designate a non-Greek, a word derived from the seemingly incomprehensible sounds – "bar bar bar" – that foreigners made when they spoke.[51] If you were Greek, it meant "anyone not you," basically, and was a way to designate the Other. In the lexicon of Latin grammarians, the term "barbarism" came to denote a seemingly foreign expression smuggled into otherwise normal, or normative, Latin, an unwelcome insertion of a nonnative word, or expression, or idiom, that did not have any basis in the "right" version of the language.[52] In Gregory's time, that question – what was the right version of the Latin language? – was becoming ever more difficult to answer.

On the one hand, Gregory transmits the notion that, since the truths of Scripture are simple truths, so too will his language be simple. On the other, his statement reveals a stark new reality: This new "empire" of notionally universal Christianity will be a tapestry sewn together by means of a language not native to many. The waves of Germanic and other tribes, plus the natural evolution of languages in peripheries that had little access to linguistic centers: Both phenomena contributed to a new and different idea. Latin would be recorded in books, its classics copied in monasteries, its contours studied in schools. The language itself would eventually become a "second" language for all who used it in the Middle Ages – a "language at arm's length," as one scholar has put it.[53] It was not a language learned at home, in childhood, from parents and nursemaids but something else, something sacred in its own way: the linguistic medium of culture, politics, and religion.[54] Because everyone would become a "barbarian," so to speak – a foreigner to the native expression of Latin – the very idea of

---

[51] Strabo, *Geography*, 8 vols., ed. and tr. Horace Leonard Jones (Cambridge, MA: Harvard University Press, 1928), 14.2.28, pp. 302–305.

[52] See Quintilian, *Institutio oratoria*, 1.5.5–33, in Quintilian, *The Orator's Education*, ed. and tr. Donald A. Russell (Cambridge, MA: Harvard University Press, 2002), 1: 124–141, and for two late ancient discussions, see Donatus, *Ars grammatica*, in Louis Holtz, *Donat et la tradition de l'enseignement grammatical: Étude sur l'Ars Donati et sa diffusion (IVe–IXe siècle) et édition critique* (Paris: CNRS, 2010), 571–674, at 653–655; Consentius, *De barbarismis et metaplasmis*, ed. Tommaso Mari (Oxford: Oxford University Press, 2021), pp. 4–109, together with Mari's "Introduction," pp. 1–41.

[53] Carin Ruff, "Latin as an Acquired Language," in Ralph Hexter and David Townsend, eds., *The Oxford Handbook of Medieval Latin Literature* (Oxford: Oxford University Press, 2012), 46–62, at 47.

[54] Ryan Szpiech, "Latin as a Language of Authoritative Tradition," in Hexter and Townsend, *The Oxford Handbook of Medieval Latin Literature*, 63–85.

the language changed, as it became a vehicle for incorporating ever more diverse peoples.[55]

As to "Donatus," with that name Gregory points to the work of Aelius Donatus, who had flourished in the fourth century CE. Among other things, Donatus wrote the *Ars grammatica*, or *Art of Grammar*, which became one of the two most important grammar textbooks for the Middle Ages (the other being that of the fifth-century author Priscian, entitled the *Institutiones grammaticae*, or *Institutes of Grammar*).[56]

When Gregory says that he does not want to "limit the words of the heavenly oracle to the rules of Donatus," he signals two things. First, he believes that sacred matters are supreme and that the form of their expression should be deemed less important than the inherent, holy content. Second, we see an estrangement from classicism. The work of Donatus, like that of Priscian, contained rules of how to write Latin in a way that was normative and in accordance with best practices in Latin's golden age, when Cicero wrote prose and Virgil poetry. Gregory is untroubled that things have moved on from that point, his goal now to communicate the truths of faith as clearly, simply, and directly as possible.

This impulse toward effective communication emerges in an anecdote in which Gregory was a protagonist. It had to do with the ancient French port city of Marseille, in Provence, which had been founded a millennium earlier by Greeks, who called it "Massilia," a name the Romans adopted when they took it over in the expansion of their dominion. It was an important city, a link by sea to North Africa, and a place where Christianity had taken root. In Gregory's era, the Christian community enjoyed the leadership of their tenth bishop, named Serenus. Serenus grew concerned that the members of his flock seemed to be worshipping images of saints. In a rage, he began destroying the statues and images. Back in Rome, Gregory heard this news and, though he admired Serenus' Christian zeal, urged him in a letter to cease this practice. Serenus, inflamed by his cause, refused to believe Gregory's letter was authentic and continued in his image-destroying campaign. Gregory, in turn, wrote another letter, sterner this time, in which he again urged Serenus to cease destroying images. Images are necessary, Gregory said – in different ways in both of his letters – because they afford access to truths at which many people could otherwise not arrive.

---

[55] Cf. Banniard, *Viva voce*.
[56] See Donatus, *Ars grammatica*, in Holtz, *Donat et la tradition de l'enseignement grammatical*; and Priscian, *Institutionum grammaticarum libri*, in Heinrich Keil, ed., *Grammatici latini* (Leipzig: Teubner, 1857), vols. 2–3.

Gregory's language is telling (here from the first letter): "And so, painting is permitted in Churches, so that those who don't know **letters** may at least 'read' by seeing on the wall what they are unable to read in **books**."[57] The two words that have been highlighted here, for emphasis, are worth foregrounding. Each word serves as a marker for change. As to "letters," the Latin term at issue is *litterae*, the plural form of the word *littera*, or "letter." That plural designation became something of a signifier.[58] It was translated painfully literally here, to bring it into relief. A more accurate representation of Gregory's meaning requires expansion. Someone who does not know "letters" means someone who does not know "literature" conceived most comprehensively. It points to a person who did not have the advantage of the broad education that Gregory – and Serenus – had enjoyed, who no longer had the stock sets of exemplars in mind, whether Virgil's heroes, or even the many works of Church Fathers like Augustine. This "illiterate" person needed guidance and shepherding. Potentially pious, he or she needed to know the narratives, examples, and stories that subtended the Christian faith. Tales of saints and martyrs, many of whom suffered death for their new faith, needed promulgation. If the only possible way to do so was through images and in-person explanation, then that was the preferred route to travel. "Letters" signified the way in which a Gregory, or a Serenus for that matter, would gain that background. For the rest, other ways needed to be sought.

To possess "letters" – to be *litteratus* in what became a standard Latin usage – meant not to be "literate" in the way that we understand that term today: to read and write, primarily in one's native language. No, to be *litteratus* meant the acquisition of the Latin language, a language that was by no means anymore the native language of many people in Christendom's vast – and growing – geography in Gregory's era. For those restricted few who would henceforth learn this language, that education was almost universally tied to Christianity. In the first instance, Latin was a language

---

[57] Gregory, *Gregorii magni registrum epistularum*, 2: 768: "Idcirco enim pictura in ecclesiis adhibetur, ut hi qui litteras nesciunt saltem in parietibus videndo legant, quae in codicibus legere non valeant." There is a rich tradition of interpretation of this passage; see Celia Chazelle, "Pictures, Books, and the Illiterate: Gregory I's Letters to Serenus," *Word and Image* 6 (1990), 138–153; Herbert L. Kessler, "Pictorial Narrative and Church Mission in Sixth-Century Gaul," *Studies in the History of Art* 16 (1985), 75–91; Markus, *Gregory the Great and His World*, 175–177; Thomas F. X. Noble, *Images, Iconoclasm, and the Carolingians* (Philadelphia: University of Pennsylvania Press, 2009), pp. 43–44.

[58] See Herbert Grundmann, "Litteratus – illitteratus: Der Wandel einer Bildungsnorm vom Altertum zum Mittelalter," *Archiv für Kulturgeschichte* 40 (1958), 1–65; English translation in Grundmann, *Essays on Heresy, Inquisition, and Literacy*, ed. Jennifer Kolpacoff Deane, tr. Steven Rowan (York: York Medieval Press, 2019), pp. 56–125.

that had been made sacred on the Cross, when, as Pilate crucified Jesus on Mount Golgotha, he mockingly affixed the title "Jesus of Nazareth, the King of the Jews," in Hebrew, Greek, and Latin (John 19:20). Then, too, Jerome's translation of the Bible into Latin allowed Latin to become the key language of the Christian faith. In the west (and for the most part), when literate elites theologized and studied the Bible, they did so in Latin. Gradually, Jerome's Vulgate Bible itself became a kind of sacred object, the source, over the medieval centuries, of countless commentaries, scriptural questions, and theological debates.

Then, there is Gregory's other key word, "books," or *codices*, in Latin. The *codex*, to use the singular form, evolved in tandem with early Christianity. When Jesus was born, the more usual form of the book was the roll, customarily made from papyrus. If you were dealing with a roll, and you wanted to find a passage toward the end of a text copied therein, you would have to unroll the whole thing. In a book, by contrast, you could turn to the needed page. As Christianity evolved, the book became the repository of Scripture.[59]

A curious thing occurred during the extended historical moment that Gregory inhabited. From the fifth to the seventh centuries, the image of the book changed in Italy, from open to closed, as the scholar Armando Petrucci noted.[60] In visualizations of Christ, the Evangelists, saints, and other important personages, the book had become a bearer of meaning. Was the book to be depicted open, as in a mosaic dating to the first half of the fifth century in the Chapel of Saint Victor, Church of Saint Ambrose in Milan? There, the saint is depicted holding a book with his name, "Victor," spanning the two pages of the open book (Figure 12.1).[61] Similarly, in the Church of San Vitale in Ravenna, another early Christian stronghold, the Evangelist Luke is depicted, again in a mosaic, holding an open book on which is inscribed: *secundum Lucam*, or, "according to Luke" (Figure 12.2). Or in Rome itself, in one of that city's oldest sites of Christian worship, the Church of Santa

---

[59] See Colin H. Roberts and T. C. Skeat, *The Birth of the Codex* (Oxford: Oxford University Press, 1983); Bernhard Bischoff, *Latin Palaeography: Antiquity and the Middle Ages*, tr. Dáibhí Ó Cróinín and David Ganz (Cambridge: Cambridge University Press, 1990), pp. 20–32, esp. 20–24; Eric G. Turner, *The Typology of the Early Codex* (Philadelphia: University of Pennsylvania Press, 1977); Trobisch, *The First Edition of the New Testament*, 69–77.

[60] Armando Petrucci, *Writers and Readers in Medieval Italy: Studies in the History of Written Culture*, ed. and tr. Charles M. Radding (New Haven: Yale University Press, 1995), pp. 25–30, to which the following paragraphs are indebted.

[61] The image can be found in Joseph Wilpert, *Die Römischen Mosaiken und Malereien der kirchlichen Bauten vom IV. bis XIII. Jahrhundert*, 4 vols. (Freiburg im Breisgau: Herdersche Verlagshandlung, 1916), vol. 3, table 83.

Endings and New Beginnings: Gregory the Great and Beyond 257

Figure 12.1 Mosaic of St. Victor, Basilica of Sant'Ambrogio, Milan, Italy, fifth century. Alamy Stock Photo.

Pudenziana, one finds an early fifth-century mosaic, in which Christ is depicted in the center, holding an open book (Figure 12.3).[62]

By Gregory's day, however, books in such illustrations began to be depicted as closed. They became symbols of the sacred nature of Scripture – it is something special, set apart – and of something more: with centuries of hindsight, they seem to stand for the new way that the Church, and in some respects learning itself, would be organized. This new model can be seen in any number of images. In Rome, in the Church of Saint John Lateran, in a mosaic completed a few decades after Gregory's death, there is a depiction of four martyrs in an oratory within the Church. Two are shown gazing out implacably at the viewer and holding closed books. Those books, in their encasement in jewels, are intended to signal not only their sacred status, but also the fact that they represent deluxe productions (Figure 12.4).[63] Similarly, in a mid-sixth-century mosaic from the Church of San Vitale in Ravenna, one observes a stunning portrayal of the Emperor Justinian, centered and surrounded by a retinue of figures (Figure 12.5). Among them, to the emperor's left, is Archbishop Maximian holding a cross

---

[62] Wilpert, *Die Römischen*, vol. 3, plates 42–44a.
[63] Wilpert, *Die Römischen*, vol. 3, plate 111.

Figure 12.2 Mosaic of St. Luke the Evangelist, Basilica of San Vitale, Ravenna, Italy, mid-sixth century. Alamy Stock Photo.

adorned with jewels. Next to Maximian there is another figure, unnamed though obviously a cleric, holding a book. Again, the book's cover is encased with jewels. Again, the book is closed.

The message of these closed books, held by figures of authority, is that one needs mediators to interpret them successfully, to open them, as it were. These mediating figures – priests, monks, and clerics in many functions – will be the guardians of learning. When they are abbots, they will supervise in their monasteries the laborious work of preserving and copying texts. When they are part of the Church hierarchy, they will pronounce as to the correct and incorrect interpretations of Scripture. They will be the ones, for the most part, who learn Latin, the language of culture. Books will have authority, and there will be authorities to interpret books.

What we see in Gregory's era is a final summing up of all that had gone before intellectually. We also observe a transformation of the many ideas,

Figure 12.3 Mosaic of Jesus as teacher, Basilica of Santa Pudenziana, Rome, Italy, early fifth century. Alamy Stock Photo.

techniques, and mentalities that began to appear in Plato's writing. They had coursed through ancient philosophy, had been the subject of much debate, and then, in the early Christian era, were appropriated and transformed. The idea that the human soul was immortal, individual, and could be shaped and improved by education and introspection remained. The notion that there was a realm superior to our own persisted, too. There, the seat of final adjudication about the quality of our lives on earth existed. Had we lived a good life? If so, we would be rewarded. If not, we would suffer punishment.

There were changes as well, changes that allowed Christianity to take root much more strongly than any ancient philosophy ever could have done. Plato and other ancients often allowed, intellectually, that there could be (and, in some cases, must be) one supreme being of some sort. Still, that monotheistic affordance had been more in the nature of an intellectual principle than a God with human-like characteristics. There was no question of that supreme intellectual principle, so far beyond us in capacities, being interested in us as individuals. The gulf was too large. And if, in the Judaic heritage, that one God was more defined – occasionally wrathful, unpredictable, and beyond human comprehension – that same God also manifested a deep concern for justice, mercy, and the fate of the vulnerable. Still, a gulf remained: The God of the Old Testament was not human in an everyday

Figure 12.4 Mosaic of four martyrs, Chapel of St Venantius, Basilica of San Giovanni in Laterano, Rome, Italy, early to mid-seventh century. Photo, Andrea Jemolo/Bridgeman images.

way. When, by contrast, early followers of Jesus came to believe what he said – that he was the Son of God, sent to redeem humanity for its flaws and inner contradictions – something new happened, when it came to philosophy, its eventual history, and its diffusion in western society.

On the one hand, some problems were solved. Or at least, there were solutions proposed that many accepted. Why, when we often know what is right, do we do what is wrong? That question is profoundly human but seems an index of our lesser status compared to any intellectually supreme being, who (knowing what was right) would never willingly do wrong. But we do "sin," meaning we often do things that reflection would tell us we should not do. Into the mix came Jesus, who was a human being. His portrait was painted in full in the gospels. He had emotions, he occasionally got angry, he felt love, and he did things that seemed very unlike what a "God" would do, things such as validating the poor, reaching out to the disabled, and in "healing" them bringing them into the fold of a larger humanity. There was little in ancient philosophy before Jesus like the Beatitudes, where the "humble" are singled out as being specially blessed. And when Paul wrote that in the Christian fold there would be "neither Jew

Endings and New Beginnings: Gregory the Great and Beyond 261

Figure 12.5 Mosaic of Emperor Justinian and his Court, Basilica of San Vitale, Ravenna, Italy, mid-sixth century. Alamy Stock Photo.

nor Greek, male nor female, bond nor free," it signaled something important: that one could conceive of all human beings as notionally equal. The conception reached back to Plato, whose denigration of the material world and validation of the human soul laid the groundwork. But Plato, like Aristotle and almost all ancient pagan philosophers, took for granted that society would be and indeed should be stratified, not a place where one could entertain such things as Paul suggested. It is true that this type of equality has rarely if ever been achieved in society and that, in other places in writing attributed to Paul, we observe startling inconsistencies with that egalitarian vision when it comes to women. And there is no doubt that like his contemporaries, Paul didn't see this spiritual equality as a stand-in for social equality, as the widespread existence and acceptance of enslavement in the ancient world shows.[64] Indeed, in his Letter to Philemon, he takes for granted that an enslaved man, Onesimus, who had been seconded to Paul by Philemon, would remain enslaved when back in Philemon's house, even as Paul evinces hope that Philemon will treat Onesimus as a brother.[65]

---

[64] See Kyle Harper, *Slavery in the Late Roman World, AD 275–425* (Cambridge: Cambridge University Press, 2011); MacCollough, *Christianity*, 114–116.
[65] Paul, Phlm, 10–21.

Yet, we should also be mindful that it was Paul, and Christianity, that introduced this idea of a notional equality to a broad, often non-literate constituency of believers in the west. It is not a coincidence that a substantial portion of Christianity's early followers were the enslaved, whose bitter lives on earth would not change fundamentally but who nonetheless found a sense of dignity in a religion that valued them, even though they had little in the way of social status.[66] So, in some ways, by Gregory's day, there were aspects of philosophy – conceived in its broad and historically authentic sense of the "love of and search for wisdom" – available to large numbers of people.

On the other hand, a great transformation was taking place, one that would take centuries to be complete. The Latin language, having emerged as the key western language of culture, became the property of an elite. More importantly, its written form did as well. The Romance languages (Italian, French, Spanish, and Portuguese) developed and evolved out of Latin in the Early Middle Ages, and German and Germanic languages developed on their own. But in western Europe, those non-Latin languages were not seen as appropriate for recording culture, by and large. Schools developed for instruction in Latin, and those schools were found for the most part in Christian institutions. This fact meant that the "monastic sensibility" that Gregory and others like him shared colored the formation of many who were educated during the medieval centuries. Learning was important but, again, that learning – of Latin, of certain carefully chosen pagan classics – was conceived of as being *for* something, not always as a good in its own right. It existed for the purpose of helping people become closer to God.

Along the way, many classic ancient texts and authors ceased being studied in depth. Some simply went out of fashion. There is – to take one example – a manuscript in the Vatican Library with the shelf mark Vaticanus Latinus 5757 (which means that it is inventory number 5757 in the "Vatican Latin" collection of manuscripts, the Vatican Library's core collection of Latin manuscripts, see Figure 12.6). It is made of parchment – treated animal skin. It is what scholars term a "palimpsest," meaning it is a manuscript that has one text, now hidden from the naked eye, that had been written down on it, only to be erased later (by being scraped off with a razor-like

---

[66] For a revisionist argument that slavery and early Christianity were mutually constitutive, see Jennifer Glancy, *Slavery in Early Christianity* (Oxford: Oxford University Press, 2002); Jennifer Glancy, "Slavery and the Rise of Christianity," in Keith Bradley and Paul Cartledge, eds., *The Cambridge World History of Slavery*, vol. 1 (Cambridge: Cambridge University Press, 2011), 456–481.

Figure 12.6 "Palimpsest," Cicero, *De Re Publica* and Augustine, *Enarrationes in Psalmos*. MS Vatican City, Biblioteca Apostolica Vaticana, Vat. Lat. 5757, f. 123r.

instrument, or as in this case, washed off); the book could thus be reused and written on once again. You can easily imagine why: A large parchment book might have comprised hundreds of sheepskins, meaning that it cost hundreds of sheep, as well as the many hours of labor needed to turn animal skins into a viable writing surface. These books were expensive and comparatively rare. If a new text came into your possession as a loan, and you wanted to reproduce it, you needed to find somewhere to copy it down. If you didn't have freshly prepared parchment at hand, you might very well reuse an old book whose contents no longer seemed useful.

Vat. Lat. 5757 represents a perfect example of one of these instances. What you see with the naked eye (see the smaller letters in fig. 12.6) is a text by Augustine. It is his *Expositions on the Psalms* and was copied around the year 700. It was important to the monks who copied it. They would have memorized the Psalms, heard them repeatedly, and thought a lot about them. There would have been great value in having by their sides the thoughts on these important religious writings of a Church Father such as Augustine.

Underneath that text of Augustine, however, is something interesting, a work of Cicero's that was otherwise almost entirely lost: his dialogue *De republica*, or *On the Republic*. The Middle Ages possessed a very small though important section of this work, called the "Dream of Scipio," part of the sixth and final Book of *On the Republic*, in which Cicero sets forth a vision of the universe (by means of the "dream" of one of his dialogue's characters) that drew the attention of a late ancient Platonist named Macrobius. Macrobius excerpted this part of Cicero's text and wrote a commentary on it, which is why the "Dream of Scipio" survived as a separate text in the Middle Ages, even as the rest of Cicero's *On the Republic* was lost.[67]

Indeed, scholars thought it was lost forever, until a scholarly cardinal and manuscript librarian at the Vatican Library, Angelo Mai (1782–1854), in 1819, discovered the Ciceronian text underneath Augustine's *Expositions on the Psalms* in this very manuscript.[68] What we have, then, is an important writing by classical Rome's most central prose writer and philosopher in a unique text. It was the kind of thing to which later scholars and thinkers, up through the era of Augustine, had access. Indeed, Augustine had employed Cicero's *On the Republic* extensively in his *City of God*.[69] Inspired by Plato's *Republic*, Cicero's work represented one of the many instances where the great Roman thinker had culturally translated Greek philosophy for predominantly Latinate audiences.

But, by the time the seventh-century monks were at work at Bobbio (a monastery near Milan, founded by a learned Irish monastic leader named Columbanus), Augustine's *Commentary on the Psalms* seemed more valuable

---

[67] See R. Caldini Montanari, *Tradizione medievale e edizione critica del* Somnium Scipionis (Florence: SISMEL, Edizioni del Galluzzzo, 2002).

[68] See Giovanni Mercati, *M. Tulli Ciceronis De re publica libri e codice rescripto Vaticano latino 5757 photoypice expressi. Prolegomena de fatis bibliothecae monasterii S. Colombani Bobiensis et de codice ipso Vat. Lat. 5757*, 2 vols. (Vatican City: Biblioteca Apostolica Vaticana, 1934); Andras Nemeth, "Recovery of Conflicting Textual Identities: Augustine and Cicero in Vat. Lat. 5757," *Miscellanea Bibliothecae Apostolicae Vaticanae* 23 (2017), 405–450.

[69] See Anne-Isabelle Bouton-Touboulic, "Cicero and Augustine," in Atkins and Bénatouïl, *Cicero's Philosophy*, 252–267, at 260–261.

to them and accordingly more worth preserving than Cicero's political thinking.[70] It would take a nineteenth-century expert at locating and deciphering palimpsests to rediscover this work of Cicero's. Cardinal Mai did a lot of this sort of thing, finding other such texts.[71] And as to Cicero, Vat. Lat. 5757 contains only about one fourth of the *De republica*. The rest may indeed be lost to history – or perhaps it is out there, waiting to be discovered, in a manuscript yet unstudied.

This example represents one of many instances where we can see early medieval readers and writers (a restricted group) making choices about what was meaningful to them. These choices had a radiating effect on the many nonliterate Christians whose outlooks were shaped by those at the top of the pyramid. Newer bodies of work, such as the many texts of the Latin Church Fathers, grew in importance, even as the corpus of regularly studied texts from pagan antiquity shrank. Virgil's *Aeneid* remained, its stories of Aeneas leaving burning Troy and founding Rome providing readers with examples of virtues and vices and spawning numerous Christian allegories.[72] And his magnificent fourth *Eclogue*, with its language of a "Virgin" returning and a "child being born," signaling the end of an age of iron and the beginning of a golden age – well, one can imagine what an afterlife that poem had in a medieval (and eventually Renaissance) Christianity always interested in finding validation for its guiding assumptions.[73]

Ovid's *Metamorphoses*, too, was another poetic text to which those privileged few who learned Latin eventually had access, imbibing along the way all the ancient myths about the pagan gods. Even there, however, it took centuries for it to be regularly read.[74] And there was no shortage of

---

[70] On Bobbio, see the impressive biography of Columbanus's biographer Jonas: Alexander O'Hara, *Jonas of Bobbio and the Legacy of Columbanus: Sanctity and Community in the Seventh Century* (Oxford: Oxford University Press, 2018).

[71] Francesco Lo Monaco, "*In codicibus ... qui Bobbbienses inscribuntur*: Scoperte e studio di palinsesti bobbiesi in Ambrosiana dalla fine del settecento ad Angelo Mai (1819)," *Aevum* 70 (1996), 657–719, esp. 672–717; Sebastiano Timpanaro, *Aspetti e figure della cultura ottocentesca* (Pisa: Nistri-Lischi, 1981), pp. 225–271.

[72] See Jan M. Ziolkowski and Michael C. J. Putnam, eds., *The Virgilian Tradition: The First Fifteen Hundred Years* (New Haven: Yale University Press, 2008).

[73] See Stephen Benko, "Virgil's Fourth Eclogue in Christian Interpretation," *Aufstieg und Niedergang der römischen Welt*, vol. 2.31.1 (Berlin: DeGruyter, 1980), 646–705; L. B. T. Houghton, *Virgil's Fourth Eclogue in the Italian Renaissance* (Cambridge: Cambridge University Press, 2019).

[74] See Robin Wahlsten Böckerman, *The Bavarian Commentary and Ovid: Clm 4610, the Earliest Documented Commentary on the Metamorphoses* (Cambridge: Open Book Publishers, 2020), esp. 1–28; James G. Clark, Frank T. Coulson, and Kathryn L. McKinley, eds., *Ovid in the Middle Ages* (Cambridge: Cambridge University Press, 2011); Frank T. Coulson and Bruno

knowledge about names and places and texts from the ancient world during the Middle Ages, whether through collections of excerpts from, commentaries about, or adaptations of ancient works.[75] Still, in the era of Gregory and immediately following, the truth is that there was a loss of interest in many ancient texts. It is worth noting, too, that there was a significant diminution of knowledge of the Greek language in western Europe. It was not a total loss, but the medieval centuries saw few western readers who could access the original language versions of Plato and Aristotle, Homer and Herodotus.[76]

Again, however, these "losses" represent choices that medieval people made.[77] The key driver behind those choices was Christianity. It provided a philosophy for all, validation for the normally disenfranchised, and a version of history – after Augustine's *City of God* – that suggested that history had direction. It was going somewhere, as were all of us individuals. It was a new and different vision of the world, one to which some of western philosophy's core ideas needed to be adopted, adapted, and transformed. The place of learning in this new landscape changed in focus. That story is for another book. But for a taste, we can turn once more to Gregory the Great, and specifically to his biography of Benedict of Nursia (480–543/47), the founder of western monasticism.

Benedict grew up as a member of his town's nobility and then turned away from its customs and habits. He discovered himself by diving deep into Christianity. Benedict's family sent him to cosmopolitan Rome to study. Even as a boy, he was someone who had "the mature heart of an old man," never having inclined toward the normal pleasures of youth. To Rome he went, to study the liberal arts.[78] Yet upon arriving, "when he discerned many traveling the dangerous ways of vice, he drew back the foot he had

---

Roy, *Incipitarium Ovidianum: A Finding Guide for Texts Related to the Study of Ovid in the Middle Ages and Renaissance* (Turnhout: Brepols, 2000); Julie Van Peteghem, *Italian Readers of Ovid from the Origins to Petrarch* (Leiden: Brill, 2020).

[75] See Silverio Franzoni, Elisa Lonati, and Adriano Russo, eds., *Le sens des textes classiques au Moyen Age: Transmission, exégèse, réécriture* (Turnhout: Brepols, 2022); Birger Munk Olsen, *L'étude des auteurs classiques latins aux XIe et XIIe siècles*, 5 vols. (Paris: CNRS Éditions, 1982–2020).

[76] See Walter Berschin, "Il greco in occidente: Conoscenza e ignoranza," in Salvatore Settis, ed., *I greci*, 4 vols. in 7 (Turin: Einaudi, 1996–), v. 3.1, pp. 1107–1115; Walter Berschin, *Greek Letters and the Latin Middle Ages*, tr. Jerold C. Frakes (Washington, DC: Catholic University Press, 1988); Pierre Courcelle, *Late Latin Writers and their Greek Sources* (Cambridge, MA: Harvard University Press, 1969).

[77] Cf. Scott Bruce, "The Dark Age of Herodotus: Shards of a Fugitive History in Early Medieval Europe," *Speculum* 94 (2019), 47–67.

[78] Gregory, *Dialogi*, 2, prologus, 2: "liberalibus studiis traditus."

just barely placed in the entryway of the world."⁷⁹ Gregory is sending the message that Benedict arrived, scoped out his new comrades and their dedication to the liberal arts, and was unimpressed by their mores.

And then there is that phrase "in the entryway of the world," or *ingressu mundi* in Latin. The "world" here becomes a stand-in for everything that the monastic life is not, or rather, in the logic of the narrative, for everything that Benedict will combat, in both his style of life and the way he eventually conceives of the place of learning. His citizenship will be, not in the City of Man, but in the City of God. And why did he "withdraw his foot" from the precipitous entryway to the world? "Lest," Gregory tells us, "in coming into contact with anything whatsoever of that type of knowledge, he fall entire into that frightful precipice."⁸⁰ The "world" – its learning, most immediately, but more broadly all its customs and habits – is something dangerous. Even a bit of its learning, on its own, can be laden with peril.

In the face of this danger, then, Benedict withdrew: "Therefore, having set aside the study of letters and left behind his father's home and wealth, he sought out the habit of holy conversation. And so, he left, knowingly ignorant and wisely unlearned."⁸¹ In these last two sentences a new world appears. First, Benedict set aside the "study of letters," the *studia litterarum* in Latin, meaning that he saw and learned what he needed to learn and decided it was enough. He "left behind his father's home and wealth": in this new dispensation, one could do things that would be otherwise startling, leaving one's family and its expectations and thus setting aside customs and habits long ingrained in the aristocracy, so that like Christ's early apostles one could drop whatever one was doing and proceed toward what was truly important (cf. Matt 4:18–22; Luke 5:2–11). For Benedict that new and highly important matter was the "habit of holy conversation." There are two key formulations here: "habit" and "holy conversation." As to habit, the Latin word in question is *habitus*. That word is the Latin translation of a Greek word, *hexis*, that for Aristotle served as one way to describe a virtue. It meant a capacity that one brought from potentiality to actuality by repeated practice. The more one engaged in it, the better at it one became. In this case, for Benedict, the "it" in question was the living of a holy life. It is also worth

---

⁷⁹ Ibid.: "sed cum in eis multos ire per abrupta vitiorum cerneret, eum, quem quasi in ingressu mundi posuerat, retraxit pedem."
⁸⁰ Ibid.: "Ne si quid de scientia eius attingeret, ipse quoque in immane praecipitium totus iret."
⁸¹ Ibid., prologus, 3: "Despectis itaque litterarum studiis, relicta domo rebusque patris, soli Deo placere desiderans, sanctae conversationis habitum quaesivit. Recessit igitur scienter nescius, et sapienter indoctus."

remarking that the Latin *habitus* also bears the meaning of a "style of dress" (hence the English locution of a "nun's habit"). When it comes to "conversation," or *conversatio* in Latin, the word has two basic meanings, both of which are indicated in Gregory's subtle use of the word. *Conversatio* meant a place where one resided with some frequency, and it also signified "conversation," in both a narrow sense – talking with people – and more broadly, meaning social interactions. Gregory signals that Benedict sought retreat from the outside world and entry into another, a world where he might live in communion with the Lord and be among those who were like-minded.

In every way imaginable, Gregory wants his portrait of Benedict to be exemplary. An example of a sudden conversion, one that in its own way must have puzzled his contemporaries. An example of what level of seriousness one should accord "letters" – meaning the study of secular literature. An example of how the monastic style of life could be considered meaningful, a life where you lived among individuals who shared your desire for God. Gregory's *Life of Benedict* was all these things.

As Gregory wrote prodigiously, sent out emissaries to serve as agents of conversion, and helped transform the papacy with vision and a natural bureaucratic mindset, he was laying the foundation for a Christian medieval Europe.

EPILOGUE

In his *Moralia in Job*, Gregory the Great wrote: "Having preserved the unity of the sacrament, the Church gathers together the faithful peoples according to the manifold variety of their customs and languages."[1] Here and elsewhere in his work, Gregory wrestled with the issue of unity and plurality in the growing Church, sometimes tolerating divergent local worship customs, other times objecting. He recognized both that the Church had an audience and that the Church's representatives needed to adapt their communication accordingly.[2] He left a legacy that had a shaping effect on the Catholic Church and, accordingly, on western thought. Gregory's lifelong ill health caught up with him in 604. This "servant of the servants of God," as he was described, died in a world of tumultuousness and change.

A continent away and about five years later, a 40-year-old man – a trader, who by his own account was not formally educated – heard a command from an angel. Muhammad was in a cave in what is now Saudi Arabia, a few miles outside the city of Mecca. He had been in the habit of retreating to secreted places to think, ever since he had received visions and come to believe that he needed time alone to meditate on them. It was not so strange a practice as it might sound to modern ears. Ancient Greek followers of the medical god Asclepius were guided through rituals of "incubation," whereby they slept and experienced healing through dreams in a restricted

---

[1] Gregory, *Moralia in Job*, 30.6.22, vol. 3, p. 1506; cit. and tr. in Markus, p. 73, tr. altered.
[2] Cf. Gregory, *Regula pastoralis*, 3 Prologus (SC 382, F. Rommel ed., pp. 258, 260, ll.2–13): "Pro qualitate igitur audientium formari debet sermo doctorum, ut et ad sua singulis congruat, et tamen a communis aedificationis arte nunquam recedat," and Gregory, *Registrum epistularum*, 2, 768.

location in a temple.³ Abraham, Jacob, Daniel, and Elijah all slept and dreamt, or fell into dreamlike states, to awaken and learn things they hadn't before known (Gen 15:12–17, 28:10–17; Dan 7–8; 1 Kgs 19: 4–8). And of course, both Moses and Elijah had private, veiled encounters with God that were connected to caves (Ex 33:18–23, 1 Kgs 19: 9–13).

When the angel Gabriel appeared, Muhammad was afraid at first. Gabriel told Muhammad to "Read" (Quran, 96:1–5) Muhammad was puzzled, but after Gabriel persisted, Muhammad understood. He was to "read" in the sense of "recite," and he was to recite the messages that the one God, Allah, was sending to the world through him. This he did. Initially the Quran was not written down. It lived in Muhammad's memory and the memories of his growing number of followers, who eagerly heard the divine revelations as Muhammad voiced them. Within about two decades of Muhammad's death, Uthman, the third "successor" (or "Caliph") of Muhammad and hence of this new religion, Islam, ensured that the Quran was compiled and standardized in written form.

Fortified by swift and decisive victories in battle, the religion and its deepening culture spread. By the time of Muhammad's death in 632, most of the Arabian Peninsula was under Islamic control. In the decades that followed, Muslim forces brought Egypt, North Africa, Persia, Spain, and parts of India into the growing Islamic realm. By the late eighth century, especially after the Abbasids founded Baghdad in 762, the cultural and political center of the Islamic world shifted eastward. During the ninth and tenth centuries, the central Asian cities of Bukhara and Samarkand (in present day Uzbekistan) served as a cultural hub.⁴ During this long period of Muslim expansion, advanced centers of learning developed – some of which later took institutional form as Madrassas.⁵ It was in these contexts that Greek philosophy flourished once again, especially that of Aristotle, whose work made its way to Muslim regions through Syriac intermediaries translated into Arabic and sometimes directly, in Greek to Arabic translations.⁶

---

³ See Hedvig von Ehrenheim, *Greek Incubation Rituals in Classical and Hellenistic Times* (Liège: Presses Universitaires de Liège, 2015); Peter Kingsley, *Ancient Philosophy, Mystery, and Magic: Empedocles and Pythagorean Tradition* (Oxford: Clarendon, 1995).
⁴ S. Frederick Starr, *Lost Enlightenment: Central Asia's Golden Age from the Arab Conquest to Tamerlane* (Princeton: Princeton University Press, 2013).
⁵ George Makdisi, *The Rise of Colleges: Institutions of Learning in Islam and the West* (Edinburgh: Edinburgh University Press, 1981).
⁶ Dimitri Gutas, *Greek Thought, Arabic Culture: The Graeco-Arabic Translation Movement in Baghdad and Early Abbasid Society (2nd–4th/8th–10th Centuries)* (London: Routledge, 1998).

Thinkers such as Al-Kindi (801–873), Al-Farabi (872–950), Avicenna (Ibn Sina, 980–1037), and Averroes (Ibn Rushd, 1126–1198), made major contributions to the history of philosophy. They regarded Aristotle as *the* authoritative thinker, though they often read him through Neoplatonic lenses, since in the intervening centuries many had commented on Aristotle's work from a Platonic perspective. Working from the shared belief that Islam was the final revealed religion, Al-Kindi, Al-Farabi, Avicenna, Averroes, and others worked to accommodate faith and reason, trying to understand how Aristotle's unquestionably brilliant work could fit into a religious framework within which some of his ideas sat uneasily.

These Islamic thinkers and more like them laid the groundwork for the same sorts of debates on faith and reason that would animate the universities of thirteenth-century western Europe. Their writings were often translated into Latin alongside the work of Aristotle in the twelfth and thirteenth centuries. Accordingly, it is worth recalling a point made at this book's outset: "western" thought has indeed come to mean something distinctive over the centuries. Yet at every historical juncture, there were conversation, interaction, and exchange – without which the problems, arguments, and frameworks associated with western thought would have taken different forms. Greek, Roman, Jewish, Christian, and Islamic traditions all played their part, even as Christianity, becoming the west's majority religion, provided the dominant framework for much philosophical thinking in the Middle Ages.

Speaking of conversation and exchange in the Middle Ages, consider this line of Latin, found in a twelfth-century manuscript book now housed in the Frankfurt University Library: *Guda peccatrix mulier scripsit et pinxit hunc librum* – "Guda, a sinner and a woman, wrote and painted this book."[7] The manuscript gathers a series of homilies – sermons – written by people like Ambrose, Augustine, and others. The cited text wraps around the portrait of a woman embedded into a large initial letter in one line. The woman is a nun, Guda herself, who is letting us know who she is: a woman who wrote, who "painted" (that is, illuminated the large initial letters), and who was a highly skilled artisan, likely responsible for not only the writing and illustration but also the overall layout of the book. Scribes sometimes identified themselves – whether modestly at the end of a manuscript in a colophon, or more creatively, as Guda did, within the text itself.[8] Guda was one of a small

---

[7] MS Frankfurt, Barth. 42, f. 110v, https://sammlungen.ub.uni-frankfurt.de/msma/content/pageview/3644769.

[8] Wilhelm Wattenbach, *Das Schriftwesen im Mittlealter* (Leipzig: Hirzel, 1896), pp. 491–534.

but significant number of female scribes in the western Middle Ages.[9] Often working within monastic settings, these women expressed themselves in a literary culture that, though dominated by men, was never theirs alone.

In the ancient world the western conversation was shaped by the monumental works that we have. And from the ancient Romans through the western Middle Ages, the Latinate, public nature of elite education meant that women's voices are less often heard than those of men. Yet, over time those voices did grow in volume. Thinkers like Hildegard of Bingen, Christine de Pizan, and others found ways, often extraordinarily, to be heard in the broad philosophical landscape. Women were always there, as conversation partners if not authors, as patrons if not the person who put things on a page, or as correspondents whose presence often stimulated writing.

Exchanges – across geographies, between women and men, and among members of different faith traditions – serve as a key theme of western medieval intellectual history. That story awaits us in our next volume.

---

[9] See Åslaug Ommundsen, Aidan Keally Conti, Øystein Ariansen Haaland, and Bodil Holst, "How Many Medieval and Early Modern Manuscripts Were Copied by Female Scribes? A Bibliometric Analysis Based on Colophons," *Humanities and Social Sciences Communications* 12 (2025), 1–5, who highlight Guda (at p. 2). The authors estimate that about 1.1% of premodern manuscripts (dating from c. 800–1626) were copied by women, a number that is probably as high as 110,000 manuscripts total (of which most, like all premodern manuscripts, did not survive), so that of those manuscripts that still exist, about 8000 will have been copied by women.

BIBLIOGRAPHY

Manuscripts

MS Frankfurt, Universitätsbibliothek, MS. Barth. 42 ("Guda-Homiliar").
MS Vatican City, Biblioteca apostolica vaticana, Vat. Lat. 5757.

Sources Cited

Ackrill, J. L., "Aristotle on Eudaimonia," in Amélie Oksenberg Rorty, ed., *Essays on Aristotle's Ethics* (Berkeley: University of California Press, 1981), 15–33.
Adams, J. N., *The Regional Diversification of Latin, 200 BC–AD 600* (Cambridge: Cambridge University Press, 2007).
Adamson, Peter, *Classical Philosophy: A History of Philosophy without Any Gaps*, vol. 1 (Oxford: Oxford University Press, 2014).
  Philosophy in the Hellenistic and Roman Worlds: A History of Philosophy without Any Gaps, vol. 2 (Oxford: Oxford University Press, 2015).
Addey, Crystal, *Divination and Theurgy in Neoplatonism: Oracles of the Gods* (New York: Routledge, 2016).
Adler, Eric, *The Battle of the Classics* (Oxford: Oxford University Press, 2020).
Alexandre, Monique, "La culture grecque, servante de la foi," in Arnaud Perrot, ed., *Les chrétiens et l'hellénisme: identités religieuses et culture grecque dans l'Antiquité tardive* (Paris: Éditions Rue d'Ulm, 2012), 31–59.
Allais, Lucy, "Problematising Western Philosophy as One Part of Africanising the Curriculum," *South African Journal of Philosophy* 35 (2016), 537–545.
Allen, Danielle S., *Justice by Means of Democracy* (Chicago: University of Chicago Press, 2023).
  Why Plato Wrote (Oxford: Wiley-Blackwell, 2013).
Ambrose, *De officiis*, 2 vols., ed. and trans. Ivor J. Davidson (Oxford: Oxford University Press, 2001).
Anderson, Matthew R., "The Curious Voyage of Christ: *Katábasis*, *Anábasis*, and the New Testament," *Les Études classiques* 83 (2015), 385–396.

Annas, Julia, *The Morality of Happiness* (Oxford: Oxford University Press, 1995).
Apollodorus, *Library*, 2 vols., ed. and trans. James George Frazer (Cambridge, MA: Harvard University Press, 1921).
Aratus, *Phaenomena*, ed. and trans. Douglas Kidd (Cambridge: Cambridge University Press, 1997).
Arenson, Kelly, *The Routledge Handbook of Hellenistic Philosophy* (New York: Routledge, 2020).
Aristophanes, *Clouds, Wasps, Peace*, ed. and trans. Jeffrey Henderson (Cambridge, MA: Harvard University Press, 1998).
Aristotle, *Aristotelis qui ferebantur librorum fragmenta*, ed. Valentin Rose (Stuttgart: Teubner, 1967).
   Ethica Nicomachea, ed. Ingram Bywater (Oxford: Oxford University Press, 1894).
   Metaphysics, 2 vols., ed. and trans. Hugh Tredennick (Cambridge, MA: Harvard University Press, 1933).
   Nicomachean Ethics, trans. C. D. C. Reeve (Indianapolis: Hackett, 2014).
   Nicomachean Ethics, ed. and trans. Horace Rackham (Cambridge, MA: Harvard University Press, 1934).
   Parts of Animals, Movement of Animals, Progression of Animals, ed. and trans. A. L. Peck and E. S. Forster (Cambridge, MA: Harvard University Press, 1961).
   Physics, Vol I: Books 1–4, trans. P. H. Wicksteed and F. M. Cornford (Cambridge, MA: Harvard University Press, 1957).
   Politics, trans. H. Rackham (Cambridge, MA: Harvard University Press, 1932).
Assmann, Aleida, "Memory, Individual and Collective," in Robert E. Goodin and Charles Tilly, eds., *The Oxford Handbook of Contextual Political Analysis*, (Oxford: Oxford University Press, 2006), 210–224.
Assmann, Jan, *Of God and Gods: Egypt, Israel, and the Rise of Monotheism* (Madison: University of Wisconsin Press, 2008).
   "Translating Gods: Religion as a Factor of Cultural (Un)Translatability," in Sanford Budick and Wolfgang Iser, eds., *The Translatability of Cultures: Figurations of the Space Between* (Stanford: Stanford University Press, 1996), 25–37.
Athanasius, "Thirty-Ninth Festal Letter," in Périclès-Pierre Joannou, ed., *Fonti: Discipline Générale antique (IVe–IXe s.)*, 2 vols. (Rome: Grottaferrata, 1963), 2: 71–76.
Athanassiadi, Polymnia, *Julian: An Intellectual Biography* (London: Routledge, 1981).
   Mutations of Hellenism in Late Antiquity (Farnham, Surrey: Ashgate, 2015).
Athanassiadi, Polymnia and Michael Frede, eds., *Pagan Monotheism in Late Antiquity* (Oxford: Oxford University Press, 1999).
Atkins, Jed W., and Thomas Bénatouïl, eds., *The Cambridge Companion to Cicero's Philosophy* (Cambridge: Cambridge University Press, 2022).
Augustine, *The City of God Against the Pagans*, 7 vols., ed. and trans. George E. McCracken, William Green, and others (Cambridge, MA: Harvard University Press, 1962–1972).
   Concerning the City of God Against the Pagans, trans. Henry Bettenson and introduction by John O'Meara (London: Penguin, 2003).
   Confessions, trans. R. S. Pine-Coffin (New York: Penguin, 1961).
   Confessions, 3 vols., ed. and comm. James J. O'Donnell (Oxford: Oxford University Press, 2012).

De consensu evangelistarum, ed. Franz Weinrich, Corpus Scriptorum Ecclesiasticorum Latinorum, 43 (Vienna: Tempsky, 1904).

De doctrina christiana, ed. and trans. R. P. H. Green (Oxford: Clarendon, 1995).

Enchiridion de fide, spe et caritate, ed. E. Evans, Corpus Christianorum, Series Latina, 46 (Turnhout: Brepols, 1969), 10:35, 49–114.

Oeuvres de Saint Augustin, Lettres 1*–29*, Bibliothèque Augustinienne, 78 vols., vol. 46B, ed. Johannes Divjak (Paris: Études Augustiniennes, 1987), let. 1a, 54–59.

On the Trinity, ed. Gareth B. Matthews, trans. Stephen McKenna (Cambridge: Cambridge University Press, 2012).

Sancti Aurelii Augustini De trinitate libri XV, 2 vols., ed. W. J. Mountain (Turnhout: Brepols, 1968).

Sermon 117, in F. Dolbeau, "Le Sermon 117 d'Augustin sur l'ineffabilité de Dieu. Édition critique," *Revue bénédictine* 124 (2014), 213–253.

Augustus, *Res gestae divi Augusti*, in Velleius Paterculus, *Compendium of Roman History* and Augustus, *Res gestae divi Augusti*, ed. and trans. Frederick W. Shipley (Cambridge, MA: Harvard University Press, 1924), 344–401.

Barnes, Jonathan, ed., *The Cambridge Companion to Aristotle* (Cambridge: Cambridge University Press, 1995).

"Roman Aristotle," in Jonathan Barnes and Miriam Griffin eds., *Philosophia Togata II* (Oxford: Clarendon, 1999), 1–69.

Banniard, Michel, *Viva voce: Communication écrite et communication orale du IVe au IXe siècle en occident latin* (Paris: Institut des études augustiniennes, 1992).

Barchiesi, Alessandro, *Homeric Effects in Vergil's Narrative*, trans. Ilaria Marchesi and Matt Fox (Princeton: Princeton University Press, 2015).

Barton, John, *A History of the Bible: The Story of the World's Most Influential Book* (New York: Viking, 2019).

Basil, *The Letters*, 4 vols., ed. and trans. Roy J. Deferrari (Cambridge, MA: Harvard University Press, 1926–1934).

Beard, Mary, ed., *Literacy in the Roman World* (Ann Arbor: University of Michigan Press, 1991).

Beatrice, Pier Franco, "*Quosdam platonicorum libros*: The Platonic Readings of Augustine in Milan," *Vigiliae Christianae* 43 (1989), 248–281.

Becker, Uwe, "The Book of Isaiah: Its Composition History," in Lena-Sofia Tiemeyer, ed., *The Oxford Handbook of Isaiah* (Oxford: Oxford University Press, 2020), 37–56.

BeDuhn, Jason, *Augustine's Manichaean Dilemma*, 2 vols. (Philadelphia: University of Pennsylvania Press, 2010–2013).

Beierwaltes, Werner, *Das wahre Selbst: Studien zu Plotins Begriff des Geistes und des Einen* (Frankfurt am Main: Klostermann, 2001).

Benedict of Nursia, *Regula Benedicti*, ed. Rudolph Hanslik, Regula Corpus Scriptorum Ecclesiasticorum Latinorum, 75 (Vienna: Hoelder-Pinchler-Tempsky, 1960).

The Rule of Saint Benedict, trans. Carolinne White (New York: Penguin, 2008).

Benko, Stephen, "Virgil's Fourth Eclogue in Christian Interpretation," in *Aufstieg und Niedergang der römischen Welt* (Berlin: DeGruyter, 1980), 2.31.1, pp. 646–705.

Berschin, Walter, "Il greco in occidente: Conoscenza e ignoranza," in Salvatore Settis, ed., *I greci*, 4 vols. (Turin: Einaudi, 1996–), 3.1, 107–1115.

Greek Letters and the Latin Middle Ages, trans. Jerold C. Frakes (Washington, DC: Catholic University Press, 1988).

Besson, Arnaud, *Constitutio antoniniana: L'universalisation de la citoyenneté romaine au 3e siècle* (Basel: Schwabe Verlag, 2020).
Bett, Richard, ed., *The Cambridge Companion to Scepticism* (Cambridge: Cambridge University Press, 2010).
  "Immortality and the nature of the Soul in the 'Phaedrus,'" *Phronesis* 31 (1986), 1–26.
  Pyrrho, His Antecedents, and His Legacy (Oxford: Oxford University Press, 2003).
  "The Sophists and Relativism," *Phronesis* 34 (1989), 139–169.
Bischoff, Bernhard, *Latin Palaeography: Antiquity and the Middle Ages*, trans. Dáibhí Ó Cróinín and David Ganz (Cambridge: Cambridge University Press, 1990).
Bishop, Caroline, *Cicero, Greek Learning, and the Making of a Roman Classic* (Oxford: Oxford University Press, 2018).
Blackburn, Barry L., "The Miracles of Jesus," in Graham H. Twelftree, ed., *The Cambridge Companion to Miracles* (Cambridge: Cambridge University Press, 2011), 113–130.
Bloomer, W. Martin, ed., *A Companion to Ancient Education* (Oxford: Wiley Blackwell, 2015).
Blumenthal, Henry J., and E. Gillian Clark, *The Divine Iamblichus: Philosopher and Man of the Gods* (Bristol: Bristol Classical Press, 1993).
Böckerman, Robin Wahlsten, *The Bavarian Commentary and Ovid: Clm 4610, the Earliest Documented Commentary on the Metamorphoses* (Cambridge: Open Book Publishers, 2020).
Bolgia, Claudia, Rosamond McKitterick, and John Osborne, eds., *Rome across Time and Space: Cultural Transmission and the Exchange of Ideas, c. 500–1400* (Cambridge: Cambridge University Press, 2011).
Bonazzi, Mauro, *The Sophists* (Cambridge: Cambridge University Press, 2020).
Bonner, Stanley F., *Education in Ancient Rome: From the Elder Cato to the Younger Pliny* (Berkeley: University of California Press, 1977).
Bouton-Touboulic, Anne-Isabelle, "Cicero and Augustine," in Jed W. Atkins and Thomas Bénatouïl, eds., *The Cambridge Companion to Cicero's Philosophy* (Cambridge: Cambridge University Press, 2022), 252–267.
Bowersock, Glenn W., *Julian the Apostate* (London: Duckworth, 1978).
Bowes, Kim, *Private Worship, Public Values and Religious Change in Late Antiquity* (Cambridge: Cambridge University Press, 2008).
Boyle, Leonard, O. P., *A Short Guide to Saint Clement's, Rome* (Rome: Collegio San Clemente, 1989).
Brakke, David, *Athanasius and the Politics of Asceticism* (Oxford: Clarendon, 1995).
  "A New Fragment of Athanasius's Thirty-Ninth *Festal Letter*: Heresy, Apocrypha, and the Canon," *Harvard Theological Review* 103 (2010), 47–66.
Bremmer, Jan N., "How do We Explain the Quiet Demise of Graeco-Roman Religion? An Essay," *Numen* 68 (2021), 230–271.
Brennan, Corey, "Tertullian's *De pallio* and Roman Dress in North Africa," in Jonathan Edmondson and Alison Mary Keith, eds., *Roman Dress and the Fabrics of Roman Culture* (Toronto: University of Toronto Press, 2008), 257–270.
Brown, Peter, *Augustine of Hippo*, 45th anniversary ed. (Berkeley: University of California Press, 2000).

Authority and the Sacred: Aspects of the Christianisation of the Roman World (Cambridge: Cambridge University Press, 1997).

The Cult of the Saints: Its Rise and Function in Latin Christianity, 2nd ed. (Chicago: University of Chicago Press, 2015).

"Holy Men," in Averil Cameron, Bryan Ward-Perkins, and Michael Whitby, eds., *The Cambridge Ancient History, Vol. 14: Late Antiquity: Empire and Successors* (Cambridge: Cambridge University Press, 2001), 781–810.

The Rise of Western Christendom: Triumph and Diversity, A.D. 200–1000, 10th anniversary rev. ed. (Oxford: Wiley-Blackwell, 2013).

Brown, William P., "The Psalms and Hebrew Poetry," in Stephen B. Chapman and Marvin A. Sweeney, eds., *The Cambridge Companion to the Hebrew Bible/Old Testament* (Cambridge: Cambridge University Press, 2016), 253–273.

Bruce, Scott, "The Dark Age of Herodotus: Shards of a Fugitive History in Early Medieval Europe," *Speculum* 94 (2019), 47–67.

"Origen Issues: The Reception of a Renegade Greek Theologian in Early Medieval Europe," *The Journal of Medieval Latin* 33 (2023), 267–303.

Brucker, Johann Jacob, *Critical History of Philosophy: "Preliminary Discourse" and "On the Socratic School,"* ed. and trans. Leo Catana (Oxford: Oxford University Press, 2024).

Historia critica philosophiae a mundi incunabulis ad nostram usque aetatem deducta, 5 vols. in 6, ed. Richard H. Popkin and Giorgio Tonelli, 2nd ed. (1766–1767, Leipzig, 1975).

Burns, Thomas S., *Barbarians within the Gates of Rome* (Bloomington: Indiana University Press, 1994).

Burnyeat, Myles, "First Words: A Valedictory Lecture," *Proceedings of the Cambridge Philological Society* 43 (1998), 1–20.

Busch, Austin, George D. Chryssides, Gregor Etzelmüller, Eric Eve, Daniel Frank, Lee M. Jefferson, Melanie Köhlmoos, Lidija Novakovic, Aaron D. Panken, Celia E. Rothenberg, W. Barnes Tatum, David Thomas, and Annette Weissenrieder, "Healing Miracles," in Dale C. Allison, Jr., Christine Helmer, Volker Leppin, Choon-Leong Seow, Hermann Spieckermann, Barry Dov Walfish, and Eric J. Ziolkowski, eds., *Encyclopedia of the Bible and Its Reception*, 29 vols. to date (Berlin: De Gruyter, 2009–), 11: coll. 474–502.

Bynum, Caroline Walker, *The Resurrection of the Body in Western Christianity, 200–1336* (New York: Columbia University Press, 1995).

Caillet, Jean-Pierre, "La transformation en église d'édifices publics et de temples à la fin de l'antiquité," in Claude Lepelley, ed., *La fin de la cité antique et le début de la cité médiévale de la fin du IIIe siècle à l'avènement de Charlemagne* (Bari: Edipuglia, 1996), 191–211.

Cameron, Alan, *The Last Pagans of Rome* (Oxford: Oxford University Press, 2010).

Cargill, Robert, *The Cities that Built the Bible* (New York: HarperOne, 2016).

Carruthers, Mary, *The Book of Memory: A Study of Memory in Medieval Culture*, 2nd ed. (Cambridge: Cambridge University Press, 2008).

Castaldi, Lucia, *La trasmissione dei testi latini del medioevo, Gregorius I Papa* (Florence: Edizioni del Galluzzo, 2013).

Catana, Leo, *The Historiographical Concept "System of Philosophy": Its Origin, Nature, Influence and Legitimacy* (Leiden: Brill, 2008).

Catana, Leo, and Mogens Laerke, "Historiographies of Philosophy, 1800–1950," *British Journal for the History of Philosophy* 28 (2020), 431–441.

Celenza, Christopher S., *The Lost Italian Renaissance: Humanists, Historians, and Latin's Legacy* (Baltimore: Johns Hopkins University Press, 2004).
  "What Counted as Philosophy in the Italian Renaissance? The History of Philosophy, the History of Science, and Styles of Life," *Critical Inquiry* 39 (2013), 367–401.
Chadwick, Henry, *The Church in Ancient Society: From Galilee to Gregory the Great* (Oxford: Oxford University Press, 2001).
Charle, Christophe, "Patterns," in Walter Rüegg, ed., *Universities in the Nineteenth and Early Twentieth Centuries*, vol. 3 of *A History of the University in Europe*, Walter Rüegg, general editor, 4 vols. (Cambridge: Cambridge University Press, 1992–2010), 33–80.
Charles, David, ed., *The History of Hylomorphism: From Aristotle to Descartes* (Oxford: Oxford University Press, 2023).
Chazelle, Celia, "Pictures, Books, and the Illiterate: Gregory I's Letters to Serenus," *Word and Image* 6 (1990), 138–153.
Cicero, *On the Nature of the Gods. Academica*, ed. and trans. Horace Rackham (Cambridge, MA: Harvard University Press, 1933).
  Tusculan Disputations, ed. and trans. J. E. King (Cambridge, MA: Harvard University Press, 1945).
Clackson, James, and Geoffrey Horrocks, *The Blackwell History of the Latin Language* (Oxford: Blackwell, 2007).
Claessens, Guy, and Fabio della Schiava, eds., *Augustine and the Humanists: Reading the City of God from Petrarch to Poliziano* (Gent: Lisa, 2021).
Clark, Elizabeth A., "Patrons, Not Priests: Gender and Power in Late Ancient Christianity," *Gender & History* 2 (1990), 253–273.
Clark, James G., Frank T. Coulson, and Kathryn L. McKinley, eds., *Ovid in the Middle Ages* (Cambridge: Cambridge University Press, 2011).
Clark, Stuart, *Thinking with Demons: The Idea of Witchcraft in Early Modern Europe* (Oxford: Oxford University Press, 1997).
Clarke, Desmond M., *Descartes: A Biography* (Cambridge: Cambridge University Press, 2006).
Cohn, Norman, *The Pursuit of the Millennium: Revolutionary Millenarians and Mystical Anarchists of the Middle Ages* (Oxford: Oxford University Press, 1970).
Colish, Marcia L., *Medieval Foundations of the Western Intellectual Tradition* (New Haven: Yale University Press, 1997).
Consentius, *De barbarismis et metaplasmis*, ed. Tommaso Mari (Oxford: Oxford University Press, 2021).
Conte, Gian Biagio, *Latin Literature: A History*, trans. Joseph B. Solodow, rev. by Don Fowler and Glenn W. Most (Baltimore: Johns Hopkins University Press, 1994).
Cooper, Kate, *Band of Angels: The Forgotten World of Early Christian Women* (New York: Overlook Press, 2013).
Cooper, John M., *Pursuits of Wisdom: Six Ways of Life in Ancient Philosophy from Socrates to Plato* (Princeton: Princeton University Press, 2012).
Copenhaver, Brian, *Philosophy as Descartes Found It* (Oxford: Oxford University Press, 2024).
Corbeill, Anthony, "Rhetorical Education in Cicero's Youth," in James M. May, ed., *Brill's Companion to Cicero: Oratory and Rhetoric* (Leiden: Brill, 2002), 23–48.

Cory, N. Clayton, "Hellenistic Philosophies and the Preaching of the Resurrection (Acts 17:18, 32)," *Novum Testamentum* 39 (1997), 21–39.
Cotter, Wendy, ed., *Miracles in Greco-Roman Antiquity: A Sourcebook for the Study of New Testament Miracle Stories* (London: Routledge, 1999).
Coulson, Frank T. and Bruno Roy, *Incipitarium Ovidianum: A Finding Guide for Texts Related to the Study of Ovid in the Middle Ages and Renaissance* (Turnhout: Brepols, 2000).
Courcelle, Pierre, *Late Latin Writers and their Greek Sources* (Cambridge, MA: Harvard University Press, 1969).
Courtois, Christian, *Les vandales et l'Afrique* (Paris: Arts et Mètiers Graphiques, 1955).
Cousin, Victor, *Cours de l'histoire de la philosophie* (Paris: Didier, 1841).
Crenshaw, Kimberlé, "Mapping the Margins: Intersectionality, Identity Politics, and Violence Against Women of Color," in Kimberlé, Crenshaw, Neil Gotanda, Gary Peller, and Kendall Thomas, eds., *Critical Race Theory: The Key Writings that Formed the Movement* (New York: The New Press, 1995), 357–383.
Crenshaw, Kimberlé, Neil Gotanda, Gary Peller, Kendall Thomas, eds., *Critical Race Theory: The Key Writings that Formed the Movement* (New York: The New Press, 1995).
Cribiore, Raffaella, *Gymnastics of the Mind: Greek Education in Hellenistic and Roman Egypt* (Princeton: Princeton University Press, 2001).
  Listening to the Philosophers: Notes on Notes (Ithaca: Cornell University Press, 2024).
Curran, John R., *Pagan City and Christian Capital: Rome in the Fourth Century* (Oxford: Oxford University Press, 2002).
Daley, Brian E., S. J., and Paul R. Kolbet, eds., *The Harp of Prophecy: Early Christian Interpretation of the Psalms* (Notre Dame, Indiana: University of Notre Dame Press, 2015).
Daston, Lorraine and Katherine Park, *Wonders and the Order of Nature: 1150–1750* (New York: Zone, 1998).
Daston, Lorraine, and Peter Galison, *Objectivity* (Brooklyn: Zone Books, 2007).
Davidson, Ivor J., "Chapter 3: Model," in Ambrose, *De officiis*, 2 vols., ed. and trans. Ivor J. Davidson (Oxford: Oxford University Press, 2001), 1: 6–19.
Davies, W. D., *The Sermon on the Mount* (Cambridge: Cambridge University Press, 1966).
De Lubac, Henri, *Exégèse médiévale: les quatre sens de l'Écriture*, 4 vols. (Paris: Aubier, 1959–1991; reedition, Clamecy: Desclée de Brouwer, 1993).
  Medieval Exegesis: The Four Senses of Scripture, 3 vols., trans. Marc Sebanc and E. M. Macierowski (Grand Rapids: Eerdman's, 2009).
De Ridder-Symoens, Hilde, ed., *A History of the University in Europe, Volume 1: Universities in the Middle Ages*, vol. 1 of *A History of the University in Europe*, Walter Rüegg, general editor, 4 vols. (Cambridge: Cambridge University Press, 1992–2010).
De Romilly, Jacqueline, *The Great Sophists in Periclean Athens*, trans. Janet Lloyd (Oxford: Clarendon Press, 1992).
DelCogliano, Mark, "Introduction" in Gregory, *Moral Reflections on the Book of Job*, 5 vols., trans. Brian Kerns (Collegeville: Liturgical Press, 2014–2019), 1: 1–45.
Descartes, *Oeuvres*, eds. Charles Adam and Paul Tannery, 11 vols. in 13 (Paris: Vrin, 1973–1976).

The Philosophical Writings of Descartes, 3 vols., trans. John Cottingham, Robert Stoothoff, Dugald Murdoch, and (for vol. 3), Anthony Kenny (Cambridge: Cambridge University Press, 1985–1991).

Dey, Hendrick, *The Making of Medieval Rome: A New Profile of the City, 400–1420* (Cambridge: Cambridge University Press, 2021).

Diels, Hermann, and Walther Kranz, eds., *Die Fragmente der Vorsokratiker*, 6th ed. (Berlin: Wedmann, 1952).

Dillon, John, "Iamblichus of Chalcis (circa 240–325AD)," in *Aufstieg und Niedergang der römischen Welt*, 36.2 (1988), 862–909.

"Iamblichus' Defence of Theurgy: Some Reflections," *The International Journal of the Platonic Tradition* 1 (2007), 30–41.

"Logos and Trinity: Pattern of Platonist Influence on Early Christianity," in Godfrey Vesey, ed., *The Philosophy in Christianity* (Cambridge: Cambridge University Press, 1989), 1–13.

Domański, Juliusz, *Philosophy, Theory or Way of Life? Controversies in Antiquity, the Middle Ages, and the Renaissance*, trans. Matthew Sharpe, Andrew B. Irvine, and Matteo Stettler (Leiden: Brill, 2024).

La philosophie, théorie ou manière de vivre? Les controverses de l'Antiquité à la Renaissance (Fribourg: Cerf – Editions Universitaires, 1996).

Donatus, *Ars grammatica*, in Louis Holtz, ed., *Donat et la tradition de l'enseignement grammatical: Étude sur l'Ars Donati et sa diffusion (IVe–IXe siècle) et édition critique* (Paris: CNRS, 2010), 571–674.

Drobner, Hubertus R., "Christian Philosophy," in Susan Ashbrook Harvey and David G. Hunter, eds., *The Oxford Handbook of Early Christian Studies* (Oxford: Oxford University Press, 2008), 672–690.

The Fathers of the Church: A Comprehensive Introduction (Peabody: Hendrickson, 2007).

Dubuisson, Michel, "Le grec à Rome à l'époque de Cicéron: Extension et qualité du bilinguisme," *Annales: Histoire, Sciences Sociales* 47 (1992), 187–206.

Dugan, John, "Cicero's Rhetorical Theory," in Catherine Steel, ed., *The Cambridge Companion to Cicero* (Cambridge: Cambridge University Press, 2013), 25–40.

Dungan, David Laird, *A History of the Synoptic Problem: The Canon, the Text, the Composition, and the Interpretation of the Gospels* (New Haven: Yale University Press, 1999).

Dunn, James D. G., *The Cambridge Companion to St. Paul* (Cambridge: Cambridge University Press, 2006).

Dunn, Marilyn, *Arianism* (Leeds: ARC Humanities Press, 2021).

Durkheim, Emile, "Religion and Ritual," in Emile Durkheim, *Selected Writings*, ed. and trans. Anthony Giddens (Cambridge: Cambridge University Press, 1972), 219–238.

Ebbersmeyer, Sabrina, "From a 'Memorable Place' to 'Drops in the Ocean': On the Marginalisation of Women Philosophers in German Historiography of Philosophy," *British Journal for the History of Philosophy* 28 (2020), 442–462.

Edmondson, Jonathan and Alison Mary Keith, eds., *Roman Dress and the Fabrics of Roman Culture* (Toronto: University of Toronto Press, 2008).

Edwards, Mark, ed., *The Routledge Handbook of Early Christian Philosophy* (London: Routledge, 2021).

Egginton, William, *The Splintering of the American Mind* (New York: Bloomsbury, 2018).

Ehrman, Bart D., ed. and trans., *The Apostolic Fathers*, 2 vols. (Cambridge, MA: Harvard University Press, 2003).
  How Jesus Became God: The Exaltation of a Jewish Preacher from Galilee (San Francisco: Harper One, 2014).
  Lost Christianities: The Battles for Scripture and the Faiths We Never Knew (New York: Oxford University Press, 2003).
  ed., *Lost Scriptures: Books that Did Not Make It into the New Testament* (New York: Oxford University Press, 2003).
Elliott, J. K., ed. and trans., *The Apocryphal New Testament* (Oxford: Clarendon, 1993).
Erasmus, *Adages, II vii 1 to III iii 100*, trans. and an. by R. A. B. Mynors (Toronto: University of Toronto Press, 1992).
Eusebius, *Ecclesiastical History*, 2 vols., ed. and trans. Kirsopp Lake (Cambridge, MA: Harvard University Press, 1926).
  Life of Constantine, trans. with introduction and commentary by Averil Cameron and Stuart G. Hall (Oxford: Clarendon, 1999).
Fafinski, Mateusz, "The Ends of History? Jerome, Geruchia, and the Rhine Crossings," *Early Medieval Europe* 33 (2025), 71–93.
Farrell, Joseph, *Latin Language and Latin Culture: From Ancient to Modern Times* (Cambridge: Cambridge University Press, 2001).
Fee, Gordon D., *The First Epistle to the Corinthians*, rev ed. (Grand Rapids: Eerdmans, 2014).
Felski, Rita, *The Limits of Critique* (Chicago: University of Chicago Press, 2015).
Ferrari, G. R. F., ed., *The Cambridge Companion to Plato's Republic* (Cambridge: Cambridge University Press, 2007).
Fowden, Garth, *The Egyptian Hermes: A Historical Approach to the Late Pagan Mind* (Princeton: Princeton University Press, 1993).
Franzoni, Silverio, Elisa Lonati, and Adriano Russo, eds., *Le sens des textes classiques au Moyen Age: Transmission, exégèse, réécriture* (Turnhout: Brepols, 2022).
Fredriksen, Paula, *Ancient Christianities: The First Five Hundred Years* (Princeton: Princeton University Press, 2024).
  From Jesus to Christ: The Origins of the New Testament Images of Jesus, 2nd ed. (New Haven: Yale University Press, 2000).
  Paul: The Pagans' Apostle (New Haven: Yale University Press, 2017).
Frilingos, Christopher A., *Jesus, Mary, and Joseph: Family Trouble in the Infancy Gospels* (Philadelphia: University of Pennsylvania Press, 2017).
Fulkerson, Laurel and Jeffrey Tatum, *A History of Latin Literature: From Its Beginnings to the Age of Augustus* (Cambridge: Cambridge University Press, 2024).
Fürst, Alfons, "*Epistulae Senecae ad Paulum et Pauli ad Senecam*," in Andreas Heil and Gregor Damschen, eds., *Brill's Companion to Seneca* (Leiden: Brill, 2013), 213–214.
Gabriele, Matthew, *Between Prophecy and Apocalypse: The Burden of Sacred Time and the Making of History in Early Medieval Europe* (Oxford: Oxford University Press, 2024).
Gager, John G., *The Origins of Anti-Semitism: Attitudes Toward Judaism in Pagan and Christian Antiquity* (Oxford: Oxford University Press, 1985).
Garber, Daniel, "Descartes, the Aristotelians, and the Revolution that did not Happen in 1637," *The Monist* 71 (1988), 471–486.
Garsten, Bryan, *Saving Persuasion: A Defense of Rhetoric and Judgment* (Cambridge, MA: Harvard University Press, 2009).

Gaukroger, Stephen, *The Collapse of Mechanism and the Rise of Sensibility: Science and the Shaping of Modernity, 1680–1760* (Oxford: Oxford University Press, 2010).
Geerard, Maurice, ed., *Clavis apocryphorum Novi Testamenti* (Turnhout: Brepols, 1992).
Geerlings, Wilhelm, and Christian Schulze, eds., *Der Kommentar in Antike und Mittelalter*, 2 vols. (Leiden: Brill, 2002–2003).
Geiger, Roger L., *The History of American Higher Education: Learning and Culture from the Founding to World War II* (Princeton: Princeton University Press, 2015).
Gerson, Lloyd P., ed., *The Cambridge Companion to Plotinus* (Cambridge: Cambridge University Press, 1996).
  Plotinus (London: Routledge, 1994).
Gill, Christopher, *Personality in Greek Epic, Tragedy, and Philosophy* (Oxford: Oxford University Press, 1996).
Gjesdal, Kristin and Dalia Nassar, "Editors' Introduction," in Kristin Gjesdal and Dalia Nassar, eds., *The Oxford Handbook of Nineteenth-Century Women Philosophers in the German Tradition* (Oxford: Oxford University Press, 2024), 1–21.
  eds., *The Oxford Handbook of Nineteenth-Century Women Philosophers in the German Tradition* (Oxford: Oxford University Press, 2024).
Glancy, Jennifer, *Slavery in Early Christianity* (Oxford: Oxford University Press, 2002).
  "Slavery and the Rise of Christianity," in Keith Bradley and Paul Cartledge, eds., *The Cambridge World History of Slavery*, vol. 1 (Cambridge: Cambridge University Press, 2011), 456–481.
Goody, Jack, "Religion and Ritual: The Definitional Problem," *British Journal of Sociology* 12 (1961), 142–164.
Gorman, Michael M., "A Survey of the Oldest Manuscripts of St. Augustine's 'De civitate Dei,'" *The Journal of Theological Studies* 33 (1982), 398–410.
Gottlieb, Anthony, *The Dream of Enlightenment: The Rise of Modern Philosophy* (New York: Norton, 2006).
  The Dream of Reason: A History of Philosophy from the Greeks to the Renaissance (New York: Norton, 2000).
Grammaticus, Virgilius Maro, *Epitomi ed epistole*, ed. Giovanni Polara (Naples: Liguori, 1979).
Grant, Robert M., "Five Apologists and Marcus Aurelius," *Vigiliae Christianae* 42 (1988), 1–17.
Gray, Patrick, ed., *The Cambridge Companion to the New Testament* (Cambridge: Cambridge University Press, 2021).
Grayling, A. C., *The History of Philosophy* (New York: Penguin, 2019).
Greenblatt, Stephen, *The Rise and Fall of Adam and Eve* (New York: Norton, 2017).
Gregory the Great, *The Book of Pastoral Rule*, trans. George E. Demacopoulos (Crestwood: St. Vladimir's Seminary Press, 2007).
  Dialogi, ed. Adalbert de Vogüé and Paul Antin, Sources Chrétiennes 251, 260, 265 (Paris: Éditions du Cerf, 1978–1980).
  Dialogues, trans. Odo Zimmerman (New York: Fathers of the Church, 1959).
  Epistolae, eds. P. Ewald and L. M. Hartmann, 2 vols., (Berlin, 1891–1899).
  Expositiones in Canticum Canticorum, in librum primum Regum, ed. Patricius Verbraken (Turnholt: Brepols, 1963).
  Gregorii magni registrum epistularum, 2 vols., ed. Dag Norberg (Turnhoult: Brepols, 1982).

Homiliae in Ezechielem / Homélies sur Ézéchiel, 2 vols., ed. and trans. Charles Morel, S.J. (Paris: Éditions du Cerf, 1990).

The Letters of Gregory the Great, 3 vols., trans. John R. C. Martyn (Toronto: Pontifical Institute of Medieval Studies, 2004).

Moral Reflections on the Book of Job, 5 vols., trans. Brian Kerns (Collegeville: Liturgical Press, 2014–19).

Moralia in Job, 3 vols., ed. Marcus Adriaen (Turnhout: Brepols, 1979–1985).

The Old English Pastoral Care, ed. and trans. R. D. Fulk (Cambridge, MA: Harvard University Press, 2021).

Règle pastorale, 2 vols, ed. Bruno Judic, Floribert Rommel, and Charles Morel (Paris: Éditions du Cerf, 1992).

Gruen, Erich, *Heritage and Hellenism: The Reinvention of Jewish Tradition* (Berkeley: University of California Press, 1998).

Grundmann, Herbert, *Essays on Heresy, Inquisition, and Literacy*, ed. Jennifer Kolpacoff Deane, trans. Steven Rowan (York: York Medieval Press, 2019).

"Litteratus – illitteratus: Der Wandel einer Bildungsnorm vom Altertum zum Mittelalter," *Archiv für Kulturgeschichte* 40 (1958), 1–65.

Guidobaldi, Federico, "Chiese titolari di Roma nel tessuto urbano preesistente," in Philippe Pergola and Fabrizio Bisconti, eds., *Quaeritur inventus colitur: miscellanea in onore di padre Umberto Maria Fasola*, 2 vols. (Vatican City: Pontificio istituto di archeologia Cristiana, 1989), 1: 383–396.

San Clemente. Gli edifici romani, la basilica paleocristiana e le fasi altomedioevali (Rome: Collegio San Clemente, 1992).

Gutas, Dimitri, *Greek Thought, Arabic Culture: The Graeco-Arabic Translation Movement in Baghdad and Early Abbasid Society (2nd–4th/8th–10th Centuries)* (London: Routledge, 1998).

Haakonssen, Knud, ed., *The Cambridge History of Eighteenth-Century Philosophy*, 2 vols. (Cambridge: Cambridge University Press, 2006).

"The History of Eighteenth-Century Philosophy: History or Philosophy," in Knud Haakonssen, ed., *The Cambridge History of Eighteenth-Century Philosophy*, 2 vols. (Cambridge: Cambridge University Press, 2006), 1: 3–25.

Habicht, Christian, *Historiography: Ancient Medieval, and Modern*, 3rd ed. (Chicago: University of Chicago Press, 2007).

Hadot, Pierre, *Études de philosophie ancienne* (Paris: Les Belles Lettres, 1998).

Philosophy as a Way of Life: Spiritual Exercises from Socrates to Foucault (Oxford and New York: Blackwell, 1995).

Plotinus, or, the Simplicity of Vision, trans. Michael Chase (Chicago: University of Chicago Press, 1993).

The Selected Writings of Pierre Hadot: Philosophy as Practice, ed. and trans. Matthew Sharpe and Federico Testa (London: Bloomsbury, 2020).

Hagendahl, Harold, *Augustine and the Latin Classics*, 2 vols. (Gothenburg: Elander, 1967).

Hahn, Johannes, Stephen Emmel, and Ulrich Gotter, eds., *From Temple to Church: Destruction and Renewal of Local Cultic Topography in Late Antiquity* (Leiden: Brill, 2008).

Hall, Edith, *Aristotle's Way: How Ancient Wisdom Can Change Your Life* (New York: Penguin, 2019).

Hall, Edith, Richard Alston, and Justine McConnell, eds., *Ancient Slavery and Abolition: From Hobbes to Hollywood* (Oxford: Oxford University Press, 2011).

Harkness, Deborah, *The Jewel House: Elizabethan London and the Scientific Revolution* (New Haven and London: Yale University Press, 2007).

Harmless, Williams, S.J., *Desert Christians: An Introduction to the Literature of Early Monasticism* (Oxford: Oxford University Press, 2004).

Harper, Kyle, *Slavery in the Late Roman World, AD 275–425* (Cambridge: Cambridge University Press, 2011).

Harris, William V., *Ancient Literacy* (Cambridge, MA: Harvard University Press, 1989).

Harvey, Susan Ashbrook and David G. Hunter, eds., *The Oxford Handbook of Early Christian Studies* (Oxford: Oxford University Press, 2008).

Hays, Christopher B., ed., *The Cambridge Companion to the Book of Isaiah* (Cambridge: Cambridge University Press, 2024).

Hazony, Yoram, *The Philosophy of Hebrew Scripture* (Cambridge: Cambridge University Press, 2012).

Heather, Peter, *Christendom: The Triumph of a Religion, AD 300–1300* (New York: Knopf, 2023).

Hebblewhite, Mark, *Theodosius and the Limits of Empire* (New York, Routledge: 2020).

Heil, Andreas and Gregor Damschen, eds., *Brill's Companion to Seneca* (Leiden: Brill, 2013).

Hengel, Martin, *Judaism and Hellenism: Studies in their Encounter in Palestine during the Hellenistic Period*, 2 vols. (Philadelphia: Fortress, 1972).

Hermanowicz, Erika, *Possidius of Calama: A Study of the North African Episcopate in the Age of Augustine* (Oxford: Oxford University Press, 2008).

Herodotus, *The Persian Wars*, 4 vols., ed. and trans. A. D. Godley (Cambridge, MA: Harvard University Press, 1926).

Herrin, Judith, *The Formation of Christendom* (Princeton: Princeton University Press, 1987).

Hesiod, *Theogony, Works and Days, Testimonia*, 2 vols., ed. and trans. Glenn W. Most (Cambridge, MA: Harvard University Press, 2018).

Hexter, Ralph J. and David Townsend, eds., *The Oxford Handbook of Medieval Latin Literature* (Oxford: Oxford University Press, 2012).

Hillar, Marian, *From Logos to Trinity: The Evolution of Religious Beliefs from Pythagoras to Tertullian* (Cambridge: Cambridge University Press, 2012).

Hiltbrunner, O., "Die Schrift 'de officiis ministrorum' des hl. Ambrosius und ihr ciceronisches Vorbild," *Gymnasium* 71 (1964), 174–189.

Homer, *Iliad*, 2 vols., ed. and trans. A. T. Murray, rev. William F. Wyatt (Cambridge, MA: Harvard University Press, 1985).

The Iliad, trans. Emily Wilson (New York: Norton, 2023).

Odyssey, 2 vols., ed. and trans. A. T. Murray, rev. George E. Dimock (Cambridge, MA: Harvard University Press, 1995).

The Odyssey, trans. Emily Wilson (New York: Norton, 2018).

The Odyssey, trans. Daniel Mendelsohn (Chicago: University of Chicago Press, 2025).

Horace, *Satires, Epistles and Ars Poetica*, ed. and trans. H. Rushton Fairclough (Cambridge, MA, Harvard University Press, 1991).

Houghton, L. B. T., *Virgil's Fourth Eclogue in the Italian Renaissance* (Cambridge: Cambridge University Press, 2019).

Huebner, Sabine R., *Papyri and the Social World of the New Testament* (Cambridge: Cambridge University Press, 2019).
Hultgren, Arland J., "The Pastoral Epistles," in James D. G. Dunn, ed., *The Cambridge Companion to Saint Paul* (Cambridge: Cambridge University Press, 2003), 141–155.
Hvidt, Niles Christian, *Christian Prophecy: The Post-Biblical Tradition* (Cambridge: Cambridge University Press, 2007).
Iamblichus, *De mysteriis*, ed. Edouard des Places (Paris: Les Belles Lettres, 1966).
  On the Pythagorean Life, trans. Gillian Clark (Liverpool: Liverpool University Press, 1989).
Ignatius of Antioch, "Letter to the Smyrnaeans," in Bart D. Ehrman, ed. and trans., *The Apostolic Fathers*, 2 vols. (Cambridge, MA: Harvard University Press, 2003), 2: 296–309.
Imrie, Alex, *The Antonine Constitution: An Edict for the Caracallan Empire* (Leiden: Brill, 2018).
Innocent I, "Letter" in Brooke F. Westcott, *A General Survey of the History of the Canon of the New Testament*, 5th ed. (Cambridge: Macmillan, 1881), 570–571.
Inwood, Brad, and Jaap Mansfeld, eds., *Assent and Argument: Studies in Cicero's Academic Books* (Leiden: Brill, 1997).
Irwin, Terrence H., "Conceptions of Happiness in the Nicomachean Ethics," in Christopher Shields, ed., *The Oxford Handbook of Aristotle* (Oxford: Oxford University Press, 2012), 495–528.
Jacobs, Andrew S., "The Lion and the Lamb: Reconsidering Jewish-Christian Relations in Antiquity," in Adam H. Becker and Annette Yoshiko Reed, eds., *The Ways that Never Parted: Jews and Christians in Late Antiquity and the Early Middle Ages* (Tübingen: Mohr, 2003), 95–118.
Janson, Tore, *A Natural History of Latin* (Oxford: Oxford University Press, 2004).
Jenkyns, Richard, ed., *The Legacy of Rome: A New Appraisal* (Oxford: Oxford University Press, 1992).
Jensen, Robin M., "Visual Representations of Early Christian Teachers and of Christ as the True Philosopher," in H. Gregory Snyder., ed., *Christian Teachers in Second-Century Rome: Schools and Students in the Ancient City* (Leiden: Brill, 2020), 60–83.
Johns, Adrian, "The Coming of Print to Europe," in Leslie Howsam, ed., *The Cambridge Companion to the History of the Book* (Cambridge: Cambridge University Press, 2015), 107-124.
Johnson, William, "Toward a Sociology of Reading in Classical Antiquity," *American Journal of Philology* 121 (2000), 593–627.
Josephus, *Life of Josephus*, vol. 9 in Steve Mason, ed and trans., *Flavius Josephus*, 10 vols. to date (Leiden: Brill, 2000–).
Kelley, Andrew J., "Miracles, Jesus, and Identity: A History of Research Regarding Jesus and Miracles with Special Attention to the Gospel of Mark," *Currents in Biblical Research* 13 (2014), 82–106.
Kelly, J. N. D., *Jerome: His Life, Writings, and Controversies* (London: Duckworth, 1975).
Kennedy, George A., *A New History of Classical Rhetoric* (Princeton: Princeton University Press, 1994).
Kenny, Anthony, *A New History of Western Philosophy* (Oxford: Oxford University Press, 2010).

Kessler, Herbert L., "Pictorial narrative and Church Mission in Sixth-Century Gaul," *Studies in the History of Art* 16 (1985), 75–91.
Klein, Almuth, "Santa Maria sopra Minerva," in Daniela Mondini, Carola Jäggi, and Peter Cornelius Claussen, eds., *Die Kirchen der Stadt Rom im Mittelalter 1050–1300*, vol. 4., Forschungen zur Kunstgeschichte und Christlichen Archäologie Band 23, Corpus Cosmatorum II, 4 (Stuttgart: Franz Steiner, 2020), 310–336.
Kloppenburg, John S., *The Formation of Q* (Philadelphia: Fortress Press, 1987).
Knauer, Georg Nicolaus, *Die 'Aeneis' und Homer: Studien zur poetischen Technik Vergils mit Listen der Homerzitate in der 'Aeneis'* (Göttingen: Vandenhoek and Ruprecht, 1964).
Koortbojian, Michael, "The Double Identity of Roman Portrait Statues: Costumes and their Symbolism at Rome," in Jonathan Edmondson and Alison Mary Keith, eds., *Roman Dress and the Fabrics of Roman Culture* (Toronto: University of Toronto Press, 2008), 71–93.
Koyré, Alexandre, *From the Closed World to the Infinite Universe* (Baltimore: Johns Hopkins University Press, 1968).
Krautheimer, Richard, *Corpus Basilicarum Christianarum Romae: The Early Christian Basilicas of Rome (IV–IX Centuries)*, 5 vols. (Vatican City: Pontificio istituto di archeologia cristiana, 1937–1977).
  Rome: Profile of a City, 312–1308 (Princeton: Princeton University Press, 2000).
Kristeller, Paul Oskar, *Greek Philosophers of the Hellenistic Age*, trans. Gregory Woods (New York: Columbia University Press, 1993).
Laato, Anni Maria, "Isaiah in Latin," in Lena-Sofia Tiemeyer, ed., *The Oxford Handbook of Isaiah* (Oxford: Oxford University Press, 2020), 489–503.
Lactantius, *De mortibus persecutorum*, ed. and trans. J. L. Creed (Oxford: Clarendon, 1984).
Laertius, Diogenes, *Lives of Eminent Philosophers*, 2 vols., ed. and trans. R. D. Hicks (Cambridge, MA: Harvard University Press, 2000–2005).
Lahrmann, Matthias, "Seneca the Philosopher," in Andreas Heil and Gregor Damschen, eds., *Brill's Companion to Seneca* (Leiden: Brill, 2013), 53–71.
Laks, André and Glenn Most, eds. and trans., *Early Greek Philosophy*, 9 vols. (Cambridge, MA: Harvard University Press, 2016).
Lang, Helen S., *The Order of Nature in Aristotle's Physics: Place and the Elements* (Cambridge: Cambridge University Press, 1998).
Lavan, Myles, and Clifford Ando, eds., *Roman and Local Citizenship in the Long Second Century CE* (Oxford: Oxford University Press, 2021).
Lear, Gabriel Richardson, *Happy Lives and the Highest Good: An Essay on Aristotle's Nicomachean Ethics* (Princeton: Princeton University Press, 2004).
Leclercq, Jean, O.S.B., *The Love of Learning and the Desire for God: A Study in Monastic Culture*, trans. Catharine Misrahi (Chicago: University of Chicago Press, 1982).
Lehtipuu, Outi, *Debates over the Resurrection of the Dead: Constructing Early Christian Identity* (Oxford: Oxford University Press, 2015).
Leppin, Hartmut, *The Early Christians: From the Beginnings to Constantine*, trans. Kathrin Luddecke (Cambridge: Cambridge University Press, 2023).
Leonhardt, Jürgen, *Latin: Story of a World Language*, trans. Kenneth Kronenberg (Cambridge, MA: Harvard University Press, 2013).
Levine, Emily, *Allies and Rivals: German-American Exchange and the Rise of the Modern Research University* (Chicago: University of Chicago Press, 2021).

Levitin, Dmitri, *Ancient Wisdom in the Age of the New Science: Histories of Philosophy in England, c. 1640–1700* (Cambridge: Cambridge University Press, 2015).

Lévy, Carlos, "Cicero and the Creation of a Latin Philosophical Vocabulary," in Atkins and Bénatouïl, eds., in Jed W. Atkins and Thomas Bénatouïl, eds., *The Cambridge Companion to Cicero's Philosophy* (Cambridge: Cambridge University Press, 2022), 71–87.

Lewis, Theodore J., *The Origin and Character of God: Ancient Israelite Religion through the Lens of Divinity* (Oxford: Oxford University Press, 2020).

Leyser, Conrad, "The Memory of Gregory the Great and the Making of Latin Europe," in Kate Cooper and Conrad Leyser, eds., *Making Early Medieval Societies: Conflict and Belonging in the Latin West, 300–1200* (Cambridge: Cambridge University Press, 2016), 181–201.

Libanius, *Autobiography*, in Libanius, *Autobiography and Selected Letters*, 2 vols., ed. and trans. A. F. Norman (Cambridge, MA: Harvard University Press, 1992), 1: 52–337.

Lilla, Mark, *The Once and Future Liberal* (New York: Harper, 2017).

Lloyd, G. E. R., *Aristotle: The Growth and Structure of his Thought* (Cambridge: Cambridge University Press, 1968).

Lo Monaco, Francesco, "*In codicibus . . . qui Bobbbienses inscribuntur*: Scoperte e studio di palinsesti bobbiesi in Ambrosiana dalla fine del settecento ad Angelo Mai (1819)," *Aevum* 70 (1996), 657–719.

Löfstedt, Einar, *Late Latin* (Oslo: Aschehoug and Co., 1959).

Long A. A., *From Epicurus to Epictetus: Studies in Hellenistic and Roman Philosophy* (Oxford: Oxford University Press, 2006).

Long A. A., and David Sedley, eds., *The Hellenistic Philosophers*, 2 vols. (Cambridge: Cambridge University Press, 1987).

Long, Pamela, "The Contribution of Architectural Writers to a 'Scientific' Outlook in the Fifteenth and Sixteenth Centuries," *Journal of Medieval and Renaissance Studies* 15 (1985), 265–298.

Openness, Secrecy, Authorship: Technical Arts and the Culture of Knowledge from Antiquity to the Renaissance (Baltimore: Johns Hopkins University Press, 2001).

Longenecker, Bruce W., *The New Cambridge Companion to St. Paul* (Cambridge: Cambridge University Press, 2020).

Longo, Mario, "A 'Critical' History of Philosophy and the Early Enlightenment: Johann Jacob Brucker," in Gregorio Piaia and Giuseppe Santinello, eds., *Models of the History of Philosophy*, 4 vols. (Dordrecht: Springer, 1992–2022), 2: 477–577.

"Storia 'critica' della filosofie e primo illuminismo: Jakob Brucker," in Giovanni Santinello et al., eds., *Storia delle storie generali della filosofia*, 5 vols. (Brescia: La Scuola, 1981–1995), 2: 527–635.

Lüdtke, Helmut, *Der Ursprung der romanischen Sprachen: Eine Geschichte der sprachlichen Kommunikation* (Kiel: Westensee-Verlag, 2009).

Lynch, J. P., *Aristotle's School: A Study of an Educational Institution* (Berkeley: University of California Press, 1972).

Ma, John, *Polis: A New History of the Ancient Greek City-State from the Early Iron Age to the End of Antiquity* (Princeton: Princeton University Press, 2024).

MacCormack, Sabine, *The Shadows of Poetry: Vergil in the Mind of Augustine* (Berkeley: University of California Press, 1998).

MacCulloch, Diarmad, *Christianity: The First Three Thousand Years* (New York: Penguin, 2011).
MacIntyre, Alasdair, *After Virtue: A Study in Moral Theory*, 3rd ed. (Notre Dame: University of Notre Dame Press, 2007).
Makdisi, George, *The Rise of Colleges: Institutions of Learning in Islam and the West* (Edinburgh: Edinburgh University Press, 1981).
Makkreel, Rudolf, *Dilthey: Philosopher of the Human Studies* (Princeton: Princeton University Press, 1975).
Marchand, Suzanne, *German Orientalism in the Age of Empire: Religion, Race, and Enlightenment* (Cambridge: Cambridge University Press, 2009).
Marenbon, John, *Early Medieval Philosophy (480–1150): An Introduction* (London: Routledge: 1988).
Markus, R. A., *Gregory the Great and His World* (Cambridge: Cambridge University Press, 1997).
Marrou, Henri Irenée, *A History of Education in Antiquity*, trans. George Lamb (Madison: University of Wisconsin Press, 1956).
Mattison III, William C., *The Sermon on the Mount and Moral Theology: A Virtue Perspective* (Cambridge: Cambridge University Press, 2017).
Mauss, Marcel, *The Gift: The Form and Reason for Exchange in Archaic Societies*, trans. W. D. Halls (New York: Norton, 1990).
 Oeuvres, 4 vols., vol. 1: *Les fonctions sociales du sacré* (Paris: Éditions de Minuit, 1968).
McGinn, Bernard, *Visions of the End: Apocalyptic Traditions in the Middle Ages*, 2nd ed. (New York: Columbia University Press, 1998).
McGinn, Bernard, John J. Collins, and Stephen J. Stein, eds., *The Continuum History of Apocalypticism* (New York: Continuum, 2003).
McLynn, Neil B., *Ambrose of Milan: Church and Court in a Christian Capital* (Berkeley: University of California Press, 1994).
Mercati, Giovanni, *M. Tulli Ciceronis De re publica libri e codice rescripto Vaticano latino 5757 photoypice expressi. Prolegomena de fatis bibliothecae monasterii S. Colombani Bobiensis et de codice ipso Vat. Lat. 5757*, 2 vols. (Vatican City: Biblioteca Apostolica Vaticana, 1934).
Merrills, Andrew H., and Richard Miles, *The Vandals* (Oxford: Wiley-Blackwell, 2010).
Metzger, Bruce M., *The Canon of the New Testament: Its Origin, Development, and Significance* (Oxford: Clarendon, 1997).
 A Textual Commentary on the Greek New Testament, 3rd ed. (Stuttgart: Deutsche Bibelgesellschaft, 1975).
Middleton, Paul, ed., *The Wiley Blackwell Companion to Christian Martyrdom* (London: Wiley, 2020).
Miller, Fred D., *Nature, Justice and Rights in Aristotle's Politics* (Oxford: Oxford University Press, 1997).
Minucius Felix, *Octavius*, in Tertullian, *Apology, De spectaculis*. Minucius Felix, *Octavius*, ed. and trans. T. R. Glover and Gerald H. Rendall (Cambridge, MA: Cambridge University Press, 1931), 314–437.
Misch, Georg, *Geschichte der Autobiographie*, 4 vols. (Bern: Francke, 1949–1969).
Mitchell, Stephen, and Peter Van Nuffelen, *One God: Pagan Monotheism in the Roman Empire* (Cambridge and New York: Cambridge University Press, 2010).

eds., *Monotheism between Pagans and Christians in Late Antiquity* (Leuven: Peeters, 2010).
Moatti, Claudia, *The Birth of Critical Thinking in Republican Rome*, trans. Janet Lloyd (Cambridge: Cambridge University Press, 2015).
"Cicero's Philosophical Writing in Its Intellectual Context," in Jed W. Atkins and Thomas Bénatouïl, eds., *The Cambridge Companion to Cicero's Philosophy* (Cambridge: Cambridge University Press, 2022), 7–24.
Momigliano, Arnaldo, *The Classical Foundations of Modern Historiography* (Berkeley: University of California Press, 1990).
Mommsen, Theodor, "Antwort an Herrn Harnack," in *Sitzungsberichte der Königlich Preußischen Akademie der Wissenschaften zu Berlin* (Berlin, 1890), 791–793.
Monoson, S. Sara, "Recollecting Aristotle: Pro-Slavery Thought in Antebellum America and the Argument of *Politics* Book I," in Edith Hall, Richard Alston, and Justine McConnell, eds., *Ancient Slavery and Abolition: From Hobbes to Hollywood* (Oxford: Oxford University Press, 2011), 247–278.
Montanari, R. Caldini, *Tradizione medievale e edizione critica del Somnium Scipionis* (Florence: SISMEL, Edizioni del Galluzzzo, 2002).
Montas, Roosevelt, *Rescuing Socrates* (Princeton: Princeton University Press, 2021).
Moraux, Paul, *Die Aristotelismus bei den Griechen: von Andronikos bis Alexander von Aphrodisias*, 3 vols. (Berlin: De Gruyter, 1973–2001).
Moravec, Matyáš and Peter West, "What is 'Western Philosophy'? Lessons from the Case of 'Analytic Philosophy,'" *Journal for the History of Analytical Philosophy* 13 (2024), 1–29.
Morrison, Karl F., *Understanding Conversion* (Charlottesville: University of Virginia Press, 1992).
Most, Glenn W., "A Cock for Asclepius," *The Classical Quarterly* 43 (1993), 96–111.
Mullen, Alex and George Woudhuysen, eds., *Languages and Communities in the Late-Roman and Post-Imperial Western Provinces* (Oxford: Oxford University Press, 2023).
Murphy, James J., Richard A. Katula, Michael J. Hoppmann, *A Synoptic History of Classical Rhetoric*, 4th ed. (New York: Routledge, 2014).
Murray, (Sister) Charles, *Rebirth and Afterlife: A Study of the Transmutation of Some Pagan Imagery in Early Christian Art* (Oxford: British Archaeological Reports, 1981).
Nadler, Stephen, Tad M. Schmaltz, and Delphine Antoine-Mahut, eds., *The Oxford Handbook of Descartes and Cartesianism* (Oxford: Oxford University Press, 2019).
Nagel, Thomas, "Aristotle on Eudaimonia," in Amélie Oksenberg Rorty, ed., *Essays on Aristotle's Ethics* (Berkeley: University of California Press, 1981), 7–14.
Nails, Debra, *The People of Plato: A Prosopography of Plato and Other Socratics* (Indianapolis: Hackett Publishing, 2002).
Nash, Ronald H., *The Meaning of History* (Nashville: Broadman & Holman, 1998).
Natali, Carlo, *Aristotle: His Life and School* (Princeton: Princeton University Press, 2013).
Natoli, Bartolo A., Angela Pitts, and Judith P. Hallett, *Ancient Women Writers of Greece and Rome* (New York: Routledge, 2022).
Nehamas, Alexander, *The Art of Living: Socratic Reflections from Plato to Foucault* (Berkeley: University of California Press, 1998).
Nelson, Eric, *The Hebrew Republic: Jewish Sources and the Transformation of European Political Thought* (Cambridge, MA: Harvard University Press, 2010).

Nemeth, Andras, "Recovery of Conflicting Textual Identities: Augustine and Cicero in Vat. Lat. 5757," *Miscellanea Bibliothecae Apostolicae Vaticanae* 23 (2017), 405–450.
Nicholas of Lyra, *Literal Commentary on Galatians*, ed. and trans. Edwin Arthur Neumann (Kalamazoo: Medieval Institute Publications, 2016).
Nightingale, Andrea, "Plato on *aporia* and Self-Knowledge," in Andrea Nightingale and David Sedley, eds., *Ancient Models of Mind: Studies in Human and Divine Rationality* (Cambridge: Cambridge University Press, 2010), 8–26.
Nirenberg, David, *Anti-Judaism: The Western Tradition* (New York: Norton, 2013).
  Communities of Violence: Persecution of Minorities in the Middle Ages (Princeton: Princeton University Press, 1998).
Nisbet, R. G. M. and Niall Rudd, *A Commentary on Horace: Odes Book III* (Oxford: Oxford University Press, 2004).
Noble, Thomas F. X., *Images, Iconoclasm, and the Carolingians* (Philadelphia: University of Pennsylvania Press, 2009).
Nock, Arthur Darby, *Conversion: The Old and the New in Religion from Alexander the Great to Augustine of Hippo* (Oxford: Oxford University Press, 1933).
Nussbaum, Martha, *The Clash Within: Democracy, Religious Violence, and India's Future* (Cambridge, MA: Harvard University Press, 2007).
  Not for Profit: Why Democracy Needs the Humanities (Princeton: Princeton University Peress, 2016).
  The Therapy of Desire: Theory and Practice in Hellenistic Ethics, 2nd ed. (Princeton: Princeton University Press, 2013).
O'Daly, Gerard, *Augustine's City of God: A Reader's Guide*, 2nd ed. (Oxford: Oxford University Press, 2020).
O'Donnell, James J., *Augustine: A New Biography* (New York: Ecco, 2005).
  "Augustine's Classical Readings," *Recherches Augustiniennes* 15 (1980), 144–175.
O'Hara, Alexander, *Jonas of Bobbio and the Legacy of Columbanus: Sanctity and Community in the Seventh Century* (Oxford: Oxford University Press, 2018).
O'Meara, Dominic J., *Plotinus: An Introduction to the Enneads* (Oxford: Oxford University Press, 1993).
O'Reilly, Katharine R., and Caterina Pellò, eds., *Ancient Women Philosophers: Recovered Ideas and New Perspectives* (Cambridge: Cambridge University Press, 2023).
Ober, Josiah, *The Rise and Fall of Classical Greece* (Princeton: Princeton University Press, 2015).
Oberleitner, Manfred, et al., *Die handschriftliche Überlieferung der Werke des heiligen Augustinus*, 9 vols. to date (Vienna: Böhlau, 1969–).
Oksenberg Rorty, Amélie, ed., *Essays on Aristotle's Ethics* (Berkeley: University of California Press, 1981).
Olsen, Birger Munk, *L'étude des auteurs classiques latins aux XIe et XIIe siècles*, 5 vols. (Paris: CNRS Éditions, 1982–2020).
Osborne, Robin, ed. and trans., *Athenian Democracy*, 2nd ed. (Cambridge: Cambridge University Press, 2023).
Östling, Johan, *Humboldt and the Modern German University: An Intellectual History* (Lund: Lund University Press, 2018).
Ovid, *Metamorphoses*, 2 vols., ed. and trans. Frank Justus Miller and G. P. Goold (Cambridge, MA: Harvard University Press, 1977).
Palmer, James T., *The Apocalypse in the Early Middle Ages* (Cambridge: Cambridge University Press, 2014).

Palmer, James T., and Matthew Gabriele, eds., *Apocalypse and Reform from Late Antiquity to the Middle Ages* (New York: Routledge, 2018).
Parker, Robert, *Polytheism and Society at Athens* (Oxford: Oxford University Press, 2005).
Parsons, Mikael C., "The Third Gospel and the Acts of the Apostles," in Patrick Gray, ed., *The Cambridge Companion to the New Testament* (Cambridge: Cambridge University Press, 2021), 134–154.
Paulus Diaconus, *Historia Langobardorum*, ed. Georg Waitz, Vol. 1 of *Monumenta Germaniae Historica, Scriptores rerum Langobardicarum et Italicarum saec. VI–IX*. (Hannover: Hahn, 1878)
Pausanias, *Description of Greece*, 5 vols., ed. and trans. W. H. S. Jones (Cambridge, MA: Harvard University Press, 1918–1935).
Pergola, Philippe and Fabrizio Bisconti, eds., *Quaeritur inventus colitur: miscellanea in onore di padre Umberto Maria Fasola*, 2 vols. (Vatican City: Pontificio istituto di archeologia Cristiana, 1989).
Perrot, Arnaud, ed., *Les chrétiens et l'hellénisme: identités religieuses et culture grecque dans l'Antiquité tardive* (Paris: Éditions Rue d'Ulm, 2012).
Petrucci, Armando, *Writers and Readers in Medieval Italy: Studies in the History of Written Culture*, ed. and trans. Charles M. Radding (New Haven: Yale University Press, 1995).
Piaia, Gregorio and Giuseppe Santinello, eds., *Models of the History of Philosophy*, 4 vols. (Dordrecht: Springer, 1992–2022).
Plato, *Complete Works*, ed. John M. Cooper (Indianapolis: Hackett, 1997).
  Cratylus, Parmenides, Greater Hippias, Lesser Hippias, ed. and trans. Harold North Fowler (Cambridge, MA: Harvard University Press, 1939).
  Euthyphro, Apology, Crito, Phaedo, ed. and trans. Chris Emlyn-Jones and William Preddy (Cambridge, MA: Harvard University Press, 2017).
  Euthyphro, Apology, Crito, Phaedo, Phaedrus, ed. and trans. Harold North Fowler (Cambridge, MA: Harvard University Press, 2014).
  Laches, Protagoras, Meno, Euthydemus, ed. and trans. W. R. M. Lamb (Cambridge, MA: Harvard University Press, 1924).
  Laws, ed. and trans. Richard Bury (Cambridge, MA: Harvard University Press, 1926).
  Lysis, Symposium, Phaedrus, ed. and trans. Chris Emlyn-Jones and William Preddy (Cambridge, MA: Harvard University Press, 2022).
  Republic, 2 vols., ed. and trans. Chris Emlyn-Jones and William Preddy (Cambridge, MA: Harvard University Press, 2013).
  Theaetetus, ed. and trans. Harold North Fowler (Cambridge, MA: Harvard University Press, 1921).
  Timaeus, Critias, Cleitophon, Menexenus, Epistles, ed. and trans. R. G. Bury (Cambridge, MA: Harvard University Press, 1929).
Pliny the Elder, *Natural History*, 10 vols., ed. and trans. Horace Rackham (Cambridge, MA: Harvard University Press, 1942).
Plotinus, *Enneads*, 7 vols., ed. and trans. A. H. Armstrong (Cambridge, MA: Harvard University Press, 1966–1988).
Plutarch, *Lives, Vol. 1: Theseus and Romulus, Lycurgus and Numa, Solon and Publicola*, ed. and trans. Bernadotte Perrin (Cambridge, MA: Harvard University Press, 1914).
Pocock, J. G. A., "*The Machiavellian Moment* Revisited: A Study in History and Ideology," *Journal of Modern History* 53 (1981), 49–72.

Poirier, John C., "The Linguistic Situation in Jewish Palestine in Late Antiquity," *Journal of Greco-Roman Christianity and Judaism* 4 (2007), 55–134.

Polansky, Ronald, ed., *The Cambridge Companion to Aristotle's Nicomachean Ethics* (Cambridge: Cambridge University Press, 2014).

Politis, Vasilis, *Plato's Essentialism: Reinterpreting the Theory of Forms* (Cambridge: Cambridge University Press, 2021).

Polybius, *The Histories*, 6 vols., ed. and trans. W. R. Paton, F. W. Walbank, and Christian Habicht (Cambridge, MA: Cambridge University Press, 2010).

Popkin, Richard, *The History of Scepticism: From Savonarola to Bayle* Oxford: Oxford University Press, 2003).

Porphyry, "Life of Plotinus," in *Enneads*, 7 vols., ed. and trans. A. H. Armstrong (Cambridge, MA: Harvard University Press, 1966–1988), 1: 2–87.

Porterfield, Amanda, *Healing in the History of Christianity* (Oxford: Oxford University Press, 2005).

Possidius, *Sancti Augustini vita*, ed. and trans. Herbert T. Weiskotten (Princeton: Princeton University Press, 1919).

Powell, J. G. F., ed., *Cicero the Philosopher: Twelve Papers* (Oxford: Oxford University Press, 1995).

Pratt, Kenneth J., "Rome as Eternal," *Journal of the History of Ideas* 26 (1965), 25–44.

Price, Richard M., "*In hic signo vinces*: The Original Context of the Vision of Constantine," *Studies in Church History* 41 (2005), 1–10.

Priscian, "*Institutionum grammaticarum libri*," in *Grammatici latini*, ed. Heinrich Keil (Leipzig: Teubner, 1857).

Quasten, Johannes, *Patrology*, 4 vols. (Utrecht: Spectrum and Westminster, Maryland: Newman Press, 1959–1986).

Quintilian, *Institutio Oratoria*, 5 vols., ed. and trans. Donald A. Russell (Cambridge, MA: Harvard University Press, 2001).

The Orator's Education, 5 vols., ed. and trans. Donald A. Russell (Cambridge, MA: Harvard University Press, 2002).

Rambo, Lewis R., and Charles E. Farhadian, eds., *The Oxford Handbook of Religious Conversion* (Oxford: Oxford University Press, 2014).

Ramsey, Boniface, O. P., *Ambrose* (London: Routledge, 1997).

Ready, Jonathan L., and Christos C. Tsagalis, eds., *Homer in Performance: Rhapsodes, Narrators, and Characters* (Austin: University of Texas Press, 2018).

Rebenich, Stefan, *Jerome* (London: Routledge, 2002).

Rebenich, Stefan, and Hans-Ulrich Wiemer, eds., *A Companion to Julian the Apostate* (Leiden: Brill, 2020).

Reed, Annette Yoshiko, "Messianism between Judaism and Christianity," in Michael L. Morgan and Steven Weitzman, eds., *Rethinking the Messianic Idea in Judaism* (Bloomington: Indiana University Press, 2014), 23–62.

Reeve, C. D. C. "Beginning and Ending with Eudaimonia," in Ronald Polansky, ed., *The Cambridge Companion to Aristotle's Nicomachean Ethics* (Cambridge: Cambridge University Press, 2014), 14–33.

Reinhardt, Tobias, "Cicero's Academic Skepticism," in Jed W. Atkins and Thomas Bénatouïl, eds., *The Cambridge Companion to Cicero's Philosophy* (Cambridge: Cambridge University Press, 2022), 103–119.

Remer, Gary, "Philosophy, Rhetoric, and Politics," in Jed W. Atkins and Thomas Bénatouïl, eds., *The Cambridge Companion to Cicero's Philosophy* (Cambridge: Cambridge University Press, 2022), 200–214.
Riché, Pierre, *Education and Culture in the Barbarian West: Sixth through Eighth Centuries* (Columbia: University of South Carolina Press, 1976).
Riedweg, Christoph, "Zum Ursprung des Wortes 'Philosophie' oder Pythagoras von Samos als Wörtschopfer," in Anton Bierl and Joachim Latacz, eds., *Antike Literatur in neuer Deutung* (Munich and Leipzig: Saur, 2004), 147–182.
Rist, John, *Plotinus: The Road to Reality* (Cambridge: Cambridge University Press, 1967).
Roberts, Colin H., and T. C. Skeat, *The Birth of the Codex* (Oxford: Oxford University Press, 1983).
Robinson, James M., Paul Hoffmann, John S. Kloppenborg, and Milton C. Moreland, eds., *The Critical Edition of Q: Synopsis Including the Gospels of Matthew and Luke, Mark, and Thomas with English, German, and French Translations of Q and Thomas* (Minneapolis: Fortress Press; Leuven: Peeters, 2000).
Roller, Matthew B., *Models from the Past in Roman Culture: A World of Exempla* (Cambridge: Cambridge University Press, 2018).
Rorty, Richard, "The Historiography of Philosophy: Four Genres," in Richard Rorty, J. B. Schneewind, and Quentin Skinner, eds., *Philosophy in History* (Cambridge: Cambridge University Press, 1984), 31–48.
  Philosophy and the Mirror of Nature (Princeton: Princeton University Press, 1979).
Rorty, Richard, J. B. Schneewind, and Quentin Skinner, eds., *Philosophy in History* (Cambridge: Cambridge University Press, 1984).
Roth, Michael, *Beyond the University: Why Liberal Education Matters* (New Haven: Yale University Press, 2014).
  "Beyond Critical Thinking," *Chronicle of Higher Education* (Jan. 3, 2010). www.chronicle.com/article/beyond-critical-thinking/
Rüegg, Walter, general editor, *A History of the University in Europe*, 4 vols. (Cambridge: Cambridge University Press, 1992–2010).
Ruff, Carin, "Latin as an Acquired Language," in Ralph J. Hexter and David Townsend, eds., *The Oxford Handbook of Medieval Latin Literature* (Oxford: Oxford University Press, 2012), 46–62.
Saldarini, Anthony J., and Amy-Jill Levine, "Jewish Responses to Greek and Roman Cultures, 332BCE to 200CE," in Bruce Chilton, Howard Clark Kee, Eric M. Meyers, John Rogerson, Amy-Jill Levine, and Anthony J. Saldarini, eds., *The Cambridge Companion to the Bible*, 2nd ed. (Cambridge: Cambridge and New York, 2012), 327–480.
Sanders, E. P., *Jesus and Judaism* (Minneapolis: Fortress Press, 1985).
Sawyer, John F. A., *The Fifth Gospel: Isaiah in the History of Christianity* (Cambridge, MA: Cambridge University Press, 1996).
Schmitt-Biggeman, Wilhelm and Theo Stammen, *Jacob Brucker (1696–1770): Philosoph und Historiker der europäischen Aufklärung* (Berlin: Akademie-Verlag, 1998).
Schnabel, Eckhard J., "Repentance in Paul's Letters," *Novum Testamentum* 57 (2015), 159–186.
Schneider, Ulrich Johannes, *Philosophie und Universität: Historisierung der Vernunft im 19. Jahrhundert* (Hamburg: Felix Meiner Verlag, 1999).

Schofield, Malcolm, *How Plato Writes: Perspectives and Problems* (Cambridge: Cambridge University Press, 2023).
  "Writing Philosophy," in Catherine Steel, ed., *The Cambridge Companion to Cicero* (Cambridge: Cambridge University Press, 2013), 73–87.
Schuddeboom, Feyo L., "The Conversion of Temples in Rome," *Journal of Late Antiquity* 10 (2017), 166–186.
Schütt, Hans-Peter, *Die Adoption des "Vaters der modernen Philosophie"* (Frankfurt am Main: Klosterman, 1998).
Schwartz, Seth, "Language, Power, and Identity in Ancient Palestine," *Past and Present* 148 (1995), 3–47.
Sedley, David, "The Dramatis Personae of Plato's *Phaedo*," in *Philosophical Dialogues: Plato, Hume, Wittgenstein*, ed. Timothy Smiley (Oxford: Oxford University Press, 1995), 3–26.
  "The Stoic-Platonist Debate on *kathekonta*," in Katerina Ierodiakonou, ed., *Topics in Stoic Philosophy* (Oxford: Clarendon, 1999), 128–152.
Sellars, John, *Aristotle: Understanding the World's Greatest Philosopher* (London: Penguin, 2023).
  The Art of Living: The Stoics on the Nature and Function of Philosophy, 2nd ed. (London: Duckworth, 2009).
  The Fourfold Remedy: Epicurus and the Art of Happiness (London: Penguin, 2021).
  Hellenistic Philosophy (Oxford: Oxford University Press, 2018).
  Lessons in Stoicism: What Ancient Philosophers Teach Us About How to Live (London: Penguin, 2019).
  ed., *The Routledge Handbook of the Stoic Tradition* (London: Routledge, 2016).
Seneca, *Epistles*, 3 vols., ed. and trans. Richard M. Gummere (Cambridge, MA: Harvard University Press, 1917).
  Natural Questions, 2 vols., ed. and trans. Thomas H. Corcoran (Cambridge, MA: Harvard University Press, 1971).
Sextus Empiricus, *Outlines of Pyrrhonism*, trans. R. G. Bury (Cambridge, MA: Harvard University Press, 1933).
Sharpe, Matthew, and Michael Ure, *Philosophy as a Way of Life: From Antiquity to Modernity* (London: Bloomsbury, 2021).
Sharples, R. W., *Stoics, Epicureans and Sceptics: An Introduction to Hellenistic Philosophy* (London: Routledge, 1996).
Shaw, Gregory, *Theurgy and the Soul: The Neoplatonism of Iamblichus* (University Park: Pennsylvania State University Press, 1995).
Shields, Christopher, ed., *The Oxford Handbook of Aristotle* (Oxford: Oxford University Press, 2012).
Sidwell, Keith, "Classical Latin Medieval Latin, Neo-Latin," in Sarah Knight and Stefan Tilg, eds., *The Oxford Handbook of Neo-Latin* (Oxford: Oxford University Press, 2015), 13–26.
Siedentop, Larry, *Inventing the Individual: The Origins of Western Liberalism* (Cambridge, MA: Harvard University Press, 2014).
Smalley, Beryl, *The Study of the Bible in the Middle Ages*, 3rd ed. (Notre Dame: University of Notre Dame Press, 1964).
Smith, Justin E. H., *The Philosopher: A History in Six Types* (Princeton: Princeton University Press, 2016).

Smith, Pamela H., *The Body of the Artisan: Art and Experience in the Scientific Revolution* (Chicago: University of Chicago Press, 2004).
   From Lived Experience to the Written Word: Reconstructing Practical Knowledge in the Early Modern World (Chicago: University of Chicago Press, 2022).
Smith, Robin, "Logic," in Jonathan Barnes, ed., *The Cambridge Companion to Aristotle* (Cambridge: Cambridge University Press, 1995), 27–65.
Snyder, H. Gregory, *Teachers and Texts in the Ancient World* (London: Routledge, 2000).
Sophocles, *Fragments*, 3 vols., ed. Richard C. Jebb, Walter G. Headlam, and Alfred C. Pearson (Cambridge: Cambridge University Press, 1917).
Sotinel, Claire, "La conversion des lieux de culte, métaphore de la conversion des populations," *Archives de sciences sociales des religions* 63 (2018), 29–48.
Squires, John T., "The Gospel According to Luke," in Bruce Chilton, Howard Clark Kee, Eric M. Meyers, John Rogerson, Amy-Jill Levine, and Anthony J. Saldarini, eds., *The Cambridge Companion to the Bible* (Cambridge: Cambridge University Press, 2021), 177–198.
Starr, S. Frederick, *Lost Enlightenment: Central Asia's Golden Age from the Arab Conquest to Tamerlane* (Princeton: Princeton University Press, 2013).
Steel, Catherine, ed., *The Cambridge Companion to Cicero* (Cambridge: Cambridge University Press, 2013).
Steinacher, Roland, *Die Vandalen: Aufstieg und Fall eines Barbarenreichs* (Stuttgart: Klett-Cotta, 2016).
Stenger, Jan R., *Education in Late Antiquity: Challenges, Dynamism, and Reinterpretation, 300–550 CE* (Oxford: Oxford University Press, 2022), 99–140.
Stephens, Walter, *Demon Lovers: Witchcraft, Sex, and the Crisis of Belief* (Chicago: University of Chicago Press, 2002).
Stern, Pnina, "*Life of Josephus*: The Autobiography of Flavius Josephus," *Journal for the Study of Judaism* 41 (2010), 63–93.
Stifter, David, and Nora White, "Early Literacy and Multilingualism in Ireland and Britain," in Alex Mullen and George Woudhuysen, eds., *Languages and Communities in the Late-Roman and Post-Imperial Western Provinces* (Oxford: Oxford University Press, 2023), 203–235.
Stock, Brian, *After Augustine: The Meditative Reader and the Text* (Philadelphia: University of Pennsylvania Press, 2001).
Szpiech, Ryan, "Latin as a Language of Authoritative Tradition," in Ralph J. Hexter and David Townsend, eds., *The Oxford Handbook of Medieval Latin Literature* (Oxford: Oxford University Press, 2012), 63–85.
Tanseanu-Döbler, Ilinca, *Theurgy in Late Antiquity: The Invention of a Ritual Tradition* (Göttingen: Vandenhoeck and Ruprecht, 2013).
Tardieu, Michel, *Manichaeism*, trans. M. B. DeBevoise (Urbana-Champaign: University of Illinois Press, 2008).
Telford, William R., *The Theology of the Gospel of Mark* (Cambridge: Cambridge University Press, 1999).
Tertullian, *De pallio*, ed. and trans. Vincent Hunink (Amsterdam: Gieben, 2005).
   De praescriptione hereticorum, ed. Pierre de Labriolle and François Refoulé (Paris: Editions du Cerf, 1957).
Thomas, "The Infancy Gospel of Thomas," 4.1–2, in J. K. Elliott, ed. and trans., *The Apocryphal New Testament* (Oxford: Clarendon, 1993), 68–84.

Tiemeyer, Lena-Sofia, ed., *The Oxford Handbook of Isaiah* (Oxford: Oxford University Press, 2020).
Tierney, Brian, *Foundations of the Conciliar Theory* (Cambridge: Cambridge University Press, 1955, repr. 1968).
Tigerstedt, E. N., *Interpreting Plato* (Stockholm: Almquist and Wissell, 1977).
Timpanaro, Sebastiano, *Aspetti e figure della cultura ottocentesca* (Pisa: Nistri-Lischi, 1981).
Toom, Tarmo, ed., *Patristic Theories of Biblical Interpretation: The Latin Fathers* (Cambridge: Cambridge University Press, 2016).
Trobisch, David, *The First Edition of the New Testament* (Oxford: Oxford University Press, 2000).
Tsuen-Hsuin, Tsien, *Chemistry and Chemical Technology, Part 1: Paper and Printing*, vol. 5 of *Science and Civilization in China*, ed. Joseph Needham (Cambridge: Cambridge University Press, 1985).
Turner, Eric G., *The Typology of the Early Codex* (Philadelphia: University of Pennsylvania Press, 1977).
Urbano, Arthur, "'Dressing a Christian': The Philosopher's Mantle as Signifier of Pedagogical and Moral Authority," in *Studia patristica* 62 (2013), 213–229.
Van der Loos, H., *The Miracles of Jesus* (Leiden: Brill, 1968).
Van Liere, Frans, *An Introduction to the Medieval Bible* (Cambridge: Cambridge University Press, 2014).
Van Peteghem, Julie, *Italian Readers of Ovid from the Origins to Petrarch* (Leiden: Brill, 2020).
Verbeke, Werner, John Marenbon, and Carlos Steel, eds., *Paganism in the Middle Ages: Threat and Fascination* (Leuven: Leuven University Press, 2012).
Verger, Jacques, "Patterns," in Hilde De Ridder-Symoens, ed., *Universities in the Middle Ages*, vol. 1 of *A History of the University in Europe*, Walter Rüegg, general editor, 4 vols. (Cambridge: Cambridge University Press, 1992–2010), 1: 35–67.
Verheyden, Joseph, "The New Testament Canon," in James C. Paget, Joachim Schaper, et al., eds., *The New Cambridge History of the Bible, Vol. 1: From the Beginnings to 600*, part of *The New Cambridge History of the Bible*, 4 vols. (Cambridge: Cambridge University Press, 2013–2015), 1: 389–411.
Vermes, Geza, *Jesus the Jew: A Historian's Reading of the Gospels* (Minneapolis: Fortress Press, 1973).
Jesus and the World of Judaism (Minneapolis: Fortress Press, 1983).
The Religion of Jesus the Jew (Minneapolis: Fortress, 1993).
Virgil, *Eclogues, Georgics, Aeneid*, 2 vols., ed. and trans. H. R. Fairclough and G. P. Goold (Cambridge, MA: Harvard University Press, 1999).
Vlastos, Gregory, "Degrees of Reality in Plato," in Gregory Vlastos, ed., *Platonic Studies* (Princeton: Princeton University Press, 1973), 58–75.
von Ehrenheim, Hedvig, *Greek Incubation Rituals in Classical and Hellenistic Times* (Liège: Presses Universitaires de Liège, 2015).
von Humboldt, Wilhelm, "Über die innere und äussere Organisation der höheren wissenschsftlichen Anstalten in Berlin," in Wilhelm von Humboldt, *Werke in fünf Bänden*, 5 vols., ed. Andreas Flintner and Klaus Giel (Stuttgart: J. G. Cotta'sche Buchhandlung, 1960), 4: 255–266.
Walsh, Robyn Faith, *The Origins of Early Christian Literature: Contextualizing the New Testament within Greco-Roman Literary Culture* (Cambridge: Cambridge University Press, 2021).

Waquet, Françoise, *Latin, or The Empire of a Sign*, trans. John Howe (London: Verso, 2001).
Ward-Perkins, Bryan, "Reconfiguring Sacred Space: From Pagan Shrines to Christian Churches," in Gunner Brands and Hans-Georg Severin, eds., *Die spätantike Stadt und ihre Christianisierung* (Wiesbaden: Reichert Verlag, 2002), 285–290.
Watts, Edward J., *The Final Pagan Generation* (Berkeley: University of California Press, 2015).
Weber, Robert, ed., *Biblia Sacra iuxta Vulgatam versionem*, 2nd ed. (Stuttgart: Württembergische Bibelanstalt, 1975).
Wellmon, Chad, *Organizing Enlightenment: Information Overload and the Invention of the Modern Research University* (Baltimore: Johns Hopkins University Press, 2015).
Wells, Colin, "The Mystery of Socrates' Last Words," *Arion* 16 (2008), 137–148.
Whitehead, Alfred North, *Process and Reality: An Essay in Cosmology* (New York: MacMillan, 1929).
Wickham, Chris, *The Inheritance of Rome: A History of Europe from 400–1000* (New York: Penguin, 2009).
Wiebe, Gregory D., *Fallen Angels in the Theology of Saint Augustine* (Oxford: Oxford University Press, 2021).
Wilken, Robert Louis, *Liberty in the Things of God: The Christian Origins of Religious Freedom* (New Haven: Yale University Press, 2019).
Williams, Megan Hale, *The Monk and the Book: Jerome and the Making of Christian Scholarship* (Chicago: University of Chicago Press, 2006).
Wills, Gary, *Augustine's Confessions: A Biography* (Princeton: Princeton University Press, 2011).
Wilpert, Joseph, *Die Römischen Mosaiken und Malereien der kirchlichen Bauten vom IV. bis XIII. Jahrhundert*, 4 vols. (Freiburg im Breisgau: Herdersche Verlagshandlung, 1916).
Wilson, Emily, *The Death of Socrates* (Cambridge, MA: Harvard University Press, 2007).
Witt, Ronald G., *"In the Footsteps of the Ancients": The Origins of Humanism from Lovato to Bruni* (Leiden: Brill, 2000).
Wolfsdorf, David, *Trials of Reason: Plato and the Crafting of Philosophy* (Oxford: Oxford University Press, 2008).
Wortley, John, *An Introduction to the Desert Fathers* (Cambridge: Cambridge University Press, 2019).
Wright, Roger, *Late Latin and Early Romance in Spain and Carolingian France* (Liverpool: Francis Cairns, 1982).
Xenophon, *Memorabilia, Oeconomicus, Symposium, Apology*, ed. and trans. E. C. Marchant and O. J. Todd and rev. by Jeffrey Henderson (Cambridge, MA: Harvard University Press, 2013).
Zanker, Paul, *The Mask of Socrates: The Image of the Intellectual in Antiquity* (Berkeley: University of California Press, 1995).
Ziolkowski, Jan M., and Michael C. J. Putnam, eds., *The Virgilian Tradition: The First Fifteen Hundred Years* (New Haven: Yale University Press, 2008).
Zosimus, *Historia nova*, ed. Johann Friedrich Reitemeier and Immanuel Bekker, Corpus scriptorum historiae byzantinae, 30 (Bonn: Weber, 1837).
New History, trans. Ronald T. Ridley (Leiden: Brill, 2017).

INDEX

activity, 27, 81, 83–84
Acts of the Apostles, 109, 169–170, 174, 195, 201
Adam (biblical figure), 22, 221, 236–237
Aeneid. *See* Virgil
Aeschylus, 25, 121
Alaric, king of the Visigoths, 224, 229
Alexander the Great, 72, 123
Alexandria, xi, 196
Ambrose, 243–244, 251, 271
Ananias, 173
antiquity, 20, 130, 148, 208, 234, 265
Apuleius of Africa, 231, 234
Arabic, xi, 270
Aramaic, 136, 148, 164
Aratus, 178–179
archbishop, 245, 257
argument, 1–4, 41, 44, 51, 53–54, 63, 68–69, 207
Aristophanes, 27
Aristotle, ix, xi, 12, 15, 19, 60, 71, **72–86**, **87–105**, 121, 123, 125, 174–175, 177, 188–189, 192, 197, 203, 226, 261, 266–267, 270–271
  Metaphysics, 73, 177
  Nicomachean Ethics, 73, 75–76, 80, 83–84, 87, 93–94, 98–99, 101, 188, 192
  Politics, 89, 91, 226
arts, 25, 27, 75–76, 117–118
  liberal arts, 15–16, 83, 266
  seductive arts, 230–231
Asclepius, 66–67, 269
Assyria, 202
Athens, 25–27, 34, 37, 46–49, 70, 72–73, 175–177, 180, 182, 191, 198
Augustine of Hippo, ix, xi, 19–21, 110, 115, 121, 133, 193–199, 202–203, 205, **208–223**, **224–239**, 240–244, 251–252, 255, 263–265, 271

City of God, 19–20, 195, 208, 223–229, 235, 237, 240–241, 264, 266
Confessions, 19, 195, 208–211, 214, 218–219, 223, 237–238
On the Trinity, 213–214
Augustus, Roman emperor, 116, 118–123, 208

barbarians, 244, 253
Barnabas, 174
Basil of Caesarea, 234
Benedict of Nursia, 266–268
Bible, 109–110, 135, 144, 170, 175, 241, 243, 256
  Book of Daniel, 155, 165, 217
  Book of Isaiah, 107, 109–115, 165
  Book of Job, 246–248
  John, 12, 227
  Joseph, 119, 149–150, 162
  Joseph of Arimathea, 165
  Josephus (37–100 CE), 208
  Luke, 12, 20, 119, 135, 139, 149–157, 161–167, 170, 256, 267
  Mark, 12, 20, 135–140, 166, 217, 244
  Mary, 119, 149–150, 162, 232
  Matthew, 12, 20, 119, 121, 135, 141, 150, 162–163, 166, 213, 227, 267
  Moses, 144–145, 151, 167, 171, 185, 205, 270
  New Testament, xv, 22, 109, 115, 119, 134, 136, 140–141, 144, 161, 165, 170–171, 178, 182, 184, 190, 195, 210, 213, 218, 227, 243
  Old Testament, xv, 107, 109, 111–112, 144, 155, 163, 165, 167, 184–185, 217, 243, 248, 259
  Paul. *See* Paul of Tarsus
  Ten Commandments, 144–145, 205
bishop, 196, 198, 202, 240, 243, 254

Brown, Peter, 200
Brucker, Johann Jakob (1696–1770), 4, 8–11, 18–19, 24

Christianity, ix–x, xv, 3, 5, 11–12, 19–21, 63, 105–109, 113, 121, 125, 133, **134–157**, 165, 167–168, 171, 173, 175, 179–180, 182, 184, 186, 190, 193–203, 209, 211, 216, 220, 224, 226, 229, 232–233, 239, 244, 251, 253–256, 259, 262, 265–266, 271
  early Christians, ix, 124, 136, 172, 178, 197, 199, 256
  Jews and, 107, 110
  philosophy and, 13–14
Christine de Pizan, 272
Church Fathers, 243, 245, 251, 255, 264–265
Cicero, xi, 1, 122–132, 251, 262–265
  De officiis, 126–127, 131, 251
  De republica, 263–265
citizenship, xi
City of God. See Augustine of Hippo
Cleopatra, 123
Confessions. See Augustine of Hippo
conquest, 118, 201, 229, 240
Constantine the Great, 200–202
Constantinople, 213, 240, 244, 248
conversation (of philosophy), 7, **11–13**, 23–24, 42
  Socrates, 53–54
Crito, 65–67, See Plato

Daniel, Book of. See Bible
De officiis. See Cicero
De republica. See Cicero
democracy, 25, 34, 226
Descartes, René (1596–1650), 4–8
  cogito, ergo sum, 5
  Discourse on Method. 4–5
  Meditations, 4, 6–7
dialogue, ix, 3, 9–10, 12, 26–29, 34, 39, 42–43, 45–49, 51–56, 63, 65–66, 68–69, 73–75, 80, 93, 97, 125–126, 168, 177, 185, 203, 217, 230, 246, 264
Discourse on Method. See Descartes

education
  Academy, 73
  allegory, 41
  art of, 43
  Augustine, 210–212
  capacity and, 188

  Christianity, 255
  common good and, 91
  complexity, 41
  elite, 272
  higher, 131
  Jewish, 143
  lack of, 255
  Latin, 129
  liberal, x
  mathematics, 43
  medieval, 133
  moral, 39–40
  of men, 40
  of metaphor, 31
  of soul, 41, 43, 259
  paideia, 39
  Plato, 33–34, 39, 42
  political, 91
  primary and secondary, 131
  Quintilian, 40, 130–131
  reform, 15
  religion, 211
  rhetorical, 131
  Socrates, 27, 39, 41, 43
  taming function, 35
  virtue, 84, 101
  way of, 36
Egypt, xi, 115, 119, 123, 144, 171, 185, 202–203, 205, 208, 232, 234, 270
England, 21, 202, 245
English, 26, 29, 42, 48, 64, 96–97, 100, 107, 120, 148, 173, 176, 181, 187, 189–190, 253, 268
Epicureanism, 125, 175–176
equality, 23–24, 92, 106, 142, 151, 183, 261
Euripides, 25, 121

Farrell, Joseph, 132
Form of Beauty, 35–36
Form of the Beauty, 38, 57
Form of the Good, 32–33, 38–39, 74, 79, 105, 203, 215
free will, xi, 156
French, 4–5, 17, 119, 254, 262
friendship, 87, 95–98

genre, ix, 27, 73–74, 126, 136, 165, 249
German, 8, 15–18, 135, 262
Germanic tribe, 202, 253
Germany, 2, 17, 21
God. See Christianity

Index

gospels, 139, 152
Gospels, x, 12, 109, 135–136, 149, 156, 164, 167, 169, 195, 217
Greece, ix, 25, 72, 116–117, 119, 122
Greek, 1, 21, 24–25, 28–39, 41–42, 44, 48, 52–55, 57, 59–60, 62–63, 67, 69, 73, 75–76, 79–81, 84–86, 88, 91–94, 96–97, 100–101, 104, 110–111, 114–116, 121–124, 126, 136–137, 140–141, 143, 146–147, 156, 159, 162, 164, 172–176, 178, 180–181, 187, 189–192, 194, 200, 203, 206, 209, 211, 213, 219, 225, 234, 242–243, 249, 253, 256, 266–267
   New Testament. *See* Bible
Gregory the Great, ix, xi, 21, 244–257, 266–269

happiness, 70, 77–78, 81–84, 98, 101, 238
Hebrew, xi, xv, 115, 136, 151, 164, 170, 185, 243, 256
Hera, 38
Heracles, 38
Heraclides of Pontus, 1
Herodotus, 266
Hesiod, 103
Homer, 37, 42, 62, 101, 103, 116–117, 121, 143, 211, 266
   Achilles, 116
   Iliad, 37, 116–117
   Odyssey, 37, 101–103, 116–117, 191, 211
Horace, xi, 107, 122
human nature, xi
Humboldt, Wilhelm von (1767-1835), 15–16

Iamblichus, 206–208, 234
ideal city, 27
Ideology, Roman, 127
Illiad, *See* Homer
individuality, 22, 35, 38, 44, 70, 74, 84, 97, 106, 146, 148, 185, 188, 194, 199, 206, 217, 238, 241, 251, 259
intellectual history, ix, 144, 167, 169, 239, 272
Isaiah, Book of. *See* Bible
Italy, 21, 123, 256–261

Jerome, Saint, 110, 199, 243, 251, 256
Jerusalem, 115, 150, 152, 156, 159, 162, 164–167, 170, 172–173, 185, 198, 227, 243
Jesus Christ, x–xi, 19, 21, 105–106, 110, 115, **134–157**, 158–174, 177, 180–184, 186–187, 190, 196–197, 213, 216–219, 222–223, 237, 242, 244, 256, 260
   birth, 106, 108, 119–121
   death, 158
   divine, x, 139, 191
   as exemplar, 134
   gaining authority, 137
   Jesus movement, 19, 23, 106, 115, 129, 170, 173, 182
   as Jew, xi, 106–107, 112
   language, 136
   life, 136–137
   message, 135
   as philosopher, ix, 12
   power of, 138
   sayings, 135, 137–138
Jew, 106–115, 143
Jesus Christ, xi, 21, 134
Jewish law, 137, 144, 151, 183
Judaism, 19, 105–108, 110, 115, 171
Job. *See* Bible
John. *See* Bible
Julian, Roman emperor, 201
Julius Caesar, 121–122, 156–157, 161, 228
Jupiter, 120, 205, 211
justice, **90–93**, 141–143
   achieving, 93
   citizen and, 49
   escaping, 112
   Form of, 74
   Forms of, 143
   of God, 110–112, 148, 171, 185, 259
   implementation, 92
   injustice, 91–92, 111, 185, 217, 227, 229
   law and, 43, 50, 142
   nature of, 50, 110, 112, 146
   office and, 131
   proportion, 91
   query of, 27, 29, 111
   reigning, 115
   restoring, 226
   for the sake of, 142
   social, 90
   taking away, 111
   as a virtue, 90, 92, 94

Lactantius, 198, 200
late antiquity, ix, 11, 133, 194, 198, 200, 232, 245
Latin language, 8, 15, 21, 116, 118, 126, 129–133, 176, 180, 210–211, 225, 241–242, **245**, 251, 253–255, 262, 265
   Vulgate, xv, 243

law
  abiding, 71, 83, 138
  on *apologia*, 48
  Aristotle, 91–93
  as a barrier, 183
  behavior and, 146, 183
  breaking of, 144
  citizen and, 49
  conventional, 77
  discipline of, 15–16, 183
  earthly, 222
  equality and, 183
  faith and, 183
  freedom and, 220
  by God, 8
  of God, 111, 171, 214
  of Jesus, 171
  Jewish, 137, 144–145, 151, 161, 183
  justice and, 91, 142
  on killing, 145
  lawfulness, 156
  lawlessness, 146
  lawyer, 151–152
  limitations, 93, 146
  necessity, 183
  Paul, 222
  Roman, 17
  the rule of, 68, 92
  of sin, 215
  Socrates, 49–51
  Spartan, 25
  the spirit of, 146
  of state, 43, 76
  state and, 92
  virtue and, 91
liberal arts. *See* arts
logic
  of argument, 2, 34, 40, 63, 68–69, 140, 191, 213, 238
  as a discipline, 15, 121
  discourse, 238
  of language, 3, 44, 73
  of narrative, 267
  space, 105, 178, 186
logos, 31, 41–42, 52–54, 56, 63, 67–68, 88, 124, 140, 207–208, 219
Luke. *See* Bible

Mai, Angelo (1782-854), 264–265
Marcus Aurelius, 198
Mark. *See* Bible

Mark Antony, 123
Mary. *See* Bible
Matthew. *See* Bible
medieval. *See* Middle Ages
Meditations. *See* Descartes
Mediterranean, 60, 70, 106, 167, 201–202, 205–206, 210
memory, xi, 14, 26, 67, 73, 107, 119–120, 127, 136, 143, 147, 158, 175–176, 178, 202, 210–211, 232, 241, 244, 270
  historical, 200
Mesopotamia, 202
messiah, 109, 115
Metaphysics (Aristotle). *See* Aristotle
Middle Ages, ix, xv, 13–15, 19, 21, 23, 107–111, 113, 119–120, 122, 127, 132, 135, 150, 176, 180, 187, 195, 221, 227, 239, 241, 243, 245–247, 249, 253–254, 256, 262, 264–266, 268, 271–272
  Early, ix, 13–14, 24, 129, 220, 232, 242, 262
  High, 83, 129, 242
Milan, 201, 243, 257, 264
mind, 6–8, 32, 36, 124, 180, 199, 204, 210, 237, 247, 250
Mommsen, Theodor (1817–1903), 17
monumentum. *See* memory
Moses. *See* Bible
Muhammad, 270

New Testament. *See* Bible
Nicomachean Ethics (Aristotle). *See* Aristotle
North Africa, xi, 119, 194, 202, 210, 224, 231, 240, 254, 270
Nussbaum, Martha, x

Octavian. *See* Augustus, Roman emperor
Odyssey. *See* Homer
Old Testament. *See* Bible
Ovid, 265
  Metamorphoses, 265

Paul of Tarsus, x–xi, 12, 19, 21–24, 109, 169–170, 172, 174–195, 198–201, 207, 214–215, 218–220, 222–223, 227, 236, 242, 260–262
  Corinthians, Letter to the, 22, 169, 186, 190, 193, 220
  Galatians, 21, 24, 169, 242
  Romans, letter to, 169, 184–185, 201, 214, 222–223
  Timothy, letter to, 22, 169

Persia, 123, 215, 232, 270
Petrucci, Armando, 256
Phaedo. *See* Plato
Philip of Macedon, 72
philology, x, 134
philosopher, ix, 1–2, 9–11, 18, 69, 78, 90, 127–129, 134, 197–198, 234–235
philosophy, ix, 1–4
  argumentation, 12, 44, 69, 175
  of Aristotle, 72, 82
  Athens, 175
  Bible and, 109, 175
  Christianity and, 12, 14, 106, 197
  concept of, 1–2, 128, 197–198
  degree of, 16
  development of, 122–123, 126, 234, 246, 259–260, 264, 266, 270
  dialogue, 79
  epistemology, 3, 6–7, 69, 220
  goal of, 19, 63, 126, 189, 203, 262
  Hellenistic schools, 106, 121, 123, 125
  history of, x, 1–5, 8, 10, 12, 17–19, 27, 43, 68–69, 144, 233, 271
  idea of, ix, 128, 199, 217
  lived practice, 11–12, 129
  metaphysics, 3, 7, 121
  method of, 26
  moral, 189
  natural philosophy, 6–7, 99
  nature of, 18, 29, 54, 67–68, 125, 127, 129, 131, 243
  pagan, 225
  of Plato, 28, 45, 54, 69, 82, 144
  respect of, 127
  root of, 106, 115, 260
  scope of, 18, 51, 76, 121–122, 127–128, 266
  status of, 69
  of Socrates, 55, 70
  training of, 122, 127, 203
  way of life, 12, 199, 245
Plato, ix, xi, 3, 5, 9, 12, 19, **25–45**, **46–71**, 72–74, 77–82, 84, 88, 90, 92–93, 97–98, 105–106, 111, 114, 121, 123–124, 136–137, 140, 142–144, 165, 174–175, 177–178, 190, 193–194, 197, 203–204, 207, 210–211, 215, 217, 230–231, 235, 252, 259, 261, 266
  Apology, 26, 34, 48–49
  Book of the Platonists, 216
  Books of the Platonists, 218
  with Christianity, x

Crito, 49–50
Echecrates, 47–48, 52–53, 67
Phaedo, 45–48, 52–53, 68, 70, 194
Platonic, 3, 11, 45, 48, 51, 55, 60, 68, 74, 143, 175, 182, 189–190, 194, 216, 218, 234, 271
Platonism, 41, 106, 182, 195, 203, 216, 220
Platonist, 6, 11, 80, 215–216, 219, 223, 234–235, 242, 264
Republic, 27–29, 33, 39, 41–43, 70, 190, 194, 230, 264
Symposium, 68, 97, 230
Timaeus, 177
Plotinus, 6, 11, 203–207, 215–216, 221, 234
  Enneads, 6, 11, 203, 206
politics, 26, 72, **76**, 77, 83, 85, 121–122, 127, 141–142, 176, 183–184, 188, **192**, 201, 227–228, 244
Politics (Aristotle). *See* Aristotle
Poliziano, Angelo, x
Polybius, 225
Porphyry, 11, 203–204, 206, 216, 234
providence, 20, 195, 223, 227, 237–238, 245
prudence, 95
psyche, 3, 41–42, 89, 214
Pythagoras, 1

Ravenna, 201, 256–257
Renaissance, x, 129, 132, 240, 265
Republic (Plato). *See* Plato
resurrection, x, 5, 165, 181–182, 190–192, 194, 225, 237
Romance languages, 262
Rome, ix, 20, 106, 115–121, 129–130, 164, 195, 199, 201–203, 208, 210, 224, 226, 228, 232, 244, 248, 250, 254, 256, 259, 264–266
  sack of Rome (CE410), 20, 228–229

Saul. *See* Paul of Tarsus
savior, 109, 113–114, 119, 150, 216
Seneca, 198–199
skepticism, 4, 123–124
Socrates, 3, 19, 25, **25–34**, 36, 39–44, **41–45**, **46–71**, 73, 81, 93, 128, 144, 199, 207, 217, 219
  daimonion, 26
Sophocles, 22, 25, 28, 121
soul, 5–6, 12, 41–44, 51–55, 57–60, 63–64, 67, 70–71, 78, 81, 83–84, 89, 94, 106, 123, 125, 159, 193–194, 204, 213, 231, 259
Spain, 119, 130, 202, 270
Stoics, 124–125, 132, 175, 182, 198–199, 251

style of life, 1, 3–4, 12–13, 78, 98, 124, 134, 140, 146, 168, 197, 199, 242, 245, 267–268
Syria, xi, 172, 270

teleology, 21, 100, 110, 115, 146, 189, 239
theology, 6, 12, 15, 168, 185
theory
  of causation, 56
  from evidence, 80
  germ, 14, 80
  of forms, 35, 38, 74, 78
  of history, 225
  of human rights, 22, 70, 185
  of knowledge, 78, 122
  of natural place, 100
  pagan, 240
  of reading, 250
  social contract, 50
  of time, 240
  of two substances, 216
tradition, xi
  ancient, xi, xv, 271
  autobiography, 195
  biblical, 169
  Christian, 5, 21, 117, 156, 220, 236
  epic, 38
  gift-giving, 96
  Greco-Roman, 109
  historiography, 123
  history of philosophy, 4
  incorporeality, 6
  of inquiry, xii
  intellectual, 107
  Jesus's birth, 162
  Jewish, 106, 112, 151, 183, 223
  Judeo-Christian, 205
  Latin, 101, 109, 225
  linguistic, 5, 81, 94, 243
  medieval, 221
  national differences, 10
  pagan, 219–220, 234, 246
  philosophical, 50, 54, 197, 219
  Platonic, 194
  religiosity, 187, 272

resurrection, 165
Roman, 199
soul, 5
teaching, 15
textual, 23, 220
virtue, 125
western, x
truth, 2, 4, 30–32, 36–37, 40, 56, 64, 78–79, 89, 99, 123–125, 155, 164, 172, 188, 198, 216, 218, 230, 249, 253–254
Turkey, 119, 123, 178, 182, 198

Virgil, **116–120**, 132, 210, 241, 254–255, 265
  Aeneid, 116–118, 120, 122, 210, 241, 265
Virgil of Toulouse (grammarian), 129
virtue, 19, 26, 81–95, 98, 104, 125, 127, 188, 192, 235, 267
  behavior and, 101
  on charity, 188
  cultivation, 199
  with friendship, 96–97
  happiness and, 98, 101, 126
  Latin and, 210
  Roman, 126, 132
  St. Paul, 218, 243
  Stoic, 132, 176

western Europe, xi, 13–14, 16, 108, 122, 129, 187, 240, 242–244, 246, 262, 266, 271
western thought, xi, 12, 90, 105, 107, 134, 142, 269, 271
wisdom, ix, xi, 1–2, 11–12, 14, 30, 34, 36, 49, 55, 63, 68–69, 78, 84, 86, 94, 128, 148, 198, 216
  search for, 11, 42, 44, 55, 75, 199, 203, 262
Wissenschaft, 16–17
  Grosswissenschaft, 17
women, 22–24, 132, 158, 166, 182, 261, 271–272
  lack of, 18, 54, 90, 132, 184

Xenophon, 27

Zeus, 38–39, 52, 103, 120, 178, 205, 211

For EU product safety concerns, contact us at Calle de José Abascal, 56–1°,
28003 Madrid, Spain or eugpsr@cambridge.org.

www.ingramcontent.com/pod-product-compliance
Lightning Source LLC
LaVergne TN
LVHW041956060526
838200LV00002B/46